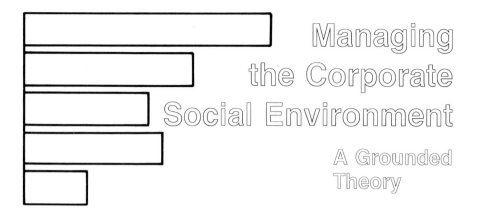

Managing
the Corporate
Social Environment

A Grounded
Theory

Robert H. Miles

Prentice-Hall, Inc., Englewood Cliffs, New Jersey 07632

Library of Congress Cataloging-in-Publication Data

MILES, ROBERT H.   (date)
  Managing the corporate social environment.

  Bibliography: p.
  Includes index.
    1. Industry—Social aspects—United States.
  2. Insurance companies—United States—Management.
  I. Title.
  HD60.5.U5M55 1986   658.4'08   86-12245
  ISBN 0-13-550880-0
  ISBN 0-13-550872-X (pbk.)

Editorial/production supervision and chapter opening
   design: Gretchen K. Chenenko
Cover design: Bruce Kenselaar
Manufacturing buyer: Carol Bystrom

The publisher offers discounts on this book when ordered
in bulk quantities. For more information, write:
   Special Sales/College Marketing
   Prentice-Hall, Inc.
   College Technical and Reference Division
   Englewood Clifffs, NJ 07632

Printed in the United States of America

10 9 8 7 6 5 4 3 2 1

ISBN   0-13-550880-0
ISBN   0-13-550872-X {PBK.}   025

PRENTICE-HALL INTERNATIONAL (UK) LIMITED, *London*
PRENTICE-HALL OF AUSTRALIA PTY. LIMITED, *Sydney*
PRENTICE-HALL CANADA INC., *Toronto*
PRENTICE-HALL HISPANOAMERICANA, S.A., *Mexico*
PRENTICE-HALL OF INDIA PRIVATE LIMITED, *New Delhi*
PRENTICE-HALL OF JAPAN, INC., *Tokyo*
PRENTICE-HALL OF SOUTHEAST ASIA PTE. LTD., *Singapore*
EDITORA PRENTICE-HALL DO BRASIL, LTDA., *Rio de Janeiro*

Dedicated to
Jane

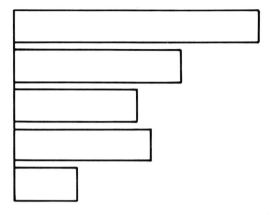

Contents

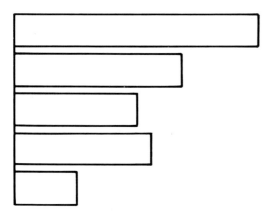

Preface

The purposes of this book are to communicate a practical framework for understanding and managing the corporate social environment and to develop a grounded theory of corporate social performance that will stimulate the advancement of knowledge in this increasingly important area of inquiry. The framework, because of the method by which it was constructed, is primarily oriented to executive leaders of large corporations who want to improve their firm's effectiveness in dealing with the broad social and political contingencies to which their businesses are exposed.

Because the framework was developed from systematic observation and close personal involvement with executive leaders, senior line managers, and external affairs professionals in large corporations, it is expressed in the language of the practitioner and it is constructed on the basis of factors over which executive leaders have some control and influence. Based on the evidence assembled in this book, these choices have lead to a framework that has both the power to distinguish among effective and ineffective corporate social performers within the same industry and the sensitivity and parsimony to facilitate organizational diagnosis and intervention for the purpose of enhancing performance in this domain. If used wisely by executive leaders, the general framework should not only facilitate a more accurate diagnosis of the strengths and weaknesses of a company's approach to understanding and managing the corporate social environment, but also increase the probability that attempts at organizational improvement will be successful.

The framework should also be of interest to external affairs professionals in large corporations whose job it is to organize and catalyze managerial learning and company responsiveness to developments in the corporate social environment. Often these professionals are tagged with the success or failure of corporate responses to the social environment even though, as the framework will reveal, there are several important factors underlying corporate social performance over which only executive leaders have control. The framework should, therefore, help these staff specialists create a greater awareness and appreciation within the organization not only about the roles they should and can play, but also about the roles required of others in the firm if progress is to be made in enhancing their company's overall social performance.

Similarly, the general framework should help line managers, who operate the business or businesses of the large corporation, better understand the kind of role they are required to play in the external affairs process. Considered in isolation, their role is not an obvious one; rather, the nature and intensity of their involvement depends on other factors considered in the general framework.

In addition, the framework should be useful to regulators and public policymakers, many of whom have only a rudimentary appreciation of the kinds of structures and processes that have been created within large corporations to deal with increasing social constraints and contingencies. Hopefully, a deeper appreciation of how large corporations have organized themselves to deal with the external social environment will enable public servants to develop more effective policies and strategies for regulating private enterprise.

Because the construct of corporate social performance is very broad, the particular focus adopted in this book is on large corporations operating in industries with unusually high exposures to the external social environment and how well they cope with industry-specific social and political contingencies that affect or are affected by their business policies and practices. It will be demonstrated that inherent in different American industries are different degrees of exposure to these industry-specific, public policy issues that form an important part of the corporate social environment. But more importantly, it will be shown that corporations operating in the same industry also vary considerably in their exposure depending on the particular business strategies they explicitly or implicitly pursue.

Recognition of these strategic differences in the level of business exposure that distinguish among member firms operating in the same industry is the first important step in any attempt by executive leaders in a particular corporation to improve the manner in which relations with elements of the corporate social environment are understood and managed. That degree of business exposure of a particular company will determine the level of top management attention, the degree of staff sophistication, the type of involvement of operating managers, and the general magnitude of resource commitments that are required to effectively manage this increasingly important domain of corporate reality.

The systematic evidence and case examples in this book will also reveal that important differences exist in managerial values from corporation to corporation, even among those competing in the same industry or market segment. The book will also illustrate that these differences in values powerfully shape the orientations that members of the corporations have toward elements of the corporate social environment and the level of effectiveness achieved in how the company understands and manages social and political contingencies affecting its business operations. Referred to as top management philosophies in this book, these values reveal the beliefs executive leaders and other key decision makers hold about the role of their corporation in American society.

Another important choice reflected in this book is a focus on large, national corporations. This decision was made for two reasons. First, large corporations have more resources, sometimes referred to as "slack" resources, for dealing with social issues impinging upon their business policies and practices. Second, because of the scope of their operations, these large national firms are visible to the general public. They employ thousands of people, have millions of customers, and can even affect the general public beyond their customer by the manner in which they produce and distribute their products and services as well as through the private decisions they make regarding product or service availability and affordability. Therefore, the ways in which large corporations approach the task of understanding and responding to the corporate social environment have a nontrivial effect on the nature of the society in which they do business.

Although the primary evidence summarized in this book was drawn from the largest companies in the United States insurance industry because of their pervasiveness in American society, the major findings appear to generalize to large American corporations operating in a wide variety of United States manufacturing and service industries that are becoming increasingly exposed to the corporate social and political environment.

Closely related to the specific objectives involving the development of a general framework and a grounded theory of corporate social performance is a more general objective. For many decades two traditional academic disciplines have endeavored from their own perspectives to explain and predict the behavior and performance of complex organizations. Organizational theorists have attempted to perform this task by examining the relationships between the external environment and organization design, while business policy theorists have relied principally on the concepts of managerial values and corporate strategy to explain the same phenomenon.

Recently, a more holistic field of inquiry known as Strategic Management has begun to emerge at the interface between these two traditional disciplines. This study adopts the nascent strategic-management approach by attempting to demonstrate the utility of merging the traditionally separate perspectives of Organization Theory and Business Policy into one that is more holistic to explain and predict an important aspect of overall corporate performance. This more holistic perspective is illustrated in the accompanying figure.

Another important feature of this book is the approach adopted for the development of the practical theory of corporate social performance. Most theory-building efforts in the area of organization and management studies have relied on methods that are quite different from the one that guided this program of research.

Most research on complex organizations has proceeded on the basis of a logical–deductive approach to theory building. This approach relies heavily on previous research and a priori assumptions as the basis for selecting variables and relationships for inclusion in the theoretical framework being developed. In general, the kinds of concepts and relationships selected for inclusion in the theory are limited not so much by the practical realities of the phenomenon under scrutiny, but by the boundaries that delimit the scope of the discipline-based literature that is searched as the prelude to theory development. Once the logical–deductive framework is con-

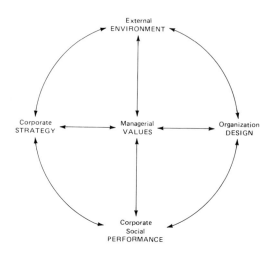

structed in this manner, data from field research are used to verify the concepts and test the relationships in the theory.

In contrast, the present exploratory study is based on an inductive approach, which seeks to develop a "grounded" theory.[1] Such a theory is grounded on the basis of empirical data generated in the field of practice. Indeed, the principal concepts and relationships are generated not so much as a by-product of a literature search (which of course is not practical for exploratory investigations), but from the field data. This type of theory is bounded not by the scope of a particular disciplinary perspective, but through the exhaustion of explanatory power as the result of a process of systematically expanding the variation in a sample of field research settings using the general method of comparative analysis. Refinement of the grounded theory is concluded when no further concepts and relationships are required to explain the phenomenon as more sample variation is added to the data base.

Because a grounded theory is based principally on empirical data collected from the field, it is unusually meaningful and relevant for practitioners and is often operationalized in their language. The grounded-theory approach is also especially useful in exploratory studies such as this one, which attempts to develop a new holistic perspective on corporate social performance.

When applied to this study of corporate social performance, the approach called first for an intensive study of one large firm's approach to corporate social performance. This intensive study served as the seedbed of concepts and relationships to be included in a preliminary framework, which was subsequently refined into a grounded theory as successive increases in sample variation were introduced by studying the best and worst corporate social performers in a major United States industry. Theory construction was concluded only after even more sample variation was added to the data base by including companies that had achieved average levels of corporate social performance. More about this approach to theory construction

1. For a more detailed explanation of grounded theory refer to Barncy G. Glaser and Anselm L. Strauss, *The Discovery of Grounded Theory: Strategies for Qualitative Research*. New York: Aldine, 1967.

and on the methods used to collect empirical data will be within the chapters themselves.

The book is organized into three major parts. Part I introduces the concepts and relationships within the general framework and applies them to a major United States industry. Chapter 1 provides a brief overview of the principal factors and relationships underlying corporate social performance. The key factors include business strategy and exposure to the corporate social environment, top management philosophy, external affairs strategy, external affairs design, and line-management involvement, and corporate history and character. The chapter also describes three key relationships among these factors, the philosophy-strategy connection, the exposure-design contingency, and line–staff balance. This brief overview is intended as a point of departure for all readers.

Chapter 2 applies three core concepts—the nature of the corporate social environment, varieties of business exposure to that environment, and prevailing top management philosophies about the role of corporations in society—to the United States insurance industry. Particular attention is paid to the ways in which an insurance company's business strategy "exposes" it to the corporate social environment.

Chapter 3 operationalizes the concepts of external affairs strategy and design, and line-manager involvement in the context of the insurance industry. Then Chapter 4 introduces the construct of corporate social performance and summarizes an assessment of the social performance of the 25 largest firms in the United States insurance industry.

Part II contains the comparative study. The general framework is refined through a comparative analysis of the host industry's best, worst, and mixed corporate social performers. This systematic investigation is based on a variety of clinical, survey, archival, and action-research methods of investigation.

The companies selected for intensive study are identified in Chapter 5. In Chapter 6 a summary of the major findings from the comparative study is illustrated using survey data. Then in Chapter 7 through 10 profiles are developed for the best-rated and worst-rated corporate social performers in the host industry, as well as for companies receiving mixed corporate social performance ratings. These chapters rely principally on the evidence provided from clinical and archival data, as well as process observation, and surface important but subtle influences of corporate history and character.

Part III shifts the focus of the investigation from comparative to developmental. Chapter 11 and Chapter 12 chronicle the development of the external affairs function in the company judged to be the overall best corporate social performer in the host industry based on five years of intensive action-research. This intensive developmental study is intended to complement the comparative study summarized earlier in this book, and it should provide insights to practitioners and scholars who are primarily interested in learning more about the organizational dynamics and managerial dilemmas underlying attempts to improve corporate social performance.

Finally, Chapter 13 attempts to pull all of the findings together into a preliminary statement of a grounded theory of corporate social performance, and to draw implications for the practice of executive leadership as well as for the academic fields of Business Policy and Organization Theory.

Before proceeding, however, I want to take this opportunity to express my appreciation to all the company executives, government regulators, trade association leaders, and industry analysts who not only had enough faith in the merits of this program of research to devote scarce personal time to it but also let information flow freely into the data-gathering process. I hope the results will be useful as they continue to improve the different practices they represent. In addition, I want to thank the many scholars representing a half-dozen disciplines who took the time to carefully review parts of the evolving manuscript and who provided forums, which enabled me to test ideas at various stages in the program of research. Five such forums were especially helpful during the final stages of manuscript preparation. On the academic side there was the Bronfman Colloquium Series at the Graduate School of Business, Columbia University and the Distinguished Lecture Series in Organizational Behavior at The Pennsylvania State University. From the perspective of management practice, I was invited to share preliminary findings from the book with public and private sector senior executives participating in President Reagan's Commission on Executive Exchange, with senior federal government executives at a workshop held at the Library of Congress under the auspices of the Government Affairs Institute, and with senior corporate executives at the annual meeting of the Public Affairs Council. The feedback and encouragement I received from participants in all of these settings is very much appreciated.

I must also recognize Raymond Corey, Joanne Segal, and Kathry Neeld May of the Division of Research at the Harvard Business School for providing the unusually large amount of financial support that a research enterprise of this scope and nature requires. Sincere appreciation is also extended to Gretchen Chenenko, my production editor, for her splendid and always cheerful editorial assistance.

Paul Lawrence deserves special recognition as a friend and mentor who encouraged me to continue what has become a very long and uncertain project. Arvind Bhambri, who served as doctoral research assistant throughout the program of research, has earned my deepest admiration for his many competences as well as for the tenacity, thoughtfulness, and good humor he brought to the project.

Most importantly, I want to thank the members of my family for the constancy of their caring and understanding. Holen, the ''Dad You're the Greatest'' signs I found posted in my study while I was laboring over this manuscript were, indeed, the Greatest! Alex, your insistence on my becoming your Little League baseball coach as the manuscript was nearing completion provided the perfect reentry vehicle for coming back down to Earth! And Jane, for holding the fort while I was in the field, for assuming the role of both parents during the endless hours of writing, for keeping the faith when even I was in doubt, and for being plucky enough to share this life journey with me, I dedicate the book to you.

R.H.M.
Wayland, Massachusetts, 01778
June 1985

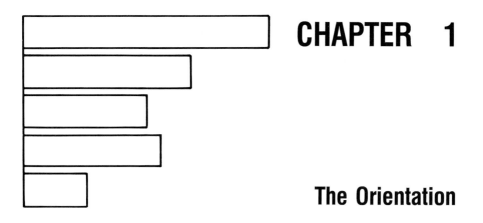

CHAPTER 1

The Orientation

Any serious exploration of business–government relations must be rooted in a deeper study of the proper role of corporations in society.

Derek Bok, President
Harvard University
1979

THE GENERAL FRAMEWORK

Executive leaders of America's largest corporations have been confronted during the last two decades with an unprecedented increase in the social issues impinging upon their business policies and practices. Not only have a variety of social regulations been developed that apply universally to all industries, but each industry has also experienced to varying degrees a proliferation of industry-specific challenges from the corporate social environment.

For most executive leaders, who were born and whose careers unfolded in another era, this social turbulence has been difficult to comprehend and manage. Yet the conceptualization and management of the proper role of different kinds of corporations in society is one of the few domains of business decision making that remains the principal responsibility of executive leaders.

That executive leaders recognize the importance of helping their corporations cope with an increasingly sensitive social environment is well documented. Recent studies of government regulation in America have justified their concern. For example, although economic regulation of business has continued to grow during the last twenty years, this traditional form of government regulation has been eclipsed in both rate of growth and intensity of resources by the new "social" regulation.[1] Other studies reported during the last few years have documented the increasing burden that these rising social expectations have placed on executive leaders of the nation's largest corporations. Many chief executive officers now spend more time on *external affairs* than on any other activities. Most have allocated significant resources to the development of elaborate corporate staff functions to help them un-

1

derstand and manage the corporate social environment.[2] But these studies have been confined to descriptions of practice and general trends. None of them have systematically examined the relative effectiveness of alternative approaches to corporate social performance.

Given the novelty of the current social challenge to large corporations and the absence of systematic field research into the differences between corporations judged to be good and poor social performers, executive leaders, their line and staff subordinates, management consultants, and even regulators and public policymakers are left with little understanding of what is required. Moreover, the emergence of industry-specific social issues and regulatory agendas, which tend to affect member firms differently depending on their business strategies, means that universal solutions are unlikely to serve two companies equally well.

A general framework that enables executive leaders to make informed choices is needed to effectively understand and manage the corporate social environment to which their companies are exposed. Such a framework should facilitate organizational diagnosis and intervention toward the improvement of a corporation's social performance. It should identify factors that significantly impact corporate social performance and that are to varying degrees subject to the influence of executive leaders. In addition, the framework should focus attention on the most critical relationships among these factors. Finally, the framework should be able to stand the test of comparative assessments of corporate social performance conducted by informed industry observers.

In this chapter I will briefly introduce such a framework. Its elements are summarized in Figure 1-1. These core elements are the product of recent developments in both corporate practice and organizational research. Together they provide a holistic approach to understanding and managing the corporate social environment. Further elaboration and refinement of this general framework will unfold in the chapters that follow and will culminate in Chapter 13 with a practical theory of corporate social performance.

Business Exposure

The starting point for understanding corporate social performance is the development of a useful, generalizable measure of a company's *exposure* to the social environment. This exposure derives from the business strategy pursued by a corporation.

The most useful and generalizable measure of business exposure that I have found is the product mix, which is inherent in a company's business strategy. Companies offer a variety of products to the marketplace.[3] The most important difference between businesses as they relate to the corporate social environment is simply whether their products are viewed as luxuries or necessities by the general public. As products become viewed more as necessities by a larger and larger segment of the general public, traditional business decisions about such things as their availability, affordability, reliability, and safety move into the public arena where the

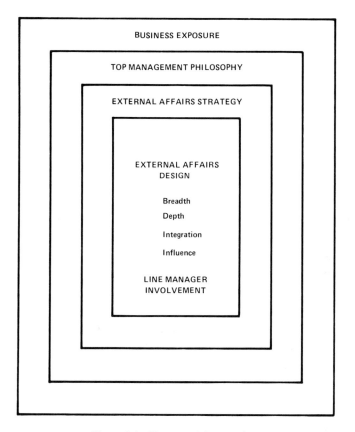

Figure 1-1   The general framework.

general public and its agents bring their influence to bear on the corporation. If, in addition, the products of such businesses or the processes by which these products are created or distributed involve potential contingencies that might adversely affect the consuming public, the corporation's business exposure will normally increase. Thus, a business mix that is heavily weighted toward products regarded as necessities, and intrinsically involving negative contingencies for the consumer, creates a high exposure for the corporate social environment.

Other dimensions of business strategy, which potentially add to a company's social exposure but which may vary in explanatory value depending on the nature of the industry under study, are customer mix and geographical mix.

In general, consumer-products companies tend to be more exposed to the corporate social environment than are companies producing commercial or industrial products. When I asked a government regulator why this is so, he replied wryly, "Corporations can't vote!" He then explained that this was because the budget for regulating the industry under his jurisdiction was limited. Consequently, he is forced to allocate most of his scarce resources to deal with complaints he receives from individual citizens and public-interest groups. He believed that commercial and industrial customers have more sophisticated purchasing functions and are staffed by professionals who are technically trained to make informed purchase decisions. By comparison, he believed that individual consumers are much less qualified to make informed purchase decisions.

A third dimension of business exposure is geographical mix. Just as political scientists and corporate managers have long realized that nations differ in the political risk to which multinational corporations are exposed, so too have executive leaders in the United States become aware of geographical risks that differ from region to region in this country. Corporations marketing consumer products regarded as necessities in urban areas are far more exposed to the corporate social environment than are those that sell similar products in nonurban areas.[4]

For example, in a study of state government regulation I discovered that regulators in urban states have far more resources and much more sophisticated regulatory agencies than their counterparts in nonurban states.[5] Urban regulators also pursue more active regulatory agendas than do regulators in nonurban states. Furthermore, consumer interest groups are generally larger and better organized in urban centers than elsewhere. The large number of such groups in the urban setting creates a complex array of competing social expectations that tends to be more diffused in nonurban areas. Thus, large American corporations whose business stakes are heavily dependent on urban markets tend to be much more exposed to the corporate social environment, especially if they offer high-exposure products to individual consumers, than are companies pursuing a strategy with similar product and customer mixes in nonurban markets.

Although all three factors are important, business exposure is not affected equally by each of them. My experience with companies in a variety of manufacturing and service industries suggests that product mix deserves the heaviest weight followed by customer mix and geographical mix. When all three are considered together, however, these fundamental elements of business strategy provide a simple estimate of exposure to the corporate social environment that is sensitive enough to discriminate not only among different American industries, but also among member firms pursuing different business strategies within one particular industry.

Scholars and executive leaders have struggled for the last century to define what is meant when someone refers to an economic activity as having become *affected with the public interest*. When an industry or business becomes identified with this evocative term, it also becomes surrounded with public attention, government regulatory initiatives, and a variety of other social and political constraints on traditional managerial prerogatives. Business exposure, and its three underlying elements, are offered here as a way to operationalize this important but elusive term. This *direct* link between business strategy and the public interest underscores the futility of pretending that the market and social contingencies and performances of large corporations in America are distinct spheres that may be understood and managed separately. *By their choices of business strategy, executive leaders wittingly or unwittingly establish a linkage between their corporation and the public interest.*

Finally, business exposure to the corporate social environment should not be regarded as a fixed constraint imposed upon executive leaders. Social issues affecting particular business policies and practices vary over time in their salience.[6] Executive leaders may choose to deal with these issues early in their life cycle when they have low salience, or later when legislative and regulatory initiatives have gathered momentum. Just as important, business exposure may be modified by executive leaders through changes they make in their corporation's business strategy. Indeed, I have witnessed chief executive officers of large corporations selling off business divisions they believed were too highly exposed to the social environment and closing offices and distribution centers in urban states where they believed the social risks outweighed the short-term profits of continuing to do business. Thus, business exposure is included in the general framework as one of the factors associated with corporate social performance over which executive leaders have some control and may exert some influence.

Top Management Philosophy

How a large corporation copes with its exposure to the corporate social environment depends largely on the other four factors in the general framework. The most important of these factors appears to be the values and beliefs of executive leaders—particularly, the philosophy they hold about the role of the corporation in society.

Firms pursuing the same strategies and consequently sharing similar business exposures, vary considerably in top management philosophy. Thus, the elements of business exposure are not sufficient to explain differences in top management philosophy. Instead, this philosophy derives in part from the relatively enduring features of a corporation's character and as well as from the personal values and political orientations of successive executive leaders; both of which may be influenced by critical events in the company's history.

Many observers of the large American corporation have suggested that executive leaders are in search of a new philosophy to guide their corporations through a social environment that has become radically transformed during the last few decades.[7] But even though many executive leaders appear to be struggling to perpetuate or modify a view of the corporation in society that was built in a different era, if you look hard enough you will find companies that have been pursuing what the same observers might call the new philosophy for a very long time.

Today, the old and the emerging philosophies coexist within the population of large American firms, and also within member firms in the same industry. These differences in top management philosophy can have dramatic consequences in terms of corporate social performance, especially under high-exposure conditions.

These top management philosophies about the role of the corporation in American society may be arrayed along a continuum that is anchored at one extreme by an institution-oriented philosophy and at the other by an enterprise-oriented philosophy. My experience in highly exposed industries shows that member firms tend to move toward the extremes of this continuum. I suspect that firms that function in less exposed industries are less explicit about their positions on this issue and may lie toward the middle of the continuum.

Institution-oriented executives view their corporation as a social institution. They believe strongly that their corporation has a duty to adapt to a changing society. Therefore, as part of their response to social issues, these executives are much more likely to consider modifying their business policies and practices than are enterprise-oriented executives. In general, executives in institution-oriented companies accord a high degree of legitimacy to social claims on their business operations and to the criticisms they receive not just from the company's immediate constituencies, but from more remote constituencies as well. They realize that the strategic choices they make (e.g., product design, market segmentation practices, and hiring and pricing decisions) often determine the status of various constituencies with respect to the corporation, rather than the other way around. More importantly, because of the large size of their corporation and the pervasiveness of its business operations, institution-oriented executives recognize that the choices they make about the purposes, policies, and practices of their organization may, indeed, serve as nontrivial sources of the changes that take place in society.

Executive leaders in these companies conceive of corporate performance in broader and longer-range terms than do their counterparts in enterprise-oriented companies. In formulating company positions and implementing company responses to social issues impacting their business, they are certainly concerned about the consequences generated for their institution; but they tend to put more emphasis than enterprise-oriented executives on the consequences for the *industry* as a whole. In general, institution-oriented executives believe that the fate of their company is inextricably tied to the fate of its industry. They are very conscious about the long-term consequences of how they respond in the present to industry-related social issues. They also tend to focus their effort on understanding the nature of social issues as they emerge, rather than on moving immediately to adopt a defensive mode to protect their self-interest and the status quo within their own company.

Institution-oriented executives also place less emphasis than their enterprise-oriented counterparts on the distinction between the market and social environments in which their company operates by bringing social awareness into the daily business operations. They merge the economic and social goals of their company by infusing both into the character of the corporation and into the planning, measurement, and reward systems they develop as part of the structural context for guiding and monitoring business operations and line manager performance.[8] The one area in which they do draw the line between market and social arenas is that they tend to avoid using the social arena to gain marketplace advantage. They believe that companies that use the social arena to create special market opportunities for themselves quickly lose credibility in dealings not only with agents of the public interest, but also among other leading firms that must attempt to reconcile their differences to maintain the social legitimacy of the industry as a whole.

Not surprisingly, many institution-oriented executive leaders refer to their large corporations as *social franchises*. They believe their corporations must continue to earn their franchise not only in the marketplace but also in the mind of the general public.

Enterprise-oriented executives contrast sharply with the executives described above. Executives espousing the enterprise philosophy seek to continue operating the large corporation as an independent economic franchise in a free-enterprise system. Their philosophy derives its support from traditional economic values in America, including economic individualism and survival of the fittest, private property rights, market competition, and the concept of limited government.

Enterprise-oriented executives do not believe that the transitions in the American econony from a multitude of autonomous and relatively impotent, small firms to a concentration of enormous wealth and power among a relatively few giant corporations, is sufficient cause to abandon their traditional philosophy of business–society relations. They continue to believe strongly that decision making geared toward maximizing the short-term economic performance of the corporation under competitive market conditions and within existing legal constraints constitutes the most appropriate response for their corporation to make to society. By dismissing the influence their great corporations have on society, these executive leaders orient much of their activity toward preserving the status quo of their traditional business policies and practices.

Social and business issues affecting their business are generally dealt with through separate channels within the corporation. Line managers are expected to focus on the achievement of business objectives, often short-term in nature, and are evaluated accordingly. The chief executive with the assistance of specialized staff units attempts to buffer business operations from social demands. Of course, all of this, as in the case of institution-oriented executives, is couched in terms of the long run. For enterprise-oriented executive leaders, short-term victories in the marketplace as well as the social arena offer the greatest potential for insuring the long-run health and survival of their corporation.

External Affairs Strategy

It is generally recognized that the values of executive leaders have an important influence on the purposes and strategies pursued by any organization.[9] Just how strong this relationship is, or what specific form it takes, however, has not been pinned down by systematic comparative research in large, complex organizatons. What is suspected is that executive values do not influence all aspects of the corporate strategy formation process equally. For example, with the ascendance of the decentralized, divisional form of organization structure in most large corporations, line managers below the executive level now participate vigorously in the development of a corporation's business plans and strategies. Moreover, the increasing diversity of businesses now operated within the large corporation forces executive leaders to depend more and more on the strategic business proposals they receive from subordinate line managers who have intimate knowledge about the nature of each business in the corporation's portfolio.[10] Although the buck continues to stop at the top, executive leaders in the large, divisionalized corporation have had to concede part of the influence over the formation of business strategy to these subordinate line managers. Somewhat less delegation, however, has occurred in the area of social strategy formation.

For strategy formation in the domain of corporate external affairs, executive leaders still retain considerable influence over decision making and action taking. This does not mean that they actually make all the decisions themselves, or personally carry out the corporation's external affairs activities. For most large corporations in America, especially those with high exposure, the burden of effectively understanding and managing the corporate social environment is simply too great to be dealt with singlehandedly by the executive leader. However, in cases of corporations that are explicit about their role in society, it is executive leaders who continue to shape and refine the business-society relationship for the corporation and who create the internal context that guides the responsiveness of subordinate line and staff employees to social issues impacting the company and its industry.

Not surprising, then, there is an especially strong relationship between top management philosophy regarding the role of a corporation in society and the corporation's external affairs strategy. This relationship is so pervasive in the evidence reported later that I have given it a special label: the *philosophy-strategy connection*.

Institution-oriented companies pursue an external affairs strategy that is collaborative and problem-solving in nature. Enterprise-oriented companies pursue an external affairs strategy that is individualistic and adversarial in nature. In some companies, these external affairs strategies are explicit; in others they are implicit and must be inferred from what executive leaders, as well as line managers and staff professionals, characteristically do when confronted with a new social challenge to their company's business activities. Finally, external-affairs strategies may be distinguished in terms of two related, underlying dimensions: the way a corporation goes about understanding the nature of social issues impacting its business and the way it manages its response to those issues.

Collaborative/problem-solving strategies.   The distinguishing characteristics of the external affairs strategies of institution-oriented companies are an emphasis on maintaining long-term relationships based on trust and open communications with a variety of external constitutencies, and a broad problem-solving perspective on the resolution of social issues impacting their business and industry. Both of these elements derive from the institution-oriented, top management philosophy, which views the large corporation as both a bonafide source and legitimate target of social change.

Representatives from these companies arrive at public and industry forums well prepared to debate from a variety of points of view the validity of industry-related social issues, and the appropriateness of alternative responses. But their preparation for and participation in these events is not exclusively oriented toward defense of the company's own business stakes; instead, it is collaborative in nature. Representatives of institution-oriented companies participate heavily not only on advisory committees to their regulators and in joint problem-solving sessions with a variety of public-interest groups, but also in trade associations that attempt to develop industry positions on social issues and regulatory initiatives that often affect member firms differently, depending on their business strategies and relative exposures.

Institution-oriented executives are quick to deny that their external affairs strategy is a purely altruistic one. They place high value on maintaining good ongoing relationships with important elements of society and they believe that a strategy oriented toward collaboration and mutual problem solving will ensure the continued prosperity of their companies as well as the long-term survival of their industry as a private, if not "free" enterprise. One benefit these companies derive that is particularly important in a highly exposed industry is that many of the more active agents of the public interest come to these companies first for consultation on initiatives they are planning to bring to the attention of the general public.

Line managers in companies pursuing this external affairs strategy attach greater importance to industry-related social issues and exhibit a greater propensity to respond by modifying their traditional business practices than do their counterparts in enterprise-oriented companies with similar exposures. Consequently, they place more emphasis during the early stages of issue development on understanding the issue, rather than on mounting a defense of their company's self-interest. They are also more concerned than their enterprise-oriented counterparts with balancing their responsibilities for meeting the financial objectives of their business divisions against the need to respond to shifting social expectations. In short, institution-oriented line managers are more willing to consider a sacrifice in short-term profits to be able to deal effectively with a high-impact social issue than are enterprise-oriented line managers. Executive leaders make it possible for line managers to perform in this manner by the structural context they create within the corporation to reinforce and reward these managers.

To be able to mount and sustain such a strategy, institution-oriented companies require a relatively sophisticated external affairs staff function. Of course, the degree of required sophistication depends on the company's business exposure to the corporate social environment. Moreover, this strategy requires a relatively high degree of line manager involvement in the external affairs process. Finally, these companies are characterized by the breadth of perspectives they nurture in the staff function itself. The corporate legal function is not permitted to dominate the way the company attempts to understand and manage relations with the corporate social environment.

Individualistic/adversarial strategies. The strategy pursued by enterprise-oriented companies contrasts sharply with the external affairs strategy. Because enterprise-oriented executives tend to deny the legitimacy of social claims on their business activities and minimize the importance of challenges they receive from external critics, their approach to managing relations with elements of the corporate social environment is adversarial in nature and relies heavily on the corporate legal function. Because the driving philosophy is to maintain or restore free-enterprise conditions in the industry, their external affairs strategy is also highly individualistic. The principal responsibility assigned by executive leaders to corporate external affairs professionals is to protect the company's self-interest and to defend or buffer its core business policies and practices against social threats. Line managers, therefore, are held primarily, accountable for short-term business results. Indeed, in companies pursuing an explicit, individualistic/adversarial strategy there is almost a complete separation between the responsibilities of line managers and staff professionals. In companies pursuing this external affairs strategy implicitly, the staff function is ''impoverished'' relative to business exposure; so the burden falls upon line managers (who, again, are primarily responsible for day-to-day operations and short-term economic results).

Enterprise-oriented companies with explicit external affairs strategies are represented on regulatory advisory committees, but the preparation and orientation of their officials is much narrower than those of institution-oriented executives. They tend to interpret the issues in terms of their company's self-interests, and when they fail to prevail in these settings they often resort to legal remedies. In contrast, many of these companies have begun to withdraw from industry trade association activities because of the associations' use of consensus decision-making processes. They fear they might have to compromise their company's own position on an issue as an association tries to reach a compromise solution that is acceptable to all of its members.

For enterprise-oriented companies that do not have an explicit external affairs strategy, participation in these public and industry forums is reversed. They tend to avoid voluntary participation in public and regulatory forums because they often are not in a position to articulate their position as well as other companies having an explicit strategy. But they depend heavily on industry trade associations to do much of their external affairs work.

Because they do not take the corporate social environment seriously, these reactive companies fail to establish an external affairs staff function that is sophisticated enough to cope with their business exposure. When new social issues emerge, these companies usually respond late and in haste, often without well-conceived positions, and almost always in the context of underdeveloped relations with regulators and other important representatives of the public interest. Unable to ''draft'' behind other companies whose positions differ from their own, line managers and corporate legal officers are forced to react at a time in the issue life cycle when the degrees of freedom for influencing the issues have sharply narrowed.[11] The typical pattern of company response then becomes the adoption of a narrow, company-specific position and the reliance on the court system to resolve the matter. Thus, reactive, enterprise-oriented companies usually find themselves pursuing by default an implicit, individualistic/adversarial strategy when confronted with a novel social issue that has the potential for high impact on their business stakes.

In the highly exposed American industries that I and others have studied, institution-oriented companies always seem to operate with an explicit external affairs strategy. In those same industries, enterprise-oriented pursue either an explicit or an implicit strategy for corporate external affairs. Executives in the latter companies resent the encroachment of society into their business affairs. However, some operationalize this resentment in a proactive manner by seeking to directly influence trends and events in the corporate social environment; whereas others attempt to ignore this arena until they are forced by a high-impact issue to mount their own defense.[12]

The fourth possibility—a major corporation espousing an institution-oriented philosophy with an implicit external affairs strategy—does not seem to exist in America's most highly exposed industries. However, it is possible, in a less socially sensitive United States industry, to conceive of an institution-oriented executive leader who has not been compelled by events to put his money where his mouth is!

External Affairs Design

The elements of the general framework that have been summarized so far provide a way of understanding the external social context to which large American corporations are exposed, the meaning executive leaders attach to that context, and their intentions for dealing with it. The framework would not be complete, therefore, if it ignored *how* executive leaders organize the internal context of their corporation to manage relations with the corporate social environment.

There are two major aspects of these internal organizational arrangements that, *given* the exposure, philosophy, and external-affairs strategy of a firm, have an important influence on overall corporate social performance. The first is the design of the core external-affairs staff function; the second is the degree of line-manager involvement in the corporate external-affairs process.

There are four basic design dimensions that help to distinguish among external affairs functions having different degrees of sophistication. They are referred to in the general framework as external affairs breadth, depth, influence, and integration. Moreover, there is an important, although contingent, relationship between these elements of external affairs design and corporate social performance. The sophistication of the corporate external affairs function must correspond to the degree of business exposure of the firm in order to achieve high levels of corporate social performance. I will refer to this relationship as the *exposure-design contingency*. Strictly speaking, however, a fit between exposure and design only predicts that a company will be able to realize the achievement of its external affairs strategy; a strategy which may or may not be viewed as appropriate or legitimate depending on who is doing the assessment of corporate social performance.

Breadth refers to the structural complexity of the core external affairs function. Operationally, breadth is the number of different staff units that specialize in corporate external affairs activities. The breadth of a company's external affairs function should be sufficient to enable the firm to cope effectively with its exposure to the corporate social environment. This principle derives from what general systems theorists refer to as the Law of Requisite Variety.[13] In the present case, the complexity of the internal structure of the large corporation must correspond to the complexity of the social environment to which it is exposed to be effective in understanding and managing relations with that environment.

Drawing on this principle, the external affairs functions of companies with heavy business exposures should be composed of a number of units, which specialize in each major segment of the corporate social environment. By the same token, companies with low business exposures should operate with relatively simple external affairs functions. To do otherwise would expose the line operatons of low-exposure companies to uncertainties and costs created more by the corporate staff function than by the actual external environment. This kind of corporate window dressing could conceivably put a low-exposure company at a competitive disadvantage with respect to other firms operating in the same niche of the industry.

The second important dimension of the design of the corporate staff function is external affairs *depth*. A company may, for example, have enough breadth to cover all of the major segments of the social environment to which it is exposed, but it may still do a poor job in this arena because its external affairs function lacks sufficient depth.

Depth is concerned with the intensity of the organizational learning process about the outside world that is established and managed within the external affairs function. The principal indicator of external affairs depth is the intensity that external affairs professionals are permitted in framing and conducting research and analysis of emerging social issues possessing high-impact potential for the company and its industry. Intensity, in turn, has two components. The first is the *range of perspectives* allowed in framing the issue-analysis process. The second is *the range of alternative company responses* that staff professionals are permitted to consider in the issues-analysis process. Thus, under high-depth conditions, the core external affairs professionals become not only facilitators of the organizational learning process, but also agents of change that may be required to adapt business policies and practices to social demands.

Highly exposed corporations require high-depth external-affairs functions in which the range of perspectives and responses considered is large. Companies with minimal exposure to the corporate social environment can manage with a shallow external affairs function. These low-exposure companies often rely on the work of outside consultants, other companies with more sophisticated external affairs functions, and industry trade associations to help them understand the few and relatively benign social issues that they experience. The relatively few changes they may be called upon to make in their business policies and practices can usually be managed on an ad hoc basis.

Influence and *integration* round out the dimensions of external affairs design. They refer to the quality of relationships that exist among core staff units in the corporate external affairs function. The absence of mutual influence and integration among the core staff units undermines and biases the corporate external affairs process. If one or a few units dominate the others, company interpretations of events and trends in the corporate social environment can become distorted and the selection of appropriate company responses can become biased in favor of the function represented by the most powerful staff group. Even so, not many corporations with sophisticated staff functions will be able to or even want to achieve perfect balance among all core staff units. What is important is that the traditional power of the corporate legal function, with its inherent adversarial orientation, be counterbalanced by the influence of nonlegal external affairs units.

Finally, the sophistication and ultimate effectiveness of the corporate external affairs functions is influenced by the degree of integration that is achieved among the activities of the core staff units. A general principle of the contingency theory of organization design is that highly differentiated structures require a relatively high degree of investment in integration if the parts are to function together effectively. Thus, as an extension of the exposure-design contingency, structurally sophisticated external affairs functions dealing with high business exposure must achieve a higher degree of integration than relatively simple external affairs functions that have to cope with low exposure to the corporate social environment.

In summary, corporations require a core external affairs function that is sophisticated enough to cope with the degree of social and political uncertainties to which its businesses are exposed. Highly exposed corporations require high levels of external affairs breadth, depth, influence, and integration; whereas corporations facing low business exposure require only simple external affairs designs. Even when the appropriate exposure-design match is achieved, however, corporate effectiveness in overall social performance may not be realized. The latter depends on the philosophy-strategy connection that guides the corporate external affairs process.

Line-manager Involvement

The last important element in the general framework is the extent to which line managers are involved in the corporate external affairs process. Generally three conditions describe the range of corporate positions on this issue

1. staff domination of the external affairs process,
2. line domination of the external affairs process, or
3. line–staff balance in corporate external affairs.

The significance of a high degree of line-manager involvement in the external affairs process varies considerably depending on the sophistication of the core staff function and the prevailing philosophy in the company about its role in society.

A high degree of line-manager involvement in a company possessing a sophisticated external affairs function is quite an important and difficult achievement. Its significance lies in the fact that both line and staff perspectives are forcefully represented in the company's external affairs process. The combination of high line-manager involvement and high staff sophistication also signals that an important option included among the variety of possible company responses to the social environment is a change in its traditional business policies and practices. In contrast, corporations characterized by low line-manager involvement and high staff sophistication exhibit a strong tendency toward pursuing a narrow, defensive, and protective external affairs posture, designed to buffer line operations from influences from the corporate social environment.

Finally, in companies that have an "impoverished" external affairs function, line-manager involvement has yet another meaning. In this situation, high involvement of line managers leads to a line-dominated, external affairs process in which only minimal attention is paid to events and trends in the corporate social environment.

The degree of line-manager involvement required depends on the sophistication of the external affairs staff function and, ultimately, on the exposure of the corporation to the social environment. In addition, the meaning of line-manager involvement in corporate external affairs depends on the prevailing top management philosophy in the company and the kind of structural context created by executive leaders to channel and reinforce the behavior of subordinate managers. Among the formal devices that have been developed to ensure integration are

1. the establishment of top management steering committees,
2. the designation of specific liason roles that link external affairs units to line operations,
3. the incorporation of external affairs goals and strategies in the annual business planning and review system,
4. the inclusion of external affairs criteria in the performance measurement and reward systems that apply to line managers,
5. the assignment of line managers to external affairs task forces,
6. the occasional rotation of line managers through temporary and full-time job assignments in external affairs units.

Finally, overarching the informal and formal approaches to line–staff integration is the symbolic role played by the executive leader in reinforcing the value of line-manager involvement in the external affairs process and in modeling appropriate managerial attitudes and behaviors.

Corporate History and Character

Before leaving the general framework, it is important to recognize the subtle but relatively enduring influence of the history and character of a corporation on its contemporary approach and effectiveness in the area of social performance. In all the companies sampled for intensive study the prevailing views held by executive leaders about the role of their corporation in society could be traced back to the manner in which key events were handled in the company's history. To a large extent, the philosophies espoused and pursued by contemporary executive leaders were more a reflection of the historical character and current culture of their institutions than of their own individual differences. Put another way, most of the executive leaders in this study had grown up in the corporation they represented. Not surprising, therefore, is the evidence that their beliefs about the role of their corporation in society tended to reflect those that could be discerned from both the historical behaviors of the corporation in responding to social and political contingencies and the top management philosophies handed down to these protégés by their organizational mentors.

The recent proliferation of both universal and industry-specific public policy issues in the American economy has, however, given current executive leaders the opportunity for more personal expression in the arena of corporate social performance. The increasing importance of corporate social and political contingencies has caused some executive leaders to seriously question and challenge traditional beliefs and approaches. Pressured by these, many executive leaders included in this investigation have attempted to make some significant changes in the way in which their corporations relate to the broad social environment surrounding their businesses. Here individual differences in the career experiences of executive leaders, such as their exposure to public forums and to new and different approaches to understanding and managing the corporate social environment, have begun to have a larger influence on overall corporate social performance.

None of these opportunities for executive leadership intervention were observed in this study to have resulted in a fundamental departure in top management philosophy. But many resulted in important directional changes in philosophy and approach, new organizational arrangements, greater explicitness in the mechanisms employed to direct line and staff attention to corporate external affairs, and other innovations enabling a corporation to better understand and manage the evolving corporate social environment. Many of these executive leader interventions can, therefore, be associated with improvements in overall corporate social performance.

The subtle but powerful influence of corporate history and character will be explored in the chapters that profile effective and ineffective corporate social performers and will be incorporated in the grounded theory that is developed at the end of the book.

FOOTNOTES

1. See for example W. Lilly and J. C. Miller, "The New 'Social' Regulation," *The Public Interest,* Spring 1977, vol. 47; and D. Kasper, "Note on Managing in a Regulated Environment" (Boston: HBS Case Services (#1-379-032), Graduate School of Business Administration, Harvard University, 1978).

2. Recent changes in the role of the chief executive officer in corporate external-affairs activities, and trends in the development of corporate external-affairs functions, have been summarized in David G. Moore, "Politics and the Corporate Chief Executive," Report No. 777 (New York: The Conference Board, 1980); Phyllis S. McGrath, "Managing Corporate External Relations: Changing Perspectives and Responses," Report No. 679 (New York: The Conference Board, 1976); and Phyllis S. McGrath, "Redefining Corporate-Federal Relations," Report No. 757 (New York: The Conference Board, 1979).

3. The reference to "product" is intended to include tangible or physical products as well as services that are provided by private-sector firms.

4. The focus in this book is on the large American corporation. Given this focus, it is appropriate to offer organizational size as a fourth element of business exposure when considering firms that vary substantially on this dimension. Business exposure may be expected to vary positively with corporate size. Large corporations are more visible to the public and their agents than are small corporations; their effects on society are more pervasive than those of smaller firms, and they often set the context of business-society and business-government relations that smaller firms in their industry must cope with. For the latter reason, consumer interest groups, the public media, regulators, and legislators tend to pay more attention to industry leaders than to smaller member firms. As a senior executive in one of America's largest life insurance companies explained to me, "Regulators tend to view us as the stalking horse for the insurance industry."

5. For a full discussion of the differences in urban and nonurban contexts refer to a recent comparative study of state regulation that is summarized in Robert H. Miles and Arvind Bhambri, *The Regulatory Executives* (Beverly Hills, CA: Sage Publications, 1983).

6. For discussions of the life cycle of industry-related, social issues refer to Robert W. Ackerman, *The Social Challenge to Business* (Cambridge, MA: Harvard University Press, 1975), esp. pp. 31–41; and James E. Post, *Corporate Behavior and Social Change* (Reston, VA: Reston Publishing, 1978), esp. pp. 21–26.

7. For recent interpretations of the origins of what is here referred to as the enterprise philosophy, as well as proposals for a new philosophy to guide business-society relations in America, refer to George C. Lodge, *The New American Ideology* (New York: Knopf, 1975); and Kenneth R. Andrews, "Public Responsibility in the Private Corporation," *Journal of Industrial Economics,* April 1972, pp. 135–45.

8. For a discussion of the "structural context" created by executive leaders to guide the behaviors of subordinate managers refer to Joseph L. Bower, *Managing the Resource Allocation Process* (Boston, MA: Division of Research, Graduate School of Business Administration, Harvard University, 1970), esp. pp. 72–74, 261–69.

9. This theoretical proposition can be traced to the classical literature on the role of executive leaders, especially Chester I. Barnard, *The Functions of an Executive* (Cambridge, MA: Harvard University Press, 1938); and Philip Selznick, *Leadership in Administration* (New York: Harper & Row, 1957); and to a variety of contemporary management scholars, including William D. Guth and Renato Tagiuri, "Personal Values and Corporate Strategy," *Harvard Business Review* (Sept.-Oct., 1965, pp. 123–32); George W. England, *The Manager and His Values* (Cambridge, MA: Ballinger, 1975); Richard Normann, *Management for Growth* (New York: Wiley-Interscience, 1977); and Kenneth R. Andrews, *The Concept of Corporate Strategy* (Homewood, IL: Irwin, revised edition 1981). In *Coffin Nails and Corporate Strategies* (Englewood Cliffs, NJ: Prentice-Hall, 1982), I was able to establish some important linkages between the dom-

inant values and beliefs of successive executive leaders and changes in the competitive strategies pursued by major competitors in the same industry. But the relationship between top management philosophy and corporate external affairs strategy has not been demonstrated on the basis of comparative field research. This relationship is established in the comparative study that follows in Part II of this book.

10. For a discussion of the bottom-up influence of subordinate line managers on the formation of a corporation's business strategy, refer to Joseph L. Bower, *Managing the Resource Allocation Process* (Boston, MA: Division of Research, Graduate School of Business Administration, Harvard University, 1970).

11. Robert W. Ackerman has referred to this phenomenon in *The Social Challenge to Business* (Cambridge, MA: Harvard University Press, 1975) as a narrowing of the executive's ''zone of discretion.''

12. A similar three-fold taxonomy of external affairs strategies has been developed by James E. Post in *Corporate Behavior and Social Change* (Reston, VA: Reston Publishing, 1978). Post refers to external affairs strategies as company response patterns. His three types, which include adaptive (reactive), proactive, and interactive response patterns closely parallel the external affairs strategies I have referred to as the implicit, individualistic/adversarial strategy; the explicit, individualistic/adversarial strategy; and the explicit, collaborative/problem-solving strategy, respectively. In Post's opinion, ''the conventional adaptive and proactive responses may be useful tactical approaches, but they are no longer effective strategic approaches to coping with [social] change.'' (p. 218).

PART I

The General
Framework:
Development
and Application

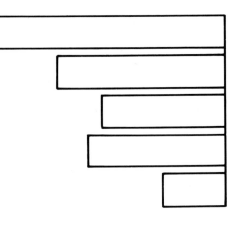

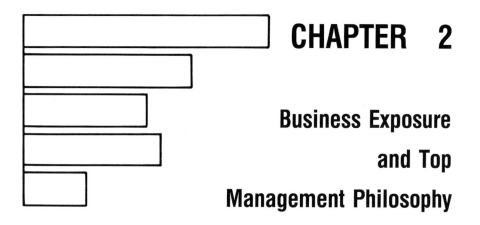

CHAPTER 2

Business Exposure
and Top
Management Philosophy

Having sketched the broad concepts of the general framework, it is the task of this chapter and Chapter 3 to demonstrate how to apply them to a particular company or industry setting. The focus of this chapter will be on the first three elements of the framework

1. the corporate social environment,
2. business exposure, which derives from the business strategy of a company,
3. top management philosophy.

These elements form the context in which a company's external affairs function must respond. A full discussion of the corporate external affairs function, its strategy and design, will follow in Chapter 3. The application of these concepts to the United States insurance industry should not only set the stage for the comparative study, but hopefully will also help practitioners, consultants, and scholars tailor the framework for the purposes of diagnosis and intervention in other industries.

THE CORPORATE SOCIAL ENVIRONMENT

Whole industries differ in their exposure to the general social environment. Some industries are generally viewed as being "affected with the public interest." The public-utility industry, the banking industry, and our host, the insurance industry are clear examples of this. As an officer of the National Association of Insurance Commissioners explained to me when this project was initiated in 1980, "Insurance covers the full gamut of society; therefore, the problems of society are basically the problems of insurance.'' As a result, the insurance industry and others whose business policies and practices are closely tied to the general public interest are usually exposed to a thick canopy of *industry-specific* government regulation. Indeed, it is the industry-specific nature of the regulation to which they are exposed that causes us to refer to them as the *regulated* industries.[1]

At the other extreme are industries whose business policies and practices are far removed from a direct and unique affection with the public interest. Although these industries are generally not subject to industry-specific regulation, during the last two decades they have begun to share with regulated industries an exposure to an increasingly complex and turbulent general social environment in the United States; one that has forced companies to begin to understand and manage an ever-expanding variety of generic public policies and government regulations. Among the more general regulatory agendas that now affect regulated and nonregulated industries alike are environmental protection, equal employment opportunity, and occupational safety and health. Each of these generic areas of relatively recent government regulation have posed some degree of threat to, and have caused at least some reconsideration of, traditional business policies, practices, and products across the broad spectrum of industries in contemporary America.

Finally, an increasing number of industries now fall between the regulated and nonregulated categories. The cigarette industry, for example, is not subject to its own, industry-specific regulatory authority. But no one would deny that the major cigarette companies have had to dig deeply to find ways to cope with the smoking-and-health controversy and its attendant legislation and regulations.[2] Even the bicycle manufacturing industry, which for decades operated at great distance from the regulatory spotlight, now is engaged in the tough task of making its products safe for use by children.

The point is that whole industries vary considerably in their overall exposure to the general social environment. Indeed, one reason the U.S. insurance industry was chosen to demonstrate and refine our framework is its exposure to an unusually diverse and heavy overlay of industry-specific legislation and regulation.

At the same time, the fit between industry exposure and the business exposure of a particular company or group of companies within the industry is never a perfect one. The few previous comparative studies of how companies in relatively homogeneous industries (e.g., the cigarette and paper-products industries) manage relations with the corporate social environment have already demonstrated that fine-grained analysis often reveals subtle but important differences in company exposure that, when recognized by executive leaders, can be exploited to a company's advantage. Indeed, close examination of these studies of apparently homogeneous industries revealed that the fit between industry exposure and company exposure is often a poor one. And in most cases, the fit is too loose to permit one to intervene at the company level for the purpose of significantly improving a particular firm's effectiveness in understanding and managing its social environment.

The principal reason for the loose coupling between industry exposure and company exposure is that companies in the same industry pursue different business strategies.[3] Indeed, contemporary observers of competitive behavior and corporate performance in the U. S. economy have argued that such differences in business strategy are necessary for member firms in an industry to locate market niches that offer them not only special competitive advantages, but also make it possible for them to persist in turbulent times.[4] The existence of such loose coupling brings us to the general framework for understanding and managing the corporate social environment.

BUSINESS EXPOSURE

The point of departure is business strategy. Although at some gross level company requirements for understanding and managing the corporate social environment vary systematically with their industry's exposure, knowledge about the specific requirements imposed on a *particular* company must be preceded by an understanding of its business strategy. It is this finer-grained understanding that is of primary interest to executive leaders in large corporations and that is engaged by the general framework developed in Chapter 1. Let us proceed then with an application of this framework to the U.S. insurance industry.

Product Mix

In the case of the insurance industry, three concrete elements of business exposure may be derived from the business strategies pursued by each major insurer. The first and most generalizable element of business exposure is a company's product mix. Two underlying dimensions of a firm's product mix contribute to its degree of exposure to the social environment. The first dimension is the extent to which the firm's products or services are viewed by the general public as necessities or luxuries. When through its product design, pricing, or distribution decisions a private firms shapes the availability and affordability of a public necessity, it exposes itself to a higher degree of social and political contingencies than that experienced by a firm making a market in luxury or discretionary products and services.

The second dimension of product mix is the extent to which the product or service offered by a firm, or the processes by which it is produced or distributed, create potential negative contingencies for the general public. The more intense and pervasive these potential negative contingencies are, the greater will be the firm's exposure to the corporate social environment.

The relationships between these product-mix dimensions and business exposure are illustrated in Figure 2-1. Business exposure increases from left to right along the diagonal. At the minimal-exposure extreme are firms such as high-fashion retailers, which market discretionary products possessing minimal negative-contingency potential. At the maximum-exposure extreme are firms such as electric utilities, which rely on nuclear power generation processes. The product they provide is a necessity for the general public, the negative consequences of service fail-

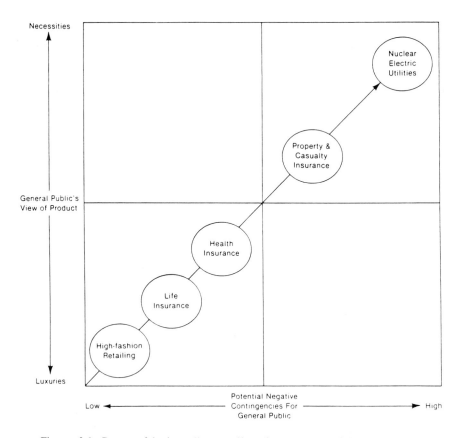

Figure 2-1 Degree of business "exposure" to the corporate social environment: product-mix dimensions.

ure are high for the general public, and the consequences of malfunction in the process by which the product is generated are potentially catastrophic. Thus, social and political contingencies, as well as the magnitude of industry-specific regulation and the intensity of industry-specific public policy issues, all vary directly with the product-mix basis of a firm's business exposure. Moreover, of the three underlying elements of business exposure developed for this study of the insurance industry, the product-mix dimensions appear to generalize most readily to other U. S. industries.

Companies in the insurance industry vary greatly in the mix of products they offer to the public. The industry is fragmented into two major categories of companies: property and casualty insurers, and life and health insurers. Moreover, within the last two decades multiple-line insurance companies have emerged from corporate internal-development and diversification strategies.

Regulatory and legislative initiatives and the public policy issues affecting the insurance industry have been much more complex and volatile for property and casualty insurers than for life and health insurers. Visits I had in 1981 with leaders of the National Association of Insurance Commissioners and with commissioners and their staffs in 12 different states revealed that no fewer than 22 major public policy issues were being actively contested in the insurance arena. As Table 2-1 reveals, property and casualty issues far outnumbered the life and health issues that were being actively contested in the industry on the eve of the comparative study of major insurers, which is reported in Part II.[5]

A legislative counsel for one of the major insurers later reflected this dichotomy in business exposure within the industry in his explanation of the exposure of

TABLE 2-1   Industry-specific, Public Policy Issues Affecting the United States
Insurance Industry: 1981

Public Policy Issues	Assigned Priority*	Type of Issue			
		Property/ Casualty	Life	Health	General
High-priority Issues					
1. Automobile insurance affordability	4.42	X			
2. Arson	4.38	X			
3. Health care cost	4.30			X	
4. Claims practices	4.24	X			
5. Automobile theft	4.03	X			
Moderate-priority Issues					
6. Cost disclosure	3.82		X		
7. Workers' compensation	3.81	X			
8. Rate regulation	3.64	X			
9. Simplified policies	3.64				X
10. Risk classification	3.52				X
11. Privacy	3.49				X
12. Preventive health care/public education	3.46			X	
13. Redlining	3.38	X			
14. Tort reform	3.36	X			
15. Products liability	3.33	X			
16. Residual markets	3.24	X			
17. Federal regulation of insurance	3.06				X
18. Suitability of alternative forms of life insurance	3.03		X		
Low-priority Issues					
19. Automobile no-fault insurance	2.78	X			
20. Private pension reform	2.73		X	X	
21. Universal Social Security coverage	2.26				X
22. National health insurance	2.21			X	

*Issue priority was rated by commissioners on a five-point scale, labeled
1 = Very Low,
3 = Moderate,
and 5 = High.

Source: Adapted from Robert H. Miles, ''Public Policy Priorities and Insurer Responsiveness,'' *Best's Review*, 1981, 82, no. 1, 12–16, 111–126, with permission from A. M. Best Co.

his company, which has a business strategy of limiting its product mix to the middle- and upper-income segments of the life insurance market. He said,

> We are not in the property and casualty business; so the inherent number of problems that we have to deal with are fewer. In an average state legislative session, we don't usually get involved in more than one or two issues. So I'm not spread as thin as, say, a person who is representing a casualty company or a multiple-line company.

One reason for the great difference in the political salience of these two product mixes is that life insurance and to a lesser extent health insurance have traditionally been viewed more as luxuries or privileges, especially in light of government-sponsored Social Security and Medicare–Medicaid programs. In contrast, property and casualty insurance in American society has become viewed more as a necessity or individual right. Property and casualty insurance products, especially their availability and affordability for the general public, affect us daily; not just when a catastrophic event occurs. We cannot drive to work—a necessity in a suburban-bound society that has not made adequate provision for mass transportation—if we are denied or cannot afford automobile insurance. We cannot obtain a mortgage to buy a home if we are denied or are unable to afford homeowners' insurance. And the affordability and availability decisions are made by the private insurance mechanism through individual company decisions, not by governmental policy. In addition, policyholder claims against life insurance products are generally fixed and predictable; whereas claims against property and casualty insurance products are equivocal, usually being settled through the processes of estimation, negotiation, and often litigation. Thus, property and casualty claims actually encourage disputes between the insurer and the insured.

The 1981 National Survey of State Insurance Commissioners revealed that property and casualty insurance issues were given much higher priority ratings by the commissioners than were life and health insurance issues.[6,7] When a crude "intensity of political pressure" index was developed, which sums the priorities commissioners assigned to current issues affecting each business line, the results were definitive. Figure 2-2 provides a dramatic illustration of the heavy relative exposure to the corporate social environment of major property and casualty insurers.

As the chief executive of one of the nation's largest property and casualty firms explained, "I don't recall any period in time when there were not crises in the automobile insurance business. That's what it's all about!"

Geographical Mix

Another important element of business exposure in the U. S. insurance industry is a company's geographical mix. Some insurers are heavily dependent on business stakes in nonurban states for their revenues and earnings. These differences in the geographical dispersion of a company's business create different company exposures to the corporate social environment.

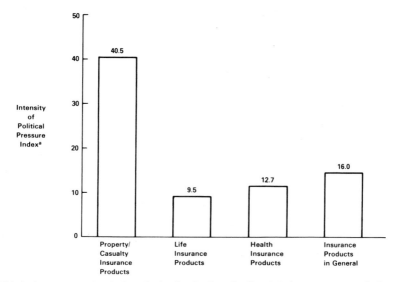

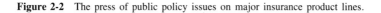

aThis index was constructed on the basis of ratings by the state insurance commissioners (National Survey of State Insurance Commissioners, 1981) of the priorities they believed major insurers should assign to each of 22 insurance-related, public policy issues. Issues were sorted into categories based on whether they primarily impacted property/casualty, life, or health insurance products, or whether they affected insurance products in general. After sorting the public policy issues into these categories, an index of the "intensity of political pressure" was calculated as the sum of the priorities assigned to issues in each of the four product-line categories.

Figure 2-2   The press of public policy issues on major insurance product lines.

Urban states are tougher to do insurance business in than nonurban states. In *The Regulatory Executives,* which summarizes the national study of the state system of insurance regulation, Arvind Bhambri and I were able to demonstrate many important ways in which urban and nonurban states differ that had an impact on the U. S. insurance industry.[8] For instance, we discovered that urban states expose insurance companies to a much more intense legislative and regulatory agenda than do nonurban states. Commissioners of insurance in urban states are much more *active* in pressing for new insurance legislation and industry reforms than were their counterparts in nonurban states.[9] These urban activists also have larger, more sophisticated department staffs than nonurban commissioners. Moreover, the state insurance departments headed by urban activists pursue broader regulatory missions, apply more aggressive regulatory strategies, and operate with far greater budgets than do those headed by nonurban commissioners.

In addition, insurance companies in urban states have a more complex assortment of well-organized consumer interest groups than do nonurban states. Indeed, the study provides evidence that urban activist commissioners often helped consumer groups become organized in order to support the commissioner's aggressive regulatory agenda. The urban–nonurban distinction, however, is not a new discovery for insurance company executives. As one senior line manager in a major insurance company based in a northeastern urban center explained, "I am sure there are people who are unhappy with insurance companies in every state, but they are significantly more vocal, more visible, and more accessible to regulators in the urban states."

Finally, the problems of dealing with the urban political context are especially burdensome for a property and casualty insurer. Indeed, many property and casualty company executives count themselves as fortunate if most of their business is located in the more remote parts of the country. As the corporate general counsel in a major midwestern property and casualty company expressed with clear signs of relief, "We traditionally have been isolated in the Midwest and, therefore, we have been less directly involved than the Northeast companies in the broad range of regulatory issues confronting the property-casualty business as a whole." Pressures have been so intense on property and casualty insurers operating in the eastern urban states, that some have restricted their operations in those states; and a few have actually pulled out their entire operations.

One of the features of the urban political context that is especially onerous for the property and casualty insurers is that, by definition, these states contain the country's largest cities which in turn have the largest problems. These problems include urban decay and the need for renewal; high population density and the corresponding high incidence of automobile accidents; and high poverty levels and the corresponding high crime rates, including theft, arson, and other forms of property destruction, which find at least one avenue of expression in the availability and affordability of various forms of property and casualty insurance. These urban centers are *high-risk areas* in the vernacular of actuarial science; a fact that insurers weigh heavily in making decisions concerning insurance product pricing and distribution, and a major point of contention with politicians and regulators whose urban constituencies are vitally interested in the renewal of American cities. As one insurance commissioner in an eastern state observed, "Some people call the Northeast corner of the United States the 'socialist' corner."

In contrast, nonurban states often present major insurance companies with far more benign political issues and regulators. As one insurance commissioner in a nonurban state explained to me, "I'm not a reformer. I guess you'd have to say that I tend to be slightly more on the conservative side. There doesn't seem to be any outcry for reform here. 'Why create a problem if there isn't one,' is my attitude. I don't hear the problem, so I'm not going to look for it. There are a number of things that need to be addressed, but all the urban ills aren't here."

Geographical mix, as expressed in the urban–nonurban state dichotomy, is a major element in the business exposure of all insurance companies. But it is especially important in understanding the business exposure of companies whose product mix is heavily oriented toward property and casualty insurance.

Customer Mix

The exposure of the nation's major insurers is also affected by the customer mix inherent in their business strategies. Some insurers sell primarily to other businesses. They are known in the industry as *commercial-lines* companies. Others sell primarily to individual consumers, and are called *personal-lines* companies.

Personal-lines insurers have been subject to more intense scrutiny by politicians and regulators than commercial-lines insurers have been, and the fundamental reason for this difference is not difficult to understand. Commercial-lines companies sell to sophisticated buyers who are employed as staff specialists in client firms. These purchasing agents understand the technical side of the private insurance mechanism, and they have the skills, the resources, and the time to make comprehensive comparisons among the products offered by many insurance companies. Personal-lines companies, in contrast, sell to individuals who understand little about the technical nature of the product and who have little time or resources to engage in comparisons among insurers and their products. As one insurance commissioner explained,

> I have focused more in the areas of personal lines of insurance. I'm a strong believer that in the area of commercial lines, sophisticated buyers dealing with the insurance industry are well able to take care of their own interests. As a matter of fact, my philosophical position on that subject is to give as little regulation as possible to the area of commercial lines.

But there are other reasons as well why regulators and politicians engaged in insurance legislation may focus more on personal lines than on commercial lines. Some observers believe that because commercial clients offer larger business potential to major insurers, commercial-lines insurance companies may give them a better deal than personal-lines companies are inclined to give to individual consumers. On the other hand, a somewhat different motive underlying the greater emphasis placed by regulators on personal lines is often identified by insurance company executives. Many of these executives view regulators as politicians who regulate in a manner that will maximize votes. When asked to explain the personal-commercial lines distinction in regulatory activity, one insurance executive replied, "That's an easy one to answer. The reason is that each individual policyholder is a voter. Companies don't vote!"

Regardless of the underlying motive, regulators and politicians do pay more attention to the business policies and practices of personal-lines insurers and do hear more complaints from individual, as opposed to commercial, customers. Therefore, this distinction is an important one in calibrating the business exposure of major U.S. insurers. Moreover, this distinction between consumer-products and industrial-products companies and their exposure to the corporate social environment appears to generalize easily across many U.S. industries.

In summary, the starting point for understanding and managing the corporate social environment is the analysis of a company's business strategy. It is the company's business strategy, as expressed in the concrete terms of its product mix, geographical mix, and customer mix, that determines the extent to which the company is "exposed" to the social environment surrounding its industry, as shown in Figure 2-3. Based on several years of clinical and survey research, as well as consulting in the insurance industry both in the U. S. and abroad, I believe that product mix is the most significant factor determining the business exposure of major insurers. However, geographical mix and customer mix are also important, when considered in conjunction with product mix, in rounding out an accurate and practically useful diagnosis of the business exposure of major insurers.

A central theme in the field of organization theory is that the effectiveness of an organization is importantly a function of the extent to which organization design is sophisticated enough to manage the environmental uncertainties to which the firm is exposed as a result of its business strategy. Later in this book, this exposure-design contingency will be revealed as a crucial factor influencing the level of corporate social performance achieved by a firm.

TOP MANAGEMENT PHILOSOPHY

Top management philosophy is another important factor influencing how a company attempts to understand and manage the corporate social environment. The primary clues that stimulated a close look at this factor came from interviews with a national cross section of state insurance commissioners during the year preceding the comparative study of major insurers.

When the commissioners were asked to identify the factors that separated the companies they had identified as the industry's best and worst corporate social per-

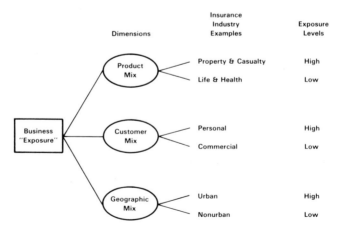

Figure 2-3   Dimensions of an insurance company's business exposure.

formers, they frequently mentioned top management philosophy. As one commissioner explained, "There is a considerable range of philosophies about insurance in the various companies. What I assume is that once the philosophy is determined, people who fit the mold do very well in the company. People who do not will find their way out. At the lower levels, the word is given and they do it. So, companies seem to behave fairly consistently internally."

This same commissioner believed that a company's external affairs strategy and structure are a reflection of top management's philosophy. "It may be that form follows function," he said. "I would say that philosophy comes first, and the organization follows. If the top two or three people in the company feel one particular way, the company will organize itself to effectively implement that philosophy. So I would look for the existence of certain types of organization as evidence of differences in top management philosophy."

Many of the commissioners, including almost all of the urban activists, preferred to go directly to top management in dealing with a major issue affecting the insurance business or its regulation. As one explained, "You have to deal with top management. There is a group of people who do nothing but travel around the country expressing the industry position and meeting with commissioners; but they're not the ones that bring about change. When a big issue comes up, I usually go to the top manager. I've had occasion to do that recently, and I've noted a very wide difference of response among the companies doing business in this state."

Field visits in the leading insurance companies confirmed the wide difference in the philosophies that were espoused and enacted by executive leaders.[10] These philosophies represent the basic viewpoint of executive leaders concerning the role of their corporation in society. Two general philosophies could be identified from the company visits. They are referred to here as the *enterprise* philosophy and the *institution* philosophy.[11]

The Enterprise Philosophy

The top management philosophy in over half of the insurance companies that were contacted for the purpose of engaging in field studies could be unambiguously classified in the *enterprise* category. Executive leaders in some of these companies held strong, explicit views about the role of their corporation in society, which they clearly communicated inside the organization as well as to outside constituencies. Perhaps the most explicit—indeed, blunt—statement of the enterprise philosophy was the one we received from the vice president of public affairs in a company that was rated among the industry's worst social performers. In a letter in which he flatly refused to allow us to visit his company, he explained the decision not to participate as follows: "We operate only in the western half of the United States, and are not subject to the most prevalent problems and issues dominating eastern thinking. It might even be closer to accurate to say that *our area is still dominated by that old time 'rugged individualism' which made America what we wish it still was.*"

Executive leaders in other companies classified in the enterprise category were less emphatic about their adherence to the free-enterprise philosophy. Some recognized at least the need to qualify the term. "I don't view us as being of the 'free' enterprise system," said one senior executive; "But rather as part of the 'private' enterprise system. I quit using the term 'free' enterprise many years ago because we're in a highly regulated environment."

Most of the less-explicit executives replied that the primary responsibility of their corporation was to its policyholders. Although this has the ring of corporate responsibility and responsiveness, an almost exclusive reliance on this criterion implies that other constituencies who have a vital interest in insurance may be excluded or ignored by these companies. Indeed, when the policyholder base of some of these companies is examined, one discovers that most of them have pursued a marketing strategy that emphasizes only a small segment, often the most affluent and least risky one, in the total population of people who need and desire insurance coverage. As an underwriting executive in a mutual insurance company explained, "I think we have an obligation to our policyholders not to subsidize other policyholders to any greater extent than the industry and the social system requires."

The chief executive officer to whom the underwriter reported drew the line even bolder between the company's policyholders and the other constituencies who are generally represented by the state insurance commissioners. He said, "You have the regulators on one side and the customers on the other. I feel more comfortable if our customers are happy than I do if the regulators are happy." Referring to the recent social and political changes that had increasingly affected the private insurance industry, the CEO said, "I think that as we go through this process, the chief executive officers in the insurance industry are going to have to stand much firmer on some issues than they have in the past and than people are going to like."

The Institution Philosophy

At the other extreme in top management philosophy were insurance companies whose executive leaders viewed the corporation as a social *institution*. Their philosophy recognized that society has the right to make certain claims on a private corporation and that the corporation has some duty to respond and to adapt its policies and practices to social and political change. As one chief executive officer espousing this viewpoint explained, "The real test of corporate responsiveness to society is how well we are doing in our basic business to meet the needs of society as well as of our customers . . . I believe we must bring social responsibility into our day-to-day operations and make it part of our business decisions." Indeed, top managers of the large insurance corporations who espoused this philosophy recognized that their large corporations also serve as nontrivial sources of social change and progress. As one of these senior managers expressed to me,

> Trying to bring corporate resources to bear on social issues is a matter of pressing urgency for each of us. We are likely to regret it bitterly in future years if we leave this job to others. As we do affect society, and by that I mean people, in a great variety of

ways, we obviously have the power to impact their lives if we wish to do so. Justice, equality, recognition, freedom, mobility and self-determination are unevenly distributed in this country today, and corporate America can do something about it—or it can be required to do something. We, individually and collectively, cannot solve all of these problems, but there are some aspects of most of them that we can influence for the better.

Whereas the enterprise-oriented managers tended to define corporate performance and effectiveness very narrowly, in terms of their immediate constituencies (e.g., current policyholders and employees) and their individual business stakes, top managers espousing the institution-oriented philosophy defined corporate performance and effectiveness more broadly. Often their concerns included the fate of the insurance industry as a whole and its general responsiveness to political and social change. For instance, when a chief executive officer espousing an institution philosophy was asked if he thought the adage, "The business of business is business," applied to the insurance industry, he replied, "You can look at it that way. Most people used to. Many people still do. But I happen to believe that it is a terribly risky point of view." The chief operating officer in the same company expressed their shared philosophy this way, "If our industry is to provide the market which the country needs, both our long- and short-range planning efforts need to be more firmly attuned to the relationship between our business and the broad political, legal, economic, and social system within which it is conducted. *We cannot be isolationists—we must realize that the industry's goals and society's goals must be brought into harmony.*"

These two executive groups also differ in the way they believe their companies should go about ensuring the long-run survival of their organizations and their industry. Enterprise-oriented executives believe it is now time to "man the walls;" to curtail the encroachment of social and political forces that emerged during the past two decades and led to the erosion of traditional managerial prerogatives. Institution-oriented executives, in contrast, believe that if their companies and the private insurance industry are to survive, they must be prepared to adapt traditional business policies and practices to social and political change. The first executive group seeks to clearly separate business and social goals, whereas the other group attempts to address both types of goals insofar as their business operations warrant and allow. The following insert reveals how the chief executive officer of an institution-oriented company explained the relationship between business and social goals to his employees.

The Social Goals of a Corporation

Corporations must set social goals just as they set business goals. Setting business goals has never been simple, but setting corporate goals is far more difficult. With traditional corporate goals, participants have a common understanding of overall objectives. They agree that such things as market share, cash flow, profit growth, quality of product or service, return on invested capital and the like are legitimate values to seek. The difference of opinions among our managers in these areas are likely to have reasonable boundaries. We are experts dealing with experts, and fortunately the more senior we are the more expert we are believed to be so that disagreements get resolved and the decisions are reasonably well accepted.

When it comes to social goals, none of us has much qualification or experience. There is no common understanding of what social values corporatons should seek. And those set on doing something for the public good seldom have enough conviction that they are right to overrule the objections, the doubters, the potential second guessers—not to mention the vigorous proponents of other corporate goals that seem, on occasion at least, to conflict with social progress.

Because social goal-setting is so new, so different and so difficult at this point, I believe it must for now be primarily a role of the chief executive. The average manager is conditioned by training and incentive programs to view profit as the solitary goal. Few managers view pursuit of social goals as necessary to personal success. Therefore, it is up to the chief executive to move the message downward, first through senior management and into the middle and lower levels of the organization. This must be done as an exercise not of autocracy but of · leadership.

Effective social goal-setting cannot be mandated in any organization—just as we found that civil rights legislation did not go very far toward changing the attitudes of a vast majority of people. I do not believe we can tell managers they must place a set number of social goals in their business plans each year and expect those goals to be pursued. It is more effective instead to create a climate in which managers willingly and thoughtfully place such goals in their plans. It has recently been my role to encourage our senior people to see that the social problems they can address creatively through their operations are considered when preparing annual plans, and that like amount of thought be given to addressing people problems as is given to addressing profit problems. If one were to read our company's annual business goals today, he would find a sprinkling of social goals mixed in with the traditional profit objectives. We have not, of course, addressed all the social problems we are able to affect. But we are doing more than we were a few years ago, and we will be doing still more in the years ahead . . .

It is important to realize that the setting of social goals is done with mixed motives. It is not merely a moral or altruistic pursuit. But, it seems to me perfectly legitimate to try to accomplish some worthwhile social goal even though we also bring about some favorable influence on our corporation. We cannot overlook the fact that our primary function of producing quality goods and services, while producing reasonable profit, cannot be ignored for very long. By the same token, we cannot make this objective our sole purpose and expect to continue earning a reasonable profit.

This division between executive groups is large and the allegiances of executive leaders in the industry are well known. These differences were played out in open forum when I presented the study findings to an association composed of the chief executive officers of the nation's largest property and casualty insurers. More-over, during my travels from company to company I discovered what amounted to two informal colleges of insurance executives. A subtle but systematic network could be discerned for each executive group. For example, when I asked executives to identify which of the largest insurance companies besides their own were doing an especially good job in the area of corporate external affairs, they generally nomi-nated companies whose executive leaders espoused philosophies similar to their own. When I probed into the backgrounds of external affairs staff professionals, many of whom had come to their current company from earlier experiences in either other companies or state regulatory agencies, I also found that many had worked with their counterparts in other companies who espoused philosophies similar to their own. And I was not surprised to learn that shortly after a senior line executive had been released from an institution-oriented company because his own philosophy did not fit, he reappeared among the senior management cadre of an enterprise-oriented company.

For all of the difference cited above, it should not be surprising that relations between these executive groups are sometimes more intense than their relations with the regulators who carry the social and political environment into the industry arena. Executives on both sides freely expressed their animosity toward one another during the field visits and interviews. Those with an enterprise-oriented philosophy fre-quently accused their institutional-oriented counterparts of "giving away the ship and the lifeboats." They viewed the institutionalists as being too conciliatory in their dealings with insurance legislators and regulators and with consumer interest groups.

Attacking the executive leader of an institution-oriented company, the vice president of government relations in an enterprise-oriented company said, "That company has a guy whose middle name is 'Conciliatory'! He is really aggravating to the industry. He'll cave in every time. He'll give up anything. He has no under-standing that we might have a position of our own that has merit." Referring to the cause of the difference between his company and the institutional-oriented one, the vice president said, "The only way I can explain the different approaches of his company and ours is in terms of the personalities at the top. He would fold and run at any chance he gets; whereas our leader would say what was really the right thing." Without prompting, he continued with rising emotion, "It all depends on your political philosophy. You have to decide how much you fold and give in to people, many of whom are not gainfully employed. They are probably out on the public dole to discredit the economic system! People should not be able to just have the whole ball game their way; not without any responsibility or accountability on their part."

Company differences in top management philosophy are very real. They are visible. They draw upon and fuel high emotions. They tend to permeate the organi-zation. And they are tangible because, as we shall see, they are closely tied to the type of strategy executive leaders assign to a company's external affairs function.

But where does top management philosophy come from, and why is it so pervasive and internally consistent in the nation's leading insurance companies?

Factors Influencing Top Management Philosophy

The comparative analyses and company histories that follow will reveal that the existence and pervasiveness of company differences in top management philosophy may be explained in large measure by a few factors that are characteristic in particular of the large, old insurance companies in America, and of large, old companies in general in this country.

In addition, because corporate social performance has been less amenable than economic performance to factual evidence and explicit, quantifiable measurement, there has been a tendency for subordinate executives to defer to the authority of the executive leaders on matters of corporate social policy. This tendency to defer to an authority figure in an ambiguous performance situation is well documented in the social psychology literature.[12]

First, the whole area of corporate external affairs, and in general, dealings with a company's nonmarket environment have traditionally been—for better or worse—the province of executive leaders in large corporations. Until the last two decades this function has typically been performed by the executive leader.[13] As the political environment has placed greater and greater pressure on private enterprise, staff units have been created to help the executive leader cope with an increasing external affairs burden. These staff units have generally served as extensions of the executive leader to whom they report and upon whom they are dependent for performance evaluation. As the new president of one of the insurance companies selected for intensive study explained, "Being president of a company gives you a unique opportunity to raise questions, to deal with emerging public issues, and to create access to information."

Thus, the chief executive officer can be expected to be a primary source of the prevailing top management philosophy in a company. Paradoxically, the comparative analysis that follows will reveal that overall company effectiveness in dealing with the increasingly turbulent social environment surrounding the U.S. insurance industry often hinges on whether the chief executive officer continues to monopolize this function or has encouraged broad participation in corporate external affairs activities from subordinate line and staff officers.

Several other factors reinforce and shape top management philosophy in the nation's major insurance companies.[14] First, much of this philosophy is carried and reinforced by the fundamental character of each corporation. These companies are quite old in both chronological age and organizational maturity when compared to companies in many other U.S. industries. Many of the nation's largest insurers were founded well before the turn of the century in response to a tangible social need which usually emerged in the immediate community.[15] As the senior vice president of external affairs in an institution-oriented company explained to me, "This company was founded by a guy whose objective was to bring insurance to low-income people. We started out with a social objective."

In many of the company cases that follow it will be shown that a large portion of the current philosophy shared by top managers can be traced to the early ideas of their company's founder. In most cases legends and stories about the social function that the company was created to perform, as well as about the deeds performed by successive executive leaders that exemplified and reinforced the company's founding purposes, have been developed and nurtured within the company for over a century.[16] Some companies actually commission periodic written histories of their progress. These legends and stories, together with the internal organizational contexts and operating mechanisms that are established and modified by successive executive leaders continue to reinforce employee attitudes, behaviors, and performance, which are consistent with the ideals embedded in the company's history and character.

Also reinforcing the persistence of the fundamental character and top management philosophy of each company is the fact that succession to executive leadership in this industry has usually been the product of long and faithful employment service in a single company. Very little movement of executives between companies may be observed, and very few young managers have been able to break into the companies' executive cadres. Thus, executive leaders, who shape and reinforce the character and philosophy of an insurance company, are often the product of long-term socialization to a company's traditional values and beliefs.

Despite the relatively enduring character of the large, old insurance companies, there is evidence that their philosophy is subject to modification. However, as one senior executive explained to me, these adaptations or modifications are better described as *directional* rather than fundamental in nature. Embedded in the company histories is evidence of at least three kinds of stimuli to philosophical development and change. First, a significant change in the business exposure of a company can initiate a reconsideration of its role in society and, particularly, in the way it approaches the task of learning about and responding to the corporate social environment. In some cases the external stimulus has emerged as an unanticipated or novel threat to one of the company's traditional product lines. Although it is conceivable that an environmental opportunity bearing similar features may also catalyze reconsideration of the company's approach, I frankly found no evidence of this in the company histories. Having to deal with an immediate or potential identified threat was by far the greatest catalyst to philosophical reexamination.

In other cases, attempts by executive leaders to diversify into new businesses or product lines have altered their company's traditional business exposure to the corporate social environment. Because the strategic choice to diversify was generally associated with an increase in the company's exposure, many leaders in diversifying companies found it necessary to reexamine their operating philosophy and to modify their external affairs mechanism to be able to cope with the enlarged social and political profile.[17]

In addition, many recent instances of executive succession have been accompanied by observable changes—often directional in nature—in a company's top management philosophy.[18] Even when the traditional pattern of executive succession was not violated by the appointment of a new executive leader, it was still possible to discern a noticeable elaboration in top management philosophy within a year or two after the event. This means that even though they have been exposed to the same internal company environment for decades of career service, different candidates for promotion to positions of executive leadership carry sometimes subtle but significant differences in personal values and political philosophies. One reason is that the candidates emerge from different functional areas within the company. Some come up through the parochial ladder of the company's business operations, whereas others have had extensive exposure to the broader social environment through previous service in corporate staff departments, such as the legal, external affairs, or planning functions. The career experience of some has been confined almost exclusively to positions within the company, whereas that of others has been marked by significant outside experience while still employed by the company. For example, executive leaders who had served in elected or appointed government posts or task forces while on leave from their company, seemed to bring to their appointment as executive leader a broader philosophy about the role of their corporation in society than those whose career had been confined within the company's boundaries.

Finally, there was one instance among the large insurance companies included in this study in which a poorly performing company had imported an executive leader from another company to turn things around. This sharp break in the company's traditional pattern of executive succession led to a substantial revision in its operating philosophy.[19] Although somewhat common in other industries, such events are quite unusual in the U.S. insurance industry, and they give enormous legitimacy to the incoming executive leader in specifying a new corporate order. Not surprising, the philosophy of our receiving company changed course in the direction of the one that characterized the company that the new executive leader had left.

In summary, although top management philosophy and the underlying character of a corporation were found to be relatively enduring in these large, old insurance companies, directional changes were often associated with dramatic shifts in either their business exposure or their traditional pattern of executive succession. Of course, such reorientations tended to be larger when changes occurred in both exposure and succession. Both types of events made it legitimate to explore the feasibility of making incremental or *directional* change. And both were generally associated with either a modification of top management philosophy or a reaffirmation and intensification of the company's deep-seated but operationally latent view of its proper role in society.

SUMMARY

In this chapter, I have applied three important elements of the general framework to the United States insurance industry. Hopefully this exercise will not only lay the groundwork for understanding the comparative investigation of corporate social performance that follows, but also provide a sound basis for applying the general framework to other industries.

First, industries vary considerably in the extent to which member firms are exposed to the corporate social environment in general. Regulated industries in the United States are those that are generally held by society to be "affected with the public interest," and are characterized by the high degree to which they are subjected to industry-specific regulators and regulations. Nonregulated industries, in contrast, are generally regarded as being only remotely affected with the public interest and, therefore, escape substantial exposure to industry-specific regulation. (It has been noted, however, that all United States industries have been exposed as never before to a variety of generic, i.e., nonindustry-specific, regulations in the social as opposed to purely economic arena during the past two decades. Therefore, the need for practitioners and scholars to more effectively understand and manage the corporate social environment has taken on more salience than in earlier eras of business history in the United States.)

These industry types form the extremes of a continuum of structures in the corporate social environment that are somewhat analogous to the economic structures of competition and monopoly that have been developed by economists to describe the corporate market environment. At one extreme on both continuua (e.g., nonregulated/monopoly), corporate discretion and managerial prerogatives are theoretically at their maximum; at the other extreme (e.g., regulated/competition), such discretion and prerogatives are substantially constrained by forces outside the individual firm. Both industry-level continuua, however, suffer similar shortfalls in their ability to prescribe, explain, and predict the behaviors and performances of different *individual* firms in the same industry.

A major thesis in the general framework presented in this book is that such industry-level designations poorly reflect the nature of the external environment to which a *particular* member firm is exposed. Similar observations have been made regarding the limitations of industry-market structures as the basis for explaining and predicting the competitive or economic—as opposed to social—behaviors of individual companies sharing the same industry market structure.

For example, in *Competitive Strategy,* Harvard Business School economist Michael Porter convincingly demonstrated that within the same industry companies behave quite differently depending on their unique competitive strategies.[20] Some companies, for example, pursue a high-volume, low-cost competitive strategy, which relies on commodity-like products; whereas others pursue a low-volume, high-margin strategy based on product differentiation. Through the explicit or implicit pursuit of different competitive strategies, executive leaders expose their firms to different economic contingencies in the overall market structure of the industry they share. To use Porter's terminology, companies within a given industry market structure pick the "battleground" in which they attempt to compete by explicitly or implicitly pursuing their own competitive strategy. It is through the selection of competitive strategy that executive leaders may choose the contingencies in the general market structure of their industry to which they are specifically exposed, as well as those they wish to effectively minimize or avoid.

The general framework for understanding and managing the corporate social environment employs a similar logic; one that is supported by the evidence from the U.S. insurance industry and from relevant studies of other U.S. industries. This framework recognizes the importance of the structure of the general social environment facing an industry. For example, it does not deny that companies in regulated industries need to employ more sophisticated external affairs mechanisms than those in nonregulated industries. But it regards such statements as trivial, seeking instead to provide advice that is relevant to the *specific* needs of *individual* companies.

The point of departure for the framework, therefore, is business strategy and the extent to which it "exposes" a particular company or group of companies to the *general* social environment surrounding their industry. The elements of a company's business strategy that were found to be most important in determining the "business exposure" of major U.S. insurance companies are product mix, geographical mix, and customer mix. By examining the sensitivities of these elements of business strategy to the *corporate* social environment of the U.S. insurance industry, it was possible to distinguish the business exposures of member firms and, as we shall see, understand and explain their relative effectiveness or ineffectiveness in terms of corporate social performance.

Although business strategy and exposure have been operationalized using terms most applicable to the U.S. insurance industry under investigation, the exercise should provide helpful insights for those who wish to apply a similar diagnosis to firms in other U.S. industries. While all three dimensions of business exposure may be relevant for many industry settings, the product-mix element appears to generalize to all industries. The relative importance of the other two elements of business exposure—customer and geographical mixes—must be judged on the basis of the nature of the industry to which they are applied.

Finally, I have developed a way of conceptualizing and assessing the differences among companies in terms of the philosophies held by executive leaders about the role of their corporations in society. To be sure, the assessment of value-laden constructs is more difficult than many of the other aspects of corporate performance, but to shy away from such important aspects of corporate behavior because of this difficulty seriously impedes—and has seriously impeded—the development of administrative science and practice.

Fortunately, a fine-grained analysis does not seem to be warranted at this stage in the development of our understanding of how executive leaders attempt to understand and manage relations between their organizations and the corporate social environment. As the comparative analysis will reveal, the gross categories of institution-oriented and enterprise-oriented top management philosophies go a long way toward explaining company differences in this arena. Moreover, the seemingly intangible construct of top management philosophy, as Chapter 3 will reveal, manifests itself in important tangible ways in the kinds of strategies executive leaders assign to their external affairs functions.

In summary, this chapter has revealed that the general social environment facing an industry provides only a first approximation of the business exposure of member firms. The point of departure for understanding the "business exposure" of a particular company is the analysis of its business strategy. The nature of a company's product mix, geographical mix, and customer mix provides a benchmark for understanding its business exposure and, therefore, for assessing the efficacy of its approach to dealing with the corporate social environment. It follows, then, that a thorough understanding of both the nature of the industry's general social environment and the extent to which a company's business strategy exposes it to various contingencies in that environment are essential before any attempt can be made to intervene into a company's approach to understanding and managing the corporate social environment for the purpose of improving its effectiveness.

Having diagnosed a company's business exposure, the next important step is to gauge its top management philosophy regarding the proper role of the corporation in society. With an accurate appreciation of a company's business exposure and top management philosophy, it is possible to understand the role played by a company's external affairs function in enhancing or inhibiting the overall corporate social performance of the company.

Chapter 3 will apply the remaining elements of the general framework— external affairs strategy and design—to the U.S. insurance industry. In general, two important relationships will be developed. First, there is a strong connection between top management philosophy and the strategy assigned by executive leaders to their external affairs function. Indeed, if one knows the viewpoint held by executive leaders about the proper role of their corporation in society, one may predict with great accuracy the external affairs strategy of the company. Second, there is an important contingent relationship between a company's business exposure, the sophistication of the design of its external affairs function, and corporate social performance. Holding other elements of the framework constant, the sophistication of a company's external affairs design must fit the degree of its business exposure in order to achieve effectiveness in overall corporate social performance.

FOOTNOTES

1. Until the 1970s, almost all federal government regulation in the United States was industry-specific in nature, as opposed to applying to business in general. For a brief summary of the recent trends in industry-specific versus general business regulation refer to Kim McQuaid, "Big Business and Public Policy in Contemporary United States," *Quarterly Journal of Economics and Business,* 1980, 20, no. 2, pp. 57–68.
2. For a recent comprehensive account of how the tobacco "Big Six" corporations have coped with smoking-and-health regulations see Robert H. Miles, *Coffin Nails and Cor-*

porate Strategies (Englewood Cliffs, NJ: Prentice-Hall, 1982), especially Chapter 3, "Domain Defense."

3. Two recent studies of relatively homogeneous industries have shown that although member firms appear to be equally exposed to the industry's political environment, selective advantages or disadvantages may be accrued to different companies depending on subtle differences in their business strategies. For detailed accounts of how companies in the United States cigarette and paper products industries are differentially exposed to their industry's corporate social environment refer to Robert H. Miles, *Coffin Nails and Corporate Strategies* (Englewood Cliffs, NJ: Prentice-Hall, 1982); and Jeffrey Sonnenfeld, *Corporate Views of the Public Interest* (Boston, MA: Auburn House, 1981).

4. The special role played by strategic management in selecting more or less effective operating domains within a given industry has been documented in Michael Porter, *Competitive Strategy* (New York: Free Press, 1981); Raymond E. Miles and Charles Snow, *Organizational Strategy, Structure and Process* (New York: McGraw-Hill, 1978); and Robert H. Miles, *Coffin Nails and Corporate Strategies* (Englewood Cliffs, NJ: Prentice-Hall, 1982).

5. The overall results of this survey have been published in Robert H. Miles, "Preliminary Report of the National Survey of State Insurance Commissioners," *Proceedings of the National Association of Insurance Commissioners,* 1981, II, 962–90.

6. A summary of the public-policy issues affecting the United States insurance industry, and the priorities attached to them by the state insurance commissioners, is reported in Robert H. Miles and Arvind Bhambri, "Public Policy Priorities and Insurer Responsiveness: Comparative Views of State Commissioners and Company Executives," *Best's Review,* Property/Casualty Insurance Edition, 1982, 82, no. 9, 20–24.

7. Based on a list of 22 insurance-related, public policy issues that were identified during field interviews with state insurance commissioners, the commissioners who participated in the National Survey were asked to rate each issue in terms of "what priority you believe major U.S. insurers should assign today to each of the following public policy issues confronting the industry." Priority ratings were scored using a five-point scale ranging from 1 = Very low to 5 = High. The issues and priority ratings for each insurance product line were as follows: *Property/Casualty Insurance*—automobile insurance affordability (4.4), arson (4.4), claims practices (4.2), automobile theft (4.0), workers' compensation (3.8), rate regulation (3.6), redlining (3.4), tort reform (3.4), products liability (3.3), residual markets (3.2), and automobile no-fault insurance (2.8); *Life Insurance*—cost disclosure (3.8), whole life vs. term insurance (3.0), and private pension reform (2.7); *Health Insurance*—health care cost containment (4.3), preventive health care and public education (3.5), private pension reform (2.7), and national health insurance (2.2); and *General Insurance Issues*—simplified policies (3.6), privacy (3.5), risk classification (3.5), federal insurance regulation (3.1), and universal social security coverage (2.3).

8. For a full account of the roles played by "activist" and "arbiter" types of state insurance commissioners, refer to Robert H. Miles and Arvind Bhambri, *The Regulatory Executives* (Beverly Hills, CA: Sage Publishing, 1983).

9. We were able to identify two different regulatory philosophies that formed the personal agendas and agency mission of state insurance commissioners. The first group of commissioners was labeled the *activists;* the second, the *arbiters.* Each group of commissioners pursued a distinctly different regulatory agenda and strategy. In addition, the

best predictor of the type of regulatory philosophy employed by commissioners was the nature of the immediate context in which they operated. Urban states tended to be represented by activists; whereas nonurban states tended to be represented by arbiters. Moreover, in cases where the fit between regulatory philosophy and context was poor, the turnover in insurance commissioners was higher than in cases where philosophy and context were congruent. For a complete discussion of how these groups of regulatory executives differ and the implications of their differences for major insurance companies, refer to Robert H. Miles and Arvind Bhambri, *The Regulatory Executives* (Beverly Hills, CA: Sage Publishing, 1983).

10. On the basis of one of the few comparative studies of managerial values that was international in scope, England concluded that, ''Personal value systems do differ in different organization contexts in ways that are generally understandable.'' However, he concluded by calling for field research to help explain how managerial value systems emerge in complex organizations and how they are modified through the process of succession to executive leadership positions. For details on this important study see George W. England, *The Manager and His Values* (Cambridge, MA: Ballinger, 1975).

11. Lee Preston has identified similar extremes in top management philosophy in his chapter on ''Corporate Power and Social Performance: Approaches to Positive Analysis,'' in *The Economics of Firm Size, Market Structure and Social Performance,* John J. Siegfried, ed., Proceedings of the Conference sponsored by the Bureau of Competition, Federal Trade Commission, Washington, D.C., July 1980, p. 37.

12. See for example the pioneering work on human obedience to authority by Stanley Milgram, ''Behavioral Study of Obedience,'' *Journal of Abnormal and Social Psychology,* 1963, 67, 371–78.

13. Some organizational theorists believe that a primary function of an executive leader is to ''infuse'' an organization with a set of values. For example, in *Leadership in Administration* (1957), Philip Selznick has argued that, ''This infusion produced a distinct character and distinctive competence. When institutional is well advanced, distinctive outlooks, habits, and other commitments are infused, coloring all aspects of organizational life and lending it a social integration that goes well beyond formal coordination and control.''

14. I have been able to demonstrate the relatively enduring nature of corporate character, and the many ways in which creative executive leaders have been able to shape and reinforce it, in studies of other U.S. industries. See, for example, my quarter-century study of the ''Big Six'' cigarette companies (Miles, 1982; especially Chapter 8).

15. In the literature on complex organizations, there is accumulating evidence that the date of organizational founding is associated with some relatively enduring characteristics of complex organizations. Arthur Stinchcombe (1965), for example, has argued that organizations are ''imprinted'' with the values in vogue during the era in which they are founded, and that such imprinting is not very responsive to subsequent changes in the social milieu in which the organization is embedded. Subsequently, Miles (1980) found similar patterns in his review of longitudinal studies of organization development. See John R. Kimberly, Robert H. Miles, and Associates, *The Organizational Life Cycle,* especially Chapter 14 (San Francisco: Jossey-Bass, 1980). Additional support for the Stinchcombe hypothesis was provided by Kimberly (1975) from a longitudinal study of sheltered workshops. He demonstrated that managerial beliefs and organizational strategies that were formed during the period of founding tended to persist even though the context in which these organizations performed had changed. Not surprising then is the

finding that, among the insurance companies selected for intensive study in this book, those with *institution*-oriented executive leaders were founded between 1853 and 1873, whereas those with explicit *enterprise*-oriented leaders were founded between 1912 and 1925. This quarter-century gap separating the social contexts in which these groups of companies were founded could account for their persistent differences in top management philosophy and corporate character.

16. In a rare study of the relatively enduring character of complex organizations, Burton Clark demonstrated the important role played by organizational stories and legends, which he labeled "sagas," in explaining organizational behavior and performance. As he explained, "Organizational saga refers to a unified set of publicly expressed beliefs about the formal groups that (a) is rooted in history, (b) claims unique accomplishment, and (c) is held with sentiment by the group." For more information about this comparative study of four-year colleges, see Burton R. Clark, *The Distinctive College* (Chicago: Aldine, 1970).

17. Evidence of the catalytic effects of changes in business exposure which result from changes in the corporate social and political environment or changes in its strategy toward greater diversification has been demonstrated in my study of the U.S. tobacco industry. Refer to Robert H. Miles, *Coffin Nails and Corporate Strategies* (1982), especially Chapters 5, 6, and 8.

18. My quarter-century study of organizational adaptation in the U.S. tobacco industry (Miles, 1982) revealed that a substantial portion of a company's dominant values and beliefs could be predicted on the basis of the political structure of its dominant coalition of executives. Political structure was operationalized in terms of the business functions represented within the dominant coalition based on the previous career experiences of its members. Noticeable shifts occurred within these companies in terms of the basic business values and beliefs that were expressed in the strategic decision-making process when a reconfiguration of the political structure of the dominant coalition occurred. This study, therefore, revealed the intimate relationship between top management philosophy and the pattern of executive succession within complex organizations.

19. Similar changes in corporate character and top management philosophy as a result of complete breaks in the traditional pattern of executive succession were observed in my quarter-century study of the U.S. tobacco industry (Miles, 1982).

20. Michael E. Porter, *Competitive Strategy* (New York: Free Press, 1981).

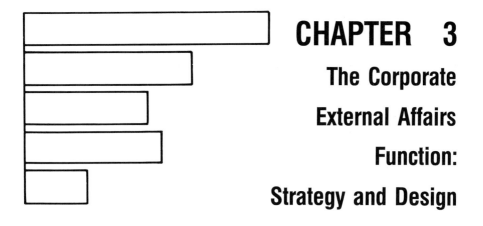

CHAPTER 3

The Corporate External Affairs Function:

Strategy and Design

At the core of a corporation's response to social and political contingencies is its external affairs function. There are two important aspects of this function that play a role in determining how well a company performs in this arena. The first is external affairs *strategy*, or the company's overall approach to external relations beyond those required by its product/markets. The second is external affairs *design*, or the organizational arrangements put into place to support the company's external affairs strategy. Both must be developed in some detail before proceeding with the comparative analysis of major insurers.

EXTERNAL AFFAIRS STRATEGY

Among the large insurance companies that participated in the study, three general strategic orientations or modes for corporate external affairs could be distinguished. Two of these strategies were *explicit*. They had been intentionally created, resourced, managed, and evaluated by executive leaders. One of these explicit external affairs strategy modes was *collaborative and problem-solving* in nature. The other explicit strategic mode was *individualistic and adversarial* in nature.

Each of these explicit external affairs strategies could be traced directly to the top management philosophy in the company. The individualistic/adversarial strategy was always associated with an enterprise-oriented philsosophy; and the collaborative/problem-solving strategy was always associated with an institution-oriented philosophy.

Moreoever, as the terminology implies, each of these explicit external affairs strategies is composed of two underlying dimensions: (1) external relationships with peer firms and (2) external relations with agents of the public interest.

The first dimension refers to how a focal company manages its external affairs activities with respect to those of other companies in the industry that are exposed to similar social and political contingencies. A focal company can generally ignore the situations of other similarly exposed firms and the consequences of its external-affairs activities for the industry or industry segment they share, and mount an external affairs strategy that is almost exclusively based on its own self-interests. This type of approach represents the *individualistic* strategic mode. In contrast, a focal company can pursue a *collaborative* approach, which more explicitly recognizes the implications of its external affairs activities for other similarly exposed firms and for the industry or industry segment as a whole.

Firms also differ in how they relate to agents of the public interest, including public-interest groups, legislators, and government regulators. Some firms adopt a *problem-solving* approach to the management of their relations with representatives of the public interest, whereas other firms adopt an *adversarial* approach to these relationships. Representative quotes taken from the interview transcripts of corporate executives and industry regulators are presented in Table 3-1 to illustrate how companies in this study differ on these two underlying dimensions of external affairs strategy.

The Reactive Companies

In addition, a few of the companies operated without an explicit external affairs strategy. Top management in these firms generally did not place a high priority on understanding and managing relations with the corporate social environment. As an external affairs officer in one of the reactive companies confided to me, "We're more devoted to the resolution of operational issues. Certainly those issues have first priority as opposed to external affairs issues. Only when an external affairs issue is perceived to have some measurable impact upon our operations do we go after it. It's sort of pragmatic. We don't have much time for ivory tower work."

Because their external affairs function is not well developed, executive leaders in the reactive companies tend to rely on the work of other companies, or the industry trade association in which they were a member, in attempting to define and defend their interests. As one senior line manager in a reactive company observed, "If you can get behind a forerunner, you can get the advantage of their experience." Occasionally reactive companies have gone out on their own when the interests and positions of other companies and trade associations departed too far from their interests; but they have generally achieved a negative reputation for doing so because they simply have not been prepared to enter this arena.

The reactive stance in corporate external affairs does not mean, therefore, that the behavior of these companies in the corporate social environment is perceived by outside constituencies as being neutral. Because these companies are not equipped

TABLE 3-1 Dimensions of External Affairs Strategy

Archetypes of External Affairs Strategy	Relationships With Peer Companies	Relationships With Agents of the Public Interest
Collaborative/Problem-Solving	Collaborative "Our *industry* has been thrust center stage to the very forefront of many of the key issues confronting society. We shrink from the challenges this situation presents at the peril of our entire private industry system." Corporate Executive Leader	Problem-Solving "Socially responsible companies *are flexible. They are willing to think through any position they take. They're not arbitrary* and they're *not hasty,* as opposed to other companies in the industry that are very traditional in their approach." Government Regulator
Individualistic/Adversarial	Individualistic "The benchmark we use in trying to develop a position on a public issue was explained to us [by our Chairman] several years ago, and it has not changed. It is *what is best for this company."* Corporate External Affairs Professional	Adversarial "*I prefer to deal with regulators in the courts.* I prefer to sue them." "What I admire about [the external affairs approach] of that company is that they'll sue the hell out of the regulators! They'll go to outside law firms and lobbyists. They hire 'gunmen,' 'hitmen,' you see. They're *free-wheeling.*" "It is really seldom that we find ourselves in a situation where we really have a question of what our priorities should be." Corporate External Affairs Professionals

or oriented toward anticipating insurance-related, regulatory, and political issues, they generally have to deal with an issue late in its life cycle.[1] As a vice president of government relations explained,

> We believe that public issues have a life cycle that follows a bell curve. You start to get public interest in an issue fairly early in the form of complaints. Then the complaints start to mount and they finally crescendo. At that point, maybe two years after the issue first emerges, it gets into the political environment. We're trying now to recognize an issue before it gets into the political environment so that we can bring to bear our public relations expertise and other communications skills. That's a major challenge, and one thing we're just beginning to develop greater skills on.

Tardy responses to important social and political issues affecting their business forces these companies into an adversarial external affairs strategy by default, because the only option available late in the game is a court suit. Moreover, the preference among reactive companies for tagging onto positions already established and identified with other companies or industry trade associations has the effect of communicating to outside constituencies that they have not thought through their position carefully. To make matters worse, because the reactive companies lack both the commitment and the resources to stay abreast of developments in the corporate social environment surrounding their industry, they are forced to allocate their somewhat impoverished external affairs talent only to issues of direct relevance to their primary product lines.

Thus, what responses they are able to make are highly individualistic ones. As a senior line manager in a reactive company revealed to me, "We are reactive in most situations. We take a defensive approach, rather than identify an issue and mount an offensive." One consequence, therefore, is that these companies have developed reputations that have tended, in turn, to weaken their bonds not only with regulators but with other companies upon which they might have to rely in future engagements in the social and political environment.

Thus a reactive company is one that has failed to establish an organizational context in which to relate to regulators and other constituencies in the corporate social environment. When an issue comes up that is relevant to such a company, its external affairs function must work through poorly established relationships with external constituencies and with uninformed and generally reluctant business managers within the enterprise. The confessions of a vice president of corporate communications in a reactive company included the following statement about the company's external affairs process: "Because we haven't defined our positions and given ammunition to the Chairman or other senior management people, we haven't wanted to go to the public forums. Basically, we really haven't had our act together in what our message is."

Only two companies in this study were attempting to operate in the complex and volatile social environment of the insurance industry without an explicit external affairs strategy. As might be expected, both were among the three companies included in the category of the industry's worst corporate social performers. Both companies had learned the hard way that more clarity of strategy and more sophistication in design was needed in the external affairs function if they were to perform effectively in the contemporary corporate social environment. Although they were unclear about how to improve their external affairs function, executive leaders and external affairs professionals in these reactive companies welcomed the invitation to participate in the comparative study in hopes of learning something that would be useful to them. As the general counsel at one of the reactive companies explained on the eve of my visit, "I've discussed your study with our president. One of the reasons we decided to participate is that we believe a study of this kind will help us focus on external affairs. We haven't done enough in this area."

I will return to the reactive approach to corporate external affairs in the company histories that follow. However, it is important now to get a fix on the two explicit strategies that were employed by insurance companies to guide their external affairs activities.

The Philosophy-strategy Connection

The strongest connection between the factors in the general framework being developed in this book is the one linking top management philosophy and external affairs strategy. As a *Harvard Business Review* article reported over a decade and a half ago, "The values that are most important to an executive have a profound influence on his strategic decisions."[2] Unfortunately very little has been done in the study of organization and management to demonstrate this relationship. In this sense, the present investigation represents a major departure.

Institution-minded executive leaders had explicitly developed collaborative and problem-solving strategies for their external affairs functions; whereas enterprise-minded executive leaders had explicitly developed individualistic and adversarial strategies for their external affairs functions. Moreover, enterprise-minded executives who had failed to create explicit strategies for their company's external affairs function found their organizations pursuing by default an implicit external affairs strategy that approximated the individualistic/adversarial approach.

The individualistic/adversarial strategy.   Enterprise-oriented companies are guided by executive leaders who wish to restore for their firms the economic independence that characterized an earlier period of history in the United States. They resent the erosion of traditional managerial prerogatives and they seek to restore separation of state and economic enterprise. As a senior staff professional in an enterprise-oriented company explained, "In many areas we think of Adam Smith's 'Invisible Hand,' and it eventually comes out right. I certainly know that's the viewpoint of the Chairman, and for good or bad, a lot of his philosophy has filtered down into this organization." They are generally suspicious of the motives of regulators who press the industry to adapt to social change, often viewing regulators as opportunists in search of visibility for the purpose of attaining higher elected public office.

Because of their political philosophy, enterprise-oriented executives create corporate external affairs functions whose primary mission it is to defend and protect the company's economic self-interests and forestall further encroachment of the social environment into the private insurance mechanism. As one enterprise-oriented executive explained to me, "My philosophy is that some of the most active state insurance commissioners want us to finance social change without the power to tax." The strategy these executives assign to the corporate external affairs function, therefore, differs in two important ways from those of institution-oriented executives.

First, the external affairs strategy in enterprise-oriented companies tends to be extremely *individualistic*. For instance, an enterprise-oriented, vice president of government affairs identified the criteria he used to determine which public policy issues to pay attention to as follows: "The philosophy I personally utilize is, number one, how do I feel an issue is going to impact *my company per se*. Number two, I will look at other issues that could generate precedents if they went through." His counterpart in another enterprise-oriented company revealed a similar approach when he explained that, "The benchmark we use in trying to develop a position on a public issue was explained to us several years ago, and it has not changed much. It is what is best for *this* company."

Many of these companies have actually withdrawn their memberships in the industry's trade associations because the positions on industry-related social and political issues taken by the associations tend to be developed on the basis of compromise and consensus among member firms whose business strategies and exposures differ. Others continue to rely on the umbrella provided by trade associations to develop positions on insurance issues, which only peripherally affect their core business lines; but they feel free to break away on issues of direct company relevance. As the executive vice president of operations in an enterprise-oriented company explained, "We're trying to work with the trade associations, but many times we have to be able to act on our own, through our own people, our own agents, our own lobbyists, our own consultants, or with a segment of the industry with which we share common interests."

In addition to assigning a narrow, parochial focus to the external affairs function, enterprise-oriented executive leaders are not predisposed to so-called mutual problem solving with elements of the corporate social environment. They prefer instead to treat such elements in an *adversarial* manner, and they tend to select as the vanguard of their external affairs thrust the corporate legal function, whose members' skills, training, and professional orientation are well suited to the adversarial approach. As the head of external affairs in one enterprise-oriented company proudly announced, "I prefer to deal with state insurance commissioners in the courts. I prefer to sue them!" When the vice president in another enterprise-oriented company was asked to identify a firm in the industry that he believed was very effective in the external affairs area, replied, "What I admire about that company is that they'll sue the hell out of regulators! They go to outside law firms and lobbyists. They hire gunmen, hitmen, you see. They're free-wheeling." Indeed, the head of one of the industry's largest company-based, external affairs functions expressed an extreme version of the adversarial external affairs strategy during a senior staff meeting in which I reported the company's overall social performance rating. As the closing comment in the meeting he said, "It might be that we would judge ourselves as effective only if *all* state insurance commissioners rated us among the *worst* five companies!"

The collaborative/problem-solving strategy. The external affairs strategy that is pursued by institution-oriented companies contrasts sharply with the one described above. Although institution-oriented companies have their own business stakes to safeguard, they tend to define their interests more broadly than enterprise-oriented companies. As one institution-oriented chief executive observed, "The insurance industry has been thrust center stage on the American political and social scene. We have been propelled—willingly or not—to the very forefront of many of the key issues confronting our society. We shrink from the challenges this situation presents at the peril of the entire private insurance business." Therefore, their relations with constituencies in the social environment surrounding the industry, as well as with other major insurance companies, tends to be *collaborative* rather than individualistic.

Executives in institution-oriented companies believe it is important to orient corporate external affairs activities toward the long-term interests of both the company and the industry as a whole. Consequently, they are willing to accept the need for adaptation in their business policies and practices in specific instances in order to be both responsive and effective over the long haul. "The changing business environment doesn't mean that we must become less businesslike or give less emphasis to profitability," said one institution-oriented chief executive. "It does mean that corporations focusing entirely on short-term profit will over the long term become less profitable. We must continue earning our franchise—not just in the marketplace, but in the minds of people."

There is, moreover, considerable evidence among the institution-oriented companies that they do in fact make short-term sacrifices in their attempts to safeguard the legitimacy of their industry. A senior actuary in such a company described the strategy by which his company had withdrawn from a very profitable line because its executive leaders believed the product did not serve the public interest. He said, "There have been instances when we as a company have taken a position that has probably cost us one heck of a lot of business. We believe it isn't enough to sell a product. It has to be what we feel is socially worthwhile." He continued by explaining that his company attempted to defend its business interests in the marketplace, not in the political arena:

> The products that we really feel are not good for the public and, therefore, that should not be sold are the ones we are actively contesting in the regulatory arena. For other products that are a threat to us, we have to determine how to respond to them in the marketplace; not in the regulatory arena.

In addition, because they believe corporate social responsibility is broader than the short-term "bottom line," institution-oriented executives tend to pursue a *problem-solving approach* with regulators who represent various public interest groups. For instance, the senior actuary continued his explanation as follows, "In addition, we want to maintain good relationships. The two objectives reinforce one another. So our approach is not completely altruistic. A corporation is a good citizen because it's good business." Thus, the external affairs strategy of institution-oriented companies is directed toward a broad perspective and toward creating and maintaining effective long-term relationships with key representatives of the public interest.

Because of the strategic orientation of their external affairs function, institution-oriented companies do not shy away from industry trade associations; instead they go to them well prepared to debate the issues and to confront the different interests that are represented by other member companies. They are also perceived by regulators as having an open mind when considering new insurance-related legislation or regulatory models. For example, when one commissioner described to me that characteristics he associated with socially responsive companies in the industry, he said, "They're flexible. They are willing to think through any position they take. They're not arbitrary and they're not hasty, as opposed to other companies that are very traditional in their approach to insurance." Executive leaders and external affairs professionals in the institution-oriented companies appear to understand and pursue this orientation. As a senior line manager in one of these companies observed,

> One way or another the state insurance commissioners have learned that they can approach companies like ours; that they can try a new idea out on us. I enjoy that position in which a state commissioner shows us a draft of a proposed regulation and says, "Before I announce this to the public, criticize it."

The importance of maintaining trust and open lines of communication between the company and the insurance regulators was emphasized by an institution-oriented, external affairs officer in an account he shared with me about how one of the company's newly acquired subsidiaries was planning to deal with a heavy-handed state commissioner in one of the most politically volatile urban states. In order to deal with this commissioner, the representative of the new subsidiary was planning to team up with his counterpart at a hard-line, enterprise-oriented insurance company (that, unknown to either person, was rated by the state commissioners as the overall worst corporate social performer in the industry). As the officer in the parent company explained,

> The external affairs representative of one of our new insurance subsidiaries came to me and expressed a desire to sue a commissioner because he had handed down a very novel regulation that directly affected the subsidiary's primary business. He wanted to get that son-of-a-bitch; to teach him a lesson! I said, "Fine. If that's what you want to do, go ahead. But at the same time, look at all these items that the company wants me

to take down to that commissioner during the next ninety days and ask him if he will expedite them on a priority basis." I also said, "I have a stinking suspicion that if you guys kick him where it hurts, he'll put these two agendas together when I go down to ask him for a favor. Now, who's going to win? Can we consider a compromise situation?"

I don't know how this is going to work out. But I hope that before this subsidiary goes ahead with its plan to sue this commissioner, the company will inform them about what the broader consequences will be."

This problem-solving aspect of the external affairs strategy in institution-oriented companies contrasts sharply with the preset positions that are revealed in the following statement by an enterprise-oriented executive, "It is really seldom that we find ourselves in a situation where we really have a question of what our priorities should be."

Another interesting feature of institution-oriented companies is the nature of the internal process of their external affairs function. The orientation in these companies emphasizes a broad perspective, relies on collaborative problem solving, and concedes the possibility that changes in business policies and practices may be required. This orientation creates the need for active involvement of nonlegal public affairs professionals and line managers as well as of professionals representing the legal function. This orientation contrasts sharply with that of the enterprise-oriented companies.

The legally dominated, adversarial approach of one enterprise-oriented company was illustrated by its CEO when he explained to me that, "State insurance departments know where we stand. They know we have no hesitancy about our positions. If we think they're doing something that won't stand up, we'll go to court. I suppose that at any point in time, we probably have six to eight state insurance departments that we're pursuing in court on some issue. Our external affairs activity is primarily performed by the Corporate Legal Department." And the corporate counsel in another company illustrated the differences between the legal and nonlegal approaches to external affairs in his company when he said, "My job is not to change the world, but to get what my company can get in the existing regulatory and legislative environment. The Public Affairs Department, in contrast, is out to improve the world, to change the process, and to improve the way America lives."

In summary, there is a very close connection between top management philosophy and external affairs strategy in the major U.S. insurance corporations, as illustrated in Figure 3-1. Institution-oriented companies explicitly pursue a collaborative/problem-solving strategy that takes a broad view of the interests at stake when a new industry-related public policy issue or regulatory agenda emerges and that seeks to create long-term, collaborative relationships with various agents of the public interest. Executives in these companies recognize that one of the legitimate responses their company must be prepared to make to public demands is a change in their traditional business policies and practices. In contrast, enterprise-oriented companies pursue explicitly or by default an individualistic/adversarial external affairs strategy, which is oriented almost exclusively to the defense and preservation of their own business policies, practices, and interests.

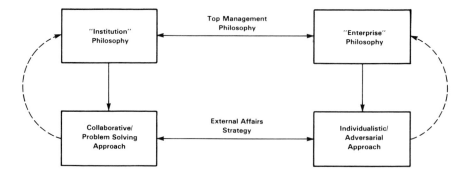

Figure 3-1   The philosophy-strategy connection in corporate external affairs.

The Philosophy-strategy-exposure Connection

The study of major insurers also revealed that the external affairs strategies of institution- versus enterprise-oriented companies have important although indirect influences on the business strategy, and consequently on the business exposure of these insurers. Institution-oriented companies for example, have tended to maintain their exposure to politically volatile urban states and to develop relationships with regulators that have helped them manage the ups and downs associated with the urban political climate. In contrast, many enterprise-oriented companies have been actively attempting to reduce their business exposure to enchance their self-interests. As one enterprise-oriented CEO confided in me, "One of my priorities is to try to move our business further West geographically, out of the Northeast part of the country—as rapidly as we can!" When asked why he placed such a high priority on changing the company's geographical mix, he said,

> I'm looking at other parts of the country where today the climate from a regulatory perspective is a more reasonable one in which to conduct a free-enterprise system. These areas would differ from places on the East Coast, such as Florida, New Jersey, Massachusetts, and New York, which I would characterize as totally consumer-oriented—particularly in personal lines, and becoming consumer-oriented in the major commercial lines.

The reverse direction of causality, however, was not observed in this industry. The fact that companies were exposed to a high degree of complexity and turbulence in the corporate social environment was not necessarily something that influenced their philosophy or external affairs strategy. None of the elements of business exposure—product mix, geographical mix, or customer mix—was an effective predictor of top management philosophy or external affairs strategy.

In summary, the views executive leaders hold about corporation's proper role in society powerfully shape the strategy of its external affairs function. In addition, there is evidence that top management philosophy has an impact on other aspects of corporate strategy, such as business strategy and exposure, although this linkage is not as strong as the connection with external affairs strategy.

EXTERNAL AFFAIRS DESIGN

The design of a corporation's external affairs function and the degree of involvement of line managers in the external affairs process make up the last important elements in the general framework. To some readers, the placement of external affairs structure and process as last in the series of company variables that are important may seem curious. What little research that is available on corporate social performance has focused almost exclusively on the development of the external affairs function itself.[3] The framework developed in this book, and all of the evidence supporting it, argues strongly that a prior assessment of the nature of the corporate social environment, the exposure of a particular firm to it, its top management philosophy, and its external affairs strategy, must proceed before one can accurately assess a company's external affairs design and begin to improve it. With this important caveat stated, the design of the external affairs function is critically important in influencing how a company responds to the corporate social environment.

Some aspects of the design of the corporate external affairs function are relatively easy to assess and document. Often one can get a fairly good sense of these design features by carefully studying organization charts, departmental mission statements, job descriptions, and other company archives. Most of the important aspects of the design of the external affairs function, however, require a closer look. To understand these design elements one must pierce the corporate veil by gaining access into the organization, interviewing key decision makers representing different functions, and observing how the external affairs function works, both internally and externally with its constituencies inside and outside the organization. Occasionally, direct involvement or intervention into the external affairs function is also needed to test and refine one's understanding of it.

All but the last approach to understanding the design of the external affairs function were applied consistently to the companies participating in the comparative study. By good fortune, I was also able to become directly involved, for a period of five years, in the development of the external affairs function within the company that later was rated as the industry's best in overall corporate social performance. Based on what I learned from all these experiences, it seems most useful to discuss the design of the corporate external affairs function, first, in terms of its basic components and then in terms of the four critical design elements over which a company's executive leadership exercises considerable control.

The Basic Components

A corporation's external affairs function is made up of two basic components. To concentrate on one component to the neglect of the other will almost certainly result in a serious shortfall in understanding both a company's external affairs function and its overall corporate social performance.

The first and most obvious component of the external affairs function consists of the people and units within an organization whose *primary* responsibility it is to help the organization understand and manage its relations with the corporate social environment. Across U.S. industries a great variety of external affairs units have emerged under an even greater assortment of labels; all of which have primarily been created to help companies deal with this increasingly important segment of the total business environment. But nowhere has the variety exceeded that which has emerged in many U.S. industries, such as food processing, prescription drug manufacturing, public utilities, banking, and insurance; businesses that are generally regarded as being heavily "affected with the public interest."

In the insurance industry an element of the corporate legal department is almost always part of the external affairs function. Also generally included are public relations and advertising or corporate communications departments. Then there are, to varying degrees, departments that have been created explicitly to address the political and social, or nonmarket, environment of the corporation. They come under a variety of departmental headings, including corporate relations, public affairs, government relations, corporate "futures," environmental analysis, legislative relations, regulatory relations, customer relations, community relations, corporate social responsibility, corporate public involvement, and almost any conceivable combination of the above.

In addition, most of the large insurance companies included in this study have established federal relations departments, many of which are located in Washington, D.C. And a few companies have begun to experiment with sophisticated analytical units, under department titles such as public policy issues analysis, which conduct in-depth studies of the nature and implications of various industry- and company-related, public policy issues and regulatory and legislative initiatives. Finally, a couple of these companies have charged such issues-analysis functions with responsibilities not only for producing an objective and useful analysis of the social and political issues confronting the firm, but also for developing recommendations for needed changes in the firm's traditional business practices. In one firm, the issues analysis function is actually held accountable for whether or not it is able to encourage business managers to implement changes in their operations. To the extent that any of these units are present in a company's structure, they are considered as part of its external affairs function.

The second major component of the corporate external affairs function consists of those people and units who are involved in external affairs activities but whose primary responsibilities lie in other areas. As the assessment of corporate social performance in the next chapter will reveal, the business policies and practices of a corporation are inextricably related to the social goals it pursues and the external affairs activities in which it becomes engaged. Therefore, in understanding a corporation's external affairs function it is critical that an account be made of the nature of the relationships between core external affairs professionals and units and other key units and actors in the organization. Of particular interest are the roles played in external affairs by the chief executive officer, by the senior executive cadre, and by managers of the company's line or business functions, and the processes of influence and integration that characterize their relations with core external affairs professionals.

The Four Design Dimensions

Although there are many ways to describe the design of a company's external affairs function, four dimensions are especially important in explaining how companies attempt to understand and manage the corporate social environment. These four dimensions represent levers at the disposal of executive leaders for improving external affairs effectiveness. Each dimension was assessed in multiple ways during the comparative study. Moreover, when an accurate diagnosis of a company's business exposure, top management philosophy, and external affairs strategy has been made, all four dimensions become essential in explaining the differences in overall corporate social performance among the nation's largest insurers.

Breadth.   The first and most visible dimension is the breadth of the corporate external affairs function. External affairs breadth refers to the structural complexity of the function. This dimension may be operationalized as the number of *different* units whose *primary* responsibility it is to manage the company's external affairs activities.

The theoretical justification for the breadth dimension lies in the well-known contingency theory of organization design.[4] Contingency theorists argue that organizations are effective to the extent that their internal structure is of sufficient complexity to cope with the complexity of the external environment to which the organization is exposed. The more complex the external environment, the greater the need is for the organization to have specialized units to deal with each major element of the external environment.[5] Translating this general proposition for our present purposes, the breadth or structural complexity of a company's external affairs function should be sufficient to cope effectively with the business exposure of the company to the corporate social environment. Companies with heavy business exposures should have great external affairs breadth; whereas those confronted with modest business exposures require much less breadth.

The major insurers presented us with external affairs functions that occupy different points along the full range of the breadth continuum. Moreover, the fit between business exposure and external affairs breadth was a good one for several companies, while for others the fit was a poor one. Corporate social performance varied systematically with the degree of fit between exposure and breadth.

At one extreme in the breadth continuum was a company that had been taken over by a noninsurance conglomerate and that had been struggling since the arrival of its new leadership to turn around its poor economic performance. When I inquired about the company's approach to external affairs, the company's newly appointed head of a one-person public affairs department simply explained that, "We have not dealt with the subject of external affairs for about two and a half years!"

Nevertheless, even in such a company, one will find the traditional public relations and advertising department and a corporate legal function; and usually a couple of people from both functions have been assigned at least part-time responsibility for handling nonmarket, or external affairs activities. A marketing research manager in the captive insurer explained his situation as follows:

> Rarely do we have a person who has just external affairs responsibilities. Its a matter that we have been given limited resources. We've got many day-to-day priorities in both line and external affairs. We would really like to take more independent positions on issues and present our viewpoints, but most of us are dissatisfied with the time and resources that we have to devote to these things. I *know* I'm dissatisfied with the amount of time I can spend on those things. But Marketing Research isn't strictly involved with public issues.

As a minimum in terms of external affairs breadth, therefore, the insurance companies in this study had given at least part-time responsibility to a few staff professionals who, most likely, are located in the traditional legal and public relations functions.

At the other extreme in external affairs breadth were companies that had developed an elaborate set of units whose primary responsibility is in the area of external affairs and whose work is specialized in and focused on different segments of the social environment confronting the company. For example, one high-breadth, corporate external affairs function contained the following eleven units all reporting to an individual who was regarded as a "superstar" in this arena: media relations, industry relations, public relations, government relations (which was subdivided into legislative relations and regulatory relations), customer relations, public affairs, research and analysis, federal affairs, and a company-sponsored political action committee (PAC) that was national in scope and that was supported through employee payroll deductions.

Not surprising, staff professionals in this company believed strongly and took great pride in informing me that they were part of the most sophisticated external affairs function in their industry. From their perspective, such a judgment is properly made on the basis of the breadth dimension of external affairs design alone. The fact that their function scored relatively low on the other three design dimensions suggested to me that these staff professionals either were unaware of the importance of the other dimensions of external affairs design or were unwilling to recognize them. I suspect that more of the latter is the case because of the arrogance these professionals openly displayed, in their conversations with me, especially with respect to the company's line managers. As one of the company's many external affairs vice presidents explained to me, "There are people who say it can't be done. In this department we always say, 'I wish you would just not stand in the way of those who are doing!'"

Depth. Corresponding to the breadth or horizontal dimension of external affairs design is what might be termed the vertical dimension. If breadth refers to the extent to which the elements of the corporate social environment are "covered" by specialized external affairs units, depth is concerned with how intensive the organizational learning process is within the external affairs function about the outside world.

The real test of external affairs depth is the *intensity* with which external affairs professionals are able to frame and conduct research and analysis on emerging, industry-related, public policy issues. External affairs depth, therefore, consists of two components:

1. the *range of perspectives* allowed in framing the issues- analysis process,
2. the *range of alternative company responses* to these staff professionals are encouraged to consider in the issues-analysis process.

External affairs professionals in some companies take a very shallow look at emerging social and political issues affecting the insurance industry. Their primary perspective in issues analysis is the company's immediate business stakes. The range of company responses that external affairs professionals are permitted to consider is usually confined to defending and protecting the company's existing business policies, practices, and products. But even this small degree of depth presumes that these huge, nationwide companies have an issues-analysis process within the external affairs function to help key decision makers learn about and respond to developments in the social and political environment. A surprising discovery in the comparative study of major insurers is that most companies do not have such a capability. As the newly appointed president of one of the worst-rated corporate social performers in the industry explained,

> The question of what will be the burning social issues of the 1980s and of how we should deal with them has been conducted for the most part through our trade association. We have really piggy-backed on them, and we have used them as our window to what the social issues are and how our segment of the industry or our company individually should deal with them. We as a company have not developed the capability of drawing back to look at the world as it is moving and develop plans and strategies. We simply have not done much of that.

Because this company had neglected the development of external affairs depth, it had literally been caught with its pants down when a recent, major controversy had emerged in the regulatory arena concerning its primary product line. Because the company was one of the nation's leading insurers in the affected product line, its tardy, defensive reaction to the controversy had undermined the credibility of the company's response and had caused the company to become typed by regulators and other leading insurers as being completely self-serving and generally thoughtless in its external affairs approach. Because the company was still recovering from this set-back when the field visit was conducted, the external affairs staff under the encouragement of the new president was attempting to learn from the comparative study how their internal process might be improved.

The company described in the previous section as having an external affairs function that was characterized as great in breadth also had a shallow issues-analysis process. It applied a very narrow range of perspectives and alternative company responses to issues analysis, focusing principally on what was best for the company at the point in time that the public issue emerged in the political arena and charging the process with identifying positions that would help defend the company's traditional way of doing things. As the vice president of government affairs explained, "The work on our company's positions on public issues is generated by a young man in my department. There are eighty position statements in the Corporate Relations Manual he develops. But to be really accurate, I'd have to say that most of the issues identified in our position index have already reached the stage in which they have appeared in the political environment."

The issues-analysis function in other companies cuts much more deeply. The analysis of issues is generally framed from a broad perspective; one that often includes the industry as a whole and the interests of nonpolicyholders as well as policyholders. Importantly, these high-depth functions represent not only the interests of the company's lawyers and public relations experts, but also those of line managers and staff professionals who have not been socialized and trained from the adversarial and representational perspectives. Just as important, the issues-analysis process in these companies is charged with the responsibility for initiating and monitoring changes, when warranted by their research and analysis, in the company's business policies, practices, and products; not merely for developing defensible positions for the status quo in the company. As a senior vice president heading the largest business division in a company characterized as having external affairs depth explained, "I think the 'proof in the pudding' for our Public Policy Issues Analysis Department really is not the research itself, though that's critical. But it is what the operating people will do in response to what comes out of that department. If we don't get organizational change out of this activity, then I guess you wonder whether it is really worth it."

In summary, high-depth external affairs functions, because of the wide range of perspectives and responses they factor into the issues-analysis process, often serve not only as *agents of organizational learning* about the external social and political environment, but also as important *catalysts to managerial thinking and organizational change* in a company's business policies, practices, and products. In contrast, shallow external affairs functions tend to be more oriented (if, indeed a company has an issues-analysis process) toward external persuasion, rather than managerial understanding and organizational adaptation.

Influence and Integration.   The last two dimensions of external affairs design describe the *quality* of relationships among staff units within the core external affairs function. These relationships may be expressed in terms of the degrees of influence and integration achieved within the organization.

Regarding relations among the core units of the external affairs function, it is important to external affairs effectiveness that no unit or subset of units dominate the ongoing process of helping the organization understand and manage the corporate social environment. For a company to be able to comprehend its social and political environment accurately, and for it to be able to clarify its position and respond effectively with respect to that environment, there should be a relatively high degree of mutual influence and integration among the various external affairs units that specialize in different parts or sectors of the external world.

When a gross imbalance in influence among these specialized units occurs, it is likely to result in a distorted perception of the corporate social environment and a biased company response to it. In the highly regulated U.S. insurance industry, for example, the external affairs function has traditionally been performed by the public relations and advertising and, especially, the corporate legal functions. If these functions are permitted to dominate the external affairs process, their primary perspectives, which emphasize company representation, protection, and advocacy, will tend to prevail in its interpretation of and response to the corporate social environment.[6]

Similarly, relationships among core external affairs units must meet some minimal standard of integration. In the absence of coordination, duplication of staff effort reduces external affairs efficiency. This visible abuse of corporate overhead aggravates the normal tensions between staff professionals and cost-conscious senior line managers. Moreover, the company may find itself pursuing different positions simultaneously in response to the same external affairs issue. These likely consequences send mixed signals to both internal and external constituencies of the external affairs function, eroding internal support for the function and external confidence in the organization as a whole.

Line-manager Involvement

Despite the obvious importance of the patterns of influence and integration within the corporate external affairs function itself, the quality of relationships established *between* external affairs professionals and senior line managers of the company's basic business operations appear to be more critical to external affairs success and overall corporate social performance.[7] As the comparative study will reveal, companies vary considerably in the degree of mutual influence and integration that has been achieved between senior line managers and corporate external affairs professionals.

External affairs activities in some firms are dominated by the perspectives of staff professionals who serve to buffer the line operations from potential perturbances from the corporate social environment. One company, for example, stood out as having the most staff-dominated, external affairs function in the industry. Under its previous chief executive officer the company had not taken the corporate social environment very seriously. Consequently it had been unprepared for the social and political turmoil that erupted around the industry during the late 1970s. When his successor, who had earlier served as head of the company's public affairs department, took over, he was determined to build an effective external affairs function around a new vice president who had served as a state insurance commissioner. As the company's senior insurance operations executive explained,

> Until [the new vice president of external affairs] arrived and started doing his show, we were seen as being absolute pushovers to regulators. We were not regarded highly by our key competitors either. Quite frankly, they regarded us with great disdain because we would give in and make it very difficult for them to try to push for more from the regulators. Since we've established our external affairs function we've been able to reestablish ourselves in a number of states as a company that is fair but firm; one that is not a pushover. If necessary, now we'll take the commissioner all the way to court!

Line managers, however, have had little influence in the conduct of external affairs in this company. As one senior line manager confided, "The senior operational managers and the regional managers who report to them rarely have any role in setting political issues. I mean *nothing!* In other words, the line managers have *no* say in these things.!'"

At the other extreme, line managers are all-powerful in corporate external affairs. Usually this condition is associated with a lack of external affairs breadth and depth; and typically the few staff professionals that do specialize in external affairs are obliged to perform their duties as prescribed by the traditional, and often parochial viewpoint of the company's business managers.

One variation of the line-dominated function, although somewhat exceptional in a highly exposed industry such as the business of insurance, might be more common in less-exposed industries. This is the CEO-dominated external affairs function. In one of the worst-rated corporate social performers in the insurance industry, the Chairman and Chief Executive Officer attempted to be the dominant source of wisdom and the principal actor in the area of corporate external affairs. "If you want an honest picture of what happens," said one senior line manager, "the company is very much dominated by its Chairman. The committees serve as sounding boards for things that are presented to a large group of top managers, but the decision-making process is pretty much all the Chairman's." Other executives in the company not only conceded that the Chairman made all the external affairs decisions, but also that knowledge of his personality influenced the analysis and recommendations offered to him by external affairs professionals. "I believe some of us feel we're more effective because we know where the Chairman is going to come out; therefore, we don't go chasing down a lot of dark alleys and coming up with zeros,'' said one staff professional. ''You pretty much know when you're putting something together how the Chairman is going to come out.''

But the CEO-dominated external affairs function is probably the exception in this industry because many observers would agree that it has been over a decade since—if ever—a single individual could be entrusted with solving all the problems posed by the increasingly turbulent social environment of the U.S. insurance industry. In most cases, therefore, the line-dominated function has emerged in companies whose external affairs depth and breadth have not kept up with developments in their business exposures.

Finally, the study revealed a few companies in which a fairly sophisticated external affairs function has been able to develop a high degree of mutual influence between staff professionals and line managers. The result is often a blend of professional objectivity and business relevance in external affairs work; one consequence of which is that, when it comes time to make a change in the company's business policies and practices in order to respond to developments in the corporate social environment, the recommendations that come from the external affairs staff are likely to be viewed by senior line managers as being both warranted and acceptable.

This balance of mutual influence between line and staff units, therefore critically shapes how effectively a highly exposed corporation responds to developments in its social and political environment. The comparative study will reveal that such a balance is, indeed, difficult to achieve and maintain; but that executive leaders have at their disposal the tools to make it happen.

The final dimension of line-manager involvement is the degree of integration that has been achieved within a company between line managers and external affairs professionals. Assuming a company has an external affairs function that is sophisticated enough to cope with its business exposure, both the extent to which external affairs units coordinate their efforts with line units and the extent to which line managers are aware of and involved in the external affairs process become important ingredients in external affairs success.

In some companies there is virtually no integration between line and staff functions. Line managers are held accountable for day-to-day business operations and market performance, while staff professionals together with the executive leader handle all external affairs activities relating to the corporate social environment. As a public affairs executive in one of these companies observed, ''The operating end of our business has not had any formal, specified method of entering into the external affairs arena. The legal function has always been there and is getting stronger.'' Indeed, so separate were the responsibilities of line and staff executives in one company that its senior external affairs officer scheduled my site visits for the only days in the year that he could be sure the entire group of senior line managers was attending an out-of-town retreat! It came as quite an initial surprise to discover when I arrived at the company that no line managers had been scheduled on my itinerary of interviews. But I soon learned that the external affairs function in this company had taken on a life of its own. With some persistence I was eventually able to interview a few line managers and to have the entire senior line management group complete the required survey. The results confirmed the almost total separation of line and staff work in the organization.

In one of the worst-rated, corporate social performers in the industry, I was invited into the company ostensibly for a round of interviews and to pick up the surveys that had been completed by line and staff executives. However, upon arriving I discovered that I was being screened by the senior external affairs officer, who announced in the preliminary interviews that he "had been too busy to set up the interviews" and who three months later phoned to say that the company had decided to withdraw from both the interview and the survey portions of the study. But during the half-day interview with this executive I learned that an assortment of three staff professionals handled all external affairs matters for this nationally based corporation, and that they merely handed down company position statements on various social and political issues to the heads of the company's regional offices, who otherwise were not involved. Thus, although frustrating, both of these company encounters yielded a considerable amount of infomation about only not the degree of line manager involvement in external affairs but also their general approach to external affairs.

In other companies, relations between line and staff functions have reached a high state of integration. In some cases the basis of integration is informal in nature. A strong top management philosophy and a pervasive corporate culture provide reinforcement to sustain a high degree of integration between members of both groups. "This belief in the involvement of line managers," said one senior executive, "is not the result of any formal procedure. It has just become institutionalized. I'm not sure how it happened, although I think it came from the top of the organization. Our last three chief executive officers led the company in that direction. It has become the way we operate. It is part of the company philosophy, part of our operations, and the way we behave."

In other cases, a formal context has been established by senior executives to regulate and reinforce line-staff integration in corporate external affairs activities. Among the formal devices that have been developed to ensure integration are

1. the establishment of top management steering committees,
2. the designation of specific liaison roles that link external affairs units to line operations,
3. the incorporation of external affairs goals and strategies in the annual business planning and review system,
4. the inclusion of external affairs criteria in the performance measurement and reward systems that apply to line managers,
5. the assignment of line managers to external affairs task forces,
6. the occasional rotation of line managers through temporary and full-time job assignments in external affairs units.

Finally, overarching the informal and formal approaches to line-staff integration is the symbolic role played by the executive leader in reinforcing the value of line-manager involvement in the external affairs process and in modeling appropriate managerial attitudes and behaviors.

SUMMARY

In summary, the design of a corporate external affairs function consists of several dimensions that are substantially under the control of executive leaders. They are referred to here as the breadth, depth, influence, and integration dimensions of external affairs design. The external affairs functions of the nation's largest insurance corporations vary widely on these dimensions. In conjunction with the other elements of the general framework, these design dimensions help explain a large portion of the variance in corporate social performance among these companies. By the same token, I believe failure to appreciate the importance of this full range of factors provides a very poor basis for diagnosing or improving the process by which large corporations understand and manage the corporate social environment to which they are exposed.

An important question for executive leaders regards the relative importance of the philosophy-strategy connection versus the exposure-design contingency in external affairs for explaining and predicting overall corporate social performance. The results of the comparative study will reveal that the philosophy-strategy connection, which represents the values of executive leaders and a company's underlying history and culture, is sufficient by itself to explain gross differences in overall corporate social performance. But the exposure-design contingency is necessary to be able to make finer distinctions among companies that differ in their overall corporate social performance. This ability to make finer-grained distinctions is what executive leaders need to appreciate if they are to effectively intervene in the development of this aspect of corporate performance and if government regulators and other agents of the public interest are to understand and effectively deal with the large corporations in society. From the point of view of scholars and educators, such an appreciation requires a melding of the traditional perspectives of two different fields of knowledge, Business Policy and Organization Theory.

Before we get too far into the grounded theory and its implications, however, the next chapter will explain the methods used in the study and how corporate social performance was operationalized and measured.

FOOTNOTES

1. For a discussion of the life cycle of public policy issues affecting an industry, refer to James E. Post, *Corporate Behavior and Social Change* (Reston, VA: Reston Publishing Co., 1978); and Barry M. Mitnick, *The Political Economy of Regulation* (New York: Columbia Univlersity Press, 1980).

2. William D. Guth and Renato Tagiuiri, "Personal Values and Corporate Strategy," *Harvard Business Review,* 1965, 43(5), pp. 123–132.
3. Three important studies of the corporate external affairs function are summarized in Francis J. Aguilar, *Scanning the Business Environment* (New York: Macmillan, 1967); Phyllis S. McGrath, *Managing Corporate External Relations* (New York: The Conference Board, 1976); and Jeffrey A. Sonnenfeld, *Corporate Views of the Public Interest* (Boston: Auburn House, 1981).
4. Paul R. Lawrence and Jay W. Lorsch, *Organization and Environment: Managing Differentiation and Integration* (Homewood, IL: Irwin, 1969).
5. A similar argument has been made from the general systems theory perspective under the "law of requisite variety." For a discussion of this perspective on organization design refer to Ross W. Ashby, "Variety, Constraint, and the Law of Requisite Variety," in Walter Buckley, ed., *Modern Systems Research for the Behavioral Scientist: A Sourcebook* (Chicago: Aldine, 1968), pp. 129–136.
6. A typology of external affairs activities that are performed by core units of a corporate external affairs function is outlined in Robert H. Miles, "Organization Boundary Roles," in C. L. Cooper and R. Payne, eds., *Current Concerns in Occupational Stress* (London: Wiley, 1980), pp. 61–96.
7. For a preliminary study of the relations between external affairs units and business divisions inside Aetna Life and Casualty that was later rated as one of the best corporate social performers in the U.S. insurance industry, refer to Robert H. Miles and Arvind Bhambri, "Organizational Maintenance and Adaptation: The Roles of Senior Line Managers and Corporate External Affairs Professionals," *Proceedings of the 40th Annual Meeting of the Academy of Management,* Detroit, 1980, pp. 216–220.

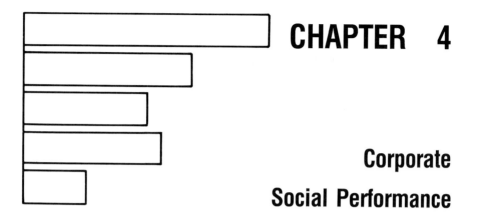

CHAPTER 4

Corporate

Social Performance

The purpose of this chapter is to reveal how the construct of corporate social performance was operationalized and measured in a major U.S. industry. This aspect of corporate performance includes not only the assessment of the responsibility that a company has exhibited historically through its behavior in society, but also its responsiveness to industry-related social and political change. Despite its growing importance in American society, and the increasing importance executive leaders in the major U.S. corporations have attached to it, corporate social performance has rarely been examined in a systematic and comparative manner.

During the late 1970s there were a variety of journalistic attempts to profile the best overall corporate social performers across U.S. industries. However, these popular press accounts generally focused on a particular aspect of corporate social performance, such as a company's record of "social" investments or its involvement in the local community, or on a particular social issue of interest, such as affirmative action or pollution abatement. None attempted the task of examining comparative social performance among competitive firms in a leading U.S. industry.[1]

The challenge behind this book was to conduct a comparative assessment of corporate social performance among the leading corporations in a major but fragmented U.S. industry. The critical questions with which I was confronted throughout the initial stage of this exploratory investigation form the outline for this chapter. They were

a. Could the individuals chosen as assessors perform a comparative assessment of corporate social performance, and would they be willing to do so?

b. How much convergence in assessments would there be for each company and how much variation in corporate social performance would there be between companies operating in the same industry?

c. What underlying meanings do assessors who are very familiar with the industry attach to the concept of corporate social performance?

d. What is the connection, if any, between a practical, industry-based assessment and the concepts and dimensions of corporate social performance that have emerged in the theoretical literature on organization and management?

e. And finally, what is the utility of conventional wisdom in the industry about the factors affecting corporate social performance?

ASSESSMENT OF CORPORATE SOCIAL PERFORMANCE IN THE UNITED STATES INSURANCE INDUSTRY

The assessment of corporate social performance was conducted on the 25 largest companies in the U.S. insurance industry.[2] These companies operate nationwide. They all control assets and earn annual revenues in the multibillion dollar range. The sample of companies was chosen to reflect the variety of business exposures in this highly fragmented industry. Some companies are engaged primarily in the property and casualty insurance business, some operate primarily in the life and health insurance fields, and some have become multiple-line insurers covering all aspects of insurance products. About half are mutual companies owned by their customers; the others are stock companies owned by somewhat more remote individual and institutional investors. Most of the companies continue to enjoy independent corporate status, having managed to avoid takeover by other companies during the third United States merger wave. A few, however, have become captives of noninsurance parent companies.

Companies and Their Social Context

The choice to focus on the nation's largest insurers was made for three important reasons. First, the behaviors of these companies whose business is national in scope, are highly visible to the general public. Moreover, the decisions they make in responding to social and political change set the stage for smaller companies sharing the same industry arena. Second, the resources of these large companies are sufficient to enable them to mount a significant approach to corporate external affairs and social performance if senior management chooses to do so. Finally, because of their national exposure, the behaviors of the country's largest insurers are known to the state and territorial commissioners of insurance who agreed to serve as the assessors of corporate social performance in the industry. These assessors have direct contact with and extensive information about the major insurers, most of which are licensed to do business in each commissioner's state or territory.

Before discussing why these individuals were chosen to perform the assessment of social performance and how the assessment was made, it is important to understand how the corporate social environment and the industry-specific regulations that create economic and social agendas for the nation's leading insurers have developed in recent times.

Of all the industries whose market performance and social legitimacy has come under serious scrutiny during the past two decades, none is more pervasive in American society than the business of insurance. The majority of U.S. citizens have at least some form of insurance coverage; virtually all of us need insurance coverage. As a television commentator on a recent NBC special entitled "Protection for Sale" explained,

> Americans spend more on insurance than they do on cars and the gas to use them. And all that money has financed an enormous industry. The combined assets of American insurance companies come to $676 billion—bigger than the oil industry, bigger than steel, bigger than the automobile business.[3]

Nevertheless, a fact that has added to the social and political controversy surrounding this gigantic and pervasive industry is that a large minority of Americans who believe they need insurance coverage either cannot afford it or are denied coverage because of business practices and management policies currently in use among the nation's hundreds of insurance companies. Clearly, if ever there were an industry that is "affected with the public interest," it is the private insurance industry.

Government regulation of the U.S. insurance industry began in 1751 in the individual states. But the precedent for state regulation was not set until the case of *Paul v Virginia* in 1869. From this decision, insurance was declared not to be interstate commerce and hence not subject to federal regulation. Individual states were thereby empowered to set their own legislative patterns and to take responsibility for the operation of insurance companies within their jurisdiction. From this landmark decision, a complicated and diverse assortment of individual state regulatory practices emerged, with individual companies negotiating individually with each state insurance commission for the right to sell different forms of insurance products.

The traditional interest of regulators has been economic in nature. The earliest focus of regulators was on the financial solvency of insurers operating in their state. The insurance product represents a promise of future benefits based on a pooling of risks associated with future losses. Therefore, the reduction of insurance company financial failures has been and continues to be a major regulatory agenda at the state level.

In addition, for most laymen the insurance product represents a complex legal and technical document. Ensuring that such contracts, and the technically sophisticated, actuarial basis upon which they are designed and priced, are comprehensible and equitable to local citizens has become a second major agenda of state regulators. Such was the nature of state insurance regulation until 1944.

In 1944, the United States Supreme Court reversed the *Paul v Virginia* decision and declared, in the *United States v Southeastern Underwriters Association* [322 U.S. 533, 1944], that the business of insurance was, in fact, interstate commerce. This reversal opened the avenue for federal involvement in insurance regulation.

To counter the threat of federal encroachment, the National Association of Insurance Commissioners (NAIC), a professional association of state regulators, drafted the McCarran-Ferguson Act in 1945. This act acknowledged the right of the federal government to become involved in insurance regulation, but stipulated that this right would not be exercised as long as the individual states performed the regulatory function in an adequate manner. Furthermore, the act guaranteed that no federal involvement would occur for a period of three years to allow the states time to review and adjust their regulatory policies.

The potential threat of federal intervention posed by the McCarran-Ferguson Act stimulated regulatory agencies at the state level to strengthen their insurance rate-setting laws, to define fair trade practices, to tighten licensing and solvency requirements, and to become more responsive to emerging public-policy issues concerning industry practices.

Despite the fact that the debate over state versus federal regulation of the insurance business has reached an intense level several times since the passage of the McCarran-Ferguson Act, the bulk of regulation still rests at the state level, with occasional intervention from various agencies on selected insurance matters. The central figure in each state is the commissioner of insurance, who initiates and administers state insurance laws and oversees the conduct of insurance companies doing business in the state.

Because insurance products are pervasive in nature touching almost every segment of society, public issues in this industry tend to become politicized easily, and both regulators and insurers are subjected to pressure from a diverse set of interest groups, including consumer interest groups, federal agencies, elected officials, state legislatures, trade associations, and the public media. In addition, the insurance industry has been going through a period of fundamental change. During the past decade and a half, major segments of the public have come to view insurance products more as rights and necessities than as privileges and luxuries. These changes in the institutional environment surrounding the industry have induced changes in the insurance companies. Of necessity, the industry has been attempting to shed its conservative image. Not only have major insurers that were single-business companies diversified into other insurance and noninsurance lines, some have also attempted to develop sophisticated systems for anticipating, understanding, and influencing the development of public policies affecting their business.

As a consequence of these developments, the role of the state insurance commissioner has expanded beyond its original mandate of monitoring the financial solvency of insurers to include market-conduct surveillance, public policy research, and consumer education. Some state regulators have set up their own research divisions to carry out studies on issues of public interest and to push for reform, while others have been more cautious in evaluating the need for change. In brief, the state commissioner of insurance occupies a role that necessitates the reconciliation of many conflicting pressures. Therefore, the decentralized system of regulation, administered independently by commissioners is diverse, and offered a unique opportunity for studying the behaviors of large insurance companies whose business is national in scope.

Under the auspices of the McCarran-Ferguson Act, the state insurance commissioner, an individual participant, has become the most important actor on this regulatory stage. Moreover, the power of this actor has been enhanced further because of the limited scope of interest and understanding of this industry and its major firms by other affected parties.[4]

Individual policyholders, who have a direct stake in the success of the industry, are generally unable to exert much influence because their involvement and interest tends to be directed at one or two insurance companies, which handle their insurance needs. In addition, the vast majority of U.S. citizens, although they have insurance coverage, are not well equipped to understand the legal and technical nature of their policies. Instead, when difficulties arise between a policyholder and a company, usually the policyholder relies on the state insurance department for assistance in resolving the matter.

Nonpolicyholders who wish to be covered by insurance but who have been denied coverage by companies usually are even less well equipped to have their grievances addressed by the industry; consequently, they too, rely on the commissioner for help. Thus, American citizens—both policyholders and nonpolicyholders—must rely to a large extent on the knowledge and clout of the state insurance commissioner to ensure that their needs are addressed by the insurance industry.

Federal agencies and actors suffer from another weakness that limits their influence on the insurance industry. These agencies tend to be issue-specific in their interests in the industry.[5] Therefore, they are generally not aware of the broad array of public policy issues confronting the industry, but only want to advance their own specific interest. Because of their relatively myopic view of the industry and the limits placed on their involvement by the McCarran-Ferguson Act, federal agencies tend to work through the state insurance commissioners to draw attention to matters of concern to them.

Choice of Assessors

In order to conduct a comparative study of the performance of companies in such a social context it was necessary to select an informed group of assessors. These individuals had to understand the public and private, social, and economic issues confronting the host industry. They had to be familiar with the 25 largest insurance companies and their business policies and practices. Preferably, because of the nature of the social context and of social values in general, these assessors needed to represent a diversity of political orientations and industry and regulatory perspectives that map reasonably well with the diversity of social values and industry expectations that are associated with doing business that is "affected with the public interest" on a national scale.

Such a set of selection criteria has no doubt frustrated the comparative study of corporate social performance in most U.S. industry settings, and the absence of suitable assessors probably accounts for the reluctance of scholars to take on the task. But in the present case, the insurance industry was selected for study in part because it is one of the few U.S. industries that remains in the private sector and can also yield such a group of assessors.

In the present study the individuals who lead the insurance reguatory agencies in the U.S. states and territories were selected as assessors. Indeed, a two-year preliminary study was conducted of insurance regulators and was fully documented in a book, *The Regulatory Executives,* before comparative study of the major insurers was begun.[6] Why were these individuals singled out as assessors? Perhaps a brief synopsis of their qualifications will provide the answer.

The individuals chosen as assessors represent a diversity of perspectives on the insurance industry and on politics in general. Thirty-eight percent of the state commissioners were Democrats, 35% were Republicans, and 27% were Independents. Thirty-eight percent represented socially active urban states, 56% represented more placid nonurban states, and 6% represented remote U.S. territories. Finally, 36% of the commissioners who served as assessors espoused an "activist" regulatory philosophy, viewing themselves as agents of the public interest and positioning their agencies at the cutting edge in consumer advocacy and regulatory reform; while the remaining 64% identified with a more conservative regulatory philosophy in which they saw their principal role as an arbiter in disputes between parties representing the public interest and the interests of the regulated industry.

Regardless of their political affiliation, state context, and regulatory agenda, these commissioners are all exposed to influences and information inputs from a variety of constituencies representing the full range of interests concerning the conduct of the regulated industry, as shown in Figure 4-1. From the perspective of the regulated industry, these assessors have to deal with representatives of individual companies, industry trade associations, and insurance agents' associations. Frequently, they also have to respond to representatives of the public interest, such as the media, consumer-interest groups, and federal agencies and officials. Finally, they all have to cope with pressures from the NAIC and their own state legislatures, both of which are forums in which public versus private interests are actively represented.

These assessors also have a good working knowledge of the technical and economic aspects of the insurance business and of the business policies and practices of the national firms. At the time of the assessment, they had been in office as head of their regulatory agency for more than four years on average. Because the large national insurance companies chosen for study operate in most of the states and territories, the assessors had had a substantial period of time in which to observe how these companies responded to the social and political issues affecting their

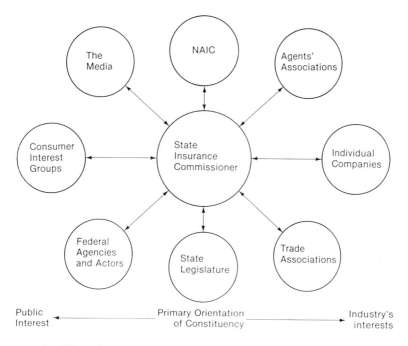

Figure 4-1   Commissioner's network of strategic constituencies.

business policies and practices. During this period of tenure most of the assessors had also been engaged in significant interactions with the major insurers concerning business practices, consumer complaints, product modifications, and regulatory developments.

Over 80% of the agencies headed by these assessors had developed sophisticated market-conduct surveillance units to complement the traditional units, which focus on the economic aspects of insurance regulation. Over three-quarters of these agencies had developed field offices distributed across the state to become more responsive to consumer complaints about the business practices of the major insurers. These structural mechanisms for monitoring the conduct of insurance companies doing business in the state are typically augmented by a variety of processes, such as in-house public policy research, toll free numbers for receiving consumer complaints, dissemination of consumer guides, and programs of consumer education, which help bring the assessors closer to the manner in which the insurance business is conducted in their states.

Adding to the technical competence of these assessors is the fact that many of them have worked in insurance companies. Indeed, the average length of work experience in insurance companies of these commissioners exceeds four years.

For all of these reasons, the state insurance commissioners were ideal candidates to perform the comparative assessment of corporate social performance among the nation's largest insurers. To enlist their support, understand the criteria they used in making such an assessment, and build trust so that these regulators would participate in the assessment, three important steps were taken. First, sponsorship of the study was obtained from the NAIC in which all commissioners were members. Shortly before the assessment was performed the president of the NAIC promoted the value of participation in the study during his national tour of the state regulatory agencies.

Second, 12 state agencies were selected for site visits on the basis of their diversity in state context and in the regulatory philosophies of their commissioners. During the visits, efforts were made to understand the regulatory environment of the industry and the meaning regulators attached to corporate social performance, and also to introduce regulators to the nature and scope of the research project. This exchange helped build trust between the researcher and the assessors that was essential to the conduct of the study. Finally, a commitment to confidentiality was conveyed to the regulators who would perform the assessment. These preliminary steps helped to ensure that even after novice commissioners were culled from the assessment group, two thirds of the commissioners were represented in the assessment of corporate social performance.

The Overall Assessment

The overall assessment of corporate social performance was conducted within the NAIC. The commissioners completed the assessment portion of the survey by studying a list of the 25 largest insurance corporations and picking out ones considered to be the industry's "best five" and "worst five" social performers.[7] The results, which are summarized in Table 4-1, reveal that the assessors were both able and willing to perform the comparative performance assessment.

Table 4-1 reveals considerable variance in the corporate social performance ratings despite the fact that the companies selected for study are all very large in size and have business operations that are national in scope. Moreover, the distribution of ratings made it easy to identify companies at both extremes of corporate social performance. This overall assessment formed the basis of the comparative study of major insurers. However, other information collected from the National Survey was useful in understanding the dimensions underlying corporate social performance and the industry-specific meanings commissioners used to make their assessments.

DIMENSIONS OF CORPORATE SOCIAL PERFORMANCE

Having obtained an open-ended assessment of comparative social performance among the nation's leading insurers, an attempt was made to link this overall assessment with some underlying dimensions of corporate social performance that have been identified by scholars who specialize in this subject. Two primary dimensions of corporate social performance characterize the developing theoretical literature.[8]

TABLE 4-1   Assessment of Corporate Social Performance

Performance Rankings of the 25 Largest U.S. Insurance Companies	Commissioner Nominations*		Overall Corporate Social Performance† (%)
	Best-Five Companies (%)	Worst-Five Companies (%)	
1	60	10	+50
2	50	7	+43
3	47	10	+37
4	23	3	+20
5	33	17	+16
6	43	27	+16
7	17	3	+14
8	27	13	+14
9	20	10	+10
10	17	10	+7
11	23	17	+6
12	13	13	0
13	13	13	0
14	13	13	0
15	13	13	0
16	3	7	−4
17	0	7	−7
18	13	23	−10
19	17	27	−10
20	10	27	−17
21	10	30	−20
22	7	33	−26
23	10	37	−27
24	0	30	−30
25	13	50	−37

*Commissioner nominations of companies into best-five and worst-five performance categories are reported as percentages of the 30 state insurance commissioners responding to this corporate social performance evaluation.

†The overall corporate social performance score is expressed as the difference between the percentage of best-five nominations less the percentage of worst-five nominations.

Corporate Social Responsibility

The first dimension is corporate social *responsibility*, which concerns the *outcomes* produced by a corporation's behaviors. In general, corporate social responsibility may be thought of as the congruence between the outcomes of corporate behavior and the norms, values, and performance expectations held in the larger social system. Thus, with reference to the historical stream of outcomes produced by corporations, some companies may be said to have behaved "responsibly," whereas others may be viewed as having behaved "irresponsibly." In the academic literature, corporate social responsibility predates the second underlying dimension of corporate social performance.

Corporate Social Responsiveness

As the social and political environment surrounding U.S. industries heated up during the 1960s and 1970s, a second dimension of corporate social performance emerged in the academic literature. Termed corporate social *responsiveness,* this dimension refers not to the outcomes achieved or the social positions adopted by corporations, but to the *processes* they have developed for understanding and responding to developments in the corporate social environment.

In theory, a corporation that has a long-earned reputation for social responsibility may fail to continue to be regarded as an industry front-runner in overall corporate social performance if it has neglected to develop the necessary internal mechanisms for responding to new trends and events in its social and political environment. This is particularly likely if the corporate social environment in which the company operates has undergone a dramatic increase in complexity and turbulence. Similarly, a corporation that has developed a sophisticated internal process, which enables it to be unusually responsive to trends and events in the social environment, may fail to score high on overall corporate social performance if it uses this process to pursue corporate ends that are viewed as irresponsible.

Given enough corporate variety in an industry, therefore, companies rated at the extremes in corporate social performance may be expected to score at the extremes in both underlying dimensions. In the present study, such variety was available in the 25 companies selected for assessment. Consequently, companies nominated by commissioners as the best five corporate social performers were expected to also be rated substantially higher on both responsibility and responsiveness than companies nominated as the industry's "worst five" performers. This question was pursued in the commissioner survey.

Differences between Best and Worst Social Performers

After the commissioners had nominated the industry's best five and the worst five performers, they rated both groups of companies on various measures representing the underlying dimensions of social responsibility and responsiveness. The specific measures used were derived from the academic literature.[9] The findings revealed that the best-rated companies scored substantially higher than the worst-rated companies on both social responsibility and social responsiveness.

The results for corporate social responsibility are shown in Figure 4-2. The most compelling result is that commissioners reported substantial differences between the best- and worst-rated companies on all measures of corporate social responsibility. However, some responsibility measures appear to be better discriminators than others.[10]

The most powerful social responsibility discriminators are

1. *company adaptation to a changing society:* the extent to which a company willingly modifies its business practices in response to changed public-policy conditions,

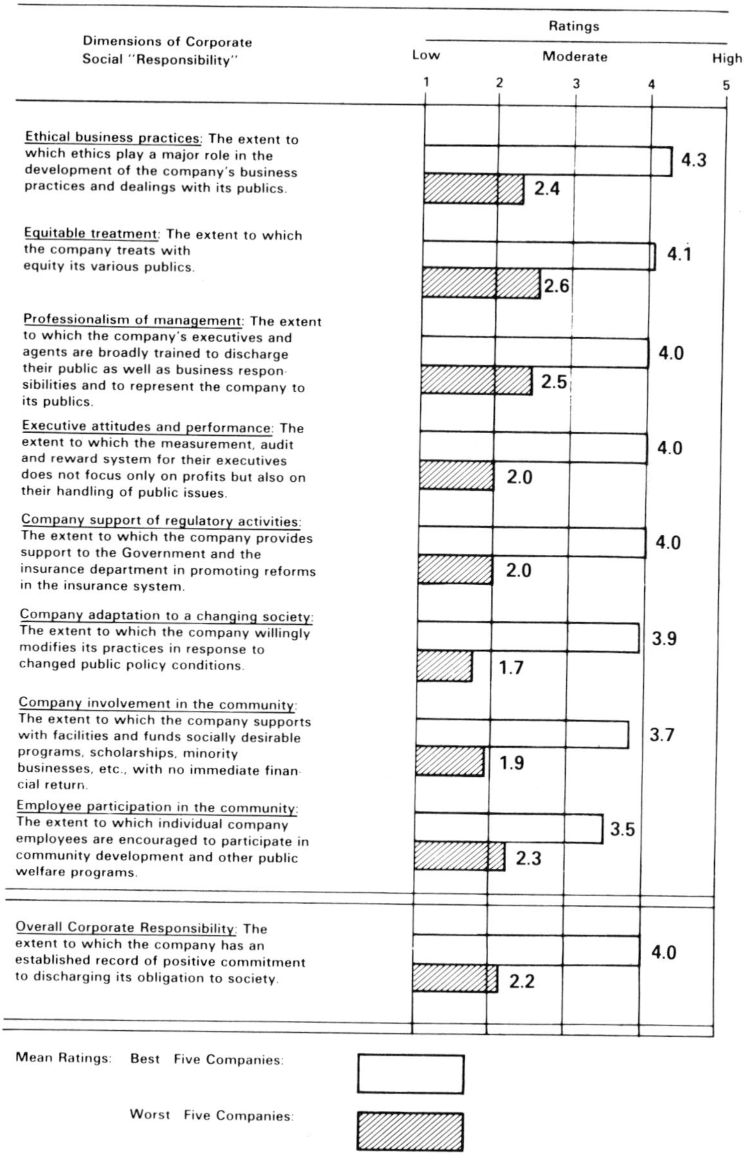

Figure 4-2 Commissioners' ratings of corporate social responsibility: best-five versus worst-five companies.

2. *executive attitudes and performance:* the extent to which a company's measurement, audit, and reward systems for its executives focus not only on profits, but also on their ability to deal with public issues,[11]

3. *company support of regulatory activities:* the extent to which a company provides support to the government and regulatory agencies in promoting needed reforms in the industry,

4. *ethical business practices:* the extent to which ethics play a major role in the development of a company's business practices and dealings with its publics.[12]

Commissioners were also asked to rate the companies they nominated as the industry's best and worst on various measures of corporate social responsiveness. As the results in Figure 4-3 reveal, the general pattern of differences for responsiveness ratings is similar to the one obtained in the responsibility ratings.

First, substantial differences between the best- and worst-rated companies occur for virtually all measures of corporate social responsiveness. However, the degrees of difference between the best and worst companies on the responsiveness measures tend to be somewhat smaller than those obtained for the responsibility measures. This pattern may indicate that commissioners place somewhat greater reliance on social responsibility than on social responsiveness in making judgments about a company's overall social performance. This implication makes sense for several reasons. First, information about a company's historical social record and general posture in the public affairs domain is more readily available to commissioners located throughout the country than is information about the company's internal processes for responding to issues in the corporate social environment. Second, the development of sophisticated external affairs functions in the major insurance companies, as in companies in other American industries, has been a relatively recent phenomenon. Therefore, information available to commissioners about the development of these internal company processes should be expected to lag considerably behind the developments themselves. Finally, the study of the commissioners themselves revealed that many of them either are not inclined or do not have the resources to develop an accurate appreciation of the internal processes that underlie the social behaviors of the insurance corporations doing business in their states.[13] Hopefully, this study will provide a framework for conducting such an investigation and the motivation among regulators for taking this important aspect of corporate social performance more seriously in the future.

Second, the measures of social responsiveness listed in Figure 4-3 also vary in their power to discriminate among the best- and worst-rated corporate social performers. The most powerful corporate responsiveness discriminators are

1. *attentiveness of company executives:* the extent to which company executives listen and are receptive to information flowing from outside the company,
2. *preparedness of company executives:* the extent to which company executives are aware of (have identified and analyzed for company impact) potential public policy issues,
3. *perceived legitimacy of outsiders:* the extent to which company executives respect the purposes of outside critics.

In summary, the assessments of overall corporate social performance of the nation's 25 largest insurers were consistent with differences between the best- and worst-rated companies on the underlying theoretical dimensions of social responsi-

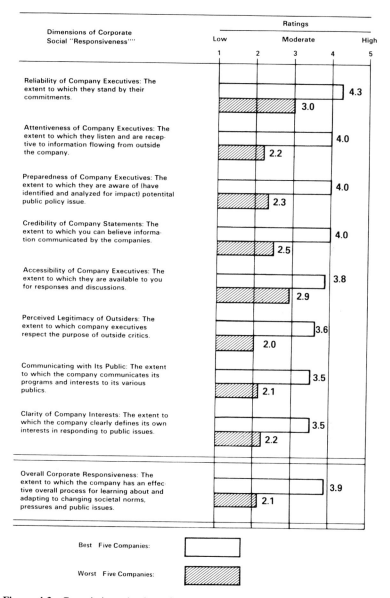

Dimensions of Corporate
Social "Responsiveness""'

Ratings

Low   Moderate   High

Dimension	Rating

Reliability of Company Executives: The extent to which they stand by their commitments.
4.3 / 3.0

Attentiveness of Company Executives: The extent to which they listen and are receptive to information flowing from outside the company.
4.0 / 2.2

Preparedness of Company Executives: The extent to which they are aware of (have identified and analyzed for impact) potentital public policy issue.
4.0 / 2.3

Credibility of Company Statements: The extent to which you can believe information communicated by the companies.
4.0 / 2.5

Accessibility of Company Executives: The extent to which they are available to you for responses and discussions.
3.8 / 2.9

Perceived Legitimacy of Outsiders: The extent to which company executives respect the purpose of outside critics.
3.6 / 2.0

Communicating with Its Public: The extent to which the company communicates its programs and interests to its various publics.
3.5 / 2.1

Clarity of Company Interests: The extent to which the company clearly defines its own interests in responding to public issues.
3.5 / 2.2

Overall Corporate Responsiveness: The extent to which the company has an effective overall process for learning about and adapting to changing societal norms, pressures and public issues.
3.9 / 2.1

Best Five Companies:

Worst Five Companies:

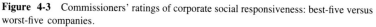

Figure 4-3 Commissioners' ratings of corporate social responsiveness: best-five versus worst-five companies.

bility and social responsiveness. Best-rated companies scored high on both dimensions and worst-rated companies scored low on both dimensions. These findings establish an important link between the actual assessment of corporate social performance in a specific industry and the more generalizable, theoretical dimensions of this construct.

INDUSTRY-SPECIFIC CRITERIA OF CORPORATE SOCIAL PERFORMANCE

In addition to obtaining an overall assessment of the corporate social performance of major insurers and linking this assessment to some important theoretical dimensions, it was possible to develop an industry-specific profile of the meaning of corporate social performance to the assessors. Twenty-nine industry-specific criteria of corporate social performance were identified from a content analysis of the transcripts prepared from preliminary interviews with a diverse group of state insurance commissioners.[14] On the basis of this preliminary study alone, it was possible to pick out a few dominant clusters of social performance criteria. However, to develop a clearer picture of the meaning attached to corporate social performance by the state commissioners, the full list of potential criteria was incorporated in the National Survey of State Insurance Commissioners.

Commissioners were asked to rate the extent to which they would rely on each of the 29 criteria in making assessments of corporate social performance in the insurance industry. They were instructed to score their reliance ratings on the assumption that they had adequate information about all 29 criteria. The average ratings of the commissioners, summarized in Table 4-2, provide an industry-specific profile of the construct of corporate social performance.[15] Three features about the way commissioners responded to this survey task are quite revealing about their views of corporate social performance in the U.S. insurance industry.

Market-conduct Activities

First, given complete information commissioners would rely most heavily on three clusters of criteria. Heading the list in Table 4-2 are criteria concerning the market-conduct activities of a company. These activities include policyholder complaints, general business practices, innovative products developed by a company to address important consumer needs, and the professionalism of a company's insurance agents and market representatives. The high reliance accorded to market-conduct activities is important because it dramatically illustrates the interdependence between a company's market performance and social performance and underscores the role of line managers in the corporate external affairs process. As one regulator explained,

> Consumer pressure and the needs of the consumer determine what areas of insurance coverage get most of the attention of a state insurance department. I think it is the combination of consumer complaints as well as pressure brought about by the newspapers, television, and radio. But even here, the pressure is initiated by the consumer.

Top Management Philosophy and Corporate Character

Top management philosophy and corporate character form another important cluster of corporate social performance criteria. Among the criteria listed in Table 4-2 that may be sorted into this cluster are: the character and reputation of a compa-

TABLE 4-2   Criteria Used by State Insurance Commissioners to Assess Corporate Social Performance

Importance Ranking*	Criteria	Extent of Reliance†
1.5	Frequency and types of complaints by policyholders	8.4
1.5	General business practices of a company	8.4
3.0	Innovative products developed by a company to address important consumer needs	7.7
4.0	The character and reputation of a company's senior management	7.5
5.0	Professionalism of company management	7.4
6.5	Degree of professionalism of agents and market representatives	7.3
6.5	Solvency of the company	7.3
8.0	Top management philosophy	7.2
9.0	Company tradition and general reputation	6.9
10.5	Behaviors and attitudes of company representatives with whom you come into contact	6.8
10.5	Criticism or praise about a company you have received from other state commissioners	6.8
12.0	The existence of organizational units within a company set up to help it understand and manage public policy issues	6.3
13.0	Criticism or praise about a company you have received from independent citizens in your state	6.1
14.0	Participation by a company in high-risk markets	6.0
15.0	The existence of public policy professionals within a company	5.9
16.0	Litigation involving a company	5.8
17.0	Participation of a company in NAIC programs	5.7
18.5	Involvement of a company or its employees in local community affairs and civic organizations	5.6
18.5	Relationship between senior company executives and field agents	5.6
20.0	Extraordinary profitability of a company or its business lines	5.5
21.5	Advertising practices of a company concerning its position on public policy issues	5.3
21.5	Advertising practices of a company concerning the promotion of its products	5.3
23.0	Company reports linking public policy issues to business practices	5.1
24.0	Whether a company is an independent corporation or a captive of a diversified conglomerate	4.9
25.5	Criticism or praise about a company you have received from organized interest groups in your state or region	4.5
25.5	Participation of a company in industry trade associations	4.5
27.0	Criticism or praise about a company you have seen in the public media	4.1
28.0	Criticism or praise about a company you have received from members of federal government bodies	3.5
29.0	Press releases from a company	3.2

*Rank order of importance: 1.5 = highest rank; 29.0 = lowest rank.

†The extent to which commissioners rely on these criteria of company social performance was based on their ratings of each criterion on a 10-point scale, ranging from 1 = to virtually no extent; to 10 = to a very great extent.

ny's senior management, the degree of professionalism of company management, top management philosophy, and company tradition and general reputation. As one urban commissioner responded when asked during the interview what he relied on in making judgements about the social performance of insurance companies, "I don't want to be antitheoretical, but I'm afraid that an awful lot of my responses would be grounded in some of the personalities within those companies." He continued by describing the philosophies of top executives of several national companies and explaining how they set the tone for the social performance of each company as a whole.

Financial Solvency

The final important criterion used by commissioners to rate corporate social performance is the traditional economic standard of insurance regulation in the United States: the financial solvency of a company. As one commissioner emphasized during the field inteviews, "The first responsibility of the commissioner is to make sure the companies licensed and doing business in the state are solvent." In reacting to the wide variety of potential criteria of corporate social performance another interviewed commissioner said,

> The most important of them all is obviously solvency, because if the company isn't solvent, everything else disappears. It doesn't make any difference whether the rates they charge are adequate, or whether the policies they sell are satisfactory. If they go broke, all the rest is academic.

Criticism or Praise about a Company

A second notable feature of the way commissioners evaluate a company's social performance is that they attach different weights to the criticism or praise about a company that they receive from different sources. They rely more as a total group on the criticism or praise they receive from their peers who serve as commissioners in other states and from independent citizens in their own state than from federal agencies and officials, the public media, or organized groups. Therefore, difficulties experienced by one commissioner in dealing with a company can prejudice or at least cause increased attention to be focused on that company by commissioners in other states where the company operates.

Public Relations versus Public Policy Expertise

The third important feature revealed in Table 4-2 is that commissioners generally prefer to discount the traditional public relations efforts of insurance companies when they make judgements about their overall corporate social performance. Given adequate information about them, company press releases, reports, and advertising campaigns were not relied on very heavily by commissioners in making these assessments. In contrast, commissioners have begun to attach moderate importance to the existence of professionals and specialized departments within a company (e.g., public policy professionals and public policy issues analysis departments) that help business managers understand changes in the political and social environments in which their businesses are conducted. This feature of the way in which regulatory executives assess companies suggests that executive leaders desiring to improve corporate social performance would do well to allocate resources more toward the internal development of substantive mechanisms for understanding and managing insurance-related, social, and political issues than toward the refinement of elaborate public relations programs.

Assessment Summary

The majority of state commissioners not only can discriminate among major insurance companies in terms of their overall social performance, but are both prepared and willing to do so. This finding attests to the growing importance of corporate *social* performance especially within industries "affected with the public interest." Moreover, these regulatory executives see clear differences between the industry's best and worst social performers on both responsibility and responsiveness dimensions, which have been identified in the academic literatures concerning corporate social performance.

But the assessment also revealed a number of important, industry-specific criteria of corporate social performance. The three most important clusters of criteria for assessing such performance in the insurance industry are: company market-conduct activities, top management philosophy and corporate character, and company financial solvency. All of this preliminary information was helpful in designing and conducting the comparative analysis of corporate social performance that followed.

SOME SUPPORTING EVIDENCE

The ratings of overall corporate social performance are as intended, therefore, quite broad in scope, covering many facets of the performance construct, and are based on the insights from extended experience with all the firms studied by an unusually well-informed and relatively powerful set of external constituencies. Nevertheless, it was important to assemble a variety of other surrogates of corporate social performance which, although necessarily narrower in scope and of less inherent quality, would lend credibility to the overall ratings by these agents of the public interest. After a good deal of searching for archival surrogates, several were found. They include

1. the openness of each firm to the social environment as gauged by the representation of women and minority members on their boards of directors,

2. content analysis of published monitoring activities focusing on selected aspects of corporate social performance,
3. selected ratios of consumer complaints to volume of business conducted in a particular state.

Although modest in scope and quality when compared to the corporate social performance ratings provided by informed regulators, these surrogates all lend support to the overall ratings made by our assessors.

Openness to Society

Recent published surveys of the composition of the board of directors of our 25 companies reveals that the companies rated high in overall corporate social performance had a substantially higher number of women and minority members on their boards of directors than did the companies that were rated lower in overall social performance.[16] For instance, 16 of the 25 insurance companies had at least one female board member. But companies rated as the top five social performers in the U.S. insurance industry had a total of seven women on their boards, whereas only one woman was a board member in the five worst-rated companies. When the social performance categories were expanded to include the best-ten and the worst-ten insurers, the same pattern was revealed. The top 10 companies accounted for 12 female directors, and the bottom 10 companies accounted for only five female directors.

Similar patterns regarding openness to society may be observed in the participation of minority representatives on insurance company boards of directors. For example, another survey of the nation's largest service companies, which was conducted during the study in 1982, revealed that the 10 best-rated social performers had a total of 11 black directors, compared to only one black director for the 10 worst-rated corporate social performers in the industry.[17]

Social Event Monitoring

Corporate social event monitoring by outside observers also appear to lend credibility to the overall ratings of corporate social performance. For example, each quarterly issue of *Business & Society Review* since the spring 1980 issue (which appeared as this program of research was getting underway) has published a "Company Performance Roundup" section, which highlights unusually effective and unusually ineffective corporate social behavior among large U.S. firms.[18] In the 20 issues since this section first appeared, the companies rated as the best-five social performers in the U.S. insurance industry received a total of nine positive citations and no negative citations. In contrast, insurance companies rated below the best-ten corporate social performers received only negative citations, including sex discrimination lawsuits from their employees and customers, episodes of organized boycotts of their products by various public-interest groups, huge punitive damage suits from dissatisfied customers, and criticism for improper consumer advertising practices. These frequencies of positive and negative citations not only lend support to the validity of the regulator-based rating of overall corporate social performance, but just as importantly the nature of the negative citations suggests that the overall rating may also generalize to aspects of corporate social behavior that were not explicitly considered by the regulatory raters (e.g., unfair labor practices and unenlightened human resource management policies).

Complaint Ratios

The frequency of consumer complaints about an insurance company should also be expected to correlate positively with its overall corporate social performance. Unfortunately, state insurance departments have only recently begun to experiment with various methods of collecting and reporting consumer complaints by company on a systematic, annual basis. Most of the early attempts were sketchy in their coverage of companies and were criticized for developing an index, the complaint ratio, which was based on dividing the number of complaints received by the dollar volume of business conducted by a company in a particular state. Recently, however, Illinois has begun to compute complaint ratios as a function of the number of policies in force. Fortunately, the two best- and worst-rated corporate social performers sold enough insurance to qualify for the Illinois volume cutoff for inclusion in the complaint-ratio report.[19] Comparisons reveal that automobile insurance complaint ratios were 65% higher that year for the worst-rated companies, and that the complaint ratios for accident and health insurance sold to Illinois consumers were 114% higher for the worst-rated companies than those of the best-rated companies. Hopefully in the future more states will develop sophisticated information processing systems that will enable them to report systematic differences in complaint ratios for the nation's major insurers; but for now, the limited data available suggest that differences in rated overall corporate social performance conform to corresponding differences in the market behavior of companies and the consumer response that such behavior elicits.

CONVENTIONAL WISDOM MISSES THE MARK

Before leaving the assessment of corporate social performance I want to examine some of the conventional wisdom in the insurance industry that was offered by regulators and company executives about what types of companies would fare well and poorly under such a comparative assessment. During various stages of the investigation, these officials shared a number of hip-pocket hypotheses about corporate social performance in their industry. I supposed at the time that these tidbits of conventional wisdom were offered to save me the time, expense, and trouble of conducting the multifaceted study I had described to these individuals. Although I was committed to do the full comparative study, it troubled me that these officials felt so comfortable with their simplistic predictions of corporate social performance.

To satisfy my curiosity, I conducted a modest preliminary analysis of the predictive power of these elements of conventional wisdom against the social performance ratings of all 25 of the nation's largest insurers. The results, which are summarized below, reveal that on most counts conventional wisdom in the industry is seriously deficient in accurately explaining and predicting corporate social performance.

Conventional Wisdom #1: Company Ownership as Predictor

Many industry observers, but especially mutual company executives, believed that mutual insurance companies are better social performers than stock insurance companies. Their hypothesis about the influence of corporate ownership was based on an assumption that because mutuals are owned by their policyholders these companies tend to be more responsive to customer needs and presumably to the general public interest than are stock companies that are owned by generally disinterested individual and institutional investors.

The results from the comparative assessment of the 25 insurers, summarized in Table 4-3, provide no support for this widely held belief. Although four of the five worst-rated firms are stock companies, the same is true for the five best-rated companies. Mutual companies out-number stock companies only in the category of "average" corporate social performance. Eighty-two percent of the mutual companies assessed fell into the average performance category, as compared to 43% of the stock companies included in the assessment. Thus, in contrast to being the worst social performers in the industry, stock companies are overrepresented relative to mutuals at both extremes of corporate social performance. Therefore, no simple relationship between company ownership and social performance was observed in the comparative assessment of major insurers.

Conventional Wisdom #2: Product Mix as Predictor

A second, frequently mentioned predictor of corporate social performance was the product mix of an insurer. The simple hypothesis offered was that because of their relatively more complex and turbulent corporate social environment, property and casualty insurers are more likely to achieve an unfavorable social performance assessment than are life and health insurers. Basically, life and health insurers have an easier task of managing the corporate social environment; therefore, they should receive higher ratings. Once again, however, no consistent pattern association emerges in Table 4-3.

Although all of the five worst-rated companies have substantial stakes and exposures in the property and casualty business, so, too, do four of the five best-rated

TABLE 4-3 Conventional Wisdom and Corporate Social Performance

Company Performance Ranking	Company Ownership: Stock vs. Mutual	Product Mix*	Distribution System	Customer Mix (%)† Personal Lines (%)	Commercial Lines (%)	Corporate Status: Independent vs. Captive
1	Stock	Multiple line	Independent agents	25	75	Independent
2	Mutual	Life/health	Direct writer	80	20	Independent
3	Stock	Property/casualty	Independent agents	15	85	Independent
4	Stock	Multiple line	Direct writer	15	85	Independent
5	Stock	Multiple line	Independent agents	20	80	Independent
6	Mutual	Property/casualty	Direct writer	90	10	Independent
7	Mutual	Life/health	Direct writer	NA	NA	Independent
8	Mutual	Life/health	Direct writer	NA	NA	Independent
9	Mutual	Life/health	Direct writer	75	25	Independent
10	Stock	Property/casualty	Independent agents	25	75	Captive
11	Mutual	Life/health	Direct writer	65	35	Independent
12	Stock	Property/casualty	Independent agents	NA	NA	Independent
13	Stock	Multiple line	Independent agents	15	85	Independent
14	Mutual	Multiple line	Independent agents	NA	NA	Independent
15	Stock	Property/casualty	Independent agents	30	70	Independent
16	Mutual	Life/health	Direct writer	30	70	Independent
17	Mutual	Life/health	Direct writer	NA	NA	Independent
18	Stock	Property/casualty	Independent agents	NA	NA	Captive
19	Mutual	Multiple line	Direct writer	75	25	Independent
20	Stock	Property/casualty	Independent agents	20	80	Independent
21	Stock	Multiple line	Independent agents	30	70	Captive
22	Stock	Property/casualty	Direct writer	NA	NA	Independent
23	Mutual	Property/casualty	Direct writer	30	70	Independent
24	Stock	Property/casualty	Independent agents	15	85	Captive
25	Stock	Property/casualty	Direct writer	85	15	Captive

*The estimate of the product mix of each company was based on total 1980 earned premiums in the property/casualty and life/health insurance lines. Sources: *Moody's Manual* (1982); *Best's Insurance Reports*, Life/Health Edition (1981); and *Best's Insurance Reports*, Property/Casualty Edition (1981). An insurer was classified as a multiple-line company if its product mix was made up of at least 20% of both property/casualty and life/health insurance lines.

†Customer mix was based on estimates provided by each company. (NA = not available, means that the company did not respond to this data request.)

corporate social performers. Life and health insurers have the edge when the performance array is divided at the middle; but this level of predictive accuracy falls far short of what is required for corporate or regulatory policy-formulation purposes. Indeed, the predominance of property and casualty companies and multiple-line companies in the best-rated category throws considerable doubt on the simple, direct relationship between business exposure and social performance hypothesized within industry conventional wisdom.

Conventional Wisdom #3: Distribution System as Predictor

A third predictor of corporate social performance often cited by regulators and company executives is the nature of a company's distribution system. Two basic types of distribution systems prevail in the insurance industry. Some companies are the *direct writers,* whose distribution systems are composed of full-time employees or exclusive agents of the company. Other companies employ an *independent agency system,* in which general agents operate their own companies, which sell or broker the insurance products of many insurers. Although some companies operate with more than one type of system, most rely exclusively on one system, and all rely primarily on a single system.

In contrast to the other elements of industry conventional wisdom, company executives offered one of two hypotheses about the relationship between distribution system and corporate social performance. On the one hand, executives in direct writers believed that having one's own salesforce inhibits company responsiveness to changes in the corporate social environment. Therefore, they argue that companies relying on independent agents have more flexibility to respond to social change and would consequently be rated as better corporate social performers than direct writers.

On the other hand, executives representing companies that rely on an independent agency distribution system tend to believe that they have less control over their independent agents and, consequently, a more difficult task of responding to industry-related social change. They hypothesize, therefore, that direct writers would tend to be rated as better corporate social performers than companies operating with an independent-agent system.

As Table 4-3 reveals, the results provide no support for either hypothesis. There is a mixture of direct writers and companies employing the independent agency system among the industry's five-worst corporate social performers. In general, companies are fairly randomly distributed along the whole performance array on the basis of their distribution systems. Therefore, no simple, direct relationship appears to exist in the industry between distribution system and corporate social performance.

Conventional Wisdom #4: Geographical Mix as Predictor

Some regulators and executives believe that the geographical exposure of a company or its senior management is related positively and directly to overall corporate social performance. They argue that companies whose business stakes are concentrated in urban areas are more likely to be receptive to the demands of public constituencies than are companies that are not very dependent on urban areas. They also argue that executives who are physically located in politically and socially volatile urban centers tend to be more sensitive and responsive to public issues and regulatory reforms than are their counterparts in companies headquartered in more remote parts of the country. They believe that having to deal with a powerful and active set of public constituencies on a day-to-day basis causes executive leaders to guide their companies toward high levels of corporate social responsibility and responsiveness.

Analysis of these relationships, however, received no more support than the other elements of industry conventional wisdom. As Table 4-3 reveals, companies rated in the top half of the distribution on corporate social performance derive 68% on average of their business from urban states, whereas those in the bottom half derive 67% of their business from urban states. The five top-rated companies average 70% dependence on urban states, as compared to 78% for the companies among the five worst rated that responded to the data request.[20] Moreover, companies that are headquartered in the geographical area regarded by many industry observers as the ''Northeastern socialist corner'' of the country (an area including New Jersey, New York, Connecticut, and Massachusetts) are not systematically rated higher than companies headquartered elsewhere. Therefore, being ''exposed'' to an intense corporate social environment, in terms of the geographical location of a company's business or its headquaters, does not by itself directly predict or explain a company's overall social performance.

Conventional Wisdom #5: Customer Mix as Predictor

Several regulators and executives also speculated that commercial-lines companies would outperform personal-lines companies in the assessment of corporate social performance. Their reasoning was similar to the one outlined in the product-mix prediction. They believed that, because personal insurance products are exposed to more conflict and controversy in the corporate social environment, commercial companies would achieve more favorable corporate social performance ratings from state insurance commissioners because they are less frequently engaged than personal-lines companies in debates, hearings, and litigation with the commissioners.

Once again, however, no support was obtained for this simple, direct relationship between another aspect of company business exposure and overall social performance. Twenty-one of the 25 companies were willing to share data on customer mix. Data were received from 10 of the 12 companies rated highest in corporate social performance and 11 of the lowest-rated companies and are summarized in Table 4-3. On the basis of the data available, no simple, direct relationship may be observed between a company's customer mix and its corporate social performance rating. An average of over 45% of the business of companies lying above the midpoint in the corporate social performance array is conducted in the personal insurance segment of the market. This same average for the companies lying below the distribution midpoint is 41%. Moreover, the majority of the worst-rated firms are commercial-lines insurers.

Up to this point, neither the distribution system used by a company nor any aspects of its "exposure" to the corporate social environment have been shown to be *directly* related to its overall social performance as industry-conventional wisdom would argue. Nor has the ownership (i.e., stock versus mutual) of an insurance company been found to be directly related to corporate social performance. However, there was one hypothesis from conventional wisdom that the evidence from the comparative assessment highlights for regulator and executive attention.

Conventional Wisdom #6: The Captive Hypothesis

Many regulators but few company executives believe that independent insurance companies perform more responsibly and responsively than *captive* insurers; i.e., insurance companies that have been acquired by noninsurance parent corporations. These regulators reasoned that captive insurers are treated as "profit centers" by their corporate parents and therefore are more accountable than their independent peers for immediate financial results and operating efficiencies. As one insurance regulator explained to me,

> With corporate takeovers, what you're likely to find is the insurance company being viewed more as a "profit center." When a company is viewed as a profit center, we become much more concerned. It becomes more important to it to generate a decent flow of cash upstream than to operate in a socially progressive fashion.

Some support for this aspect of conventional wisdom may be observed in Table 4-3. None of the top five corporate social performers is a captive company; whereas three of the industry's worst-five corporate social performers are captives of noninsurance parent corporations. Moreover, of the five captive companies among the nation's 25 largest insurers, only one is rated among the industry's top 17 corporate social performers.[21]

The fact that 50% of the insurance companies rated in the bottom third of corporate social performers in the industry are captives, when coupled with the increasing interest in the acquisition of U.S. insurance companies by noninsurance conglomerates and diversified majors, should raise concern among both industry regulators and company executives. Many acquisitive conglomerates may look to the insurance industry as a source of acquisition candidates that can provide a steady and substantial cash flow from investment operations. Executives in such acquisitive conglomerates may have little previous exposure to or sensitivity toward the special obligations of a company that operates in an industry that is substantially interlocked with the public interest.

SUMMARY

This chapter has revealed that it is possible to assess corporate social performance by comparing companies operating in the same industry with roughly comparable resources. This assessment was enhanced in the present case by selecting an industry that is confronted with a high social profile and a relatively large group of assessors who have sufficient responsibility, knowledge, and resources for comparing the overall social performance of member firms.

Indeed, the reason for choosing the U.S. insurance industry for demonstrating the utility of the general framework was because its characeristics are well suited to conducting a reliable and valid assessment of corporate social performance. The assessment yielded some distinctive categories of corporate social performance that were used as the basis for selecting companies for intensive study. As the intensive studies which follow will reveal, the exaggerated nature of the social environment of this industry also made it possible to pick out differences in the more subtle but important elements of the approach each major company had developed for understanding and managing relations with its social context.

This chapter has also revealed that regulators can be an important source of information about comparative social performance in an industry, particularly if they are exposed to the full range of social as well as economic issues confronting member firms. However, other studies have shown that when the scope of regulators' appreciation of the full breadth of the corporate social environment surrounding an industry is less substantial, such an assessment can be made by pooling the evaluations from multiple outside constituencies, each of which may be interested in only a part of the whole of corporate social performance.[22] Again, the insurance industry was chosen as the setting for this demonstration project because of the availability of a large group of maximally exposed assessors.

It is also refreshing to discover that the individuals chosen as assessors not only had the ability to, but were also willing to perform the overall assessment of corporate social performance in the U.S. insurance industry. Their willingness to tackle head-on this allegedly intangible and elusive construct attests to its growing importance in American society. In addition, it was possible to establish some important linkages between the actual assessments and the theoretical literature on corporate social performance, and to generate and prioritize a number of industry-specific criteria of this aspect of corporate performance.

Finally, the comparative assessment has revealed that there is a very weak linkage between actual corporate social performance and conventional wisdom among industry regulators and company executives about corporate social performance. Only one of the widely held hypotheses concerning a direct link between several overall characteristics of a company and its overall social performance was supported for this nation's largest insurers.[23] The general absence of overall patterns of association, however, should not diminish the importance of the captive hypothesis which did receive considerable support. In the midst of increasing interest, the acquisition of insurance companies by diversifying companies in other industries should be a stimulus to legitimate concern among insurance company executives as well as regulators. Beyond this discovery, however, the absence of simple, direct connections between the other predictors from industry conventional wisdom and actual corporate social performance focuses attention on the general framework that is being developed and refined in this book and the intensive comparative studies of the industry's best and worst social performers that follow.

FOOTNOTES

1. Two studies published in the early 1980s, however, were quite useful in informing the present investigation. In *Coffin Nails and Corporate Strategies* (1982) I was able to examine the response of a whole industry to a major threat from the corporate social environment. Because of the continuing sensitivity of tobacco company executives to the smoking-and-health controversy, however, I was unable to conduct a comparative analysis of the social performance of the performance of the tobacco "Big Six" corporations. The study was useful in the present context because it revealed subtle but important differences in external affairs strategies within a highly homogeneous industry. The other study, conducted by Jeffrey Sonnenfeld, a faculty colleague at the Harvard Business School, featured the first comparative assessment of social performance within a major U.S. industry. In *Corporate Views of the Public Interest* (1981), Sonnenfeld demonstrated that it is possible to systematically compare industry competitors on the basis of corporate social performance. His conceptualization of the differences in external affairs design between these companies operating in a fairly homogeneous industry was useful in developing the general framework in this book. The comparative assessment of corporate social performance in a fragmented industry and the development of the full framework, however, had to await the results of the present investigation. This general framework melds the elements of corporate strategy discovered in my study with the elements of organization design in the Sonnenfeld study to predict and explain company differences in overall corporate social performance.
2. The determination of company size was based on company assets. A list of the 15 largest property/casualty insurers was developed along with a list of the 15 largest life/health insurers. After consideration of the fact that some multiple-line companies appeared in both lists, the two lists were merged to identify the 25 largest U.S. insurance companies. (Source: *Best's Review*, Property/Casualty Edition and Life/Health Edition, 1982.) Both premium volume and assets were employed as possible criteria for choosing the 25 insurance companies. Neither criterion, by itself, was adequate due to lack of

direct comparability between life/health and property/casualty insurers. The much higher assets-to-premiums ratio in life/health companies relative to property/casualty companies generated too many life insurance companies if exclusive reliance was placed on assets and not enough if exclusive reliance was placed on premium volume. For example, Prudential, a dominant life insurer, has assets of about $60 billion compared to $24 billion for Aetna, a multiple-line insurer, with about the same premium volume. The final compromise was based on the researcher's judgment to include in the company sample industry leaders in both market segments. Therefore, the 10 largest life insurance companies in assets (Source: "Leading U.S. Life Companies," *Best's Review - Life/Health Edition,* June 1979) and the 17 largest property/casualty companies in industry premiums (Source: "The 200 Leading Property/Casualty Companies and Groups," *Best's Review - Property, Casualty Edition,* June 1979) were selected to provide a list of seven companies that had a major presence only in life/health market, 11 companies that had a major presence only in property/casualty and seven companies that had a major presence in both markets. It may be noted that the 17th largest property/casualty insurer's premiums exceeded that of the 10th largest life insurer, and that the overall population of life/health and property/casualty companies in the U.S. number approximately 1950 and 2900, respectively.

3. "Protection for Sale: The Insurance Industry," NBC Special, reported by Chris Wallace, April 17, 1982.

4. A recent public opinion poll revealed that only one out of ten media leaders, congressmen, consumer leaders, and members of the general public in the United States consider themselves as very familiar with and knowledgeable about the insurance industry. (Louis Harris and Associates, Inc., *A Survey of Leadership and Public Attitudes Toward Various Aspects of Regulation of Insurance,* 1980.)

5. This conclusion was reached rather quickly after an initial round of interviews in 1981 with the heads of several insurance-related agencies in federal government departments.

6. For a detailed description of this context and the roles played by the state commissioners refer to Robert H. Miles and Arvind Bhambri, *The Regulatory Executives* (Beverly Hills, CA: Sage Publications, 1983).

7. The immediate stimulus question to the corporate social performance assessment in the National Survey of State Insurance Commissioners was: "As the most informed group in the insurance regulatory environment, we would like to ask you to identify the five insurers from the list of the biggest 25 insurers that *you* think have been the "best" social performers and the five that have been the "worst" social performers. We understand that this is a highly judgmental task based on a variety of bits and pieces of information that come to your attention, and this will be kept in mind in our analysis." Using this stimulus, commissioners checked off their nominations of the five best and five worst corporate social performers in the insurance industry. Thirty of the 34 commissioners participating in the national survey completed the corporate social performance assessment portion of the survey. Of the four remaining commissioners, two were novices (i.e., they had been in office for less than six months), one was a territorial commissioner who did not interact with many of the companies being evaluated, and one completed the assessment form incorrectly.

8. The stream of research that treats responsibility and responsiveness as separate dimensions of overall corporate social performance includes the following works: D. Votaw and S.P. Sethi, *The Corporate Dilemma* (Englewood Cliffs, NJ: Prentice-Hall, 1973); S.P. Sethi, "Dimensions of Corporate Social Performance: An Analytical Frame-

work," *California management Review,* (Spring 1975); R. Ackerman, *The Social Challenge to Business* (Cambridge, MA: Harvard University Press, 1975); R. Ackerman and R. Bauer, *Corporate Social Responsiveness: The Modern Dilemma* (Reston, VA: Reston Publishing Co., 1976); A.B. Carroll, "A Three-Dimensional Conceptual Model of Corporate Performance," *Academy of Management Review,* 1974, 4, no.4, 497–505; T.J. Zenisek, "Corporate Social Responsibility: A Conceptualization Based on Organizational Literature," *Academy of Management Review,* 1979, 4, no. 3, 359–368; and J.A. Sonnenfeld, *Corporate Views of the Public Interest,* (Boston: Auburn House, 1981).

9. The specific measures of the social responsibility and social responsiveness dimensions were derived from a recent review of the literature on corporate social performance in Jeffrey A. Sonnenfeld, *Corporate Views of the Public Interest* (Boston: Auburn House, 1981).

10. The estimates of the discriminatory power of the eight measures were based on the difference in the average ratings from commissioners of the performance of the five best rated and five worst rated companies on each measure. For example, this difference was greatest for the *company adaptation to a changing society* measure (2.2) and least for the *employee participation in the community* measure (1.2) of corporate social responsibility.

11. Although the academic literature was the principal source of the items included under the responsibility and responsiveness measures, I am not in total agreement with the theoretical dichotomy. For example, I believe that executive measurement and reward systems are part of the "process" by which a company responds to the corporate social environment and should, therefore, be properly considered as part of the social responsiveness dimension. However, in the present discussion this item is listed under corporate social responsibility in order to establish the linkage between the current findings and the traditional academic literature.

12. In contrast, involvement in local community activities by either the company or its employees was a relatively weak discriminator between the industry's best- and-worst-rated, corporate social performers. Indeed, several commissioners who were interviewed prior to the National Survey were skeptical about investments of corporate time and money in the local community. They often observed that such investments were typically made in the community in which these national corporations were headquartered from profits earned from customers who were located throughout the country.

13. For a complete discussion of the regulatory agendas and resources of the state insurance commissioners refer to Robert H. Miles and Arvind Bhambri, *The Regulatory Executives* (Beverly Hills, CA: Sage Publications, 1983).

14. These criteria were derived from a content analysis of the taped transcripts of preliminary interviews conducted with a national cross section of state insurance commissioners.

15. An early report of some of these findings was published in an industry journal to provide timely feedback to insurance regulators and company executives. Refer to Robert H. Miles, "How Do State Commissioners Assess the Corporate Social Performance of Major Insurers?" *Best's Review,* Property-Casualty Edition, November 1981, 82, no. 7, 32–127.

16. Beth W. Ghiloni, "The Corporate Scramble for Women Directors," *Business and Society Review,* Fall 1984, no. 51, 86–95.

17. Milton R. Moskowitz, "The 1982 Black Corporate Directors Lineup," *Business and Society Review,* Fall 1982, no. 43, 51–54.

18. Milton R. Moskowitz, "Company Performance Roundup," *Business and Society Review,* Spring 1980 through Winter 1984.

19. Consumer complaints are defined by the Illinois Department of Insurance as "written correspondence primarily expressing a grievance against an insurance company." The complaint ratio is computed by dividing the number of consumer complaints the Department receives concerning a company by the number of policies in force, or more technically as the number of complaints per 10,000 policies in force. The specific data reported were taken from "Complaint Ratios for Life, Accident and Health Insurance Released," *Regulatory News,* published by the Illinois Department of Insurance, January 14, 1981.

20. The nation's 25 largest insurers have substantial business stakes in urban states. This fact creates a restriction of range in the urban exposure of the assessed companies.

21. Only stock companies are eligible for acquisition by other corporations. Mutual insurance companies are wholly owned by their policyholders whose shares are not publicly traded.

22. See, for example, the technique used to pool the comparative assessments of corporate social performance in the U.S. forest products industry by diverse external constituencies in Jeffrey A. Sonnenfeld, *Corporate Views of the Public Interest* (Boston: Auburn House, 1981).

23. This examination of simple hypotheses associated with the prediction of corporate social performance, of course, is confined to the sample consisting of the largest U.S. insurers. An examination of the utility for explaining corporate social performance among the many smaller insurance companies must be future research.

PART II

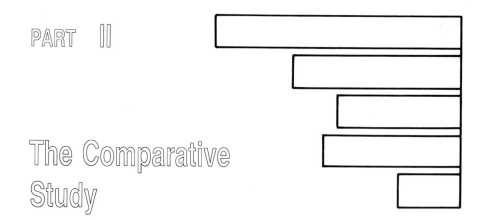

The Comparative
Study

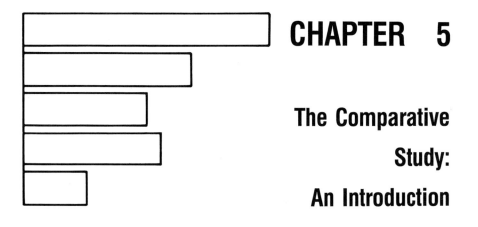

CHAPTER 5

The Comparative Study: An Introduction

The comparative study consisted of an intensive investigation of companies that have achieved different records of corporate social performance. The initial design focused on the extreme corporate social performers—companies rated as the host industry's best and worst social performers. But as the subsequent discussion will reveal, a third category of companies, which was interesting and distinctive because they fell into the midrange of corporate social performance, was added to the sample to provide a finer-grained demonstration and refinement of the grounded theory. Expansion of the company sample was concluded after these midrange companies were investigated because no further gains in theory development could be achieved given the overall nature and scope of the program of research.

CONDUCT OF THE STUDY

The comparative study was based on five principle sources of information. First, several years were spent as an action-researcher in the development of the external affairs function of the company that was subsequently rated as the best corporate social performer in the host industry.[1] I had sensed during my work with this company that it was doing a particularly good job in relating to external social contingencies, especially in understanding and managing the major public policy issues affecting its core businesses; but I became curious about how well it was doing in this arena relative to industry peers with similar resources. This in-depth, action-research opportunity also enabled me to understand how line and staff units interact to perform the corporate external affairs function, as well as the roles executive leaders play in setting the internal context of corporate social performance. Finally, this early work provided me with a broad perspective on corporate external affairs and social behavior.

All of these experiences from the early work with one company were part of the motivation to conduct a broad-based comparative study of corporate social performance in the insurance industry. Moreover, this intensive experience in helping executive leaders in one major insurance company develop and refine their corporate external affairs function made it possible for me to identify some of the important but sometimes subtle features of the external and internal contexts of corporate social performance in this industry. This special window into the way things work later made it possible for me to quickly "read" the approaches adopted by other companies to corporate social performance.

Second, based on preliminary interviews and site visits in a national cross section of state regulatory agencies, which were followed by a more systematic National Survey of State Insurance Commissioners, I was able to obtain both quantitative and qualitative insights about public expectations, social issues, and corporate social performance in the U.S. insurance industry.[2] This information was useful not only in selecting companies for the comparative study, but also in selecting variables for inclusion in the preliminary framework and in anticipating key relationships among those variables that might eventually emerge in the grounded theory of corporate social performance.

Third, a variety of archives were searched to obtain relevant company and industry data, which were necessary both to operationalize some of the categories in the framework and to corroborate my clinical impressions and process observations.

With all of these data sources assembled, the next-to-last sources of data were the companies selected for comparative study and their line managers and staff professionals.[3] Each selected company was required to host two to five days of site visits to facilitate a modest amount of process observation and a round of interviews with all senior line managers and senior corporate external affairs executives. These site visits were preceded by the collection of relevant company records and by the completion of a survey by all senior line managers and corporate external affairs professionals.[4] Analysis of the archival and survey data was conducted prior to the site visits in order to focus the interviews and process observations during the fieldwork in each company.

Finally, after all data were assembled and organized, I returned to each company to present a summary of the comparative findings to all senior line managers and staff professionals. Their reaction to this feedback served as the final source of data for the generation of the grounded theory. It was only during these post-study presentations that I revealed the company's rated level of corporate social performance.

All of these data sources formed the basis of the comparative study, the development of the general framework to guide executive leaders and their colleagues, and ultimately the grounded theory of corporate social performance. In the remainder of this book, the evidence is organized and presented in two different ways.

First, in Chapter 6 an overview of the framework is illustrated principally with survey findings. Then in Chapters 7 through 10, companies sorted into three different levels of corporate social performance are compared principally on the basis of the evidence drawn from on-site clinical research, process observation, and archival analysis. These company profiles illustrate not only the important differences between the best, mixed, and worst performers, but also reveal important insights from company histories, which help explain their different present-day approaches to corporate social performance.

SELECTION OF COMPANIES

Based on the overall assessments of corporate social performance of the nation's 25 largest insurers, a decision was initially made to focus on the companies rated at the industry extremes. Five companies could be clearly identified (see Table 4-1) as the industry's worst social performers. However, only the companies rated among the top three could be judged to clearly be among the industry's best social performers. Beyond that cluster of companies, social performance ratings fell off dramatically. So, all eight companies were contacted to enlist their participation in the comparative study. Subsequent experience in attempting to negotiate entry and conduct the necessary research in these companies yielded by themselves a crude, albeit consistent, validation of their corporate social performance ratings.

As the overall assessment of corporate social performance would suggest, the three best-rated companies were the first to respond positively to the letter of invitation. Indeed, senior executives in two of these companies called to set up the site visits before I was scheduled to telephone them. Participation by all best-rated companies was complete with respect to all access and data-collection requirements.

Enlisting the support of the industry's worst-rated companies was another story. Of the five companies contacted, one flatly refused to participate. The second company tentatively agreed to participate, but continued to postpone setting a time for the field visit. Nine months later, this company pulled out of the negotiations abruptly. A third company kept things hanging for six months, then conceded to complete the surveys, host the site visit, and scheduled the required interviews with senior line managers and external affairs professionals. But when I arrived at the site, I was informed by my host, who was the company's senior external affairs officer, that he had been too busy to distribute the surveys and set up the interviews. With some persistence I was able to leave the company with a half-day, taped interview with my host, and with a renewed promise to set up the site visit and to have the surveys completed and returned. Repeated attempts over the next three months to resume contacts with this executive went unanswered. The company was dropped from the sample when a letter was received from the executive indicating that his company did not wish to participate further in the study.

The remaining worst-rated companies also took more time than the best-rated companies to decide to take part in the study. After project schedules were set, however, both companies participated fully in all aspects of the investigation. When the chief executive officers of both companies were asked why they had decided to participate, both indicated that they did so in hopes of learning something that might be of value in improving their company's external affairs function.

The comparative study begun, therefore, with all three of the best-rated companies and two of the five worst-rated companies. However, it did not take long to discover striking differences between the two groups of companies on most of the factors included in the general framework. Therefore, a decision was made to perform a finer-grained comparative analysis of corporate social performance.

To do so meant that more companies had to be added to the project. After examining the remaining companies in Table 4-1, a decision was made to add a third category of companies. They are referred to as the "mixed" companies because they achieved a relatively high percentage of nominations at both extremes of corporate social performance. Two companies that met this criterion were selected for intensive study. Both of the mixed companies were rated as being in the middle of the corporate social performance continuum that was anchored at either extreme by the best- and worst-rated companies. One company was chosen because its mixed rating was more positive than negative. The other was chosen because its mixed rating was more negative than positive.

Both mixed companies agreed to participate in the comparative study, and both completed all of the study requirements. However, the length of the preliminary negotiations fell between the time spans required to negotiate entry into the best- and worst-rated firms. Moreover, difficulty was encountered in the more negatively rated mixed company in obtaining access to and surveys from senior line managers.

The final sample of companies employed in the comparative analysis is broken down by social performance category in Table 5-1.[5] Complete data from all sources (i.e., clinical, archival, and survey) were obtained from these companies that participated fully in all aspects of the study.

Preliminary Company Profiles

Although the three categories of companies differed markedly in terms of overall corporate social performance, the business exposures and most of the general corporate attributes of the individual companies varied widely with no consistent relationship to their social performance ratings. For example, Table 5-2 reveals that the sample is roughly split between stock and mutual companies and between companies having independent-agent distribution system and direct writers. Only one captive insurer, however, was netted in the sample, and this company was one of the industry's worst corporate social performers.

The companies selected for intensive study also varied considerably, but unsystematically, with respect to corporate social performance, on two of the three dimensions of business exposure to the corporate social environment. In terms of product mix, property-casualty specialists, life-health specialists, and multiple-line

TABLE 5-1   **Companies Selected for the Comparative Study**

Corporate Social Performance Category	Company	Overall Social Performance Rank †	Overall Corporate Social Performance‡ (%)
Best Companies	Aetna	1	+50
	Prudential	2	+43
	St. Paul	3	+37
Mixed Companies	Delta*	11	+6
	Endicott*	19	−10
Worst Companies	Falmouth*	21	−20
	Gannett*	23	−27

*The names of the mixed and worst companies are disguised to preserve their anonymity. Any similarity between the fictitious names and the real names of existing insurance companies is purely coincidental. Explicit permission was obtained to use the real names of the best-rated companies for the purpose of providing positive role models to companies desiring to improve their corporate social performance.

†The company's rank among the 25 largest U.S. insurers based on the corporate social performance ratings from the state insurance commissioners (Table 4-1).

‡The overall corporate social performance score is expressed as the difference between the percentage of best-five nominations and the percentage of worst-five nominations (Table 4-1).

companies are roughly equally and quite randomly represented in the three social performance groups. The company sample is also split on the basis of customer mix. Some deal primarily with personal insurance lines and individual consumers, whereas the others deal primarily in commercial insurance lines and corporate customers. In contrast, little variation may be observed in the primary indicator of geo-

TABLE 5-2   **General Corporate Attributes of Companies Selected for Intensive Study**

Corporate Social Performance Category	Company	Company Ownership	Distribution System†	Company Status
Best companies	Aetna	Stock	Independent agents	Independent
	Prudential	Mutual	Direct writer	Independent
	St. Paul	Stock	Independent agents	Independent
Mixed companies	Delta*	Mutual	Direct writer	Independent
	Endicott*	Mutual	Direct writer	Independent
Worst companies	Falmouth*	Stock	Independent agents	Captive
	Gannett*	Mutual	Direct writer	Independent

*Fictitious company names.

†Included in the direct writer category are companies that distribute their products through either a company salesforce or exclusive agents. Direct writers therefore tend to have more direct control over their distribution system than do companies that distribute product through independent agents.

TABLE 5-3 Business Exposures of Companies Selected for Intensive Study

Corporate Social Performance Category	Company	Product Mix†	Geographical Mix‡		Customer Mix‡		Immediate Geographical Exposure of Executive Leaders	Overall Business Exposure§
			Urban States (%)	Nonurban States (%)	Personal Lines (%)	Commercial Lines (%)		
Best companies	Aetna	Multiple-line company	70	30	25	75	High	High
	Prudential	Life/health generalist	70	30	80	20	High	Moderate
	St. Paul	Property/casualty specialist‖	65	35	15	85	Low/Moderate	Low
Mixed Companies	Delta*	Life/health specialist‖	50	50	65	35	Low/Moderate	Low
	Endicott*	Multiple-line company	65	35	75	25	Low/Moderate	High
Worst Companies	Falmouth*	Multiple-line company	85	15	30	70	Low/Moderate	High
	Gannett*	Property/casualty generalist	73	27	30	70	High	Moderate

*The names of the mixed and worst companies are disguised to preserve their anonymity. Any similarity between the fictitious names and the real names of existing insurance companies is purely coincidental. Explicit permission was obtained to use the real names of the best-rated companies for the purpose of providing positive role models to companies desiring to improve their corporate social performance.

†The estimate of each company's product mix was based on its total 1980 earned premiums in the property/casualty and life/health insurance lines. Sources: Moody's Manual (1982); Best's Insurance Reports, Life/Health Edition (1981); and Best's Insurance Reports, Property/Casualty Edition (1981). An insurer was classified as a multiple-line company if its product mix was made up of at least 20% of both property/casualty and life/health lines.

‡Geographical-mix and customer-mix estimates were obtained by survey from the senior external affairs professional in each company and were corroborated during interviews with the company's senior line and staff executives.

§The empirically based formula used to estimate overall business exposure weighted product mix twice as heavily (see Table 3-1) than either geographical mix or customer mix. First, the exposure created by a company's product mix was numerically scored as follows: multiple-line (100%), property/casualty (50%), and life/health (25%). The following formula was applied to arrive at a company's general business exposure: company exposure = [2(product mix) + (geographical mix) + (customer mix)]/4. The general business exposure for Aetna, for example, was computed as follows: Aetna exposure = [2(100%) + (25%) + (70%)]/4 = 74%. The calculated exposure for the other six companies were: Prudential (50%), St. Paul (45%), Delta (42%), Endicott (85%), Falmouth (79%), and Gannett (51%). After arraying the companies on the basis of this crude estimate of general business exposure, consideration was given to the breadth of the company's product line and market segment and to the immediate exposure of its executive leaders. The narrowness of St. Paul's and Delta's product lines and market segments, together with their location outside the northeastern corridor, further reduce their overall business exposure.

‖These companies have concentrated their product mix in a very narrow range of products that are delivered to a relatively small market segment.

graphical mix. All of these companies, by the fact that they are the nation's largest insurers, have relatively heavy business stakes in the socially complex and politically volatile urban centers. However, when the immediate geographical exposure of executive leaders is considered, some unsystematic variation may be observed among the performance categories in terms of the location of the company headquarters.

A company's overall business exposure to the corporate social environment was estimated, favoring strongly the product mix dimension, from the overall profile summarized in Table 5-3. The estimate provides the benchmark from which the general framework is applied in the comparative summary in the next chapters and to the company profiles in the subsequent chapters.

FOOTNOTES

1. The initial motivation to become involved with this company was to write a teaching case that focused on the creation and early development of an innovative public policy issues analysis function that was being added to the company's external affairs function. It was only after becoming involved in the initial casewriting interviews that I became intrigued with what the company is trying to do in the area of corporate social performance. Because of the initial feedback I was able to provide the founders of the new department about line and staff reactions to its initiation, the chief operating officer commissioned me to continue to function as a consultant to the staff of the new department. Although my formal consulting relationship, which began in 1978, lasted only for the first year of the new department, I continue to have access to company line and staff managers and executive leaders for the purposes of longitudinal process observation and interviews in exchange for the feedback I provide about the evolution of the company's external affairs function.

2. The national study of the state commissioners of insurance is summarized in detail in Robert H. Miles and Arvind Bhambri, *The Regulatory Executives* (Beverly Hills, CA: Sage Publishing, 1983).

3. Contact was initiated by a letter to the chief executive officer of each company selected for intensive study. The letter outlined the purposes of the study, the requirements of the company, and the sponsorship of the program of research. The letter also explained that both individual and company identities would be treated as confidential; and that an effort would be made to maintain company anonymity in subsequent reports of the study findings unless permission had been sought and obtained from the company to have its identity revealed. Finally, the letter explained that the site visits would terminate with a debriefing to all participants of the preliminary findings based on the clinical and survey data obtained from the company. (The reactions from company officers received during the debriefing, of course, also provided valuable data.) Telephone contact was initiated with or by the company within ten days following the mailing of this letter.

4. The company surveys were administered prior to the company visits during 1981. The overall response rate was quite high with 73 out of 82 (89%) senior line and staff executives completing the questionnaire. Each company was mailed between 9 and 16 questionnaires, depending on the number of relevant senior line and staff officers in the firm.

A fairly even split between line and staff functions was achieved in the questionnaire responses, with 53% of the responses coming from external affairs staff professionals and 47% from senior line managers. Feedback on the results of the survey analysis was included in the debriefing I conducted in a meeting with senior line and staff executives at the end of the last day of the site visits.

5. All seven companies selected for intensive study were highly visible to the assessors, in that they received a high percentage of extreme nominations from the commissioners. By adding the percentages of nominations each company received in the extreme "best" and "worst" corporate social performance categories, the corporate "visibility" averages for the three groups of companies selected for intensive study were as follows: Best (n = 3) companies (61.3%); Worst (n = 2) companies (43.5%); and Mixed (n = 2) companies (42.0%). For the 17 companies not selected for intensive study, the average corporate visibility index was only 34.0%.

6. The reason for giving greatest weight to product mix has been revealed in Chapter 2 under Table 2-1. Product mix is the best indicator of the number of different public policy issues that a company is exposed to as a result of its business strategy. Geographical mix and customer mix refer more to the intensity of the exposure created by a company's business mix. Finally, little variation may be observed between the largest U.S. insurers in terms of their stakes in (exposure to) the nation's politically and socially volatile urban centers. It must be emphasized, however, that these estimates of overall business exposure in the insurance industry may be relatively high when compared to the business exposure of leading firms in many other U.S. industries.

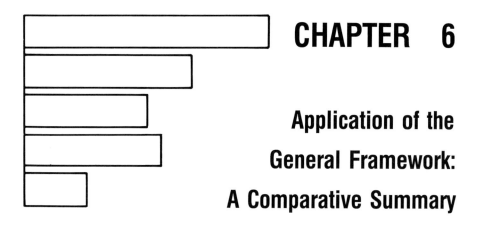

CHAPTER 6

Application of the
General Framework:
A Comparative Summary

This chapter includes a summary of the overall findings of the comparative analysis using the general framework. Comparative results from the survey data are used to illustrate the differences among the best, mixed, and worst corporate social performances.

This summary will reveal that the general framework is quite powerful in explaining and predicting company differences in corporate social performance. Moreover, its utility to executive leaders is enhanced because the general framework focuses attention for purposes of organizational diagnosis and intervention on just three sets of relationships, which are to varying degrees subject to control and influence by executive leaders. These three features of the general framework are

1. the philosophy-strategy connection,
2. the exposure-design contingency,
3. the patterns of influence and integration that link elements of a company's core external affairs function to its line operations.

THE PHILOSOPHY-STRATEGY CONNECTION

The most dramatic difference between the "best" corporate social performers and the "mixed" and "worst" companies is the philosophy-strategy connection: *All of the best-rated companies explicitly pursue an institution-oriented top management philosophy coupled with a collaborative and problem-solving, external affairs strategy*. All of the mixed corporate social performers are guided by an explicit enterprise-oriented philosophy and an explicit individualistic/adversarial external affairs strategy.

Finally, all of the worst-rated companies operate with an enterprise-oriented top management philosophy and with a reactive external affairs strategy. The reactive nature of their relatively impoverished external affairs function has resulted in the emergence of an implicit individualistic/adversarial external affairs strategy. This reactive nature is the result of their tardy responses to emerging social issues affecting their businesses, which has frequently forced them into a defensive and protective mode for which the only available recourse late in the life cycle of the issue is court action.

The differences in top management philosophy between these company groups were pronounced in the discussions with senior line managers and external affairs professionals. These philosophical differences were also discernible on a relative basis in the survey responses of company officials, despite the fact that such responses are subject to social desirability bias. Institution-oriented executives, for example, believe that their companies play a more pervasive role in society than do enterprise-oriented executives. The former see their organizations as being not only legitimately required to respond to social change, but also as sources or stimuli to social change through the influence of their business policies and practices on society. Therefore, institution-oriented senior line managers, who are primarily responsible for their company's operating performance, tend to have a higher degree of commitment than their enterprise-oriented counterparts to understanding (rather than simply influencing) the corporate social environment. This pattern can be observed in the average survey responses of senior line managers in Figure 6-1.

Institution-oriented executives also believe more strongly than enterprise-oriented executives that the industry in which they all operate faces major social issues that require fundamental business changes in order to survive (Figure 6-2). In addition, institution-oriented managers in the best-rated companies believe more strongly than enterprise-oriented managers that they should be concerned about responding to shifting public expectations in addition to managing their operations to achieve the company's financial objectives. These differences in managerial beliefs are reflected in the average survey responses summarized in Figure 6-3.

Finally, institution-oriented executives are more likely than their enterprise-oriented counterparts to consider as a legitimate corporate response to new public policy issues a change in their company's business policy and practices. As the survey responses in Figure 6-4 reveal, this managerial difference in willingness to adapt business policies and practices persists even when such a response may require the sacrifice of company profitability.

As the company profiles in Chapters 7–10 will show, these differences in top management philosophies are reinforced formally through the development of business unit planning and review systems and of managerial performance measurement and reward systems toward greater emphasis on social goals and external affairs activities, and through organization and job design. They are also reinforced informally by the symbolic roles played by executive leaders and the relatively endur-

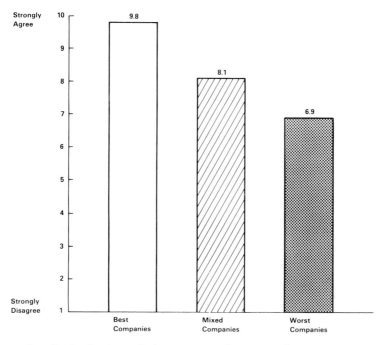

Survey Question: "It makes good business sense to expend resources to make sure my company understands the public issues confronting its businesses."

Figure 6-1 Senior line manager survey responses about the allocation of company resources to understand public issues.

Figure 6-2 Senior lines manager survey responses to the statement: The insurance industry faces some very major social issues today and should make fundamental changes in order to survive.

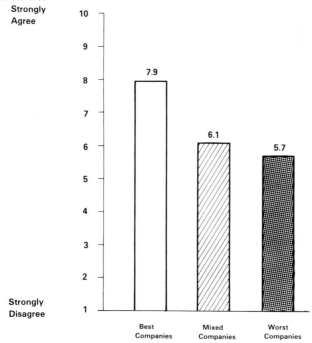

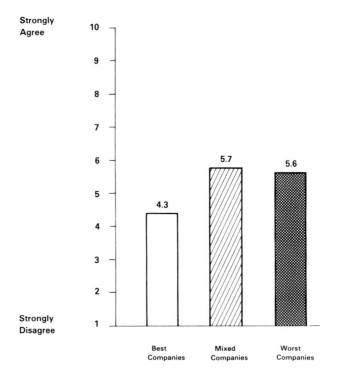

Strongly
Agree

Strongly
Disagree

Best
Companies

Mixed
Companies

Worst
Companies

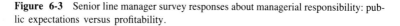

Survey Question: ''I believe that my primary concern should be on maximizing
the financial objectives of my company's product lines and not on responding-
to shifting public expectations.''

Figure 6-3   Senior line manager survey responses about managerial responsibility: public expectations versus profitability.

ing features of corporate character in each firm. In most cases, these formal and
informal reinforcers are mutually reinforcing.

These differences in top management philosophy also translate into corresponding differences in each company's external affairs strategy. Moreover, they
may have an indirect influence on the structure (i.e., breadth and depth) and process
(i.e., influence and integration) of each company's external affairs design.

Perhaps the most dramatic way to illustrate the differences between the
collaborative/problem-solving approach to external affairs used by the best-rated
companies and the individualistic/adversarial strategy employed by the mixed- and
worst-rated companies is to examine the receptivity of line managers to the purest
representatives of the public interest—consumer interest groups. As the average
survey responses in Figure 6-5 reveal, senior line managers in the best-rated
companies attach far more importance to the role of consumer interest groups in
helping their company understand the corporate social environment than do managers in the mixed- and worst-rated companies.

But this pattern also generalizes to a wide variety of relationships with other
strategic constituencies in the industry. The best-rated companies, which rely on a

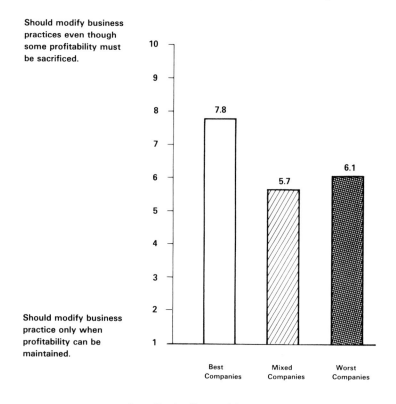

Should modify business practices even though some profitability must be sacrificed.

Should modify business practice only when profitability can be maintained.

Best Companies   Mixed Companies   Worst Companies

Survey Question: "In terms of changing a business practice in response to a major public policy issue, what do you think an individual company's posture should be?"

Figure   6-4   Senior line manager survey responses about sacrificing company profitability to respond to a major public policy issue.

collaborative/problem-solving, external affairs strategy, tend to be more actively involved in discussions and negotiations at both the industry trade associations and the National Association of State Insurance Commissioners, and with other companies and a variety of public-interest constituencies (such as federal agencies and the public media) than do the mixed- and worst-rated companies. Executives in the former companies are generally regarded as being more prepared for these occasions, coming to them with a broader perspective and a more open agenda, than are the latter companies. In addition, representatives of the industry's best corporate social performers generally place a good deal more emphasis on maintaining favorable long-term working relationships with their company's strategic constituencies than on "scoring" a short-term company victory, when compared to their counterparts who pursue an individualistic/adversarial approach.

Finally, both of the industry's worst corporate social performers continue to function without an explicit external affairs strategy. The reactive nature of these companies with respect to social and political change affecting their product lines is revealed in their responses to the company survey. For example, the state insurance

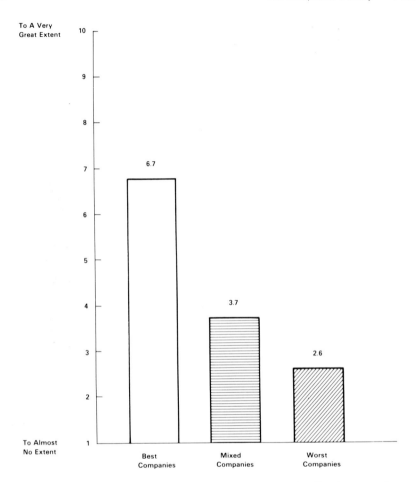

Figure 6-5 Senior line manager survey responses to the question: To what extent do consumer interest groups help your company understand the public policy issues it faces?

commissioners are the most powerful actors in the industry's social and political arena. Therefore, one would expect representatives of a company pursuing an explicit external affairs strategy, regardless of the approach taken, to stay in close touch with commissioners in order to anticipate the emergence of new social issues and regulatory agendas and to become involved in the early negotiations concerning these events. When the survey responses of senior line managers and external affairs professionals are combined, systematic differences in the initiation of company contact with these regulatory executives may be observed. As Figure 6-6 reveals, contact with the commissioners is much more likely to be initiated by the companies (i.e., the best and mixed companies) pursuing external affairs strategies. In the case of the reactive, worst-rated companies, senior executives report that contact is more likely to be initiated by the commissioners than by their company.

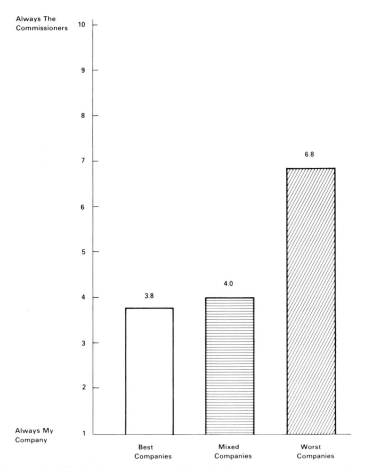

Figure 6-6 Who initiates contact on public policy issues: company versus state insurance commissioners. *Note:* Responses based on total sample of senior line managers and senior external affairs professionals.

Similarly, external affairs professionals, who are more likely than line managers to become involved in relationships with regulatory agencies, are also more likely to await direct communication from the regulatory agency concerning an industry-related public policy issue or regulation problem if they represent the worst-rated companies than with explicit external affairs strategies (Figure 6-7).

Finally, reactive companies are more likely than companies with explicit external affairs strategies to have impoverished external affairs functions. One important reason for this difference is reflected in Figure 6-8. Executives in companies guided by explicit external affairs strategies believe more strongly than their counterparts in the reactive, worst-rated companies that having corporate-level external affairs units and staff professionals is essential for company effectiveness in understanding and managing the corporate social environment.

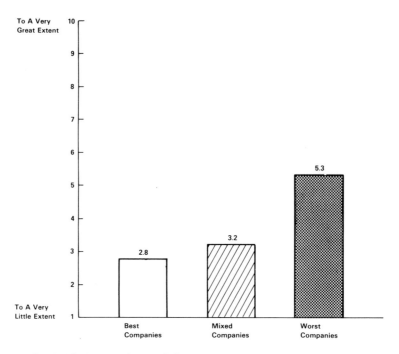

Question: "To what extent do you await direct communication from the State Insurance Department or other external agency before initiating action?"

Figure 6-7 Explicitness of external affairs strategy: views of external affairs professionals.

Figure 6-8 Senior line managers and corporate external affairs professionals survey responses to the question: How essential to effective understanding and management of public affairs issues is it to have in place at the corporate level units or professionals that specialize in this activity? *Note:* Responses based on total sample of senior line managers and senior external affairs professionals.

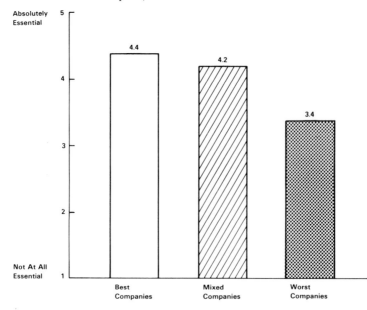

All of these deficiencies in the reactive external affairs strategies of the industry's worst social performers combine to force these companies into an implicit external-affairs strategy that relies on a protective and defensive mode when important social issues emerge and that resembles in most important respects the individualistic/adversarial strategy.

In summary, the *philosophy-strategy connection* is a powerful predictor of corporate social performance, as revealed in Table 6-1. Companies guided by an institution-oriented top management philosophy and pursuing an explicit, collaborative and problem-solving external affairs strategy outperform companies guided by an enterprise-oriented philosophy and an individualistic and adversarial strategy. Moreover, corporate social performance may be further distinguished on the basis of whether a company's external affairs strategy is formulated and implemented explicitly, as in the case of the best- and mixed-rated companies, or implicitly, as in the case of the worst-rated companies, which pursue external affairs in a reactive manner.

This second-order distinction of the philosophy-strategy connection brings us into the area of external affairs design and to the second important set of relationships in the general framework—the exposure-design contingency.

TABLE 6-1   The Philosophy-Strategy Connection: A Comparative Summary

Corporate Social Performance Category	Top Management Philosophy	External Affairs Strategy
Best companies	Institution oriented	Collaborative/problem-solving (explicit)
Mixed companies	Enterprise oriented	Individualistic/adversarial (explicit)
Worst companies	Enterprise oriented	Individualistic/adversarial [implicit (reactive)]

THE EXPOSURE-DESIGN CONTINGENCY

Although the philosophy-strategy connection is directly related to the corporate performance of a firm, no such direct relationship exists between external affairs design and corporate social performance. Having a sophisticated external affairs mechanism does not guarantee performance effectiveness. Instead, *there is a contingent relationship between a company's business exposure and external affairs design and the level of corporate social performance it achieves.* However, this performance contingency becomes important in explaining company differences only after accounting for top management philosophy and external affairs strategy.

A host of theoretical perspectives on organization design, including contingency theory, general systems theory, and information-processing theory, all converge on the prescription that organizational effectiveness is contingent upon the fit achieved between the nature of the external environment and the design of the organization. Organization's confronting complex and dynamic environments require sophisticated structures—greater structural specialization and correspondingly greater levels of coordination—in order to effectively understand and manage the contingencies posed by the environment. In contrast, such high levels of structural specialization and integration are not required by organizations confronted by simple and stable external environments. Indeed, such structural sophistication may create inefficiencies relative to the operating costs of leaner competitive organizations sharing the same context.

But as I have demonstrated, the business strategy pursued by a particular company may "expose" it to a set of contingencies that differs substantially from the contingencies with which organizations operating in the same industry context, but with different business strategies, must cope. Thus, the first step in gauging the exposure-design contingency for a particular company is to examine its business strategy; and in the case of corporate social performance, the extent to which the business strategy exposes the company to contingencies in the corporate social environment.

Companies with high business exposures to the corporate social environment need high levels of breadth and depth in the design of their external affairs functions. High breadth assures the company that it has specialized external affairs units that are uniquely qualified to anticipate and understand each of the many important contingencies or sectors in the corporate social environment to which the company is exposed. High external affairs depth, on the other hand, means that the company has in place a broad framework, including multiple perspectives for analyzing and interpreting the meaning and significance of social environment contingencies, which may be used to select among a broad repertoire of alternative company responses. In contrast, companies with low exposure to the corporate social environment generally require less external affairs breadth and depth in order to perform effectively in this domain. (The ability to get by with unsophisticated external affairs function, however, appears to depend on the role played in the corporate external affairs process by line managers. This qualification will be taken up in the next section, which focuses on the process dimensions of external affairs design.)

The comparative analysis of the best-, mixed-, and worst-corporate social performers in the insurance industry provides substantial support for the exposure design contingency. Table 6-2 summarizes the small business exposures and external affairs structures of the companies selected for intensive study. For all of the best corporate social performers, there is a strong degree of fit between the level of business exposure and the breadth and depth of the external affairs function. In contrast, the lack of fit between business exposure and external affairs design increases progressively through the mixed- and worst-rated companies.

Companies were scored high on the breadth dimension if first, they had structurally complex external affairs functions composed of multiple core units, each specializing in a different aspect of the company's external affairs activity or sector of the corporate social environment. Second, external affairs functions that scored high in breadth were also composed of units that employ a number of professional-level specialists whose primary responsibility is corporate external affairs.

TABLE 6-2   The Exposure-design Contingency:
The Degree of Fit Between Business Exposure and External Affairs Structure

Corporate Social Performance Category	Company	Business Exposure	External Affairs Structure*			
			Breadth	Fit†	Depth	Fit†
Best companies	Aetna	High	High	Good	High	Good
	Prudential	Moderate	Moderate	Good	Moderate	Good
	St. Paul	Low	Low	Good	Low	Good
Mixed companies	Delta	Low	Low‡	Good	Low	Good
	Endicott	High	High	Good	Low	Poor
Worst companies	Falmouth	High	Low‡	Poor	Low	Poor
	Gannett	Moderate	Low/moderate	Fair	Low	Poor

*Categories of external affairs structure were developed on the basis of clinical interviews and observations and on company archives. For more details, refer to the company profiles in subsequent chapters.
†This column summarized the degree of fit that has been achieved between business exposure and external affairs breadth or depth in each company.
‡This company has a chairman-dominated external affairs process.

In contrast, companies with low external affairs breadth had only one or two specialized units, usually including the traditional public relations department and a subunit of the corporate law department. In most cases these units tended to be one- or two-person departments or they were staffed by professionals with only part-time responsibility for corporate external affairs. In the latter case, for example, one company included one person from the corporate law department, the public relations and advertising department, and the marketing research department in its corporate external affairs function. However, discussions with these individuals revealed that their day-to-day activities are devoted principally to supporting the product/market activities of the companies' insurance divisions. Thus, despite the fact that the three best corporate social performers varied considerably in the structural sophistication of their external affairs breadth, members of their core external affairs units devoted their time, as shown in Figure 6-9, more exclusively to external activities than did their counterparts in the mixed- and worst-rated companies. Moreover, staff professionals in the best- and mixed-rated companies, which all pursued explicit external affairs strategies, spent a higher percentage of time engaged in external affairs activities than did their counterparts in the reactive worst-rated companies.

A first approximation of external affairs breadth could be gleaned from the company's organization chart. Subsequent reviews of job descriptions, unit head counts, and interviews with individuals identified with the external affairs function produced a more accurate description of the breadth of this function. All of this evidence revealed that no direct relationship exists between external affairs breadth and corporate social performance, and indicated the need to account for business exposure before making judgements about the appropriateness of external affairs breadth.

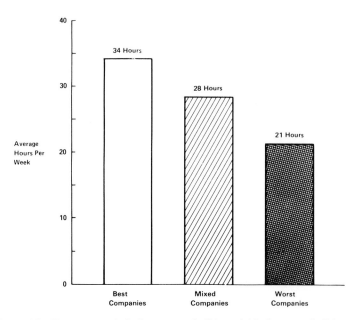

Figure 6-9 Time spent exclusively on external affairs activities by external affairs professionals. (Average hours spent per week by an individual member of the core external affairs unit.)

The most striking discovery of the comparative analysis of external affairs structures, however, is the finding that only one of the companies selected for intensive study has achieved a *high-depth* external affairs function. External affairs depth, you may recall, refers to the intensity with which external affairs professionals are able to frame and conduct research and analysis on emerging industry-related public policy issues. Intensity in this regard includes both the *range pf perspectives* allowed in framing the issues-analysis process and the *range of alternative company responses* that may be considered in formulating company positions on the issues.

As a highly exposed, multiple-line (i.e., diversified) company, Aetna needs a high-depth function. Indeed, managers in its different insurance divisions often find themselves pursuing external affairs tactics that are internally inconsistent. For example, in the late 1970s it was discovered that the health insurance division was pursuing an aggressive media campaign against escalating health-care costs. Meanwhile, the property and casualty insurance division was experiencing a consequential rash of policy cancellations in its medical liability and malpractice line by doctors who were outraged by the media campaign. Aetna, therefore, has used its high-depth function to monitor these real, as well as potential, interdependencies in an effort to create an overall corporate approach to external affairs.

Aetna was also among the nation's leading property and casualty insurers that was caught flat-footed during the mid-1970s when the highly publicized manufacturer's product-liability crisis emerged in the public media. The media alleged that the high cost and apparent lack of availablity of product-liability coverage for manufacturers, in an era of escalating consumerism and government regulations, threatened the industrial sector of the U.S. economy and raised serious doubts about the legitimacy of the private insurance mechanism.

Executive leaders at Aetna were shocked to discover that they could not respond in a timely and definitive fashion to these allegations, and that they had no mechanism in place for ensuring that the company anticipated, understood, and responded to such public policy crises that might threaten not only one of its major product lines but also the private insurance industry in which it had very high stakes. Serious development of a high-depth, external affairs function, therefore, was initiated as part of the company's response to this alleged crisis.

Finally, just before the outbreak of the product-liability crisis, two of Aetna's executive leaders had served on White House task forces. Both the chief executive officer and the chief operating officer had left these experiences with a belief that important but seemingly ambiguous public policy issues that affected their business could be effectively framed and analyzed in advance of their impact and that a mechanism and process, similar to those they had experienced on the presidential task forces, could and should be developed within the external affairs function of the company.

It is this mechanism, together with the company's philosophy and external affairs strategy, that have had made it possible for Aetna, which has one of the highest exposures to the corporate social environment in the industry, to be judged as the overall best corporate social performer among major insurers. Fortunately, I served as an action researcher and consultant to this process for a period of five years including its initiation. Because this aspect of external affairs structure is so critical to effective corporate social performance for highly exposed companies, I will return to it briefly in each company profile, and I have set aside all of Part IV to discuss how the high-depth function in Aetna was created and managed over its first five years of existence.

In summary, the contingent relationship between business exposure and external affairs structure provides an important, supplementary explanation of company differences in corporate social performance. Although the philosophy-strategy connection systematically separates the very best performers from all the others, the exposure-design contingency helps to make finer distinctions among companies that differ along the full range of corporate social performance. In particular, the mixed-rated companies, for which there is a good fit between business exposure and external affairs breadth, perform better in understanding and managing the corporate social environment, than do the worst-rated companies for which there is a lack of fit between exposure and breadth.[2] This pattern means that executive leaders may be misguided if they strive to achieve some universal ideal in the design of their external affairs function. This study indicates that they should instead attempt to tie the breadth and depth of this function to the business strategy and the degree of exposure it creates for the company.

INFLUENCE AND INTEGRATION
IN CORPORATE EXTERNAL AFFAIRS

The process dimensions of a company's external affairs design are treated as a separate category of factors in the general framework because they appear to be a complex product of top management philosophy and external affairs strategy, and a necessary complement to the structural dimensions of external affairs design.

Influence and integration *within* the external affairs function vary somewhat from firm to firm as the company profiles will reveal, although not nearly as much as influence and integration *between* core units of the function and the company's line operations. With regard to intrafunctional relations, Figure 6-10 reveals that mutual influence and coordination among core elements of the function are generally higher for companies pursuing an explicit external-affairs strategy (i.e., the best- and mixed-rated companies) than for the reactive (i.e., worst-rated) companies. This pattern is consistent with the argument that in order to pursue an explicit external affairs strategy, executive leaders must ensure that the specialized perspective within the external affairs functions and the various activities pursued with respect to different sectors of the corporate social environment are represented and reconciled in the external affairs decision-making process. Otherwise core external affairs units may become engaged in independent activities that may be inconsistent or contradictory in their effects on corporate social performance.

In some companies, specialists in different external affairs units seldom talk

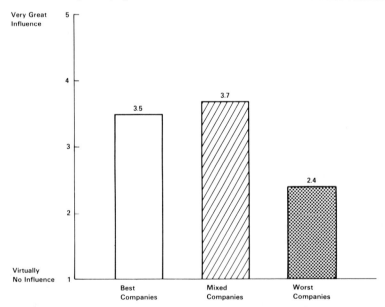

Figure 6-10 Mutual influence among core external affairs units. External affairs professionals survey responses to the question: How much influence do the other corporate external affairs departments have on the decisions made in your department?

to each other; they are often physically separated. In one company, for example, staff professionals in the federal affairs unit located in Washington, D.C., rarely had any contact with the unit specializing in state regulatory affairs that was located in the parent company's headquarters in the Northeast. In some companies coordination is achieved principally through informal contact, whereas in other companies formal settings have been created in which external affairs units regularly brief each other and solicit advice on their agenda. And in a few companies, unit members sit on task forces and act as consultants to other units to help with their progress on external affairs projects. Finally, some external affairs units report to the same senior executive, whereas in others their reporting channels differ. All of these variations have an impact on the patterns of influence and integration within the external affairs function. Indeed, the company analyses will show that their impact varies with the nature of each company expressed in terms of other dimensions of the general framework.

LINE-MANAGER INVOLVEMENT

The more important effects of the integration and influence dimensions on overall corporate social performance, I believe, have to do with the quality of relations *between* members of the core external affairs function and the company's line managers. *The impact of line-manager involvement on corporate social performance depends on how a company stacks up on the other factors in the general framework.* This conclusion should in no way be interpreted as diminishing the potential influence of line-manager involvement. To the contrary, the statement means that being able to understand or predict its influence requires a prior diagnosis of the company based on the other factors in the general framework.

The comparative study reveals three basic forms of *line-manager involvement* in the external affairs process, as summarized in Figure 6-11. At the left hand extreme, the company's approach to understanding and managing the corporate social environment is dominated by the *line-management point of view.* Line managers must make decisions regarding what social issues to pay attention to and how the company will respond to them. Often they rely on scattered staff elements to provide support for their decision-making and action-taking activities. Usually this support is modest because the staff units they call upon are already overworked and are generally limited to the traditional line-support functions, including marketing, public relations (narrowly conceived), and law. Occasionally, the whole line-dominated approach to corporate external affairs continues to be dominated by a single individual, the chairman.

The consequences of the line-dominated approach are predictable if the prevailing management philosophy about the role of the corporation in society is also known. If the prevailing philosophy is enterprise-oriented, the line-dominated approach is likely to generate a defensive and protective posture with respect to the status quo of the traditional business policies and practices of the line operations. Little challenge is mustered for organizational adaptation to social change. Second,

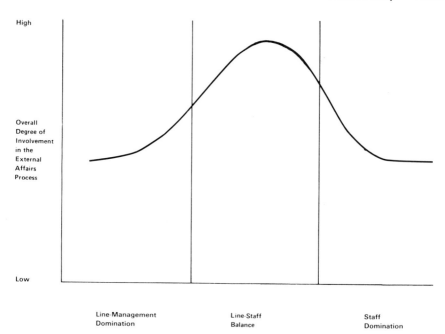

High

Overall
Degree of
Involvement
in the
External
Affairs
Process

Low

| Line-Management | Line-Staff | Staff |
| Domination | Balance | Domination |

Figure 6-11   The three basic forms of line-manager involvement in the corporate external affairs process.

the approach tends to be driven almost exclusively by company self-interest. Consequently, the responses of the company are likely to be judged by outsiders as extremely individualistic and adversarial. Finally, because line managers spend most of their time focusing on business operations, these companies tend to be very reactive in responding to industry-related social change.

Only two types of companies appear to be able to "get by" with a line-management approach to corporate external affairs. Either their business exposure is very low (as in the case of Delta), or their line managers are imbued with an institution-oriented philosophy about the role of their corporation in society (as in the case of St. Paul). For the latter to work, business exposure must also be relatively low; otherwise, line managers become overwhelmed with competing social and operational responsibilities. The worst-performing reactive companies tend to operate with this type of external affairs process.

The *staff-dominated* external affairs function occupies the opposite extreme in Figure 6-11. In these companies, responsibilities for understanding the product/market and social environments are separated and assigned to line managers and external affairs professionals, respectively.

Highly exposed companies that are guided by an enterprise-oriented, top-management philosophy and an *explicit* individualistic/adversarial strategy, tend to operate with a staff-dominated external affairs process, as revealed in Figure 6-12. Line managers attempt to maximize the short-term performance of the company's

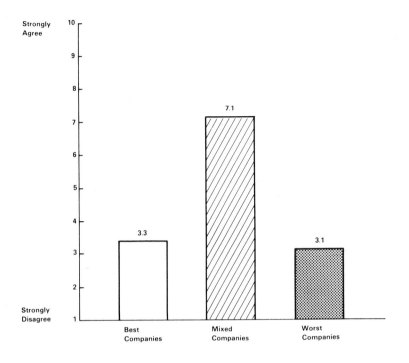

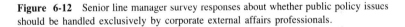

Survey Question: "I believe the primary responsibility in my company for coping with public policy/public affairs issues should rest with our external affairs (e.g., government relations, public affairs, corporate communications, public relations, etc.) departments, and not with the line or business divisions.

Figure 6-12 Senior line manager survey responses about whether public policy issues should be handled exclusively by corporate external affairs professionals.

traditional business operations, while external affairs professionals attempt to buffer and protect the business core from interference from the corporate social environment. Little challenge is presented by the core external affairs function to the traditional policies and practices of the company's business operations; instead, the function is in place to create more favorable external conditions for those operations.

As the company case histories will reveal, Endicott pursues the purest form of staff-dominated external affairs of all the companies intensively studied. This was the company whose senior external affairs executive scheduled my site visit and interviews when all of the senior line managers were scheduled to be out of town!

External affairs breadth at Endicott is high; however, external affairs depth, which involves the process by which a company learns about its external social environment, is minimal. Neither business divisions nor line managers are measured and evaluated on the basis of their ability to cope with social events and trends.

Finally, there are companies whose external affairs function falls in the middle of Figure 6-11. Their core functions are characterized by both high staff involvement (e.g., high breadth and depth) *and high* line-management involvement. Line managers are measured and evaluated on the quality of their contributions to the corporate external affairs process. Often succession to top management positions requires rotation through external affairs units and participation on high-level task forces, which focus on external affairs issues and events. Indeed, involvement in corporate external affairs is viewed as an essential opportunity for management development and as an important criterion for executive succession within the firm.

Staff professionals in these companies are evaluated not only on the quality of their contributions to management understanding of the external social environment, but also in terms of their catalytic efforts in stimulating organizational adaptation to the corporate social environment. These dual responsibilities are illustrated in Figure 6-13 for the three companies in the comparative study that were judged to be highly exposed to the corporate social environment. Senior line managers at Aetna, the best-rated institution-oriented company, perceive their external affairs function both as providing a lot of help and as creating a lot of uncertainty for them. In contrast, senior line managers in the highly exposed, mixed- and worst-rated companies perceive their external affairs functions only as support activities, not as catalysts to their thinking and to operational change.

Thus, line and staff professionals are expected to collaborate in these

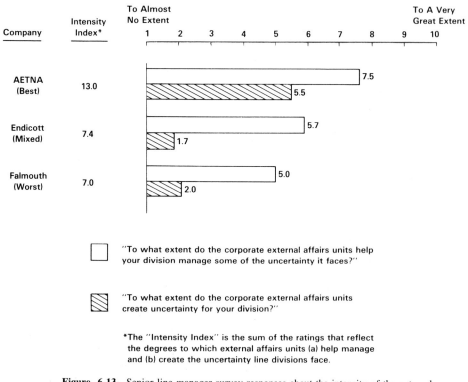

Figure 6-13 Senior line manager survey responses about the intensity of the external affairs process in three highly exposed companies.

companies toward the resolution of industry-related social issues. As Figure 6-14 reveals, institution-oriented line managers in the best-rated companies regard themselves as a primary source of information concerning new, industry-related public policy issues. In this manner, on an ongoing basis, these companies confront the fundamental tension between short-term operational efficiency and long-term organizational adaptation and legitimacy that lies at the heart of institutional effectiveness.

The achievement and maintenance of this kind of *line–staff balance* in corporate external affairs will always require the support and encouragement of executive leaders. Through the symbolic roles they play, their day-to-day behaviors, and the decision-making contexts they create, executive leaders model and reinforce the need to manage, rather than ignore or avoid, this ongoing tension between institutional efficiency and legitimacy.

In addition, it is obvious from the company histories which follow, that the specific elements of the internal contexts they create for this activity will vary from situation to situation. For example, Aetna's traditional dependence on a highly decentralized profit-center structure of business divisions required the creation of an

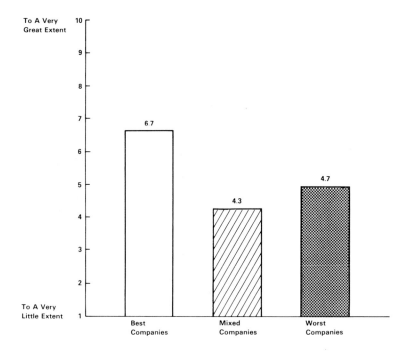

Note: Out of a list of twelve potential sources of information about public policy issues, line executives were rated as the second most important source in the best companies, eleventh in the mixed companies, and ninth in the worst companies. All companies rated the state insurance commissioners as the most important information source on company-related public policy issues.

Figure 6-14 Senior line manager survey responses to the question: To what extent do line executives serve as the source of information about new public policy issues?

intensive overlay of performance measurement and reward systems, as well as a highly sophisticated core external affairs function, to achieve the same high level of line-staff involvement that was possible in St. Paul because of its centralized operations, its relatively small size, and its thick internal culture which had for decades reinforced heavy public involvement of its rising line managers.

Two of the more important differences in line-manager involvement between these three classes of companies surfaced in the analysis of the company surveys. As Figure 6-15 reveals, staff professionals in the companies pursuing explicit external affairs strategies (i.e., the best- and worst-rated companies) all stay involved with company-related public policy issues for a substantial interval of time. In contrast, staff professionals in the reactive, worst-rated companies stay involved in these issues for a somewhat shorter interval. But the big differences in Figure 6-15 occur for senior line managers.

Senior line managers in the best-rated, institution-oriented companies stay involved with external affairs issues far longer than do senior line managers in the mixed-rated, enterprise-oriented companies. The former tend to emphasize a line-staff balance in the corporate external affairs process, whereas the latter tend to operate with staff-dominated functions. Finally, senior line managers in the reactive,

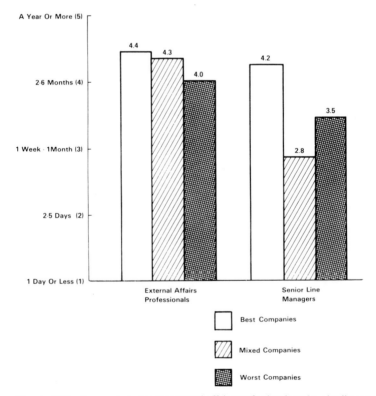

Figure 6-15 Survey responses by external affairs professionals and senior line managers to the question: How long do you generally stay involved with a particular public policy issue?

worst-rated companies tend to occupy the midrange in line-management involvement. They do so because their companies tend to operate with impoverished external affairs functions.

The other important set of differences among these company groups lies in the area of employee rewards for being able to understand and deal with external affairs issues. Company differences in such areas as divisional planning and review systems and employee performance evaluation systems are clearest from the clinical data generated in the on-site visits. But they are also visible in the survey data summarized in Figure 6-16, which reveals the extent to which personnel believe their

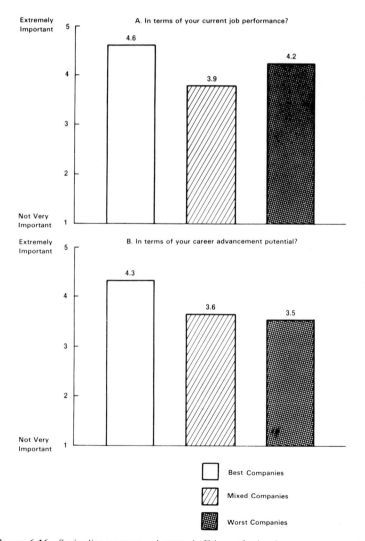

Figure 6-16   Senior line manager and external affairs professionals survey responses to the question: How important is your ability to understand and deal with public affairs issues? *Note:* Total sample.

individual contributions to corporate external affairs are factored into their performance evaluations and assessments of career advancement potential. Although the
differences in survey reports are not pronounced, in both instances they favor the
best-rated, institution-oriented companies.

SUMMARY

This overview of the findings from the comparative study demonstrates the utility of
the general framework for organizational diagnosis aimed at understanding how
large corporations manage relations with the corporate social environment. The application of the framework to a U.S. industry also reveals three critical relationships
that may be used to guide both organizational diagnosis and intervention for the
purpose of improving corporate social performance. These relationships are the
philosophy-strategy connection, the exposure-design contingency, and the degree
of line-management involvement.

But even this brief summary has revealed that the application of the framework cannot be a mechanical one. Large corporations are exceedingly complex social and economic systems, and the interactions among a large number of factors—
some originating inside the corporation, and others imposing themselves from
outside—influence overall corporate social performance. Therefore, the general
framework constitutes only a way of beginning to order these factors for
organizational diagnosis and intervention by executive leadership.

The next four chapters, which summarize the variety of approaches developed
by the best, mixed, and worst companies, reveal some of the important subtleties
and occasional paradoxes that must be understood if the general framework is to be
applied intelligently and practically to the improvement of corporate social performance.

FOOTNOTES

1. The underlying mechanism in external affairs depth has been discussed recently in the
   literature as "issues management." The new role of social issues specialist has been
   discussed in R. Ackerman and R.A. Bauer, *Corporate Social Responsiveness* (Reston,
   VA: Reston Publishing Co., 1975). Moreover, general treatments of issues management may be found in "The Fundamentals of Issue Management" (Washington, D.C.:
   Public Affairs Council, Monograph 12-78); S.P. Sethi, "A Conceptual Framework for
   Environmental Analysis of Social Issues and Evaluation of Business Response Patterns," *Academy of Management Review,* 1979, 4, no. 1, 63–74.
2. External affairs breadth does tend to vary somewhat systematically with the explicitness
   of a company's external affairs strategy. In general, the more explicit a company's external affairs strategy the greater will be the breadth of the external affairs functions in
   order to enable the company to pursue its strategy.

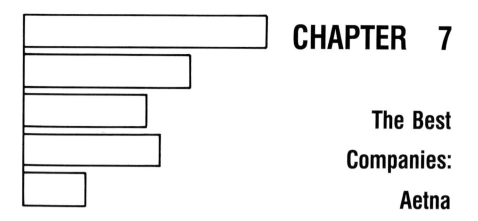

CHAPTER 7

The Best Companies: Aetna

The insurance industry has been thrust center stage on the American political and social scene. We have been propelled—willingly or not—to the very forefront of many of the key issues confronting our society at the present time. We shrink from these challenges which arise from the changing mores of American life at the peril of the entire private insurance business. For my part, I welcome this reality and I urge our industry to accept its responsibility. In order to do so, we need, in my judgment, to rethink what this responsibility entails and take a fresh look at how we go about discharging it.

William O. Bailey
Chief Operating Officer

Aetna was rated as the best overall corporate social performer in the U.S. insurance industry. It achieved this distinction despite the fact that its exposure to the corporate social environment is one of the highest in the industry.

As one of the nation's largest, multiple-line insurers, Aetna is exposed to all major segments of the insurance industry. Because of its multiple-line status corporate management must reconcile not only the diversity of social issues that impact its various business divisions, but also the occasional conflicts that arise among the divisions as each attempts to mount its own responses.

A clear picture of what it is like to manage under such high-exposure conditions was initially revealed to me when an Aetna vice president described what his life was like during the early 1970s when he served as a liaison between the corporate law department and the property and casualty insurance division. He said,

The nature of my liaison work with the Property and Casualty Division was extremely topical. I could read the front page of the daily newspaper and probably guess what I would be working on that day. I was dealing with immediate problems that involved public reactions and outside pressure groups. And, considering that we are a multiple-line company, anything I did in the casualty area had ramifications with respect to the life and group insurance divisions.

Aetna's social performance is all the more remarkable in light of the company's high visibility in both public and private forums. It was the most highly visible company from the point of view of state regulators.[1] But it was also the most frequently mentioned company when industry executives were asked to identify major insurers that were doing an especially good job of understanding and managing the corporate social environment. On the one hand, executives in other best-rated companies closely identified with Aetna's overall approach to corporate social performance and believed that Aetna had developed the most sophisticated issues-analysis mechanism in the industry. On the other, executives in the lower-rated, enterprise-oriented companies pointed first to Aetna as their major rival in the corporate external affairs domain. Thus, Aetna has achieved its distinction as industry leader in corporate social performance even though it is the most highly visible corporation in the U.S. insurance industry.

In brief, Aetna cannot escape the public controversies surrounding its industry. For any corporate management such exposure and visibility would be problematic. That Aetna has been able to cope effectively under this extreme situation while other highly exposed industry majors have not, creates a special opportunity to examine the elements underlying successful performance under conditions of high business exposure. Having access to such a company for comparative research purposes, therefore, was especially critical for the demonstration of the general framework. However, my access and involvement with Aetna was not confined to the comparative study alone.

During the five years leading up to the publication of this book I had been engaged as an action-researcher and consultant to Aetna's executive leaders. My principal involvement focused on the continued development, elaboration and refinement of the company's external affairs process. This activity included assistance in the design and launching of an innovative external affairs department and its integration with existing staff units and with the line operations of the company. Because of the intensity of my involvement, the opportunity presented by Aetna to learn about effective corporate social performance will be summarized in this chapter and treated in substantial detail in Chapters 11 and 12.

AETNA IN PROFILE

The principal factors underlying Aetna's success are not difficult to isolate. First, Aetna's fundamental character and traditions have strongly endorsed both corporate social responsibility in decision making about business policies and practices and public involvement of line managers. These elements have been refined by Aetna's present executive leaders in light of recent changes in the corporate social environment surrounding its industry. To meet the demands of an increasingly turbulent social environment, which emerged during the 1970s, Aetna's executive leaders have added social *responsiveness* as an important element of the company's character. All of these elements are now guided by Aetna's traditional, institution-oriented philosophy and are operationalized in terms of an explicit, collaborative and problem-solving, external affairs strategy.

Second, the company has developed a highly sophisticated external affairs design. The core of this function, which is made up of corporate-level staff specialists, has achieved a high degree of breadth and depth, and is characterized by strong patterns of mutual influence and integration among the several specialized staff units. Added to the sophistication of the core function is a high degree of institution-oriented, line management involvement in the external affairs process.

In light of the company's high degree of business exposure, this configuration of factors has enabled Aetna to carve out a unique place for itself in the corporate social environment. Its business policies, practices, and products are viewed as being highly responsive to the demands of the changing social environment of the industry. Moreover, the company is able to assume leadership in shaping a private insurance mechanism that meets current social demands and appears likely to survive over the long haul. State regulators, both conservatives and activists, tend to seek out in advance Aetna's opinions on regulatory agendas and legislative initiatives they plan to introduce into the insurance industry. Aetna's participation in the activities of the National Association of Insurance Commissioners is also highly valued by regulators.

The patterns that emerge among these elements of Aetna's approach to the corporate social environment provide substantial support for the general framework proposed in Chapter 1.

Business Exposure

Aetna operates with one of the highest business exposures of all the companies selected for intensive study—substantially higher than the exposures of either of the other best-rated companies.[2] Not only is Aetna one of the country's largest multiple-line insurers, with assets and annual revenues ranging in the billions of dollars; but it is headquartered in the capital of a major northeastern state. Adding to its exposure is the fact that over 70% of its business has traditionally been derived from the politically and socially volatile urban centers of America.

Exacerbating its exposure to the corporate social environment is the fact that Aetna's largest business stakes remain in the property and casualty business. Moreover, the majority of the commissioners of insurance in urban states are activists. Activists do not regard insurance companies as part of their constituencies; instead, they focus on the interests of individual policyholders, individuals who have been denied insurance coverage, and organized consumer-interest groups. Activists initiate more comprehensive and revolutionary agendas in the regulatory and legislative arena than do their counterparts in nonurban states, and they have more abundant resources and more sophisticated regulatory agencies to support their agendas than do nonurban commissioners.[3] Under this extreme performance situation, Aetna has had to develop a highly sophisticated and institutionalized approach to understanding the corporate social environment. Fortunately, Aetna has not been impeded in this effort by a reluctant corporate history.

Company History and Character

Aetna was founded over a 100 years ago by a former judge whose company career was punctuated with significant experiences in community and political affairs. The company was one of the few major insurers to pay all claims during the catastrophic urban fires at the turn of the century and it managed to avoid employee layoffs during the Depression years. As recently as two decades ago, Aetna's chief executive officer urged employees to give tithes of their time as well as their money for the public good. Throughout its long history, the company's character has fundamentally endorsed the values of social responsibility and public involvement.

These social elements of corporate character, however, came under strain during the 1960s because of the tremendous number of company- and industry-related, public policy issues that emerged to threaten the traditional business policies and practices of this large, multiple-line insurer. With the goodwill that Aetna had earned with regulators and other external constituencies, the company was able to move to a more anticipatory and interactive approach to corporate external affairs during the period 1960–1980. In many respects, this goodwill earned over the years through responsible practice and public involvement provided the organizational slack needed to make an orderly transition to becoming a highly responsive corporation.[4]

The Aetna chief executive officer who retired in the mid-1970s, was credited with having anticipated the shift toward greater turbulence in the corporate social environment surrounding the U.S. insurance industry; a trend that had begun in the 1960s. "One of the contributions of the former CEO," said one senior Aetna executive, "was that he recognized the impact that government and society was beginning to have on corporations. Even under his reign we were in a process of thinking though what is the proper role of the corporation in society. We created our Corporate Responsibility Committee at the Board of Directors level, and we became committed to Affirmative Action not because the law required it, but because there was a feeling that things like this were appropriate. The current chief executive officer feels this way strongly, as does the chief operating officer."

The current chief executive officer, John Filer, an attorney by profession who served as a state senator before joining Aetna's law department, has maintained a high external affairs profile. As examples, during the time of this study, Filer served as a trustee of the Urban Institute, as a member of the Board of Governors of the Nature Conservancy, as a director of the National Minority Purchasing Council, as chairman of the American Council of Life Insurance, as a trustee of the Committee for Economic Development, and as chairman of the National Alliance of Business. He created one of the first Corporate Social Responsibility staff departments among large U.S. corporations and his career has involved a number of significant outside experiences, including White House and private foundation committee work, trusteeships with a variety of public-interest and minority organizations, and leadership roles in both industry trade associations and all-industry associations (such as the Business Roundtable and the National Alliance of Business).

His appointment of William O. Bailey, the company's chief operating officer and second-in-command, was somewhat unusual. Bailey replaced his boss, the former president of the company's insurance operations, before the president reached retirement age. The former president was not retained as a board member, as was the tradition at Aetna. When asked why the shift in the traditional pattern of executive succession was engineered in this manner, a former special assistant to the CEO explained that Filer valued Bailey's ''vision and breadth, and his capacity to operate in an environment that is going to be different from the one we had in the past.'' Other senior executives remarked that the two executive leaders complemented and reinforced one another.

Having risen from a distinguished career in the company's line operations, Bill Bailey complements the corporate staff perspective of John Filer. But Bailey also brings to the COO position an unusually high commitment to and broad appreciation of the relationship between Aetna and American society. He, too, had been active on White House committees where he was schooled in the processes by which public policies are formulated and implemented; and he had become active in public-interest forums and industry trade association activities.

Aetna's senior corporate staff executive described the complementarity of the company's two executive leaders as follows: ''If you look at the public issues arena here at Aetna, Filer is very knowledgeable, well known in Washington, and certainly in our state and in our industry. Bailey is also very well known in insurance circles and, I happen to think, is probably the most knowledgeable property and casualty executive in the business. Together, they bring a certain insight and direction to our external affairs activity.''

These executive leaders engineered two important changes in Aetna's traditional character and structure. Building upon the timely insights of their predecessor, they developed an external affairs function that was not only responsible and committed to public involvement, but also highly responsive to the increasing diversity and intensity of social issues impacting the company's varied business divisions. An excerpt from a memorandum sent jointly from Filer and Bailey to all senior line and staff managers underscored the requirement for developing greater company responsiveness to insurance-related social issues. They said, ''We must move from a history of worthwhile and relatively isolated and uncoordinated acts of volunteerism to a more fundamental commitment—one that recognizes that each [business] division's central mission in the years ahead must encompass the concept of public involvement.'' Importantly, this call for greater corporate commitment to social issues came at a time when many of Aetna's managers were struggling to cope with a serious downturn in the property and casualty business, increased pressures for cost reduction, and unprecedented market competition in the form of widespread product innovation.

These executive leaders also insisted on, and eventually achieved, better overall integration of the company's line operations at the corporate level. A strong set of economic values had also become part of the company's evolving character. Traditionally, highly decentralized product-line divisions had been regarded as independent profit centers. However, despite the new turbulence in the corporate social environment, line divisions had continued to develop their own responses to social issues, creating crises at the corporate level. For example, when the health insurance division responded to escalating health-care costs by initiating a national campaign to stimulate public pressure on the health-care industry, Aetna's property and casualty division suffered a rash of cancellations in medical liability policies from outraged physicians. The new executive leaders believed that this level of complexity and interdependence in the corporate social environment, could only be managed by increasing the level of coordination at the corporate level. Pressures from the marketplace to become more cost competitive reinforced the decision to move toward greater corporate centralization and consolidation. The modifications in corporate character and structure, however, enabled Aetna to avoid conflicting responses to social issues by its operating divisions and to develop a company-wide approach to external affairs.

Top Management Philosophy

Aetna line and staff executives are guided by an institution-oriented, top management philosophy that has strongly been reinforced by the company's executive leaders through both their personal role behaviors and the structural context for decision making they have created. This philosophy recognizes the legitimacy of social claims on a large and pervasive corporation and Aetna's duty to be responsive to those claims. "Our society rightfully expects us to contribute fully to the search for more basic solutions that will enable the public to get the coverage it needs at a price it can afford to pay," said Bill Bailey. "To the extent that we are unable to fulfill that need, we fail in our primary mission and erode the support of the public on which our continued existence depends."

So strong is the commitment of Aetna's executive leaders to this philosophy that they have frequently featured it as a major theme in the speeches they give to various external groups representing the industry or the public interests. For example, during the period 1975–78, Bailey took this message to a national meeting of independent agents' associations. Commenting on the failure of the insurance industry to effectively respond to rising consumerism and public scrutiny, he said,

> It seems to me that we should have learned two important lessons, both of which should have been readily apparent but obviously were not. The first lesson is that the external environment plays a major role in the destiny of the insurance industry. The

second and more important lesson is that our industry needs to be more perceptive about and more responsive to social, economic and political trends. . . . Only by anticipating, responding and adapting can we shape our destiny in this often hostile external environment. . . . We cannot afford to be isolationists—we must realize that the industry's goals and society's goals must be brought into harmony.

When I asked Bailey, who also serves as president of all of Aetna's insurance divisions, how he would describe his role, he said, "I am having to spend more of my time worrying about the kind of world we are going to live in; the kind of business environment that all business is going to function in; and the kind of social developments that are going on, so that we can preserve a strong operational entity that can really perform to its capability, and is not hemmed in by external pressures and complications."

As the descriptions of the external affairs strategy and design that follow will reveal, the commitment of Aetna's executive leaders to an institution-oriented philosophy goes far beyond their personal statements and role behaviors. During the half decade or so that they have run the company, they have modified the structural context for decision making to channel and reinforce the activities of line and staff employees in support of the philosophy. One important aspect of this context has been the merging of economic and social goals in the corporate planning and review process. John Filer explained his role in this process and its underlying rationale as follows:

Because social goal-setting is so new, so different and so difficult at this point, I believe it must, for now, be primarily a role of the chief executive. The average manager is conditioned by training and incentive programs to view profit as the solitary goal. Few managers view pursuit of social goals as necessary to personal success. Therefore, it is up to the chief executive to move the message downward, first through senior management and into the middle and lower levels of the organization. This must be done as an exercise not of autocracy but of leadership.

Effective social goal-setting cannot be mandated in any organization. I do not believe we can tell managers they must place a set number of social goals in their business plans each year and expect those goals to be pursued. It is more effective instead to create a climate in which managers willingly and thoughtfully place such goals in their plans. It has recently been my role to encourage our senior people to see that the social problems they can address creatively through their operations are considered when preparing annual plans, and that like amount of thought be given to addressing people problems as is given to addressing profit problems. If one were to read our company's annual business goals today, he would find a sprinkling of social goals mixed with the traditional profit objectives. We have not, of course, addressed all the social problems we are able to affect. But we are doing more than we were a few years ago, and we will be doing still more in the years ahead.[5]

When asked whether the inclusion of social goals in the company's business plan was an altruistic gesture or simply a matter of good business in a highly exposed situation, Filer responded,

This is important, not from a sense of obligation or moral duty, but as a continuing investment in our long-term profitability and growth. The private sector in this country, including the corporate community, must be more involved and effective in addressing public or social issues either alone or in cooperation with government. Failure to do so will inevitably produce a resurgence of undesirable government efforts or seriously adverse social consequences.

These philosophical orientations and agendas of Aetna's executive leaders translate directly into the company's external affairs strategy.

External Affairs Strategy

Aetna's strategy for corporate external affairs is explicit in its reliance on a collaborative/problem-solving, as opposed to an individualistic/adversarial, approach to the resolution of company- and industry-related social issues. "I have strong views on what we should be doing," said Bill Bailey. "We need to listen better to what the public is telling us but, at the same time, we have to provide public leadership as well as reponse to public opinion. We have to avoid being defensive. Instead, we need to challenge our own traditional assumptions and defend our practices only when they are truly defensible. We have to invest more brainpower and energy in our analysis of emerging public issues rather than let others shape and define them for us. We have to anticipate issues and find innovative directional responses in advance of a crisis—real or perceived."

Executive leaders at Aetna have encouraged recognition throughout the organization that traditional business policies and practices are not sacrosanct. As Bailey continued, "If insurance is to continue performing its mission, changes will have to be made in the insurance mechanism, in the systems served by insurance and also in some public attitudes and expectations."

To make progress on this agenda, Aetna has assumed a leadership role in the industry. Its broad business portfolio engages most of the social issues impacting the industry as a whole, and its long-term business stakes are ultimately inseparable from the fate of the private insurance mechanism in the United States. Therefore, Aetna is quite active in the industry trade associations, where its representatives attempt to encourage companies with diverse business stakes and interests to collaborate in developing broad and responsive positions on industry-specific social issues. "To be effective in these efforts, our industry must have the discipline to stop divisive quarreling among ourselves over minor differences and recognize that fundamental solutions, refined over time, must be found to the major problems confronting us," said Bailey. "Our inability as an industry to come forward jointly with clear alternatives and basic solutions on critical issues only prolongs and heightens the problem while worsening the public's perception of our sincere concern for its interests."

But Aetna's collaborative approach to corporate external affairs is not limited to industry forums. It extends well into a variety of regulatory and public-interest arenas as well. For instance, a former president of the National Association of Insurance Commissioners commented on Aetna's participation on NAIC Advisory Committees as follows:

> Aetna is one company that monitors NAIC activities quite well. They're willing to serve on Advisory Committees that the NAIC forms to give us input. From that direct view Aetna's performance has been good. They appear to be objective and straightforward. Theirs is not a slanted, biased kind of view simply to gain some company benefit.

The company's external affairs function is sufficiently sophisticated to enable Aetna to focus on industry-related issues at an early stage in their development, while the company's "zone of discretion" for determining how to respond to them is large. As Bailey explained,

> One should have, ideally, a very good antenna system for recognizing emerging problems, grab them away, if you will, from the political arena early so they can be better defined and worked on. If one waits, as has been the tradition, pretending that a problem really isn't there, then a public institution will become convinced that it is there, and will start to define it so narrowly that they are the only ones who can possibly come to grips with it. So, the earlier in the development process you can jump in and start getting involved, the better off you are.

At the time Aetna line managers and staff professionals begin serious work on an issue such as a new regulatory initiative, there is usually sufficient opportunity to explore a number of options with both industry and public or regulatory groups. Indeed, representatives of both interest groups often seek out Aetna's advice on social issues or regulatory proposals before developing their own positions.

From the perspective of Aetna's executive leaders, the collaborative/problem-solving strategy serves two purposes. "We must assume the leadership role in informing the public of the good and bad implications of the changes which are taking place so that public policy and attitudes will reflect a balanced and objective assessment and not focus solely on the benefits of change," Bill Bailey said. "We must also research and make public in understandable form the alternative choices available in order to create an informed climate in which consideration of reform can be achieved through governmental or social processes."

Pursuing such a strategy under high-exposure conditions requires not only a sophisticated external affairs "core," but also a line-management function that embraces the institution-oriented philosophy and that is involved in the external affairs process. As one senior staff executive at Aetna explained, "If our executive leaders are going to be credible with an industry trade association group of executives, and prompt them to take action, we have to be fully prepared here to support them. The really first test is whether our operating people are willing to do something."

External Affairs Design

The core external affairs function at Aetna has achieved a high degree of breadth, depth, mutual influence, and integration. Over the years it has encouraged greater involvement of line managers and has received, in turn, increasing receptivity among Aetna's basic business divisions.

Breadth. The core staff function consists of four primary external affairs units, each specializing in a different aspect of the corporate social environment, but having boundaries between one another that executive leaders have preferred not to draw definitively. The oldest units, Corporate Communications (formerly Public Relations and Advertising) and Government Relations, perform the traditional external affairs functions, broadly conceived as representing the corporation to its publics and defending the core line function from unwarranted intrusion from the corporate social environment. The newer units, Corporate Social Responsibility and Public Policy Issues Analysis, both created by the current executive leaders, have a very different kind of mission. Two of their important functions are to facilitate managerial learning about the corporate social environment and to catalyze organizational change. Finally, these core staff units are complemented by the work of two standing committees, the Environmental Analysis Group and the Marketing Study Group, that are led by and primarily composed of senior line managers. They too have been added to the traditional external affairs function by the current executive leaders.[6]

The Government Relations department is staffed by attorneys whose responsibility it is to

1. represent the company,
2. interpret current legislative and regulatory developments at the state and federal level,
3. engage in lobbying efforts on behalf of the company at federal and state level,
4. participate when feasible in the drafting of new insurance-related legislation.

Its primary focus is current and near term in nature. The department head described the primary responsibility of his unit as "getting changes implemented outside, desirable issues adopted, and others defeated." The unit is organized along product lines and many of its senior members have specific liaison responsibilities with particular business divisions. Unit members frequently accompany line executives during their visits with regulators, legislators, and other public representatives. Finally, the Government Relations department is responsible for managing the efforts of retained lobbyists in Washington, D.C. and other strategic locations across the United States.

The Corporate Communications Department performs an expanded public relations function and develops and manages all advertising activities. Under the leadership of a recently appointed former line executive, who had successfully run two of Aetna's largest property and casualty regional offices, this department has engaged in a new form of advertising, referred to as "issues" or advocacy advertising, which is designed to raise the level of public awareness of problems in society that affect the insurance business.[7] This program differs from traditional product advertising in that the former attempts to influence attitudes and opinions of the general public, whereas the latter is targeted at customers and potential customers.

Commenting on the role of the Corporate Communications Department, the new department head said, "My objective as a senior communications officer, certainly, is to make Aetna look as good as it possibly can. But when it doesn't look good to me, I think I have an obligation to scurry around and bring that to the attention of the divisional people or, if I need to, the 'Top Floor'."

The Corporate Social Responsibility Department was created by John Filer, in the words of its present head, "to address the question of how to institutionalize corporate social responsibility; how this ought to be going on throughout the company, not just in a specialized staff function."[8] Among its major functions are

1. establishing, managing, and evaluating the company's Affirmative Action program,
2. developing and managing Aetna's social investments programs (from a fund set aside from retained earnings to support proposals for the creation of new minority enterprises),
3. formulating policy for corporate philanthropy and proxy voting.

For a time, this department also served an ombudsman role by sending its members to settle supervisor-employee disputes in the company's line divisions. It was also a department in which the company's Affirmative Action program could be placed to receive high visibility and attention throughout the company before being returned to the Corporate Personnel Department shortly before the conclusion of this comparative study.

Finally, the Issues Analysis Department was created by Bill Bailey in 1978. It serves as

1. a clearinghouse for social issues affecting the company and its industry,
2. a center for managing the analysis of issues having high impact potential,
3. a facilitator of line-management learning about the corporate social environment and the role of Aetna in society,
4. an occasional catalyst and consultant on needed changes in the traditional policies and practices of the company's line divisions. (I will have more to say about the way this department operates in the section that follows on external affairs depth.)

The Environmental Analysis Group (EAG) and the Marketing Study Group (MSG) were established to expand the breadth and horizon of the corporate planning function. The EAG is composed of senior line and staff executives who meet several times a year to identify factors (e.g., economic, demographic, social, political, etc.) that have a high potential for influencing the company and its industry over the five-to-ten-year horizon. This group met intensively for its first year and a half to develop a satisfactory framework for analyzing trends in the suprasystem and distilling them into "most favorable," "least favorable," and "most likely" scenarios. The information was fed back into the business divisions to help them formulate long-term plans. At the time of the comparative study the framework had become established and the Corporate Planning Department prepared annual forecasts. These forecasts are reviewed and revised by the EAG before being distributed to the line divisions for use in their annual business plans. Because of its membership, the EAG continues to serve as one of several sources of line-staff and staff-staff coordination in Aetna's external affairs process.

The last corporate-level external affairs component, the MSG, was created to develop a company-wide perspective on the products and markets of all the business divisions. Although somewhat peripheral to the core external affairs function, the MSG reinforced the move by executive leaders to get more corporate-level control and coordination among the product–market activities of the various divisions and to formulate a more integrated marketing strategy for the company as a whole. The work of this high-level group was, therefore, regarded by Aetna executives as important for the work of the formally designated external affairs units.

Depth.   Aetna has achieved the greatest degree of external affairs depth of all the companies selected for intensive study. The intensity of Aetna's organizational learning process about the corporate social environment is far greater than that achieved in other highly exposed corporations in the industry (for example, see Figure 6–13). External affairs professionals at Aetna are encouraged to frame and conduct research and analysis of emerging social issues from a variety of perspectives and potential responses. Indeed, Bill Bailey was emphatic about Aetna's approach to understanding emerging, industry-related social issues in an internal memorandum he circulated among all senior line and staff professionals several months before my site visit. He said

> It is necessary to have our corporate activities viewed from the perspective of the total impact of the company on all of our public constituencies rather than being segmented as business activities on the one hand and corporate social responsibility activities on the other.

The Issues Analysis (IA) department was created to ensure that this broad perspective is applied on an ongoing basis throughout the corporation.

One of the reasons the Issues Analysis unit has been able to perform this function is that it is evaluated by the chief operating officer on two potentially conflicting performance criteria: the objectivity of its analysis of social issues affecting the company and its industry *and* the extent to which its recommendations for changes in Aetna's business policies and practices are implemented in the operating divisions. Another reason for its success has been the adoption of a task-force approach to the resolution of social issues that relies heavily on the intensive participation of high-potential line managers who are recruited in the early and middle stages of their careers for extended periods of task force duty. In addition, the IA Department has been involved directly in the annual division planning processes for most of its existence. Liaisons from the IA Department now consult with divisional planners in the development of business plans that are responsive to relevant events and trends in the corporate social environment. Finally, the competence and earned respect of its carefully selected but revolving core staff have enabled IA to negotiate its difficult task in the potentially hostile context of a divisionalized corporate structure.

For all these reasons, IA has been able to sustain the highly politicized roles of facilitator of managerial learning and catalyst of organizational change with respect to the corporate social environment. Moreover, there is considerable evidence that experience on IA task forces has had a positive effect on the ability and willingness of rising line managers to understand and deal with business-related social issues after they return to their normal jobs in the operating divisions. One major Aetna division has even developed its own issues-analysis function, which is now led by a former member of IA's core staff. And by the end of its first half decade, IA had been asked by the divisions to assume a leading role in helping them resolve fundamental business and investment issues. Thus, IA's role as an agent of learning and change now extends beyond the external affairs domain.

Social or public policy issues affecting Aetna and the U.S. insurance industry are formally inventoried by IA in a rough matrix, like the one shown in Figure 7-1, on an annual basis from input from the company's line and staff operations as well as the active issues monitoring and analysis activities of IA staff members. The intensity of IA work on issues depends on where they fall in the matrix. Generally, issues affecting more than one of Aetna's business divisions, plus issues in the high-high cell and cells adjacent to it receive the greatest attention.

For these high-priority issues, IA commissions and leads task forces composed of high-potential, middle-level line managers and relevant staff professionals. These task forces do the analytical work and make recommendations concerning alternative company responses. Outside consultants are often brought in to provide specialized expertise, and in many cases the task force goes to the field to obtain relevant information at its source.

IA's work on the insurance redlining issue fell into this category. *Redlining* refers to the alleged practice in the insurance industry of denying property and casualty coverage to whole geographic areas assumed to be high in risk. The term refers figuratively and literally to the act of drawing a red circle around, say, a series of city blocks in a high-risk urban area to indicate that no homeowners or theft coverage is to be sold to any residents in the designated area.

Aetna took this social challenge seriously. The Redlining issue was not only directly related to one of its primary product lines, but also to the property and casu-

Company Impact Potential

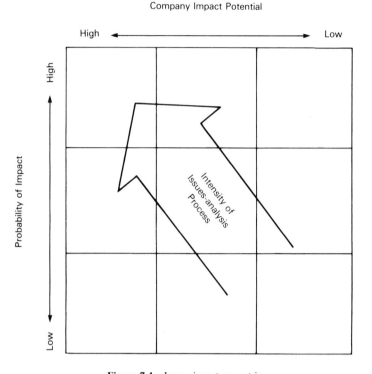

Figure 7-1 Issues inventory matrix.

alty segment of the industry as a whole. Executive leaders assigned the issue to IA for analysis and recommendations. A task force was created and middle-level managers from Aetna's property and casualty division were recruited and given release time to join staff experts on a task force. The process involved both conceptual and empirical work.

First, the definition and analysis of the issue was broadly framed, and a substantial amount of effort was put into this part of the process. When they reached the point that they understood the issue and the reasons underlying its emergence, the task force went into several of Aetna's field offices that were located where much of Aetna's business was concentrated. There they discovered some evidence of inappropriate practice. As a result, their recommendations included some important changes that were needed in the business policies and practices of the property and casualty division.

One of the changes required field representatives to send all applications for certain types of property and casualty coverage to the home office for review. Formerly, representatives were permitted to make these decisions at the local level. Members of IA, as well as line managers who had returned to their normal jobs in the affected division after the task force report was released, were required to assist in the design and implementation of the new monitoring system in the casualty division. This part of the IA process was closely followed by the chief operating officer to encourage responsiveness in the business division.

A number of line-staff and division-corporate "exchanges" are facilitated by IA's task force approach. These features of IA's work create a high-depth external affairs process and stimulate a line–staff balance in external affairs activities that is appropriate for the company's high exposure and consistent with its top management philosophy.

Because the IA staff is in the leadership role and is primarily responsible for the task force process and outcomes, participating line managers are forced to examine the parochialism that they might bring to bear on an issue if the process were managed within the potentially affected operating division. This ordering of roles ensures a certain level of breadth in the conceptual and analytical work of the task forces as well as objectivity in the recommendations they make for company responses. By the same token, heavy line manager involvement brings an element of realism and practicality to the process that might be lost if this work were performed exclusively by corporate-level staff specialists. The dual performance criteria assigned to IA by the chief operating officer reinforces the essential line-staff balance in task force work.

To fully meet this challenge, IA added to its task force approach two important liaison functions. First, before the initiation of a task force the IA leader negotiates a progress briefing arrangement with the senior line manager of the affected division. IA's attempt is to avoid surprises that might lead to unnecessary friction between the unit and a division executive whose business policies and practices are under scrutiny. Second, each member of the IA staff has been assigned a specific liaison responsibility with one of the major business divisions in the company. Each of these relationships is negotiated between the staff professional and the division executive. In some cases the IA member is invited to participate in the line executive's weekly staff meetings; in other cases the liaison function is less routine. Together, these liaisons provide an open, ongoing channel of communication between IA and all of the line operations. They also serve to increase the expertise of IA staff members on a divisional basis and thereby enhance IA's task force work and implementation role.

Integration and influence.   Aetna has achieved a high degree of integration and mutual influence among the core units in its external affairs function. The company's external affairs professionals attach a higher degree of importance to the relations they have with other external affairs units (see Figure 9-5) and report the highest level of mutual influence among the core external affairs units (see Figure 9-4), than do any of their counterparts in the other companies selected for intensive study.

These high levels of mutual influence and integration have been achieved despite the fact that, at the time of this study, the core units had different reporting relationships within the corporate structure. IA reported to the chief operating officer. Corporate Communications and Corporate Social Responsibility reported to the senior vice president of corporate administration, while Government Relations was located in the corporate law department.

In 1978, when I asked why the core units had not been consolidated under one senior external affairs executive, the response I got most frequently was that each unit was being encouraged to develop its own niche and internal process. For example, when I put the question to the senior vice president of corporate administration, who managed two of the core units and served as head of the Environmental Analysis Group, he replied, "There are a couple of reasons we haven't consolidated the units. The first has to do with the maturing of those units. Each of them is really learning how to operate. Second, there isn't any compelling reason for pulling them together because of the overriding strength of the key individuals." Bill Bailey concurred with this rationale when he explained to me that "a certain amount of redundancy" would be tolerated to allow the units to invent their own processes and develop their own competences, as well as to allow their leaders, three of whom were young by Aetna standards, to develop themselves.

Thus, the sources of high influence and integration among the core units of Aetna's external affairs function reside elsewhere, in the informal culture of the institution and in a variety of formal aspects of the structural context created by the current executive leaders. First, all of the key staff professionals have grown up together in the company. Very few outsiders are brought in at their levels; instead, a premium is placed on earned respect as a basis for career advancement. Second, the core units regularly exchange activity summaries and solicit comments on proposals from one another. Leaders of the core units also have overlapping memberships in a variety of external-affairs committees. IA's task forces often include representatives from the other core units and when they do not, other units provide consultants to the task force on an as-needed basis.

Leaders of the core units also meet biweekly as a group with Aetna's executive leaders and senior line managers to discuss their work in progress and to exchange views on recent developments in the corporate social environment (see boxed insert). In addition, although the core units do not share the same direct reporting relationships, their leaders regularly attend the weekly staff meetings of the senior vice president of corporate administration. These staff meetings serve two purposes. They keep the unit heads informed about one another's activities and they keep them abreast of other things going on in the corporation as a whole.

Finally, just after the site visit for this comparative study, all core external affairs units were consolidated under a new vice president of Law, Communications, and Public Affairs. (The former senior vice president, who had been heavily involved in corporate external affairs activities, was transferred to manage Aetna's most exposed business division.) Here the core units continue to enjoy considerable autonomy in the way they define and pursue their external affairs activities, even though their processes have become well defined. Presumably, this shared reporting relationship has enabled the units to achieve even higher levels of influence and integration than is revealed in the survey statistics compiled before the units were reassigned.

Aetna's PIG

Shortly after the formation of the Issues Analysis Department, the head of the new department initiated a series of biweekly meetings that many people referred to as "issues luncheons." Aetna's executive leaders, the heads of its business divisions, as well as the vice president of corporate planning and the heads of the core external affairs units were invited to attend as their schedules permitted.

The topics discussed during these luncheons, which occasionally became breakfasts as the itineraries of executive leaders and senior line managers demanded, were more or less random, although the common theme was corporate external affairs.

In 1978 I attended one of the first meetings. As an example of what goes on in these luncheons, I'll briefly outline the meeting's agenda. The meeting started with a discussion of a presentation the senior vice president of the property and casualty division was preparing on Aetna's position on the issues of automobile insurance availability and affordability, to be delivered at a meeting of the National Association of Insurance Commissioners later that week. He sought and received constructive suggestions from the other line and staff members present before the discussion shifted to the chief executive officer who pressed the group for less external affairs research and more emphasis on the implementation of recommendations. Then the topic shifted to what other companies were doing on several issues and how Aetna compared to them. Next, the chief executive officer asked for a progress report on one of the Issues Analysis task forces. During the response, the senior vice president of the life insurance division asked whether the task force was aware of a relevant survey that had been conducted by the Marketing Study Group. The IA head replied, "Only vaguely," and promised to follow up later that week. Then there was a brief discussion prompted by the chief executive officer of the company's equal employment opportunity program, followed by a drift back into the NAIC presentation. Toward the end of the luncheon, the head of Government Relations briefed the group on the increasing interest of the Federal Trade Commission in the insurance industry. The CEO concluded the meeting by reminding everyone that they should not lose sight of the business objectives they had committed themselves to earlier in the year!

Over time, the agenda for these meetings became more formalized, with noticeable competition for a place on the schedule. In 1982, when I was invited by the group to present a preliminary version of the general framework, an executive summary was prepared by the Issues Analysis Department, sent to me for comment, revised, and distributed to all attendees a week before the meeting. The group continues to meet regularly under the affectionately appropriate nickname of PIG: the Public Issues Group!

Line-manager Involvement

Given the foregoing analysis, it should be obvious that there is a high degree of institution-oriented, line-manager involvement in Aetna's external affairs process (Figure 7-2). When combined with the company's sophisticated external affairs function, this high level of managerial involvement results in an effective line–staff balance in corporate external affairs that ensure a more objective process of learning about the social environment and that reinforces analytical relevance and realistic recommendations from the perspective of affected business divisions.

This constructive tension between rigor and relevance in corporate external affairs is reflected in the comparative survey results for the highly exposed companies (refer to Figure 6-13). Aetna's senior line managers not only reported receiving the greatest amount of help from their external affairs units in managing the uncertainties they faced, but also reported that their external affairs units created the greatest amount of uncertainty for them to have to cope with. This built-in tension between relevance and rigor is the essence of the intensity of line-staff relations that is created by a high-depth external affairs function.

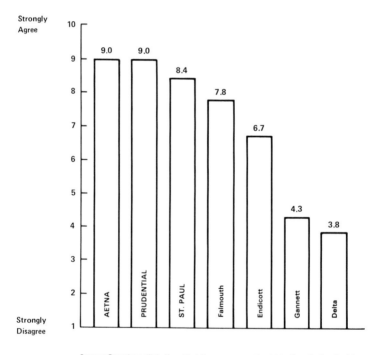

Survey Question: "I believe that line managers should be *heavily* involved in helping my company understand and manage the public policy issues it faces."

Figure 7-2 Senior line-manager beliefs about how heavily they should be involved in the corporate external affairs process.

Because of the overriding institution-oriented philosophy of the company, external affairs units have been able to chart a course that avoids both cooptation by the operating units and irrelevant "ivory tower" work. Moreover, an important by-product of Aetna's unusual approach to line manager involvement is that the external affairs perspective has become increasingly institutionalized in the way operating managers approach their daily tasks. This process of institutionalization and the effort by executive leaders to move the company from a posture of responsibility to one of responsiveness have been reinforced by the decision to incorporate social issues in Aetna's business planning and review process (Figure 7-3).

Perhaps the best way to sum up the attitudes about line manager involvement in corporate external affairs at Aetna, is what the senior corporate staff executive had to say about this issue during the company interviews. He said,

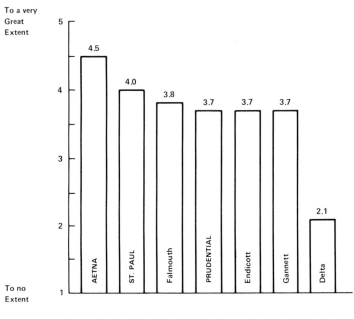

Survey Question: "To what extent does the company's formal planning and review process as it relates to your department explicitly include public affairs and public policy issues which relate to your line of business?"

Figure 7-3 Senior line-manager survey responses about the degree to which their company incorporates social issues in the business planning and review process.

It would be a great mistake for this company to conclude that our response and our approach to the public arena should be done through staff areas. We've got to have this awareness on how we conduct our day-to-day business, or we won't do this well, because the business has to operate in the climate of today.

If line managers are not deeply involved and committed, the staff people doing the external affairs work are going to spend all their time firefighting. So, my position is that, if the business divisions will do a quality job of responding to complaints against their own operations and will make required changes in the way they conduct their business that is creating a legitimate problem for the consumer, we are better served as a company. My job as the staff is to make sure they are doing these things.

FOOTNOTES

1. Refer to Table 6-3 for estimates of the business exposures of all the companies selected for intensive study.
2. For a comprehensive summary of a recent comparative study of the state commissioners of insurance, including their regulatory philosophies and agendas, refer to Robert H. Miles and Arvind Bhambri, *The Regulatory Executives* (Beverly Hills, CA: Sage Publications, 1983).
3. For a discussion of the role of organizational slack in facilitating the process of strategic adaptation refer to Robert H. Miles, *Coffin Nails and Corporate Strategies* (Englewood Cliffs, NJ: Prentice-Hall, 1982), esp. pp. 158, 192, and 248–54.
4. For an expanded statement by Aetna's chief executive officer about the connection between the economic and social goals of a large American corporation, refer to the insert in Chapter 2 (p. 20) entitled "The Social Goals of a Corporation," excerpts from a chapter contributed by John Filer to Thornton Bradshaw and David Vogel, eds., *Corporations and Their Critics* (New York: McGraw-Hill, 1981), pp. 269–76.
5. From the perspective of regulators, the philosophies of executive leaders powerfully shape the external affairs strategies pursued by major insurers. For instance, when I asked a veteran commissioner of insurance in an urban state to list the best corporate social performers in the insurance industry, he replied, "I don't want to be antitheoretical, but I'm afraid that an awful lot of my response would be grounded on some of the personalities within those companies." When I probed to learn what he meant by "personalities" I received the following response, "On that list Aetna would turn up on almost every issue. I have a feeling that it is largely the result of John Filer and Bill Bailey."
6. For a study conducted in 1978 of the functions performed by Aetna's six external affairs units, refer to Robert H. Miles, "Organization Boundary Roles," in C. Cooper and R. Payne, eds., *Current Concerns in Occupational Stress* (London: Wiley, 1980), pp. 61–96.
7. The head of the Corporate Communications Department has become a rotational position for senior line managers who can benefit from a company-wide and external affairs experience.
8. When asked what he meant by institutionalizing corporate social responsibility throughout the company, the department head shared the following example: "The first thing that we have institutionalized reasonably well is the equal employment opportunity function; the employment and promotion of minorities and women, and now, with equal attention to the handicapped and age discrimination cases. The equal employment

opportunity objectives are actually part of the business plan objectives of every one of the operating units in the company. We get quarterly results back and deal with the divisions and with the EEO coordinators in the divisions.'' He continued, ''Corporate Social Responsibility also conducts career workshops for minorities and women, first of all, to help them understand what opportunities are available to them in the corporation, and second, to help them develop the skills required to attain those goals.''

CHAPTER 8

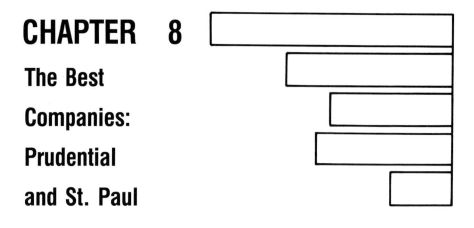

The Best Companies: Prudential and St. Paul

During the time of this study, Prudential and St. Paul were operating with business exposures that were quite different from that of Aetna. However, all three top-rated performers were diagnosed using the general framework as possessing similar overall philosophies and strategies for understanding and managing the corporate social environment.

First, all three companies pursue an institution-oriented, top management philosophy that explicitly recognizes the legitimacy of social claims on their traditional business policies and practices. Second, all three operate with an explicit external affairs strategy that encourages collaboration with industry peers and problem solving in exchanges with important representatives of the public interest. Third, all three companies have achieved a good degree of fit between their business exposure and the design of their external affairs function. Although the best-rated companies differed in the sophistication of their core external affairs function, these differences were consistent with the traditional business exposure of each company. Finally, counter-balanced against a sufficiently sophisticated external affairs staff function in each company is a relatively high degree of line-manager involvement; involvement that is motivated by a strong managerial identification with the institution-oriented philosophy and character of each firm.

PRUDENTIAL

Social institutions, like political institutions, can endure only if they prove their social utility by successful adaptation and readaptation to the everchanging conditions and circumstances of political and social life.

From the personal memoirs of
Prudential's founder

Despite enormous financial success and a position as one of the largest insurance companies in the world, Prudential continues to be guided by the social purpose for which it was founded: to provide basic life insurance coverage to the working class of America.[1] The company began operations by selling so-called ''debit'' insurance; small-coverage, low-cost life insurance that was paid for by low-income families, often during monthly home visits by a Prudential debit agent who was based in the local community. Through this debit system many Prudential agents developed close relationships with the policyholders in their territory and consequently, bonds of trust with the American general public.

During the past 25 years Prudential has gradually upgraded its customer mix by targeting lower-middle and upper-middle income groups. By the time of this study, Prudential's size and scope of operations justified a considerably broader mission statement, but one that derived from its founding purpose:

> The Prudential is to be a quality provider of a broad range of financial products and services. Our products and services will provide financial protection against risks that threaten individuals, families and groups or will enhance their financial security through a variety of savings and investment alternatives. We will offer our products and services in all markets where we can provide value to our customers and earn a reasonable return. We believe that achievement of this mission is enhanced in a work environment in which employees exercise creativity and initiative, and we are committed to providing such an environment.

By the time of the site visits, one senior line manager described Prudential this way, ''It's kind of a 'middle-America' operation.'' Although Prudential's increasing size and diversity have caused the company to establish more sophisticated mechanisms for maintaining and responding to the public trust, the company's founding philosophy and character continue to be the main source of its outstanding record of corporate social performance.

The other factor that contributes to Prudential's effectiveness in this domain is its business exposure. Despite its enormous size and complexity, Prudential has continued until recently to concentrate its business stakes in life insurance business. Recent attempts to diversify into other insurance product lines still have not contributed much to the company's overall business performance. Therefore, Prudential's business exposure to the corporate social environment surrounding the insurance industry as a whole has traditionally been moderate—lower than that of the multiple-line Aetna, but higher than that of St. Paul, the property and casualty specialist.

Top Management Philosophy and Company Character

The carefully nurtured values of Prudential's founder, and the broad range of contact with the general public dictated by its evolving business strategy, have reinforced a company character that places central value on corporate social responsibility. This fundamental corporate value has selected and developed over long periods of employment service a succession of executive leaders who champion the institution-oriented philosophy regarding the role of Prudential in society. The company has even gone so far as to have its history written every 25 years since its founding as a way of keeping track of its fundamental philosophy and character.[2]

Under these circumstances it should not be surprising that the views of the company's recent chief executive officers accord well with the lead quote from the founder's memoirs. For example, the CEO who served during the tumultuous 1970s expressed the following view about the proper role of business in society:

> Business has responsibilities to many constituencies (stockholders, employees, suppliers, consumers, and the general public), and needs to be responsive to the needs and desires of *all* of these groups. Business has, in effect, a franchise granted to it by society and that franchise will be continued only so long as society is satisfied with our handling of it. We must think of the corporation as a socioeconomic institution rather than as an economic institution which has some incidental social responsibility.

This view of the corporation as a "social franchise" that must be responsive to the changing needs and desires of multiple stakeholders also appeared in the first speech made by Prudential's current CEO to the company's senior officers.[3] In that speech he affirmed that the basic principles or "guideposts" of Prudential are,

> To be responsive to the needs and wants of many publics with which we deal . . . while carefully balancing the interests of all parties in achieving social good.
> To lend our leadership, know-how, resources, and ingenuity to the development and implementation of programs that deal effectively with the social problems of our times.

Prudential executive leaders have continued an informal policy of periodically sending letters and memoranda—referred to as the "pumpkin papers"—throughout the organization, which express their strong points of view on corporate social responsibility and on the particular industry-related social issues of the day. In addition, Prudential's external affairs function is responsible for disseminating internal publications that summarize company positions on public issues affecting the company and its segments of the industry.

But at Prudential these espoused philosophies transcend speeches and written policies. First, executive leaders refer to themselves, and are referred to by their subordinates, as "activists" in the insurance industry. They carve out a large role for themselves in external affairs. They sit on major public policy committees and participate actively in a variety of public forums inside and outside the industry. Moreover, they expect their senior line subordinates to assume a lot of responsibility in this arena at the regional level. As one senior vice president explained,

> We are always supporting the community and are involved to a great extent in social investments, community education, and so forth. When I was a regional vice president in the New England Office, I served on 18 civic boards. . . . I think I spent more time outside the office visiting cultural centers than I spent in the office.

In addition, executive leaders at Prudential actively model the behaviors they want from their subordinates through the pattern of day-to-day decisions they make. Rising managers are carefully socialized through their association with executive leaders. As one senior vice president reflected on his own role in this process,

> This philosophy of "doing good" is really pervasive among the top management. People get "Prudentialized" by repeated exposure to particular decisions made by top managers. For example, I was working in one state when we realized that we had violated a broker licensing law. My subordinates were concerned and suggested that they begin to rectify the situation over the next couple of years. But I said, "To heck with all that. Let's just go to the person who deals with this and tell him that we've made an honest mistake, and see what we can work out." It is this kind of decision that reinforces the culture that pervades Prudential.

Finally the sheer size and high public visibility of Prudential—approximately one out of every five or six Americans is somehow covered by the company's insurance products—creates a greater awareness within the firm about the consequences of its decisions regarding business policies and practices than in many of the smaller firms intensively studied. "Because Prudential is so big," said one vice president, "the stands we take on public issues are irreversible because of the publicity that the company attracts. Company reputation becomes much more important and, simultaneously, also more sensitive in the public eye." Indeed, because of this high visibility, Prudential has developed a widely shared benchmark for determining what public policy issues to pay attention to and how to respond to such issues. This benchmark is phrased in the form of a question that many officers quoted verbatim during the field interviews. It simply asked Prudential executives,

> Would you be comfortable if this appeared on the front page of *The New York Times?*

External Affairs Strategy

The derivative of Prudential's institution-oriented character and philosophy is an explicit, collaborative and problem-solving strategy in corporate external affairs. Also reinforcing its approach to external affairs is Prudential's large size and corresponding high public visibility. As one senior line manager observed, "We take a long-range view of things. . . . I'm sure that some of the things that Prudential does could be criticized simply because we're so big. Other companies could do the same things and nobody would pay much attention to them."

Another line executive expanded on the issue of the company's size and public visiblity by noting that Prudential had become the "stalking horse" of the life insurance industry. He said,

> We *feel* the visibility. We have been to some extent forced to attend to more public issues than, say, a small life insurer that is not visible and that does not come to people's attention. I also think we are regarded by the federal government as the "stalking

horse" for the industry. They're going to attend to us, and if they deal with us effectively perhaps the rest of the life insurance industry will fall in line. Therefore, we recognize our responsibilities for setting standards for the industry. We feel the responsibility in many areas for setting an example—for taking leadership.[4]

Prudential line and staff executives take a broad view of their corporate responsibility. First, they are involved in active and ongoing collaboration with a wide variety of industry groups in both governmental and private-sector forums. "We actively participate in the NAIC task forces and advisory committees and we spend a great deal of time at the industry trade associations," said a senior line manager. "The Public Affairs Department has a major role in these activities. But spread throughout the organization are people representing different functions who serve on committees and get actively involved."

In addition, Prudential executives take a broad approach to problem solving in their work on social and public issues affecting the industry. Because of the size and pervasiveness of this company, many of the positions it has taken reflects the perspective of the life-insurance industry as a whole as well as that of the company itself. As one line executive explained, "We have the function of leading the industry and trade associations to take positions they might not otherwise take." But he was quick to add that, "We like to think that we have an open mind, and that there is a free discussion in the industry trade associations. We certainly don't feel we have all the answers."

Third, Prudential shares a long-range perspective with the other two best-rated companies. Senior line and staff executives at all three companies believe strongly that the need to adapt traditional business policies and practices to changing conditions in society is a reasonable part of continuing to earn their franchises. Therefore, these companies seek to steer their competitive rivals away from stonewalling or avoidance tactics that might eventually lead to an external assault on the private insurance mechanism. One Prudential executive offered the following example of his company's view on the need to be responsive to pressing public issues:

> When we encountered an industry deadlock on the issue concerning which formula for cost disclosure is most appropriate for the life insurance industry, Prudential worked awfully hard to get some industry action on the premise that, if we don't take a positive action and try to do the best we can as an industry, somebody's going to do it *to* us!

Finally, Prudential executives believe it is important for them to separate the intentions of their activities in the marketplace from those in the political and regulatory arena. They strive to avoid using the political/regulatory arena as a setting in which to pursue market advantages for their products. "The products that we really feel are not good for the public and should, therefore, not be sold are the ones we actively contest in the regulatory arena," said one line manager. "For the products of other companies that are a threat to us, we're going to have to determine how to respond to them in the marketplace; not in the regulatory arena." Another senior executive underlined Prudential's view of appropriate company behavior in the political and regulatory environment when he recalled that, "There have been many instances in which, as a company, we've taken a position that has cost us one heck of a lot of business. It isn't enough to be able to sell a product. It has to be what we feel is socially worthwhile." Numerous, detailed stories of positions taken by Prudential on product-related issues were obtained from its executives, all confirming this element of the company's explicit approach to corporate external affairs.[5] On this basis alone, companies like Prudential and the other best-rated companies stand in stark contrast to companies that pursue a highly individualistic external affairs strategy.

By taking a problem-solving approach to corporate external affairs—one which adopts a broad, long-term perspective—Prudential has been able to achieve an enviable relationship with important representatives of the public interest. "We want to do right; but the other part of it is that we want to maintain good relationships," said Prudential's chief actuary. "The two objectives reinforce one another. So, our approach is not necessarily or completely altruistic. This corporation is a good social citizen because it's good business."

State and federal regulators, the primary and most technically sophisticated representatives of the public interest on insurance matters, feel that they can trust companies like Prudential. They value Prudential's open-mindedness in debates concerning appropriate positions on industry-related public policy issues. They seek the advice and counsel of Prudential's executives and representatives when they are developing new regulatory models and legislative initiatives. As one legislative counsel explained,

> One way or another the state commissioners of insurance have learned that they can approach the Prudentials of the world; that they can try out a new idea on us. I enjoy being in a position in which a state insurance department shows us a draft of a proposed regulation and says to us, "before we announce this to the public, criticize it."

This collaborative and problem-solving approach to external affairs, and the desire to maintain effective, long-term relationships with representatives of the public interest, were apparent even when Prudential was considering the acquisition of a large, noninsurance company. Although not required to do so, Prudential's chief executive officer sounded out the insurance commissioner in the company's headquarters state before proceeding to make the deal.

External Affairs Design

Until 1965, responsibilities for corporate external affairs were shared by the chief executive officer and several members of Prudential's Law Department. However, with rising consumerism and increasing awareness and criticism of the U.S. insurance industry by the general public, Prudential found that the combination of these external affairs resources and the institution-oriented philosophy of its line managers was no longer sufficient to cope with the company's increasing exposure.

Therefore, in 1965 a Corporate External Affairs Department was created in which all state and federal activities were consolidated.

This integrated department lasted, however, only until the appointment of Prudential's next chief executive officer in 1969. With the new appointment, the external affairs department was dismantled and its components were assigned to different parts of the headquarters office. Many of the attorneys who had been transferred to the External Affairs Department were returned to the Corporate Law Department.[6]

Breadth.   Since 1974 the corporate external affairs function has been divided between two corporate-level departments. These departments contain a variety of specialized staff units, each focusing on a major segment of Prudential's corporate social environment. Together they constitute a high-breadth external affairs design.

The Government Affairs (States) section of the Law Department is responsible for all company relations with state-level regulators and legislators. The company's overall lobbying effort at the state level—referred to internally as regulatory and legislative relations—is coordinated by this section and is supported by legal counsels located in each of Prudential's geographically dispersed regional offices.

The Public Affairs Department, which is the other major component of the company's external affairs function, has become more complex since its creation in 1974. As one senior line manager explained, "The Public Affairs Department has grown in responsibility, and under our current CEO is double underlined as one of our major departments." This department handles all lobbying at the federal level through the company's Washington, D.C. office. The department is also responsible for all other company-based external affairs activities. These activities, which are organized into units reporting ultimately to James Gillen, the senior vice president of public affairs, include consumer affairs, community affairs, corporate contributions, social investments, public relations, advertising, survey research, and editorial and artwork services.

Gillen outlined the breadth and activities of what he considered to be the principal components of Prudential's Public Affairs Department follows:

External Affairs Design at Prudential

Consumer Affairs has only a couple of people, but we have a very sophisticated system for monitoring the complaints we receive. We get something like 15-16,000 complaints each year. The head of that unit monitors these things. We classify complaints as to whether they are valid or invalid. If our people followed our rules and did everything they were supposed to do, we say the complaint is invalid. But then we look at it and say, "Well, maybe there is something wrong with our rules." The Consumer Affairs units tends to focus on the invalid complaints. This leads to responsiveness to customers. They also send a memorandum to the unit that is involved with the problem in which they make a recommendation for change. Sometimes the recommendation is accepted; some-

---

times it is not. Third, when we are considering new products, Consumer Affairs reviews these things. Finally, the head of the unit and his staff are members of a number of consumer organizations. They go to meetings to hear what consumer groups think is going on.

Community Affairs is pretty much what the name implies. Obviously, we have problems in our headquarters community [Newark, NJ] because of the kind of community it is. This unit was started after the urban riots in the late 1960s. Its basic function was to find a way for us to interact with our home city; to bring Prudential's resources to bear where they could help build good relations. The current thrust of the unit is heavy involvement in ways to refurbish the city, to rehabilitate the city, and to attract money to it. For other communities, the Public Relations and Advertising departments in our regional offices engage in a similar function for the local community, and there is some coordination between the Community Affairs unit here and the regional units.

Advertising. We do not employ issues advertising. We have felt that this is not the right way to advertise. Our philosophy is that we spend advertising dollars to sell our products, not to sell our ideas.

The *Contributions* unit is another piece of the way we attempt to project our image. We have set up a foundation . . . and we have established a complex set of guidelines on what things we will make contributions to and what we won't. We put heavy emphasis on the contributions in our headquarters state, heavy emphasis on health and education and lesser emphasis on culture, and pretty good emphasis on minority activities.

Public Relations handles the media. We have been on a program for a couple of years of trying to develop good relations with the media. We follow a scrupulous policy of honesty; of not bothering them with unimportant stuff; and of being open with them as much as we can possibly be without compromising our business.

Government Relations is our Washington, D.C. office. It is a straight lobbying operation. They monitor key legislation; principally legislation, not regulation. State regulatory matters are handled principally in the Law Department and through lawyers. Our D.C. lobbyists have an agenda of 20–30 major items that they follow. They maintain contacts with the key legislators and they generate material or they get it from somewhere else. They provide these materials to the legislative staffs to support different company positions. The principal areas where we are involved are social security, pension laws, or any federal legislation dealing with insurance.

At the time of the comparative study, the Public Affairs Department defined its staff role in terms of three major responsibilities

1. To monitor the outside environment to discern early warning signals and signs of change in that environment, and to communicate effectively throughout the company;

2. To review all company policies and programs that have public affairs significance and to strengthen these when needed;
3. To communicate fully and openly so that company thinking and company action will be as well understood as possible, both inside the company and in the outside world.

In brief, the principal roles of the external affairs units within Prudential aside from their external lobbying activities, are to monitor, analyze, review, and communicate. Thus, with the exception of lobbying that is oriented toward influencing the outside world, the external affairs function within Prudential is placed in a "pure" staff role. They advise line managers, but they are not permitted to direct line managers to make changes in their business practices and policies. So far, Prudential has relied principally on the ingrained, institution-oriented philosophy of line managers to insure that they make required adaptations in the way in which they conduct business. And all the evidence from the comparative study indicates that this combination of external affairs staff breadth and management philosophy, together with the moderate business exposure of the company, have enabled Prudential to maintain an external reputation for high corporate social performance.

The role assigned to external affairs staff in Prudential contrasts substantially with the one assigned to external affairs professionals at Aetna. With the primary stakes of Aetna residing in the socially and politically volatile property and casualty business, its line operations have been subjected to much more pressure for change than the traditional life-insurance operations of Prudential. Moreover, the companies have different corporate structures. Prudential continues to operate with a "negotiated" internal environment under a functional corporate structure. In contrast, Aetna operates under the principal of operational autonomy with a divisional structure. Thus senior line managers at Aetna, who head the major business divisions, tend to be more oriented than their functional counterparts at Prudential to short-term operating performance. Because of these differences, Aetna executive leaders have given more authority to their core external affairs units. Several of Aetna's staff units are evaluated on the basis of whether their recommendations for changes in the business policies and practices of line divisions are implemented. Under the principal of functional staff authority, Aetna's external affairs units are expected to perform the roles of catalyst and consultant to changes required in the company's line operations in addition to the roles outlined above for Prudential staff units. In order to carry off this larger role, Aetna's staff units make broader and more formal use of line-manager involvement in the corporate external affairs process than do their counterparts at Prudential.

Depth.   External affairs depth at Prudential is moderate. The process by which the company identifies, prioritizes, analyzes, and responds to emerging public policy issues affecting its business was created three years before the site visits, and is informal and generally unsystematic. In part, this approach flows from the demands of Prudential's business exposure. The life-insurance segment of the industry has been characterized by fewer and slower-developing, public issues than other industry segments, especially the property and casualty segment. As one of Prudential's senior line managers observed, "When it comes to public issues, you can waste an awful lot of time trying to predict the future. These issues tend to evolve, and even if something radical happens, we always seem to have enough time to adapt or react."

At the time of the site visits the locus of issues management lay with the Public Affairs Department's veteran "futurist." However, this individual was scheduled for retirement within a few weeks, and no plans had been agreed upon for his replacement or for the development of the issues-management process.

Members of the Government Affairs section of Prudential's Law Department generally regarded the Public Affairs futurist as the issues-management contact person; but they conceded that they had not been involved in the creation and design of the issues-management process. As one legislative lobbyist explained,

> We have a looseleaf booklet that probably contains a hundred different issues that are in the process of evolving. It involves finding a problem and then tracking it as it evolves. One person in Public Affairs generates this booklet and he updates it on an annual basis and periodically during the year. If a major development occurs, he circulates the current company position to all interested parties and says, "Give me changes; give me additional data that you think ought to be reflected in the background material." So, it's a living, growing, changing issues booklet.
>
> If you want to either create a new public issue and get it in the booklet or change a company position, this person in Public Affairs is the coordinator. He would get approval from the Executive Office. Everybody in the company has a copy of that booklet.

When Prudential executives were asked who decides what is an issue and how much attention is paid to it, one member of the Government Affairs section said, "We don't have guidelines. We can't show you a book about how you proceed on these problems." When asked who is responsible for identifying emerging public issues, a similar response was obtained: "Sometimes an issue is first recognized in the Law Department. Today there is a great deal of responsibility to recognize these issues in the Public Affairs Department. And it may also be that the Executive Office or the line operations first recognizes the issue."

Some line managers were not aware that Prudential has an issues-management process. They tend to talk about the issues booklet and the periodic newsletters they receive about the status of particular issues, all of which are published by the Public Affairs Department; but they are unclear about the underlying process. As one senior line executive speculated when asked about Prudential's approach to issues management,

> We *might* have an issues inventory in the company. If so, I'm not aware of it. The Public Affairs Department does put out a company position book for executives to use if they are speaking for the company or if they have to deal with outside interviews. It also gives line executives an opportunity to voice their opinions.

Like so many other things at Prudential, the issues-management process is informal, involving "lots of back-and-forth" among line and staff executives who have grown up together under the guidance of a common company character and philosophy. As one senior line manager explained,

> Personally, I'm not sitting here looking for public policy issues for the company to deal with. We don't have a formal process within the line operations for identifying public policy issues. From time to time the Public Affairs Department asks for our input. But within the line organization, we don't sit down to do this.
>
> The way these issues come about is in the course of our operations. I feel quite comfortable going to the Law Department, which deals with the states, and the Public Affairs Department, which deals with the federal government, and saying, "Look, this regulation is going to cause us a lot of problems, and it doesn't really make sense. I don't see where it helps the public." Or alternatively, if the Law Department of Public Affairs hears about something, they may come to me and say, "This is what's going on. What's your reaction to it?" So there's a certain amount of back-and-forth.

During the site visit, Gillen, the recently appointed senior vice president of public affairs, seemed to recognize where improvements were needed in Prudential's external affairs function. In particular, he believed that the issues-management process was neither adequately used nor developed within the company. But he also recognized the traditional limits Prudential placed on corporate staff units. Gillen's ambivalence is reflected in the statement he made about his objectives in the area of external affairs depth and how it compared to the depth that had been achieved by the industry's best overall corporate social performer.

> We don't have anything like Aetna's Issues Analysis Department. That is one of my objectives.
>
> But about 10 to 12 years ago we had a very large planning staff. As a result, there was a sense in the company that the staff was directing a lot of people rather than supporting them. We have not recovered from that experience.[7]
>
> Therefore, I don't know whether the company will be receptive to that kind of department. But at least it ought to be tried.

Taking a significant step in the direction of increased external affairs depth will constitute a major departure in the way the core function has traditionally been permitted to operate within Prudential. Increased business exposure, through a change in the company's business strategy and product mix may require greater experimentation in the area of external affairs depth. It may require a fundamental change in the way the company's futurist described the current issues-management process:

> We send out a report and hopefully we sensitize people. But essentially it is their responsibility. We are a staff group—an advisory group. We have no clout or authority to exercise over line people. We have not tried to. We do not work that way.

Integration and influence.   Integration and influence *within* Prudential's core external affairs function are judged to be moderate. (See Figures 9-4 and 9-5, in Chapter 9, for survey data on influence and integration within the core external affairs function of all companies intensively studied.) For instance, two important sets of external relationships (i.e., federal versus state government relations) are managed in different corporate departments. Commenting on the quality of integration between these core external affairs departments, a staff executive had this to say, "There are quite a number of issues that have both a federal and a state aspect. As separate departments we do reasonably well, but I'm not sure there is always sufficient coordination."

Not only are these important external affairs departments physically and organizationally separated, but they also contain members whose missions and orientations differ substantially. Attorneys involved in state regulatory and legislative relations, for example, tend to be engaged in activities designed to defend, protect, and represent the company's existing business policies and practices; whereas a number of members of the Public Affairs Department are viewed inside Prudential as pursuing different missions and orientations. One external affairs professional in the Corporate Law Department explained the differences this way: "My job is not to change the world, but to get the best that my company can get from the existing environment, within the existing regulatory and legislative process. The Public Affairs Department is out to improve the world, to change the process, and to improve the way America lives."

When asked how integration takes place within the Public Affairs Department, Gillen replied, "It varies," He described the integrative process within the core function as follows: "Coordination of all these activities is informal at this point. I am hoping to put it on a more formal, systematic basis so that we can exploit opportunities." When asked for clarification, Gillen explained that,

> The Public Affairs Department is seven years old. It was just sort of thrown together, and there has been a lot of turnover at the top levels. Right now we've got strong people in all of these units. But I have the sense that they are not as integrated as they should be.
>
> Part of the problem is that our physical locations are separated. And we don't have any long-range plans. I have hired a consultant to try to find some way to make this informal thing more systematic. But the individuals in the department are sufficiently sensitive so that the process works pretty well anyway; and we do have a staff meeting once a month.

Line-manager Involvement

Influence and integration *between* the core external affairs function and Prudential's line operations also vary considerably and are largely informal in nature. The quality of line-staff relations was described by a senior line manager as a "back-and-forth" process. He said, "If it's a matter of getting a state insurance department's approval, we always consult with the Government Affairs section of the Law Department. There's a lot of back-and-forth all the time. It really isn't so much that we're thinking public policy. It just sort of grows out of the demands of the job and the decisions you have to make. And, of course, we've kind of grown up without counterparts in the Law Department and the Public Affairs Department.''

In part, the pervasive, institution-oriented management philosophy in the company diminishes the need for elaborate formal mechanisms for line–staff integration. As one of the company's actuaries explained, ''I've worked for Prudential for over thirty years. Public consciousness has always been part of my job. The job is to treat people fairly. Being an actuary has meant that the whole question of equity is just part of my job.'' When another senior line manager was asked how this strong identification with the company's philosophy had developed among line managers, he said,

> This belief among line managers is not the result of any formal procedures. It has just become institutionalized. I'm not quite sure how that happened, although I believe it came from the top of the organization. The last three chief executive officers have led the company in that direction. It has become the way we operate. This is part of the company philosophy, part of our operation and the way we behave.

In part also, the company's business exposure has traditionally been moderate; the life insurance industry has been able to avoid some of the social volatility and unpredictability experienced by the property and casualty segment of the insurance business. Life insurance issues have emerged slowly, providing line-staff collaboration inside companies like Prudential to develop gradually.

Finally, Prudential line managers are evaluated and promoted in part on the basis of their achievement of specific performance objectives in such areas as community involvement and affirmative action. As one senior line manager explained, ''There are some very direct parts of a manager's evaluation that are directed toward accomplishing social goals. We set very definite goals in terms of minority spending and equal employment opportunity, how well they react to outsiders, their involvement in outside activities, and so forth. The manager's achievement or nonachievement of these goals is very definitely a part of the evaluation process and affects salary, rewards, and promotions.''

All of these aspects of line-manager involvement appear to be quite satisfactory given the current exposure, traditional reputation, and ingrained management philosophy at Prudential. These factors have made it possible for Prudential to operate with a pure-staff external affairs function and with an informal, as opposed to systematic, approach to integration within the differentiated core function and between that function and the line operations. Moreover, the company's traditional exposure has not placed great demands on the external affairs function for systematically involving line managers in a proactive issues-management process. The moderate level of external affairs depth that is achieved by ''lots of back-and-forth,'' although somewhat reactive, appears to be sufficient to meet the nature of the demands posed by the segment of the insurance industry in which Prudential has its principal stakes. As one external affairs professional quipped, ''It's relatively easy to be a nice guy in the life insurance business.''

Reflections

Consistent with the overall patterns associated with the industry's best corporate social performers, Prudential

1. operates with an institution-oriented, top management philosophy regarding the role of the company in society,
2. pursues an explicit, collaborative and problem-solving strategy in corporate external affairs,
3. has achieved a good fit between its business exposure and external affairs design.

In addition, line-manager involvement in the external affairs process is quite high, despite being informal, unsystematic, and somewhat ad hoc.

Several areas, however, may be identified for the enhancement of Prudential's approach to understanding and managing the corporate social environment. A more systematic approach to integration within the core external affairs function could probably be achieved without creating much additional burden on corporate overhead. More important is the need to replan and develop a systematic issues-management process that explicitly outlines the manner in which line managers are to be involved.

More importantly, Prudential in recent years has been adding to its portfolio a number of new insurance and noninsurance subsidiaries. Some of these subsidiaries have been developed internally by deploying people who have grown up within the pervasive philosophy of the parent company; others have resulted from external acquisitions. As these subsidiaries grow and mature, accounting for greater and greater stakes for the parent company, there will be a need to integrate their activities into Prudential's overall external affairs framework. Indeed, the company's external affairs professionals have already encountered difficulties with some subsidiaries who manage their own external affairs activities somewhat independently from those of the parent company. For example, a staff professional in the parent company's headquarters described the difficulties he had encountered as a result of the independent actions of a subsidiary as follows: ''The lines of communication that exist between that state department of insurance and Prudential do not exist between that department and [one of our insurance subsidiaries]. In the latter case, there is an animosity—a lack of trust on both sides—that is novel to our general operation.''

Update

A year and a half after the field visits to Prudential, an attempt was made to determine if Gillen had been able to make progress on the agenda he set for the Public Affairs Department. During the interviewing period, developments in Prudential's business strategy and in its environment had increased the company's business exposure. Prudential's stakes had increased in businesses other than life and health insurance, most notably in property and casualty insurance and reinsurance operations. Moreover, its merger with Bache, a large investment and securities brokerage firm had moved it into center stage of the emerging financial services industry. These developments increased the need for the refinements Gillen wanted to make in the Public Affairs Department when he took over shortly before the initial field visits.

First, Gillen put the Public Affairs Department through its own strategic planning process. Second, he established an Issues Management Department, headed by an individual who was previously in charge of futures research at an industry trade association. In addition to this director the department now has three professional-level employees: an emerging-issues analyst, who coordinates environmental scanning activities; a librarian, who is building systems to improve issues monitoring capabilities; and an individual holding MBA and Ph.D. credentials, who tracks financial and deregulation issues.

This staff meets twice a month to identify emerging trends, issues and events and discuss the development of issues further along in the life cycle. The work of these core issues-management professionals is supplemented by data base subscriptions, federal and state legislative scanning services, and, in the case of major issues, by task forces made up of managers possessing required expertise.

Material prepared by the new department is presented to senior managers who consider its relevance for the company's business operations. Subsidiaries are involved in this process. In addition, the issues-management staff works closely with Prudential's executive office and the Washington office in developing company responses to public policy issues. In the near future, Prudential plans to incorporate the work of the new department on current and emerging issues in company newsletters to be distributed to all managers.

Commenting on the development of the Issues Management Department which she directs, Ronna Lichtenberg said,

> To date, our services have been used most often by the Executive Office, the top six people in the company. Policy recommendations in two important areas have been taken to and approved by this group. The system is designed to begin to reach more and more managers in the company, now that senior management support is clear.

Through the creation of this department, Gillen has begun to make progress on his agenda: to create external affairs depth within Prudential, greater coordination within the corporate external affairs function, and greater line-manager involvement in the external affairs process—all of which appear to be required by the company's increasing exposure to the corporate social environment.

THE ST. PAUL COMPANIES

> *What I tend to be personally proud of in this company is that when we recognize we've made a mistake we will correct it. . . . The real sense of responsibility throughout this organization—from top to bottom—is that our people are comfortable about blowing the whistle without fear of retaliation. They know our senior management will correct a mistake no matter how painful it is at the time.*
>
> Senior External Affairs
> Professional

St. Paul is one of the smaller companies in the comparative study, and its approach to understanding and managing the corporate social environment is the most unusual. The success of this company cannot be attributed to a sophisticated staff function or to heavy resource allocation in the area of corporate external affairs. Indeed, because of the absence of a sophisticated external affairs apparatus most St. Paul executives expressed surprise when they learned in the final debriefing that their company ranked alongside Aetna and Prudential in overall corporate social performance.

But it did not take long to understand why St. Paul's social performance was judged so positively. First, the company has a very low business exposure. Despite its strategic concentration in the property and casualty insurance business, its product lines are quite focused in areas that have not been highly sensitive to many of the public issues affecting the industry as a whole. Moreover, most of its products are sold to technically sophisticated commercial clients. Thus, St. Paul's traditional business exposure has not required an elaborate external-affairs staff function.[8]

Second, like Aetna and Prudential, St. Paul is guided by a long-term commitment to an institution-oriented, top management philosophy that is deeply ingrained in the fundamental character of the corporation and in the managerial belief system that guides day-to-day behavior. As one senior line manager observed, "All of us are involved in the personality of this company." Moreover, on the few occasions when St. Paul has become exposed to important social and political issues, the institution-oriented philosophy of its top managers has been manifested in the form of an explicit external affairs strategy; one that has been distinctly collaborative and problem-solving in nature. "The standards flow out of this company through tradition," said a senior external affairs executive. "St. Paul has a long tradition of a certain kind of behavior. From the business side, it involves a long history of product innovation and of being a responsible corporate citizen." The shared value that was mentioned most frequently during interviews with these line and staff executives is integrity.

Third, and perhaps the most important factor for the insight it provides, is the heavy involvement of line managers in St. Paul's external-affairs process. The small external affairs staff that the company has assembled is viewed as both the catalyst and the support for line management decision making and action taking. As the president of the company's largest business division explained,

> The purpose of our external affairs staff is to identify the need for, and to truly integrate into the line functions, a responsiveness to public issues. You're never going to get the responsiveness if it's a staff function. The people in our line functions *believe* this is their responsibility. They view members of our external affairs staff as resources.

In most cases such a high degree of line-management involvement in the absence of external affairs breadth and depth signals that a company is principally interested in defending and protecting the status quo of its operations, as opposed to responding and adapting business policies and practices to social change. In St. Paul's case, the high degree to which the institution-oriented philosophy has been internalized by line managers, and reinforced by a "thick" corporate character, has created a managerial cadre that is highly sensitive to the legitimacy of social claims on company policies and practices. In this sense the intentions and consequences of high line-management involvement in the external affairs process is markedly different in institution-oriented and enterprise-oriented companies. To understand how this line-management orientation developed within St. Paul it is necessary to review the major events in the company's recent history.

Catalytic Events in St. Paul's Recent History

Two recent events served to catalyze heavy line-management commitment to an institution-oriented philosophy and involvement in the corporate external affairs process. One involved an internal change in St. Paul's organization structure. The other was an external event that impinged upon the company's major and somewhat unique product line.

The first event involved St. Paul's pattern of organizational evolution. Until the beginning of the last decade, the company operated with a highly centralized organization structure. Line managers at all levels were located in the corporate headquarters, from which they oversaw the activities of independent insurance agencies that sold St. Paul's products and that were located throughout the country. Under this structure, line managers developed and progressed up the career ladder under the guidance of executive leaders who actively championed an institution-oriented philosophy.

When St. Paul decided as part of its corporate growth strategy to reorganize in favor of a decentralized structure, the most promising of its rising line managers were transferred from the corporate office to head the new, geographically dispersed field offices. With this movement of line managers, who had been socialized through long service in the central office, St. Paul was able to facilitate the diffusion of its strong management belief system into the field, closer not only to its customers and to the independent agents who sold its products, but also to regulators and legislators in the states where it conducted business.

To reinforce field managers' commitment to the company's philosophy, executive leaders took a number of steps designed to communicate a clear signal. For example, an elaborate claims-processing system was developed for administration at the field-operations level. The company even gave each field office a special budget to be used at the discretion of the field manager for making social investments in the local community.

But even with this planned change in St. Paul's internal structure and the early efforts to reinforce field management responsibility for external affairs issues and events, it is likely that such a commitment among managers, although strong at first, would have eroded with time. Instead, a dramatic event in the corporate social environment to which the company was exposed emerged to catalyze and even intensify the involvement of field managers in the corporate external affairs process.

Until the early 1970s, St. Paul's low business exposure had enabled it to avoid many of the external affairs issues that had begun to impact the insurance industry as a whole. Consequently, the company had placed little emphasis on the development of a sophisticated staff function for helping line managers understand and respond to developments in the corporate social environment. The company had continued to conduct external affairs in a responsible manner; however, its responsiveness to the corporate social environment had never been seriously challenged. This traditional context changed abruptly with the emergence of a novel, industry-related public policy issue. The issue directly affected a product line in which St. Paul had a heavy business stake. Moreover, St. Paul was more committed to this product line than were other major insurers. Therefore, it could not rely on help from its trade associations to understand and respond to the legislative and regulatory threat posed by the issue. Nor could its line managers rely on the existing external affairs function to bring the company's position to the attention of regulators and legislators in the various states.

After formulating a position on the issue, St. Paul's executive leaders had no alternative but to rely on field managers to present the company's arguments and recommendations to the regulators and legislators in all the states in which St. Paul products were sold. The discovery that almost all of the field managers were able to do this successfully not only gave these managers confidence that they could perform effectively in the external affairs arena, but also greatly strengthened their commitment to do so in the future.[9] From that moment in corporate history, line managers have been heavily involved in the process by which St. Paul understands and manages relations with the corporate social environment. As one senior line manager recalled,

> We did a good job. We helped the state insurance departments. Therefore, the next time they needed help on a problem they tended to call St. Paul in, including our local field managers. Regulators got to know us—as a company and as individuals in the field.

As the quote suggests, this occasion also marked the beginning of a new element of St. Paul's reputation among outside constituencies. Already regarded by outside constituencies as a responsible company, St. Paul had now earned the additional distinction of being responsive.

One added benefit of the company's move to the decentralized structure is that now some of the field managers are being promoted to senior executive positions at the corporate headquarters. Their presence and influence there has had the effect of closing the long loop between the formulation and implementation of external affairs strategies at the corporate level and actual market conduct and new product development and distribution that bring the company into direct contact with the general public and that are closely monitored by state regulators. As one individual who had completed this loop explained, "I used to resent the external affairs staff, especially the way their bureaucratic procedures were superimposed on field operations. But I gradually began to appreciate how they could help me anticipate things. They are good business."

External Affairs Design

The core external affairs function at St. Paul is minimal when compared to those in most of the other companies studied. "We're not very specialized," said one senior line manager. "People in the field assume responsibility for external affairs issues affecting the company. It's not the structures and procedures around here that account for our success. It's the involvement of senior executives and field managers in the external affairs process."

The core of this function principally consists of two senior staff professionals and two corporate-level staff units, all located in close proximity both to each other and to senior line managers in the company's headquarters. St. Paul's general counsel is responsible for regulatory and legislative relations in the company's home state; and a former state insurance commissioner, who carries the title of director of government affairs, handles regulatory and legislative matters in the other 49 states.

The company also has a Corporate Responsibility Committee and a Public Relations and Communications Department. The committee is composed of the chief executive officer, the chief operating officer, the five executive vice presidents, and two external affairs officers. In 1974 the committee developed a statement of corporate social responsibility that was distributed throughout its ranks. The Public Relations and Communications Department tends to place as much emphasis on internal communications as it does on traditional external activities. As the vice president of this department explained, "We communicate rather well within this company. Basically, we share information and we see each other a lot. We don't treat knowledge as power to be protected." This dual emphasis is especially important because of the company's decentralized structure, consisting of geographically dispersed field offices. "What we are trying to do," continued the vice president, "Is to communicate more thoroughly than we have been doing to all our employees about the public issues impacting our businesses." Field managers receive a monthly newsletter that informs them of the company's positions on current issues, and the head of government affairs recently published and distributed St. Paul's first issues reference book to all staff professionals and line managers.

Commenting on the status of the core external affairs function, one senior staff member said, "We're really stretched thin. You might mention this in your debriefing to senior managers in the company." Indeed, external affairs professionals at St. Paul reported the highest levels of role overload and job stress of all staff professionals in the companies surveyed.

Reinforcing Mechanisms

To help reinforce broad concern for and involvement in the external affairs process, despite the development of only a minimal core function, St. Paul has implemented a number of supporting mechanisms. For example, in 1974 the company inaugurated an innovative consumer complaints system that managers describe as "timely, sensitive, responsible, and responsive claims handling." The system is viewed as both a line-management function and an executive function. Field managers are responsible for administering the system, and their effectiveness in doing so is measured as part of their formal performance appraisal. Indeed, executive leaders emphasized St. Paul's "tight reporting line to the troops in the field." This reporting line has been strengthened in recent years by the use of outside consultants who are retained "to assess what people in the field are perceiving and misperceiving in the public affairs area."

The field-based claims handling process is reviewed semiannually by a senior vice president in the office of the president at corporate headquarters. Because of the seriousness with which field and senior managers take this part of their overall responsibility, executive leaders at corporate headquarters report that they are seldom surprised by regulators or consumer interest groups.

Other reinforcing mechanisms include active role modeling by executive leaders and symbolic promotions to senior executive positions of officers who have demonstrated a recognition of the business legitimacy of public issues and events. When asked how the corporate mind-set had developed to embrace the institution-oriented perspective, many St. Paul managers pointed to the consistent signals given to them by a long succession of executive leaders. One senior line manager said, "The attitudes and involvement of top management are the most important things;" and another said, "there has been a long series of chief executive officers at St. Paul who have viewed their public commitment as seriously as their bottom-line commitment. Therefore, we have little tolerance for managers who don't relate or listen to the whole public issues area." Given this active role modeling at the top, it is not surprising that people who are promoted to top management are generally recognized for their achievements in helping the company understand and manage its social environment.

In addition, senior line managers and external affairs professionals share responsibility for identifying and analyzing issues that might potentially affect company operations. In the past these efforts have been ad hoc in nature. Cross-functional task forces have been assembled on an as-needed basis into what St. Paul executives refer to as "R & D groups" to study issues and to recommend company action. The typical process was described by a staff professional this way:

> A lot of us are involved in monitoring external affairs issues. The process is rather unstructured. Many people have written into their accountabilities the responsibility to watch out for certain things; and there is duplication in these accountabilities. But at least we get several points of view.

This somewhat reactive approach to issues management has been consistent with the company's low business exposure. It has also been helped by the early-warning system that has developed informally as a consequence of field manager responsibility for local external affairs events and trends. But the potential weakness remains. As one staff executive put it, "We don't have a lack of knowledge about public issues. Our problem is one of translating that sensitivity into timely action."

Finally, St. Paul has recently taken a few steps toward becoming more proactive in this area. The company is experimenting with "interface meetings" between senior line managers and staff officers, which have been instituted to provide an ongoing forum where external affairs issues are discussed and prioritized. St. Paul has also been trying to integrate its external affairs process with the overall strategic planning and review process. Most executives agree that so far the results have been disappointing; but at the time of the site visits they were busy planning a second attempt.

When put into the context of the company's unique historical developments, it is easy to understand why any additions to the core staff function in external affairs are gingerly pursued. Both line and staff executives take great pride in the consensus they have achieved around a core set of institution-oriented values. Both believe that line managers have an important role to play in the corporate external affairs process. And they tend to agree with the company's president when he observes that in the external affairs process, "Shared responsibility forces integration and minimizes turf fighting." For all of these reasons, I was not surprised during my closing interview with St. Paul's senior external affairs executive when he confessed, "I'm afraid to tamper with this too much because I might turn off the wrong key."

Reflections

Despite the current success of St. Paul's unique approach to understanding and managing the corporate social environment, some potential weaknesses emerge from the diagnosis. First, it is doubtful that the minimal external-affairs core will be sufficient to enable the company to cope with an expanded business exposure. If for instance, the company should begin to drift away from its narrowly focused business strategy—following the lead of other insurance majors who have diversified into both insurance and noninsurance businesses—both the complexity and unpredictability of its business exposure will increase. With the core external affairs function already stretched to the limit, it is doubtful that without additional resources this core will be able to continue serving as the catalyst and integrator of line-management involvement in the social and political arena. Not only will external affairs breadth have to increase, but also the depth of the company's issues identification and analysis activity will have to be more heavily resourced and staffed. In fact, both line and staff executives at St. Paul already agree that a current priority for the external affairs area is the development of a mechanism and framework for identifying and prioritizing relevant social and political issues and that requires collaboration between line managers and external affairs professionals. Many of these executives believe that the company has been fortunate in avoiding major surprises.

Just as important is the need to recognize the multiple influences of the company's structural evolution from centralized to decentralized and geographically dispersed operations. There are signs that the need for careful socialization into the corporate value system of rising field managers may be breaking down. Current field operations executives were developed through many years of service in the corporate headquarters before being sent to establish the geographically dispersed regional offices. Their eventual successors, who are now branch managers, have been recruited and developed in the field offices. Because managerial values are so important in the way St. Paul responds to the corporate social environment, the company's executive leaders have become concerned about what should be done to ensure that rising field managers operate with the same philosophy as their bosses who were trained at corporate headquarters. As one senior manager in corporate headquarters observed.

> The "imaging" is not as clear for the emerging generation of managers in our regional operations. They've never been exposed to our senior management role models.

So far the company has attempted to bridge the generation gap by communicating written policies to its rising field managers and by sending out audit teams to assess their performance. But most agree that these efforts are insufficient. Indeed, some corporate executives have already observed differences in the responsiveness of regional offices to social and political issues affecting their local operations. St. Paul is therefore searching for other means to preserve the managerial philosophy and company character that have served it well in the past.

Update

A year and a half after the initial field visits, contact was made with St. Paul. During the interim the company had added new insurance product lines, but it continued to choose highly specialized property and casualty products and to pursue business expansion within the insurance business. Because of the highly specialized nature of its property and casualty business, St. Paul's business exposure remains substantially lower than those of Aetna and Prudential.

Modest developments, however, have occurred within the corporate external affairs function. A Corporate Affairs Division was created. It consists of four departments:

1. Community Affairs, which serves as staff to the Corporate Responsibility Committee, monitors the social environment for issues and trends that may impact the company, administers community grants, and organizes volunteers for community action,
2. Communications, which handles internal and external communications on property-liability insurance matters,
3. Corporate Public Relations, which is responsible for external communications regarding civic affairs and corporate finance,
4. Government Affairs, which remains a one-person unit.

The general counsel continues to be responsible for legislative and regulatory affairs in Minnesota while the head of the Government Affairs Department is responsible for legislative and regulatory affairs in the other forty-nine states. As Kent Shamblin, who heads St. Paul's Corporate Affairs Division, summarized,

> Yes, that's a slim operation. We think we've gotten better at prioritizing and identifying where we must take a proactive role.
>
> I think we've made considerable progress . . . in integrating the external affairs process into overall corporate planning and in setting our priorities in line with the critical strategic goals of the line units. The head of Government Affairs has very frequent contact with some line units and less with others, depending on the ''business exposure,'' current issues, and so forth.

SUMMARY

The profiles of the best corporate social performers, summarized in Table 8-1, are different, depending on the business exposure of each company. But the overall patterns derived from the application of the general framework are the same for all best-rated companies. They share the same business-strategy connection; one which differs from those of the mixed- and worst-rated companies. Each of the three companies has achieved a good fit in the exposure-design contingency. Later chapters will show that this degree of fit diminishes progressively as one moves through the mixed-rated and worst-rated companies. Finally, all three best-rated companies have encouraged a line–staff balance in the external affairs process to add perspective and encourage responsiveness and relevance in the core staff function. As we shall see, the mixed- and worst-rated corporate social performers have been unable to achieve this blend of line–staff integration and influence.

TABLE 8-1 Comparative Summary of the Best Companies

Companies	Business Exposure	Management Philosophy	External Affairs Strategy	External Affairs Design		
				Breadth	Depth	Line–Staff Balance
Aetna	High	Institution-oriented $\longrightarrow$	Collaborative and problem-solving $\longrightarrow$	High	High	High
Prudential	Moderate			Moderate/High	Moderate	Moderate/High
St. Paul	Low			Low	Low	High

FOOTNOTES

1. This case description was prepared in collaboration with Arvind Bhambri, who assisted in the site visits and field interviews and researched the company's history.

2. As the senior vice president of public affairs explained, "Every 25 years we have had a history written of the company. It talks about a corporate culture; and there is no question that there is such a thing. It is clear that Prudential's culture is distinctive." Justification for the development and continued refinement of a corporation's history may be found in G.D. Smith and L.E. Steadman, "Present Value of Corporate History," *Harvard Business Review,* November–December 1981, pp. 164–73.

3. The concept of the company as a "social franchise" also appears in the views of the corporation in society that were expressed by the chief executive of Aetna.

4. Many other Prudential executives referred to this distinction in the roles played by large companies like their own and smaller companies in the industry. For example one said, "We have found that the smaller companies don't have as broad an interest in some of these things as do the larger companies and that some of the smaller companies are much more narrowly directed at protecting their own interests." However, the only interpretation the comparative findings yield is that the relationship between company size and external affairs strategy depends on top management philosophy and corporate character. Companies similar in size to Prudential are arrayed throughout the social performance continuum provided by industry regulators. The only systematic correlate of their choice of external affairs strategy is top management philosophy. Moreover, one of the smallest (i.e., St. Paul) of the 25 companies studied, which also had one of the narrowest product lines, pursued a philosophy and strategy that was very similar to the ones of Aetna and Prudential. Thus, it is company philosophy and character, not size, that appears to govern how a company interprets its responsibility and determines how it will respond to developments in the corporate social environment.

5. Among the many stories told by Prudential's executives was the following one: "The Pension Reform Act, passed in 1974, allowed individuals to set up their own retirement accounts. We sold a lot of endowment insurance policies as a means of complying with that Act. Then we discovered that if the individual became employed by a company with a plan, he was not able to continue endowment, and if he let his personal policy lapse he would lose a substantial amount of money because of the agent's commission that had been paid. We refused to sell those products once we discovered what was happening, even though we made a tremendous amount of sales in that product line. I think ultimately that the law might have been changed to prohibit the product; but we had stopped voluntarily quite some time ahead of that."

6. Apparently, the breakup of the integrated external affairs department in 1969 was made more on the basis of internal politics than organizational efficiency. As one external affairs professional recalled, "Part of the breakup in the old department had to do with the need to promote people in our Washington, D.C. office. To promote them you had to move them aside to make vacancies in the organization. For example, one of my subordinates who was heading up the D.C. office was promoted to the same level as me; therefore, he couldn't report to me anymore. He had to report to someone else; and that was the beginning of what is now the separate Public Affairs operation." My own experience from consultation and from intensive study of major insurers is that another factor associated with the failure to achieve a structurally integrated external affairs function is that attorneys become uneasy about their professional status when they are

asked to move out of the corporate law department. They tend to view such a move as "falling out of the professional legal career track." Finally, some executive leaders have kept professional lawyers separated from the rest of the core external affairs function because these leaders are aware that the values and orientations of corporate attorneys, instilled in adversarially oriented legal training, differ from those needed in other parts of the core function. All of these factors, together with the simple availability of the right person with the right talents at the right time, tend to constrain optimal mutual influence and integration with a company's core external affairs function.

7. The attitude toward corporate staff that was expressed by the senior vice president of public affairs was also expressed by Prudential's chief executive officer in an internal statement on future company directions that he prepared in 1978: "We will not have a separate planning department. I believe that organizations with such a department have really chosen the wrong path. Planning is an essential part of every manager's job. I have not yet seen planning effectively integrated with other mangement functions when planning is done by a separate entity. . . . Under those conditions planning provides neither guidance nor commitment to operating managers."

8. St. Paul line and staff executives were quite aware of the unusually low business exposure of their company. As one executive explained, "We're not a personal-lines company. We deal primarily with commercial lines. [Also] we traditionally have been isolated or insulated in the Midwest. Therefore, we have been less directly involved than the Northeast companies in the broad range of regulatory issues confronting the industry as a whole."

9. The following recollection was shared by the senior external affairs officer about one of the few exceptions to the success field managers had in representing the company when the catalytic external-affairs issue emerged. He said, "I can recall one instance concerning the issue in which a local manager had done something that had been brought to the attention of a state insurance commissioner. It came to our attention at corporate headquarters. The first thing I knew the senior line manager had called a meeting between his people and the public affairs staff. He posed the question, "What is the right thing to do?" And we tried to sort it out. Was this a decent business decision? Was it responsible? Should we stand behind our guns? Or is it something we honestly can't say we're comfortable with? We made the latter conclusion, tough as it was, and we told the local manager where we thought he was wrong and we dispatched a communication to the state insurance commissioner. This action did us good in the long run. Even in the short term I believe it did us good because the commissioner was impressed that we would voluntarily correct what we perceived to be a mistake."

CHAPTER 9

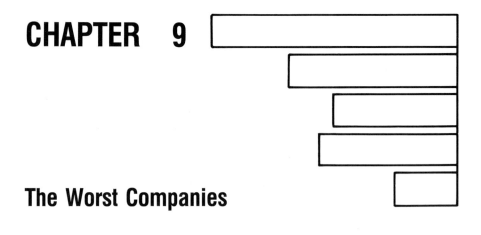

The Worst Companies

The profiles of the worst-rated companies provide a stark contrast to those of the best-rated companies in the U.S. insurance industry. The worst corporate social performers operate with an enterprise-oriented, top management philosophy. However, they do so with a reactive external affairs strategy. Because they respond late in the life cycle of social and political issues, and then only to issues that directly impact their major product lines, their external affairs strategies may be judged on most counts as implicitly individualistic and adversarial in nature.

Relative to their business exposures, both companies rely on impoverished external affairs functions to help them understand and manage relations with the corporate social environment. In one case the function is chairman dominated, and although the chairman is informed by line managers, the function lacks the support and perspectives of seasoned external affairs professionals. In the other case, the company has become overly dependent on its trade association; consequently, it has found itself unprepared to defend its own interests when they depart from the consensus-based positions adopted by the trade association membership. In this company, a small band of attorneys react on an ad hoc basis to public issues with minimal involvement of line management.

The company profiles will reveal, therefore, that external affairs strategy, structure, and process in both companies lack the clarity, breadth, and depth that is required for them to meet the challenges of their business exposures.

FALMOUTH

We are reactive in most situations. We take a defensive approach, rather than identify an issue and mount an offensive.

Senior Line Manager

172

Falmouth is a highly exposed, multiple-line insurance company whose business is conducted primarily in urban centers. The company has also become the captive of a noninsurance parent corporation; an event that followed several years of poor operating performance. The recent history of Falmouth's acquisition and its aftermath helps explain a lot about its current approach to understanding and managing the corporate social environment and why it is ranked 21st in overall corporate social performance among the nation's 25 largest insurance companies.

The Philosophy-strategy Connection

A combination of at least three factors have caused the emergence of a strong enterprise-oriented philosophy that is widely shared within the company. Indeed, when compared to the other companies selected for intensive study, Falmouth has been attempting to operate as though the corporate social environment did not exist. Several years of poor operating results, together with acquisition by a financially oriented parent corporation, have resulted in a strong bottom-line emphasis throughout Falmouth. Moreover, an executive was brought in from another insurance company by the new parent with a mandate from the parent corporation to turn around Falmouth's operating performance. Thus, despite the recent proliferation of issues and events in the corporate social environment to which the company is exposed, Falmouth's executive leaders have been dedicated to operational and financial improvements.

Under these circumstances, it was not surprising when the senior external affairs attorney described the company's approach to external affairs in this way

> We're more devoted to the resolution of operational issues. Certainly those issues have first priority as opposed to external affairs issues. Only when an external affairs issue is perceived to have some *measurable* impact upon operations do we go after it. It's sort of pragmatic. We don't have much time for ivory tower work!

Indeed, survey results reveal that Falmouth executives are considerably more resistant than their counterparts in other companies to changing a business policy or practice in response to developments in the corporate social environment; especially when such a change might adversely affect company profitability, as Figure 9-1 reveals. "We're not a governmental institution!" explained an external affairs professional. "And I don't think anybody pretends that we are. In many areas we think of Adam Smith's 'invisible hand;' and it eventually comes out right."

Because the company has not taken the corporate social environment as seriously as have many of the other companies studied, an external affairs strategy at Falmouth must be deduced implicitly from its internal structures and processes and recent corporate behaviors. Such an assessment reveals a reactive strategy; one by which Falmouth responds late in the issue-development cycle and then only to issues that directly impact the company's primary self-interests. As one of Falmouth's part-time, external affairs professionals explained, "We haven't form-

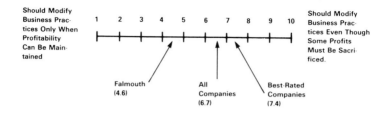

Survey Question: "In terms of changing a business practice in response to a major public policy issue, what do you think an individual company's posture should be?"

Figure 9-1 Senior line manager beliefs about how responsive their companies should be to changes in the corporate social environment.

ally dealt with external affairs issues in several years [since the takeover]. The operating side of our company has not had any formal process for addressing external affairs issues. However, the law department has been there and is getting stronger."

The effects of the company's almost exclusive focus on turnaround in its insurance operations have not been confined inside the company. They have also been visible in the company's relations with industry trade associations that could otherwise help Falmouth fill some of the current gaps between its business exposure and external affairs capability. Consistent with its focus on operational efficiencies, Falmouth has withdrawn its memberships in major trade associations. As one senior executive observed, "We aren't a member of a property-casualty trade association because they require too much money for too little return."[1] Indeed, the company has generally avoided participation in any industry forum in which positions on external affairs issues are discussed. "Because we haven't defined our positions and given ammunition to the Chairman or other senior management people," explained the new head of corporate communications, "We haven't wanted to go to the public forums because we really haven't had our act together on what our message is."

Chairman-dominated External Affairs Function

Decision making within Falmouth concerning external affairs as well as insurance operations continue to be dominated by the company's chairman. Under his direction the company's external affairs strategy has been highly individualistic because of the operational focus.[2] It has also become adversarial in nature because whatever responses are made to the corporate social environment are determined by the operationally oriented Chairman, and formulated and implemented by an equally operationally oriented legal function. As a senior operations executive explained,

> We have not been joiners. It reflects the very independent and very capable nature of the Chairman. He likes to go in his own direction. He doesn't want to commit himself and let somebody else play his hand. That's about the simplest way to explain why we're not involved more heavily in the trade associations.

One way in which the company has benefited from the work on external affairs issues conducted outside the firm, however, is through the relationships the Chairman maintains with his peers in a few other insurance companies. As in auto racing, Falmouth frequently is able to draft behind an industry frontrunner on an issue. "He's in contact with his peers," said one senior line manager. "And they're talking about these issues all the time." But another company executive confessed that "It has been our good luck that our interests have just happened to be coincident with some other companies on a lot of external affairs issues." Indeed, he emphasized the company benefits of "getting behind an industry forerunner, and learning from their experience." One of the corporate attorneys concurred somewhat more bluntly when he explained that, "We have not generally had to invest heavily in external affairs because the other companies have been doing it for us!"

An Impoverished External Affairs Design

With an enterprise-oriented philosophy, an operationally focused executive cadre, and an extremely reactive external affairs strategy that may be individualistic and adversarial in nature, it should not come as a surprise that Falmouth continues to operate with what can be described simply as an impoverished external affairs design. No unit separate from the corporate legal department is exclusively responsible for external affairs activities. Within the legal department there are two units that focus on what has traditionally been called operationally oriented external affairs activities. One unit deals with day-to-day regulatory matters, involving compliance with enacted state laws and regulations affecting the company's business lines. The other, Corporate Relations, is responsible for monitoring proposed state and federal legislation and developments within the industry trade associations and the NAIC, and for both state and federal lobbying. This unit is headed by a former state insurance department attorney to whom four company attorneys and an actuary report.

Beyond the legal function, however, only two operationally oriented units have some responsibility for corporate external affairs. A small market research unit, which conducts competitive analyses, collects intelligence from field operations, and reports directly to the vice president of marketing, occasionally becomes the home of special projects involving the analysis of external affairs issues. However, the latter is clearly a part-time one for this unit, and the decision to task the unit with the analysis of external affairs issues is highly selective, informed by senior line management, and ultimately made by the chairman. "A total philosophy of getting involved in external affairs issues is not pervasive in this company," explained the head of marketing research. "In some cases our approach has been reactive; in others, it has involved carving out a niche." When asked what type of issues get selected for study by his unit, he said,

> We take it as a given that, *if* we are going to be affected by a public issue, *if* the industry is not taking a stance, and *if* we have an opinion to make, we will go after it. Given those assumptions there is an overriding drive in the company to take an external-affairs position. *If* self-interest is at stake, we'll most certainly take a stance if needed.

The other unit that is involved in corporate external affairs at Falmouth is the Corporate Communications Division, which is also located in the marketing function. Although this division devotes most of its attention to traditional public-relations and product advertising activities, and communications with the independent agents in the company's distribution system, a one-person unit had been created within it to begin to serve as an issues analysis function. At the time of the site visit a former line manager had been assigned to this new position only a matter of weeks. His appointment had been made by the chairman, ostensibly for the purpose of relieving the latter from an overload situation in the area of corporate external affairs. As the new appointee explained, "The Chairman, in convincing me to take this position, had demanded that I develop an issues-analysis function. I think he is getting very tired of the tedium of being the only answer to every question. But I'm not sure how credible his interest really is in shedding some of this responsibility now. I've got to take him at face value when he says he wants the function to be developed, and I am going to develop the function."

Much of the time I spent with this new staff executive was devoted to a discussion of his plans for creating Falmouth's first issues-analysis function. However, when I contacted the company two years later to gauge his progress, I was informed by a senior executive that, owing to the downturn in the U.S. property and casualty business, "The Corporate Communications area has become even more operations-oriented. The head of the department submitted a definitive corporate external affairs proposal to senior management earlier this year, but it was assigned a lesser priority, in deference to new advertising initiatives and an innovative program to fortify the company's relationship with selected independent insurance agents."

In the absence of an issues-analysis function, which is active in identifying and analyzing external affairs issues, and making recommendations for managerial action, Falmouth continues to rely on an unstructured approach to issues identification based on the instincts of the chairman and his senior line managers and the legislative summaries prepared by the corporate legal function. Of the two sources, the line operations led by an active chairman make most of the decisions about which issues warrant company attention.[3]

In many cases the company does not become aware of an issue until very late in the issue life cycle. "The original surfacing of a public issue," explained one senior line manager, "will come from the law department's summary of impending legislation. If it triggers our interest, we'll get together to decide whether to study the issue." Thus, issue identification within Falmouth often does not begin until an issue has become highly politicized to the point that legislation has been initiated to support it.

The second step in the process involves the reactions of operations executives, principally in the marketing and underwriting functions.[4] Based on their assessments, an ad hoc meeting may be convened to discuss the issue. A summary of this discussion is later presented to the corporate executive committee, which is composed of the chairman, the general counsel, and the heads of underwriting, marketing, finance, administration, claims, and field operations.

The reaction of the executive committee to the preliminary issue summary determines whether discussion and company action on the issue ceases or goes into coordination. Coordination is the term used by Falmouth senior executives to describe what happens to an issue when it is formally delegated from the executive committee to a coordination committee that is usually managed by the head of the market research unit. This small unit, which has only part-time responsibility for external affairs activities, organizes a multifunctional study of the issue, and submits monthly status reports to the executive committee. But as the head of this unit conceded, ''Rarely do we have a person who has just external affairs responsibilities. My area reacts to issues. It brings up issues if there is concern about them. But market research isn't strictly involved with public issues.''

In some, but not all cases, this process ends when the chairman announces that the company has taken a position on the issue. ''Our approach is to provide the Chairman with a consensus based on the participation of line and functional areas,'' said a company executive.[5]

In conclusion, the external affairs function at Falmouth must be judged as both line-dominated and impoverished.[6] External affairs breadth and depth are minimal in this highly exposed company. For these reasons, there is little wonder why external affairs professionals at Falmouth reported the lowest level of satisfaction with the work performed by their departments among all the companies selected for intensive study, as shown in Figure 9-2. When asked why their level of satisfaction was so low, Falmouth staff professionals pointed to the lack of staff breadth and depth in light of the company's high exposure to the corporate social environment. As one senior staff executive explained,

> We would like to get more involved in some external affairs activities, but we have other commitments. We have limited resources. We know we've got many day-to-day priorities in both line and external affairs. We would really like to take more independent positions on issues and present our viewpoints, but most of us are dissatisfied with the time and resources we have to devote to these things. I *know* that I'm dissatisfied!

Not surprisingly, both senior line managers and external affairs executives at Falmouth associated the lowest perceived career and advancement opportunity with their work on external affairs activities among all the company executives surveyed.[7]

The low degree of breadth and depth at Falmouth, when compared to its heavy exposure and strong operational focus, also means that the few people who are at least partially responsible for corporate external affairs are able to spend very little time on those activities. Indeed, the company surveys revealed that Falmouth external affairs professionals spend less time per week on average engaged exclusively in external affairs activities than do their counterparts at any of the other

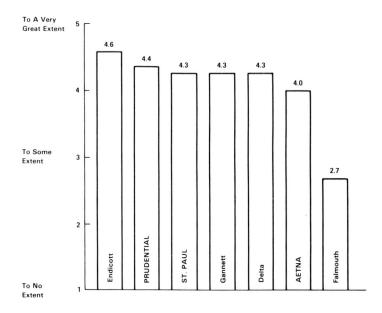

Figure 9-2 Survey responses of external affairs professionals, about how satisfied they are with the work done in their own department.

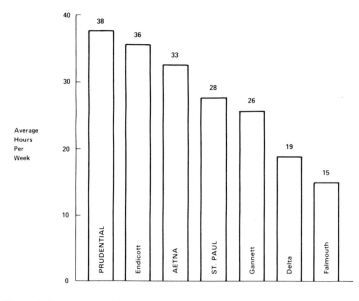

Figure 9-3 External affairs professionals survey responses on how many hour on average they spend per week on external affairs activities.

companies that were intensively studied (Figure 9-3).[8] Moreover, Falmouth external affairs executives reported the highest degree of instability in the amount of time they devote to corporate external affairs activities.

Update

But the story of Falmouth's social performance does not end here. A follow-up study, which inquired about subsequent developments in the company's approach to corporate external affairs, was conducted on the eve of the publication of this book. In addition to the discovery that the planned issues-analysis function had never gotten off the ground, I was astonished to learn that *no one* currently held a full-time, external affairs job. When I inquired further, one of the members of the former Corporate Relations unit described the deterioration of Falmouth's external affairs function as follows:

> The low profile of the company in external affairs was reduced even further with the reorganization of the law department in mid-1982, eliminating in a structural sense the Corporate Relations unit, which had primary corporate responsibility for the external affairs function. Employees of that unit who were engaged in those activities on a full-time basis have been reassigned to law department divisions providing legal counsel to corporate operations. While they have been asked to continue external affairs activities, those elements are second in priority to operations assignments. The corporate communications department continues to be involved in external affairs as part of its overall responsibility for corporate public relations. . . .

> Hopefully, the "survival mentality" that now pervades the property/casualty insurance industry will only be a passing moment in history. Maintaining a glimmer of external affairs activity while directing most of our energies toward operational concerns certainly makes the most sense for this company right now.

GANNETT

The question of what will be the burning social issues of the 1980s and of how we should deal with them has been conducted for the most part through our trade association. We have really piggy-backed on them, and we have used them as our window to what the social issues are and how our segment of the industry and our company individually should deal with them. As a company we have not developed the capability of drawing back to look at the world as it is moving and develop plans and strategies.

Senior Executive

Gannett is a large property and casualty generalist headquartered in the urban northeast. It has a moderately high degree of business exposure which in recent years it has found to be increasingly difficult to manage. The company was rated 23rd out of 25 in terms of its overall social performance. As the following discussion of Gannett's approach to dealing with the corporate social environment will reveal, the key variables and relationships in the general framework are useful in explaining a large measure of the company's poor social performance.

The Philosophy-strategy Connection

Top management philosophy at Gannett is enterprise-oriented. Indeed, the company was founded by a group of corporate executives who wanted to meet some of their pressing insurance needs. As in the cases of the other enterprise-oriented companies studied, but particularly the mutuals, Gannett executives are oriented primarily toward policyholder benefit. "I think we have an obligation to our policyholders" said one senior executive, "not to subsidize other policyholders to any greater extent than the industry and the social system require." Indeed, one of the explicit priorities of the relatively new chief executive officer has been to alter Gannett's business and geographical mix to reduce its exposure to socially sensitive, property and casualty product lines and politically volatile, urban areas. As he explained,

> One of my priorities is to try to move further West, out of the Northeast part of the country, as fast as we can! I'm looking at other parts of the country where the climate from a regulatory perspective is a more reasonable one in which to conduct a free enterprise system.

In addition to his attempt to reconfigure Gannett's business exposure, the CEO had begun to take a firmer and more independent stand than his predecessors on public policy positions. Commenting on the erosion of traditional managerial prerogatives under pressure from the increasingly turbulent social and political environment surrounding his industry, the CEO said, "Chief executive officers in the insurance industry are going to have to stand much firmer than they have in the past on some issues than most people are going to like." And take a much firmer, independent stand is exactly what Gannett has been attempting to do during the past few years. As one of the company's legislative lobbyists explained during the field interviews, "The benchmark in trying to develop a company position on an issue was explained to me several years ago, and it has not changed much. It is what is best for *this* company."

But the new approach has not worked for Gannett. Instead of freeing the company from social and political encroachment, the approach has put the company on a politically endangered species list, as far as regulators and executives in many rival companies are concerned. One important reason for this unanticipated consequence is that although the company is tougher, it has taken its stands by reacting late in the issue life cycle. As one of Gannett's senior external affairs executives explained, "Our response to the regulatory environment has been on an ad hoc basis. We tend to react to issues on a specific basis." This reactive approach was conveyed more bluntly by one of the company's legislative lobbyists when I asked him what triggered company attention to a public policy issue. He replied, "In my opinion it is a seat-of-the-pants reaction."

This reactive approach manifests itself in two primary tactics that are used by the company to deal with social and public policy issues that engage its business interests. The first is the company's traditional relationships with its trade associations. The second is the degree of sophistication of its external affairs function.

Overdependence on Trade Associations

The company depends more than any other firm studied on industry trade associations to understand and manage the corporate social environment. When I asked how the company managed its external affairs, the typical reply I received was, "That's going to be tough for me to answer because we don't really have a very formalized external affairs structure. We rely on our trade association for most of our formal external affairs positions. Through our committee work in the trade association, we develop the policy positions we wish to take, and the association implements them for us."

These observations from the field work were reflected in the results of the company surveys. First, Gannett line and staff executives reported the highest frequency of direct contact with industry trade associations. Second, they attached the highest degree of strategic importance, among all external constituencies, to their relationships with industry trade associations. Third, they rated relations with trade associations as more indispensable for an effective company response to public policy issues than did members of the other six firms studied (Figure 9-4). Finally, Gannett executives reported that they received more help than did their counterparts in the other companies in managing uncertainties in the corporate social environment from industry trade associations.

This high degree of dependence on trade associations, however, cuts two ways for highly exposed companies such as Gannett. On the positive side, reliance on the trade associations has saved Gannett much of the cost that would otherwise have been associated with the creation and maintenance of a sophisticated external affairs function. Indeed, much of the cost of staff work on association committees has been passed on to other members of the association. In addition, as long as these committees have continued to develop positions on issues that are consistent with Gannett's business strategies and stakes, the company has been able to benefit from lobbying in strength.

The negative side of high dependence on trade associations comes about when the association develops a position that is in conflict with the peculiar interests of a member company. It is this potential liability, together with the absence of a strong, company-based, external affairs capability that many senior managers at Gannett believe accounts for what was to them a shockingly low company rating on corporate social performance.

During the half-decade preceding the assessment of corporate social performance, a politically dormant but highly profitable product line in which Gannett had very high business stakes was propelled into the political arena by reform-oriented regulators. Because their regulatory initiative meant change in the competitive structure of the product line, these regulators were supported by companies that

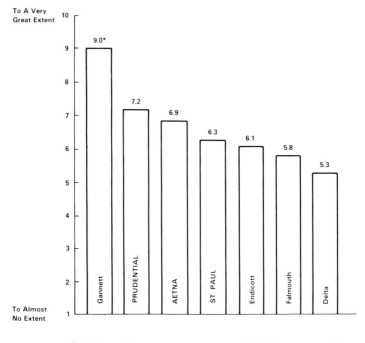

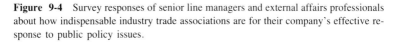

*Grand mean of the company average responses of senior line managers and
corporate external affairs professionals.

Figure 9-4 Survey responses of senior line managers and external affairs professionals
about how indispensable industry trade associations are for their company's effective response to public policy issues.

might gain market share during the change period and, of course, were not opposed
by companies that were not affected by the proposed change. One important effect
of the proposed legislation, however, would be to potentially undermine Gannett's
traditional market dominance and competitive edge in the affected product line.
Thus, Gannett could not afford to ignore the issue; nor could it support the
consensus-based position adopted by its trade association. Instead, the company
was faced with having to mount its own defense late in the issue life cycle against
heavy opposition, with both flanks exposed because of its weak external affairs capability. If ever there were a situation in this industry in which company could be
said to have literally led with its chin, this was it.

External Affairs: Design and Strategy

Gannett's excessive dependence on trade associations was a traditional one
that reflected the strong preferences of its former executive leaders. However, when
the current chief executive officer assumed his position only a few years before the
comparative study, one of his goals had been to strengthen the company's external
affairs function. Toward this end, he had instructed the company's general counsel,

who oversaw Gannett's external affairs activities, to develop a more sophisticated function.

Unfortunately, before this developmental process had begun the company was hit by the public issue that threatened its primary product line. In haste, the general counsel hired an outsider with experience as a public affairs counsel to head a new public affairs unit within the law department. However, the appointee lasted only a matter of months before leaving the company because of what Gannett officials refer to as personal problems. As one executive explained,

> We hired an individual to head up a public affairs effort not knowing exactly where he was headed. It was a broad idea to have the company develop a capability for dealing with social issues to some extent independently of the trade associations. But he turned out to have personal problems, and he is no longer with us. So our first budding effort, which involved going outside to hire a person, has been sidetracked.

Thus, in the midst of its most significant external affairs adventure, Gannett found itself fighting the state regulators and legislators as well as most of its industry rivals with an impoverished external affairs function.

The core of that function is directed by the general counsel and housed in the corporate legal function. The function consists of the general counsel and two legislative relations professionals who report to him. One professional is responsible for monitoring events in the legislature in which the company is domiciled. The other handles relations with trade associations and the NAIC, including committee work, as well as routine rate filings with state insurance departments.

Beyond the legal function there is a small public relations unit. But as the general counsel explained, "Public relations is a minimal operation around here. In addition to a head, it is composed of a staff person from the Claims Department and three ladies."

Perhaps things might not have gone as poorly for Gannett in the corporate social performance arena if the relatively minimal external affairs operation had been better coordinated as well as complemented by a high degree of line-management involvement. Neither intrafunctional coordination nor line-management involvement, however, characterized Gannett's external affairs function.

For example, company survey results in Figures 9-5 and 9-6 reveal that elements of Gannett's external affairs function are characterized by less mutual influence and internal integration than any of these functions located in the other companies. Moreover, senior line and staff executives at Gannett believe less strongly than their counterparts in the other companies that line managers should be heavily involved in the corporate external affairs process (Figure 9-7). Although the new CEO has announced that line managers will become more involved in external affairs, no rationale or plan has been developed to guide their efforts in this area. Moreover, the corporate planning function at Gannett, which could serve as a supplemental source of line-staff integration in the external affairs process, focuses exclusively on financial, as opposed to social, objectives.

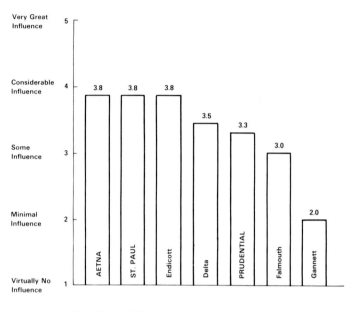

Survey Question: "How much influence do the other corporate external affairs departments have on the decisions made in your department?"

Figure 9-5 Survey responses of external affairs professionals on their perception of the degree of mutual influence among corporate external affairs units.

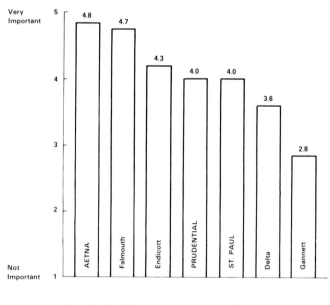

Survey Question: "How important are relations with other corporate external affairs units in terms of their effect on your department?"

Figure 9-6 Survey responses of external affairs professionals on how important they feel integration among corporate external affairs units is.

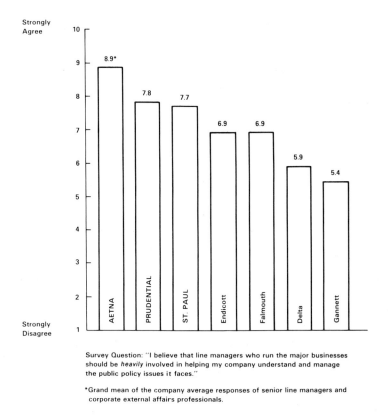

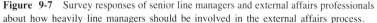

Survey Question: "I believe that line managers who run the major businesses should be *heavily* involved in helping my company understand and manage the public policy issues it faces."

*Grand mean of the company average responses of senior line managers and corporate external affairs professionals.

Figure 9-7   Survey responses of senior line managers and external affairs professionals about how heavily line managers should be involved in the external affairs process.

Despite the fact that several Gannett executives believed that the lack of formal external affairs breadth and depth was compensated for by the use of ad hoc committees and task forces, the survey results reveal that top management steering committees that focus strictly on external affairs issues are less well established at Gannett than at the other companies surveyed. In addition, external affairs professionals at Gannett reported the lowest frequency of reliance on task forces within the company to deal with public policy issues. Finally, senior line managers at Gannett reported the lowest frequency of contact with corporate external affairs units of all the managers surveyed.[9] These survey results complete the picture of Gannett's reactive and impoverished approach to understanding and managing the corporate social environment by revealing not only minimal mutual influence and integration within the company's external affairs function, but also between this function and the company's line operations.

From any perspective, this minimal external affairs capability is grossly inadequate to meet the demands of the company's business exposure. Gannett's primary product lines in the property and casualty segment of the insurance business are among the most socially sensitive and politically volatile in the United States.

Moreover, its stakes are extremely high in urban centers, especially those located in the northeast.

To exacerbate matters, the company operates nationwide with about a dozen regional profit centers, which are overlaid with a functional headquarters structure. Each regional profit center carries the full product line and operates like a medium-sized insurance company. With this high degree of decentralization it would take a strong corporate-level, external affairs function to attract and guide the attention of operating managers. As the senior vice president of field operations conceded, "There is a lack of communication as to who is supposed to do what in public affairs: the field offices versus the home office." Thus, the current external affairs function is inadequate with respect to both the company's business exposure and its structural decentralization.[10]

Finally, all of the above must be amplified because of the strong, legally based, adversarial orientation of the external affairs function that is guided by Gannett's general counsel. "I tend to take a minimal position on public affairs issues," said the general counsel. "It never occurred to me that anybody in this company would know what our position is on most things. We address external affairs issues on an ad hoc basis. We don't do much issues analysis in terms of looking down the road to see what's coming up."

Given Gannett's moderately high business exposure and its minimal external affairs breadth and depth, the company's approach to external affairs when it cannot secure the cooperation of its trade association becomes a fait accompli. "I prefer to deal with state commissioners in the courts," said the company's senior external affairs officer. "I prefer to sue them!" Indeed he took great pride in this approach to external affairs. Continuing with obvious conviction, he said,

> I don't know any particular way of combating an issue that a commissioner has been signalling for a long time until you get to it. Then you have to confront it. You're talking to a lawyer. I *love* to sue people, and this is my way of managing this kind of problem. I have sued commissioners all around the United States. I've even sued the United States government. And I have been very successful at it.

Reflections on the External Affairs Debacle

When Gannett executives were briefed at the end of the field work on the company's low standing on overall corporate social performance: they were shocked. Many were angry and embarrassed. Most blamed the hard independent stand the company had recently taken on the public issue affecting Gannett's primary business. As a group these executives were concerned that their new approach to corporate external affairs may have negated all the "chips" that the company had tried to build up with its external constituencies over a period of decades. All wanted to know what the company could do to restore the company's goodwill and normalize its external relations.

When the company was contacted several months after the debriefing it was obvious that the negative feedback on Gannett's social performance had catalyzed considerable rethinking about the company's approach to external affairs. A new model, however, had not emerged to replace the one in place. The reflections of one of Gannett's new senior executives illustrate managerial thinking in the company at the time. He said,

> This company has for years tried to nurture a certain reputation with the regulators apart from the trade associations. Regardless of whether you are an enthusiastic member of a trade association, you must deal with individual regulators on individual issues. We have tried for years to nurture those relationships. Some of those relationships were the ''good old boy'' kind. But beyond that we tried to develop relationships based on mutual trust, that implied, ''We are aware of your regulatory problems and the pressures you feel. We want to deal effectively with you and help you solve your problems and do things in a cooperative environment in the public interest. We also want you to know, Commissioner, that we are honest. We have a high degree of integrity. Our word means something. We are not going to pull any fast ones on you. We are not going to try to manipulate you. We are in it for the long haul.'' For years and years, we were very successful doing that.
>
> But as you have recorded, somehow something seems to have changed, and there is enough feedback to know that whatever we've been doing hasn't worked. We can quibble about the degree of the problem, but there is something out there—an attitude toward this company—that is inconsistent with what we have tried to do.

When asked why the unfavorable change occurred in the way outside constituencies view the company, the executive replied,

> I think that a company's stand on one issue can tend to paint a new picture; to change the perception about what a company is all about. This company's stand on one issue has pretty much overcome all other history concerning what the company is and what it stands for.
>
> It is astounding to me that our actions on one issue would cause all of the chips we have accumulated over the years to be cashed in on a single issue; but that may well be the case.
>
> The perception came out that our company is simply rattled; that it's had this goose that's been laying golden eggs for years and years, and now somebody is throttling the goose!
>
> I am not sure whether we should have committed ourselves to being exposed to having all of our chips cashed in at one time on a single issue. I am not sure whether the thinking that went into our response to that issue was impaired by the fact that we did not have an external affairs organization in place that could have made judgments and provided information to the company's senior management. However, I believe having a stronger group in place to deal with social issues would have been helpful. If we had had that organization at the front end, we'd have gotten some early feedback from our actions. But we didn't.
>
> God, I don't know what it is that we need to do. But we need to do something different! And I don't think my yelling will somehow stop like a little sore that goes away. My problem to some extent is to change the perception of other people in the organization.

TABLE 9-1   Comparative Summary of the Worst Companies

Companies	Business Exposure	Top Management Philosophy	External Affairs Strategy	External Affairs Design		
				Breadth	Depth	Line–Staff Balance
Falmouth	High	Enterprise oriented	Reactive	Low	Low	Chairman dominated
Gannett	Moderate	↓	↓	Low/ Moderate	Low	Staff dominated

SUMMARY

The profiles of the worst rated companies are summarized in Table 9-1. The dramatic differences between these profiles and those of the best-rated companies in Chapters 7 and 8, provide considerable support for the general framework. When controlling for business exposure, the best and worst corporate social performers were found to differ substantially on all other elements of the general framework. The best performers pursue an institution-oriented, top management philosophy; the worst performers pursue an enterprise-oriented philosophy. The best performers have adopted an explicit external affairs strategy that is collaborative and problem solving in nature; the worst companies have settled for a reactive approach to external affairs that is implicitly individualistic and adversarial in nature. In addition, there is a good fit between the business exposure of the best-rated companies and the breadth and depth of their external affairs function; whereas the fit between business exposure and external affairs design in the worst-rated companies is poor. Finally, the best-rated companies have achieved a line–staff balance in the corporate external affairs process whereas the worst-rated companies have not.

But these obvious differences between the extreme performance groups do not reveal much about the relative importance of different elements in the general framework. Nor do they provide the kind of sensitivity in understanding that is required to make selective improvements in a company's overall approach to understanding and managing the corporate social environment. To perform this sensitivity analysis, information comparable to that which was obtained from the best and worst performers was sought from companies that fell along the middle of the corporate social performance continuum—from the companies that received a "mixed" rating on overall corporate social performance. This information on the "mixed" corporate social performers is presented in Chapter 10.

FOOTNOTES

1. Based on the company survey, Falmouth line and staff executives reported that they received the least amount of help from industry trade associations in managing external affairs uncertainties of all line and staff executives in the study.

2. When asked in the company survey which was more important, business operations or external affairs activities, external affairs professionals at Falmouth placed greater relative importance on business operations than did their counterparts in any of the other participating companies.

3. External affairs professionals at Falmouth reported receiving the highest degree of influence on their activities from line operations among all companies, based on an analysis of the company surveys.

4. Falmouth external affairs professionals reported greater company reliance on line managers to perform the external affairs function than did their counterparts in any of the other companies completing the company survey.

5. Despite the fact that Falmouth's external affairs function is dominated by the company's chairman and chief executive officer, senior line managers and external affairs professionals at Falmouth reported that, relative to other management topics, public affairs issues are less important to their CEO than did line and staff executives in any of the other companies surveyed.

6. On the company survey, Falmouth senior line executives reported that they received more attention and support from top management than did their counterparts in any other company selected for intensive study. In contrast, Falmouth external affairs professionals reported that they received less attention and support from top management than did their counterparts in any of the other companies studied. Moreover, external affairs professionals at Falmouth reported the least amount of understanding of their function by senior line managers when compared to the survey responses of external affairs professionals in the other companies.

7. They shared this low degree of career and advancement potential only with Delta, one of the mixed-rated companies discussed in the next chapter. It should be noted that Delta and Falmouth may be distinguished from the other companies on one important basis: they are the only firms that operate with a chairman-dominated external affairs function.

8. Senior line managers at Falmouth also spent less time on average on corporate external affairs than did their counterparts in the other companies. For example, survey results revealed that Falmouth senior line managers spent only 2–5 days on a particular public policy issue whereas senior line managers in the best-rated companies generally spent 5–30 days on a particular issue.

9. Similar results were obtained for the frequency of contact among core elements of Gannett's external affairs function. Of all companies surveyed, Gannett external affairs professionals reported the lowest frequency of contact with each other.

10. Gannett, like many other mutual insurance companies, employs policyholder advisory boards within each of its regional operations. These committees are made up of policyholders regarded by Gannett executives as "people of substance in the areas we serve." Thus they represent a very narrow segment of the general public served by Gannett, and they may even be quite unrepresentative of Gannett's policyholder base. These regional boards are briefed quarterly on the company's financial performance as well as its community programs and positions on social and public issues. Thus, these boards may be considered as peripheral elements in the company's external affairs process. However, no systematic framework has been developed within Gannett for clarifying their role in corporate external affairs or for integrating them into this process.

CHAPTER 10

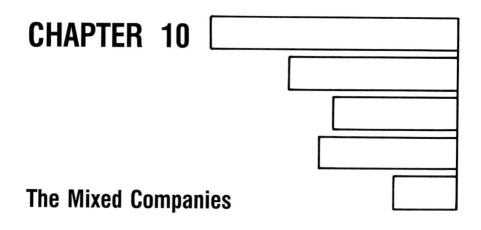

The Mixed Companies

Two companies were selected from the list of the 25 largest U.S. insurers because they received mixed ratings on overall corporate social performance. These firms fell within the midrange of social performance, each receiving a relatively high percentage of both best and worst ratings. For one company, Delta, the mixed performance rating was positively skewed in favor of best ratings; for the other, Endicott, the mixed performance rating was negatively skewed with more worst than best ratings.

As expected, both companies occupied the midrange between the best- and worst-rated companies in terms of the diagnosis provided by the general framework. Internal consistency among the factors included in the framework was highest among the best-rated companies, lowest among the worst-rated companies, and only partially achieved in the mixed-rated companies. For example, like the best-rated companies, these two firms exhibited a good fit between their business exposure and the breadth of their external affairs function. However, both Delta and Endicott operated with external affairs functions that were low in depth. In the case of Delta, the positively rated mixed company, low depth coincided with a low business exposure; but for Endicott, the negatively rated mixed company, there was a poor fit between external affairs depth and business exposure. Neither mixed company had achieved a working balance of line–staff influence in the external affairs process.

But the greatest difference between Delta and Endicott and the best-rated companies concerned the philosophy-strategy connection. Both mixed companies were guided by an enterprise-oriented top management philosophy that was operationalized through an explicit, individualistic and adversarial, external affairs strategy.

These patterns, which distinguish the companies occupying the mid-range of the corporate social performance continuum from those lying at its extremes, provide a fine-grained demonstration of the potential power of the general framework for understanding and managing the corporate social environment. The following profiles of Delta and Endicott reveal their distinguishing features as well as some of the important but subtle forces that underlie each company's concept of and approach to corporate external affairs.

DELTA

We've had a tendency, for right or wrong, to view ourselves as a stand-alone in the industry because our focus is so narrow and our product differentiation is quite marked. We have not been all that excited about jumping in bed with the industry. Their interests are not necessarily our interests; so we're going our own little way.

Senior Line Manager

Delta is a life insurance specialist that pursues the narrowest market segment with the most restricted product line of all the companies in the comparative study. It focuses almost exclusively on the sale of relatively large-coverage, life insurance policies (called *ordinary* insurance in the industry) to well-educated, upper-income individuals in professional and managerial professions. It is headquartered away from the socially sensitive and politically volatile urban centers in the northeast, although a relatively high percentage of its business is conducted in urban states. Overall, because of its somewhat unique business strategy, Delta's business exposure to the corporate social environment is quite low; the lowest among the companies selected for intensive study.

Indeed, both line and staff executives voiced complaints about the detail and length of the questionnaire they were asked to complete and return for analysis prior to my site visit. Because this was the only company from which I received negative reactions to the survey, I asked Delta executives what bothered them most about the questionnaire. The executive vice president's reply was typical. He said that most of the questions were irrelevant for Delta executives because, ''We have a narrow product line and our emphasis is on ordinary, personal insurance. That's the nature of our beast.''

Exposure, Philosophy, and External Affairs Strategy

Because of its low business exposure, Delta executives appeared hard pressed during the interviews to identify insurance-related public policy issues that were high in relevance for the company. The only issues that were receiving active attention at the time of the field visit were inflation and taxation; hardly industry-specific issues but which nevertheless carry important implications for the financial decisions of individuals at the high-income end of the life insurance market that Delta serves.[1]

Beyond these general public policy issues, Delta had recently been involved in two industry-specific issues in a manner that reflects its enterprise-oriented top management philosophy and its highly individualistic approach to corporate external affairs. The company had been engaged in a major push on both regulatory agendas without the support of the rest of the life insurance industry, which is composed of firms offering coverage to a broader segment of the general public and are consequently exposed to both more and different social and political issues and risks than is Delta.

In one instance, Delta had been strongly in favor of more intensive and restrictive regulation on the issue of life insurance cost disclosure. Its motives, however, had not been entirely altruistic. Delta's exclusive focus on the high-income segment of the market meant that it was dealing with more affluent and better-educated customers than were most of its large, nationally based rivals. Delta consequently experienced a lower lapse rate in policy renewals, earned a substantial portion of its annual premiums from its existing policyholders who had decided to increase their insurance coverage, and generally faced less portfolio risk and operating costs than its peers among life insurance majors. The latter, which assume more of the risk in the U.S. life insurance market, would not compare favorably with Delta under a cost-disclosure campaign.

Despite the consumer benefits of reduced insurance costs and stricter cost disclosure, Delta's bid has not been entirely successful with the state regulators. Many of these regulators, together with industry rivals, viewed Delta's external affairs thrust on the cost-disclosure issue as an expression of company self-interest. Regulators in particular tend to focus their attention on society's disadvantaged. Indeed, the whole cost-disclosure push may have backfired because it caused some regulators to take a closer look at Delta's restrictive underwriting policies. Regulators have also become increasingly concerned with "replacement" practices in the industry, which involve the replacement of higher-priced insurance of one company that is owned by a policyholder by agents of another company offering similar, but lower-priced coverage. As a result of this particular regulatory thrust, Delta has begun to rigorously enforce the standards under which its exclusive agents may sell replacement policies. Moreover, as result of all of these developments, some Delta executives have become concerned about the possibility of the emergence of a new public policy issue that would have high relevance and impact potential for their company. As one senior line manager observed,

> We may eventually be vulnerable because of the fact that either knowingly or unknowingly we've done a fantastic job of segmenting the market. Our costs are low because we sell a large policy to a limited group of people who keep coming back for more insurance. We are not servicing the lower end of the market. In contrast, an outfit like Prudential covers a broad range; so they are going to have higher costs and higher-priced insurance. But this issue has not been raised, and *I can assure you* that we are not going to raise it!

The sophistication and affluence of this firm's policyholders also recently created another company-specific issue that Delta attempted to actively engage. Delta policyholders quickly began to turn to low-interest policy loans when more attractive, secure investment alternatives emerged during the early 1980s (e.g., high-yield corporate and municipal bonds and money-market funds). As cash flowed out of the company's reserves in the form of low-interest policy loans on demand from policyholders, Delta mounted a nationwide lobby with state commissioners and legislators to raise the interest rates on policy loans. They pushed initially for a variable interest rate, but lacking once again the support of other life insurance majors, Delta's lobbyists settled for an 8% rate in states where they could get it.[2]

These recent incidents signal the highly *individualistic* approach to corporate external affairs at Delta; one that the following discussion will reveal is conceived and enacted almost exclusively by individuals with legal or technical backgrounds and orientations and that generally avoids the compromise positions adopted in the life insurance trade associations.

This individualistic orientation in corporate external affairs is supported by a widely shared enterprise-oriented top-management philosophy. All line and staff executives agree that the primary, if not sole criterion, for responding to insurance-related public policy issues is policyholder benefit. "It is relatively seldom," explained the company's legislative counsel, "that we experience a situation in which we really have a question of what our priorities should be." Although this pronouncement like the one about cost disclosure has the ring of corporate responsibility, it is a fact that many of the social issues confronting the insurance industry as a whole are concerned more with citizens who need insurance but who cannot afford or are denied coverage than with those who already have secured needed coverage. Although these issues threaten the private insurance mechanism as a whole, they are beyond the current scope of Delta's highly individualistic approach to corporate external affairs.

Delta, therefore, avoids involvement with industrywide issues and with industrywide associations, which engage in consensus-based decision making concerning public issues and regulatory initiatives. "As far as issues engaging the insurance industry as a whole, or the regulation of the industry, we have stayed away from them," said a company senior vice president. "We have not had strong representation within the trade associations. We've tended to go to them when we need them, but we've stayed the heck away from them the rest of the time. The same applies to our involvement in the NAIC."[3] Indeed, another senior executive shared that on some of the few occasions that Delta has gone to the trade associations, it has done so as a stalling tactic. It has asked the association to mount a study of an issue in order to give the company slack time with which to formulate and initiate its own position on an issue.

In terms of the company's relationships with regulators, Delta line and staff executives like to believe that they conduct themselves in a professional manner. "It is important to maintain good relations with the state insurance commissioners," said one senior line manager, "because if you have their support you can get things through the state legislature more frequently." He continued, however, by conceding that, "Taking a bold, free-enterprise stand on issues can be a handicap in maintaining those relationships. But we don't worry about some states in which all insurance companies have a bad image." When an external affairs professional was asked how he thought the company was viewed by state regulators, he replied, "We probably have a pretty high profile in many of the state insurance departments, and I think they perceive us quite favorably, although not uniformly. We actually had to get to the point of suing one commissioner. We licked him, of course; and once other commissioners saw what we were doing, we got approval for our project in every state."

On balance, the external affairs strategy pursued by Delta is more individualistic than adversarial in nature. What enacts and drives an external affairs activity is company self-interest. Because of its unique business strategy and exposure, Delta is seldom accompanied by its industry peers in its relatively few forays into the corporate social environment. Delta executives prefer to maintain good relationships with industry regulators and to become involved with them early in negotiations concerning emerging issues and regulatory initiatives that are high in company relevance. Because relatively few issues or initiatives fit the company-relevance criterion, Delta is frequently able to pursue external affairs on its own terms, which include avoiding whenever possible consensus-based decision making and position taking with other life insurance majors. But Delta is also prepared to take regulators to court if it cannot otherwise achieve its agenda; and it's well equipped to do so. Another unique characteristic of this company is that a large majority of both its external affairs professionals and its senior line managers are lawyers with substantial work experience in the corporate law department.

External Affairs Design

The corporate external affairs function at Delta is a very simple operation. Its structure is low in breadth and depth and is chairman dominated.

There are no core external affairs departments; instead, members of the corporate law department team with members of the technically oriented actuarial function to analyze the relatively few issues that affect Delta's narrow business line and focused market niche. These teams also lobby regulators and legislators on behalf of the company.[4] The locus of initiation and decision making, however, does not reside with these ad hoc teams. They do the legwork for a senior management steering committee that serves as a forum for discussion in which the perspectives of the different functional areas within the company are expressed.[5] The committee meets on a schedule that is dictated by the flow of company-related, external affairs issues and events. All final decisions regarding the determination of whether to mount an issues-analysis effort, to engage in an intensive lobbying effort, or to take a company position on an issue, however, are made by Delta's chairman. As one senior vice president explained,

> If you want an honest picture of what happens, the company is very much dominated
> by its Chairman. The [top management steering committee] is pretty much a sounding

board for things that are presented to a large group of top managers. It provides a vehicle for a lot of disciplines in the company to speak. In the committee everyone speaks his piece and the Chairman makes the decision.

In light of the company's traditional business exposure, this unstructured, chairman-dominated approach to understanding and managing the corporate social environment is viewed as satisfactory by many of the company's senior managers. As one senior executive summarized for me, "Until the problems of government affairs become more complicated or more time consuming, our unstructured approach will keep cranking it out." Indeed, the dominant role played by the chairman is also welcomed by some of the company's external affairs professionals who prefer not to be chasing around for answers to external affairs questions when they know the chairman already has them! As one external affairs professional explained,

> I believe some of us feel that we're more effective because we know where the Chairman is going to come out and we don't go chasing down a lot of dark alleys and coming up with zero. We pretty much know when we're putting something together how he's going to come out on it.

The trigger or mechanism for getting top management attention to focus on a public policy issue is difficult to locate among the fragmented elements of the corporate external affairs function. Routine issues are generally handled by lawyer–actuary teams or by individual lobbyists in the field without active involvement of the top management steering committee. Nonroutine issues, however, come to management's attention through a variety of sources. The chairman is frequently the source of attention when he charges the committee or a subordinate staff team to focus on an issue. Other times, an issue attracts the attention of someone in the corporate law department. A senior vice president explained what usually happened then: "When knowledge comes to us that something is pending, the law department has rules about the persons to whom the information is to be circulated. But there is no one on the list who is designated to take action or to decide what to do. The information will go to six or eight people, and presumably one of them will recognize the need to do something."

Many executives believe that this unsystematic approach to issues management is still effective for Delta. But some have doubts about whether this is the best way to organize the external affairs function. These beliefs and doubts were summarized in the reflections of a company actuary who said,

> Our strength basically comes from the fact that we're a small company that has grown big. It is easy to talk to other people here. If something comes up, we all get together and decide what to do. It's done on a very informal, first-name basis. I guess the weakness would be the lack of formal organization, where someone has the buck and its his job to get this done. We have to rely on the hope that somebody will say, "Gee, we'd better do something here." Otherwise, something could fall through the cracks.

The part-time work of company lawyers and actuaries on external affairs issues is complemented by the full-time work of three individuals whose primary responsibilities lie in the external affairs area. One is a legislative counsel based in the corporate law department who has spent most of his time during the past 18 years as a regulatory lobbyist dealing almost exclusively with the insurance department and legislature in the company's home state; with somewhat less intensive responsibility for monitoring developments (e.g., new regulatory agendas and models) within the NAIC. He is supported at the state legislature by two free-lance lobbyists. One is a former Republican member of the state legislature; the other, a former state Democratic chairman.

The other attorney is based in the chairman's department, although he spends most of his time in Washington, D.C. He works on the general issues of taxation and inflation, normally indirectly in conjunction with the lobbying efforts of many other companies and industry groups. The third external affairs professional serves as a utility player, shifting his attention from federal to state activities as conditions warrant. His title of vice president, with no further description, implies that he serves as a high-level staff professional who works on issues of importance to Delta's chairman, to whom he reports. For instance, he served as the official company host for the site visit and the administration of the company survey.[6]

Two other small departments are peripherally related to Delta's external affairs function. A single-person department deals with customer inquiries and complaints and reports to the senior line manager in charge of insurance operations. This department monitors the market conduct and business practices of the company's exclusive agents. But as the head of the department explained, "We're in a delicate position because our company licenses general agencies who in turn license agents. We have no direct control over those agents because we are literally working through a general agent. Therefore, the only policing activity that we have over agents is to make recommendations to the general agent that an agent should be terminated or should no longer be permitted to sell a particular type of product." Finally, no systematic integrative mechanism has been developed within Delta to ensure coordination between this somewhat isolated, focused department and either the ad hoc teams or the senior management steering committee that are responsible for conducting the company's external affairs activities.

The other peripherally related department is public relations and advertising, which reports to the vice president of marketing. This department, however, focuses principally on managing the traditional public relations and advertising activities needed to support Delta's line operations. Moreover, its head was brought in from another industry. He was not regarded by his colleagues as knowledgeable about the insurance business and the unique corporate social environment surrounding it. In assessing the influence of both these departments, one Delta executive concluded, "These departments are viewed as relatively ineffective in the external affairs area and noninfluential in external affairs decision making."

Executive Reflections on the External Affairs Function

When given the opportunity to take a critical look at the company's current approach to external affairs, Delta executives identified several areas that they believed needed improvement. First, some of the individuals who are involved in the day-to-day, external affairs process believed that not enough attention and focus was being devoted to this function.[7] As one external affairs professional explained, "When external affairs is a part-time responsibility for many people, it is really anyone's responsibility. As a company we are spread too thin. External affairs requires thought, direction, and more formal time allocation, instead of a lot of part-time responsibilities."

His concern also included the lack of involvement of line managers.[8] "In the line operations we're so busy 'doing' that we don't have much time to think," he said. "I believe this reflects a short-sighted management philosophy; one that views line managers as individuals who don't need time to think, but who are here just to get things done." One of his suggestions for improving this situation was to rotate line managers through external affairs positions. "They can bring the line perspective to external affairs," he said. "And having had external affairs experience, line managers could bring something back to the line operation. That is what we are missing, very much so."

Another frequently mentioned area for improvement concerned the lack of coordination among the various elements involved in corporate external affairs. As one Delta executive explained, "Presently there is *no* coordination except that provided hit-or-miss by the Chairman. Government relations activities are proliferated among several staff and line departments and much of it is handled by amateurs. Our public relations staff generally is ignorant of the insurance business and of legislative and regulatory matters."

Third, a few managers recognized the need for more external affairs depth. One executive argued forcefully for the need to "more clearly identify responsibility for raising and managing issues." And another expressed his concern about the changing nature of the insurance business in which Delta operated. He said, "The world is changing. The tax laws are changing. Definitions of group insurance are changing. New definitions have been adopted by the state insurance commissioners. And I believe these are things we cannot continue to ignore."

Some Delta senior line executives also felt that the chairman should allow them to delegate down the line more of the decisions regarding day-to-day operations so that they can spend more time on critical external affairs issues. "I have a strong feeling," observed one senior line executive, "that the top officers of the company do not spend as much time on these issues as they ought to. We need to be delegating as much of the everyday operating decisions as we can down the line, so that vital external affairs issues can have the time of top management that they really deserve."

Finally, some of Delta's executives had begun to recognize the need for more systematic measurement and evaluation of the roles played by company executives in corporate external affairs. "I don't think we pay as much attention as we ought to in the evaluation of performance to how managers deal with public issues." Indeed, in terms of the extent to which the company's planning and review system explicitly incorporates external affairs issues, Delta line and staff executives report the lowest level of attention to these issues of all companies selected for intensive study, as revealed in the company surveys. Moreover, both line and staff executives at Delta report the lowest level of perceived career and advancement potential as a consequence of their work in the area of corporate external affairs.[9]

It is not surprising, therefore, that an oversight committee composed of Delta policyholders recently questioned the company's approach to understanding and managing its relations with the corporate social environment. In the committee's 1981 report, one of the issues raised for top-management attention read as follows: "Senior management now assumes a greater role in representing the company to its external constituencies. . . . Whether the conventional pattern of a Chairman/President leadership structure will be responsive to these burdens is a matter deserving careful consideration. A thorough assessment of alternative structures should be made by senior management . . . before final decisions are made."[10]

Despite all of these shortcomings, the low breadth and low depth of Delta's external affairs structure generally fit the degree of its business exposure, which is low. Moreover, because the process is chairman dominated and borne principally via a top management steering committee, at least the company's senior line managers become involved in discussions concerning the most critical external affairs issues confronting the company. These factors alone probably account for much of the reason why Delta's mixed corporate social performance rating is positively skewed. Moreover, the company's low business exposure to social and political issues in the industry together with its sophisticated customer mix give Delta a relatively low profile in the corporate social environment and among the state insurance commissioners. In general, these organizational characteristics help to support an external company reputation for corporate *responsibility*.

However, Delta's highly individualistic, legally driven, enterprise-oriented strategy has become highly visible during recent lobbying efforts in the corporate social environment. The company's hard-line stands on recent issues of critical importance to its peculiar self-interests have generated criticism and suspicion among outside constituencies about its *responsiveness* to events and trends in the corporate social environment.

Whether Delta can continue to operate in this manner without risking further deterioration of its reputation with important constituencies and with its industry peers is a legitimate question that, as the policyholder review committee has recommended, deserves top management consideration.

Other developments within the industry are also beginning to increase the burdens already shouldered by Delta's chairman. For example, recent mergers between life insurance companies and financial brokerage firms have resulted in hybrid companies that may be able to offer more attractive packages of insurance and financial services than Delta can provide.[11] Such packages would be particularly appealing to Delta's sophisticated customers. Also, rapid changes in the investment side of the insurance business may begin to sap more senior management energy and expertise. As Delta executives attempt to respond to these developments they may also increase the company's exposure to the social and political environment. These current and potential future developments raise serious doubts about the efficacy of Delta's chairman-dominated approach to just about everything.

ENDICOTT

> *It might be that we would judge ourselves as effective only if all the state insurance commissioners rated us among the worst-five companies.*
> Senior External Affairs Officer

In contrast to Delta, Endicott is a highly exposed, multiple-line insurer that depends largely on personal insurance products, most of which are sold in states east of the Mississippi River. The company's current executive leader not only rose from the line-management ranks, but also spent a significant part of his career as head of Endicott's public affairs department. As might be expected, he has focused considerable attention since becoming president on building a stronger external affairs function.

This developmental effort has enabled Endicott to couple its traditional, enterprise-oriented, top management philosophy with an explicit external affairs strategy. This strategy is more individualistic and more adversarial than any encountered in the companies selected for comparative study. It is backed not only by a committed executive leader and a high-breadth external affairs design, but also by a new, company-sponsored, political action committee (PAC).

Management Philosophy and External Affairs Strategy

Executive leaders at Endicott share a deep-seated, free-enterprise view of the role of their company in society. Both the current president and the new senior external affairs officer are convinced that government regulation has become excessive in the insurance industry and that fundamental managerial prerogatives have been eroded by conciliatory responses by leading companies to emerging, insurance-related, public policy issues. These beliefs are reinforced by the previous experiences of these highly influential executives.

The president had served as the head of Endicott's small public affairs function during a period in which the company had been repeatedly surprised by new public issues and innovative regulatory initiatives that directly affected its major product lines. On several occasions, Endicott representatives had sallied forth into the social and political environment only to be rebuffed because of their inability to articulate and press for acceptance of their positions. One senior executive reflected on this difficult period as follows: "Until the vice president of external affairs arrived and started doing his show, we were seen as being absolute pushovers to regulators. Also, we were not regarded highly by our key competitors. Quite frankly, they regarded us with great disdain, because we would give in and make it very difficult for them to try to push for more from the regulators."

The new vice president of external affairs is an experienced attorney who had also served as a state insurance commissioner, during which time he had been heavily involved in the activities of the NAIC. In his opinion, the central office of the NAIC had become "a new branch of government." When asked to describe the new vice president of external affairs, one company executive said, "He feels strongly that the insurance industry has been overrun by regulation. When he joined us he believed that the company had to gear up to deal in the corridors of political power."

Given the shared view of the role of Endicott and the nature of its social environment, it should not come as a surprise that this company has developed perhaps the most individualistic and adversarial external affairs strategy of all the firms in the intensive study. Within months of his arrival, the new vice pesident of external affairs began to develop a high-breadth external affairs function that is oriented primarily toward lobbying tailored to each of the segments of the corporate social environment that the company believes is important to its business stakes and protecting the status quo in its line operations. Under his leadership the company had also assembled one of the most substantial employee-based, political action committees in the industry.

When asked to identify companies that were doing an especially good job in the area of corporate external affairs, Endicott executives were quick to point to companies that also pursued a highly individualistic/adversarial strategy. Indeed, the vice pesident of government affairs piqued my attention when he described the competitor he admired most as follows:

> What I admire about the company is that they'll sue the hell out of regulators! They go to outside law firms and lobbyists. They hire gunmen, hitmen, you see. They're free-wheeling!

When these same executives were asked about the companies that had caused trouble in this domain, they identified insurers that were led by executive leaders whom they regarded as being "too conciliatory." When pressed to explain the differences between the two company groups, the government affairs executive replied, "The only way to explain the different approaches [of companies] is in terms of the personalities at the top. . . . It all depends on your political philosophy. You have to decide how much you fold and give in to people, many of whom are not gainfully employed. They are probably out on the public dole to discredit the economic system!''

The bare-knuckles approach to external affairs at Endicott is perhaps best illustrated by the response made by the new vice president during my debriefing, in which I reported the company's low-mixed rating on corporate social performance. His blunt response at this gathering of the heads of all of Endicott's core external affairs units was, "It might be that we would judge ourselves as effective only if all the state insurance commissioners rated us among the worst-five companies!"[12]

The philosophy-strategy connection at Endicott is also reflected in certain reorientations in its overall business strategy and in its relationships with industry trade associations. Not only has the company recently withdrawn business from "highly politicized" states, but it has repositioned itself to shift its business concentration from east to west of the Mississippi where its leaders believe that is more growth potential and less political and social risk. Endicott has also begun to chart its own course with respect to industry trade associations. As one external affairs professional explained,

> We've been getting *killed* by relying on the trade associations; some of the people in the trade associations don't want to make the state insurance departments mad. Our position is that if you're in a fight, you'd better let the insurance department know they're being opposed in one way or another. So, we now exercise our *own* leadership. No doubt about it.

The new posture of Endicott with respect to the corporate social environment sets the company apart from most of its competitors. The company has begun to take a bold, free-enterprise approach, bolstered by an intensified external affairs strategy that has provided a lot of excitement not only within its core external affairs function but also within the industry. This bold departure from Endicott's historical posture in corporate external affairs is perhaps best summarized in the point of view expressed by the current vice president of government affairs, when he said,

> Too frequently company executives say, "We don't really get involved much in politics." The life insurance companies are most likely to give you that response. They want to stop the really big things. But too frequently, when you take that attitude, you're killed before you even know what's hit you. Most of the companies are not making any commitment to the political environment. However, when it catches up with them, all of a sudden they're very likely to come right to us.

External Affairs Design

Endicott operates with a high-breadth external affairs function that is well suited to its heavy exposure to the corporate social environment. This function is a vastly more sophisticated version of the function that had been in place less than five years earlier. As one of the company's senior staff professionals observed, "The corporate external affairs department has been developed during the last three years. The company had been too reactive so a superstar was brought in." Moreover, the external affairs function is self-contained. All of the core units report directly to its architect, the senior external affairs officer, who in turn reports directly to Endicott's president.

Contained within Endicott's core external affairs function are the following units:

- public relations, which is made up of public affairs, media affairs, and internal corporate communications,
- government affairs, which is broken down into (state) regulatory relations, (state) legislative relations, and federal relations,
- industry relations,
- customer relations,

Also included are a couple of small units that deal with external relationships that are unique to Endicott's business strategy and product lines. Thus, this high-breadth function is structurally differentiated according to the segments of the corporate social environment that create the most important contingencies for the company's primary business lines.

Responsibility for external affairs is drawn quite clearly around these core units. Both the traditional corporate legal function and the product advertising function, which reports to the vice president of marketing, lie outside the core external affairs function. As we shall see, so do Endicott's basic line operations.

Staff professionals within the core function take considerable pride in their work. Most of these staff professionals are attorneys or MBA's that have been handpicked by the senior external affairs officer. None have had substantial line-management experience in the company.

Among all companies surveyed, external affairs professionals at Endicott were the most satisfied with the work performed by their units. They also perceived the greatest degree of career and promotional potential from their work. Moreover, when questioned about how important to the success of their company external affairs activities are relative to the performance of the firm's basic businesses, core staff professionals at Endicott attached much greater importance to external affairs activities than did their counterparts in the other companies surveyed.

Given the consolidated and focused nature of this core function, external affairs activities at Endicott are among the most tightly coordinated in the companies studied.[13] Although the core function has grown rapidly during the past five years, the fact that all units report directly to a highly committed and involved external affairs superstar facilitates coordinated action. That this person also handpicked his subordinates reinforces their pursuit of his external affairs values and agenda.

Endicott's new political action committee.   In addition to a new and expanded core external affairs function, Endicott has recently organized what company officials refer to as a "grass-roots" political action committee (PAC) to support its lobbying effort at the corporate level. At the time of the study, the company boasted a PAC membership of 7,000 employees, which was supported through payroll deductions and organized by region. When asked how the company was able to enlist such broad-based support for its new PAC, the vice president of government affairs replied,

> Just last year members of my staff went to all our regions. We made 75 presentations to all of our executive and administrative personnel. Two weeks before we got to them they received a letter from the company president in which he said, "We hope that you'll consider supporting this." When we arrived, we gave them the "soft approach." There was no arm twisting or anything like that. But we asked them to go for payroll deductions. We went out on this two years in a row.

The vice president continued by explaining that PAC members receive monthly bulletins, "which tell them what is happening in the political arena that might impact on the business of insurance and on their jobs." He said, "On occasion we issue an action call, which asks members to become directly involved with a state or federal legislator. There is nothing like this network in our industry."

The corporate external affairs function also maintains a "political contact index," a file that summarized employee relationships with state and federal legislators. "We file them by congressmen," explained the government affairs officials. "We just go to the file and pick one out; and we can get to that person very quickly." The company has even produced films that encourage its rank-and-file employees to assume a more active lobbying role on behalf of Endicott.

Some Important Design Flaws

These potential strengths, however, reveal some of the weaknesses in Endicott's external affairs design. Some of these weaknesses result directly from Endicott's top management philosophy and external affairs strategy; others may be attributed to the early stage of development of the company's expanded external affairs function.

Lack of line-manager involvement.   Because of the strong, enterprise-oriented view of Endicott's role in society, relatively low emphasis is put on the possibility of changing a business policy or practice in response to events and trends in the corporate social environment. Instead, the external affairs strategy principally emphasizes *representing* the company's unique business interests and *protecting* the status quo of its line operations from social and political threats. Not surprisingly, Endicott's external affairs activities are conceived and enacted with minimal involvement from the company's line operations.

Indeed, Endicott may be distinguished from all the companies studied on the degree of separation between elements of its line and staff operations. This fact was brought forcefully to my attention when I arrived for the company visit. As mentioned before I discovered that the dates chosen by the senior external affairs executive were the only ones during the year when virtually all of Endicott's senior line managers were scheduled to be away for a line-management retreat. With some reluctance this executive arranged for me to meet with one senior line manager and, subsequently, to have the other senior line managers complete and return the company survey. Their survey responses confirmed by suspicion about the lack of line-manager involvement in corporate external affairs.

When the survey responses of all companies were compared, senior line managers at Endicott scored highest on the extent to which they believed that the responsibility for helping the company understand and manage public affairs issues lies with external affairs staff professionals, as opposed to line managers. These same line managers report that they are less likely than their counterparts in the other companies to be consulted when external affairs units are formulating their plans and developing new programs. Moreover, Endicott's senior line managers reported that their external affairs recommendations are less likely to be factored into the formal planning and review process used by the company to monitor and evaluate their operations than did their line-management counterparts in the other companies. A similar situation exists in terms of the current measurement and reward system for line managers. As one company official explained,

> Right now we have in the creation process a Compensation Committee. Some of the things we are putting in the rating system are contacts with legislators and regulatory officials. So, we are working on this. But right now you don't get any damned reward at all for doing these things.

Given the almost complete separation of operating and external affairs responsibilities at Endicott, it should not be surprising that both its senior line managers and its corporate external affairs professionals report the least amount of mutual understanding of each other's function among all line and staff executives surveyed. The consequences of this lack of line–staff integration in corporate external affairs activities is dramatically illustrated in Figure 10-1, which reveals that Endicott senior line managers believe that their external affairs function is far less responsible to their operational needs than do senior line managers in the other companies studied.

The effects of this line–staff dichotomy in external affairs are potentially exacerbated by Endicott's decentralized line operations. Products are delivered through a dozen or so regional offices located throughout the United States. Each regional office operates like a semiautonomous profit center. Therefore, its business practices and market conduct activities, which figure heavily in the state commissioners' assessments of overall corporate social performance, may vary widely from those of other regional offices and may be quite inconsistent with the signals communicated to external constituencies from the headquarters staff. As one of the company's senior executives explained,

> The senior line managers and the regional managers who report to them rarely have any role in setting any of these political issues. I mean *nothing!* In other words, the line

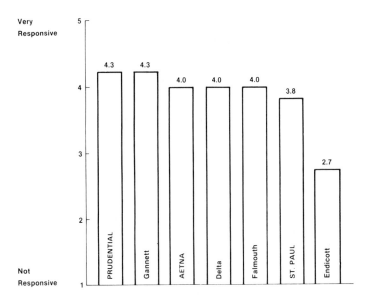

Figure 10-1   Survey responses of senior line managers on how responsive they feel the corporate external affairs function is to their needs.

managers have *no* role in these things! There is struggle going on within the company right now on the issue of who sets corporate policy on these things.

Lack of external affairs depth.   External affairs depth is another problem for Endicott, and one that is generally recognized by the new staff. As one staff professional observed, "We're now trying to recognize a public issue before it gets into the political environment so that we can bring to bear our public relations expertise and other communications skills. That's a major challenge, and one that we're just beginning to develop greater skills on."

The company has developed a position index that contains one-page summaries of its official positions on approximately 75 issues. However, the approach to developing these positions is managed by a junior staff member and is generally confined to the Government Affairs Department, in which issues are parcelled out to various members of the staff. Very little committee work is involved, and very little line-management input is sought. As one staff member explained, "We figure you're not going to get a blasted thing done by committees; so most of the work on an issue is done inside the government affairs group."

Issue identification is another problem facing Endicott's external affairs function. "We believe that public issues have a life cycle that follows a bell curve," said the vice president of Government Affairs. "You start to get public interest in an issue fairly early in the form of complaints. Then the complaints start to mount and they crescendo. At that point, maybe two years after the issue first emerges, it gets into the political environment." When asked at what point in the issue life cycle

Endicott generally begins to take notice, the vice pesident responded, ''To be really accurate, I'd have to say that most of the issues described in our position index are those that have already appeared in the political environment.''

In summary, Endicott's recent attempts to cope with its high business exposure have met with mixed success. The expanded breadth of its core external affairs function now matches its high degree of exposure. But both the guiding philosophy and external affairs strategy of the company, together with the early stage in the development of the new core function, have combined to create some important shortcomings in how Endicott attempts to understand and manage the corporate social environment.

To be sure, the early stage of development of the core external affairs function contributes to this shortfall. As one external affairs professional observed, ''One of our main challenges is to be more substantively oriented to public issues; but we are currently learning from implementation.'' However, the strategic orientation toward protecting and defending the status quo of the company's business operations, provides a rationale for minimizing the involvement of line managers in the process by which the core external affairs function develops its plans and programs. This same orientation probably accounts for the minimal involvement of line managers in the process of issues identification and analysis.

SUMMARY

The mixed-rated companies fall in the middle of the internal-consistency continuum between the best-rated and worst-rated corporate social performers when they are subjected to a diagnosis that is guided by the general framework. In general, Table 10-1 reveals that they have achieved external affairs breadth that is commensurate with their current exposure to the corporate social environment. Moreover, they are more similar to the best-rated companies than to the worst-rated companies in terms of one important aspect of the philosophy-strategy connection. They, together with the best corporate social performers, pursue an explicit external affairs strategy that derives directly from the views of their executive leaders about the role of the company in society. But similarities between the best- and mixed-rated companies end here.

The mixed-rated companies pursue the same top-management philosophy and external-affairs strategy as do the worst-rated companies. These two groups differ, however, in that the mixed companies do a better job in pursing their philosophy and strategy than do the worst companies. For the mixed-rated companies, an enterprise-oriented philosophy is tied to an explicit external affairs strategy that is individualistic and adversarial in nature. For the worst rated companies, the same philosophy-strategy connection exists, only the strategy is not explicit. Moreover, there is a better degree of fit between business exposure and some elements of external-affairs design for the mixed companies than for the worst corporate social performers.

TABLE 10-1 Comparative Summary of the Mixed Companies

Companies	Business Exposure	Management Philosophy	External Affairs Strategy	External Affairs Design		
				Breadth	Depth	Line–Staff Balance
Delta	Low	Enterprise oriented →		Low	Low	Chairman dominated
Endicott	High		Individualistic/Adversarial →	High	Low	Staff dominated

These patterns of similarities and differences provide a finer-grained demonstration of the power and utility of the general framework than the simple comparisons of the best and worst companies alone. *The nature and explicitness of the philosophy-strategy connection appears to be more powerful as a predictor of corporate social performance than the degree of fit achieved in the exposure-design contingency.* Moreover, the effects of high line-manager involvement in corporate external affairs appears to depend substantially on the particular form of top-management philosophy and corporate character of the firm.

Together, the full range of company comparisons reveals that considerable variance in corporate social performance can be accounted for by the general framework, and that this framework has promise as a tool for organizational diagnosis and intervention by executive leaders to help their organizations understand and manage the corporate social environment.

FOOTNOTES

1. The president of Delta, who had been on the job only a couple of weeks at the time of the site visit, struggled hard to identify some social and political issues that were important to his company. After mentioning the company's emphasis on policyholder benefit, he hit upon the subject of corporate "social" investments. As evidence of the company's commitment to socially worthwhile investments he explained that, "We turned down Atlantic City gambling investment opportunities."

2. The president of Delta explained the company's bold response to the policyholder loan issue as follows: "We were hit harder than the other major life insurers because we have more sophisticated policyholders. Therefore, we wanted to get the interest rate ceiling on policyholder loans raised. But the American Council of Life Insurers (ACLI) was not willing to go along. So we went on our own. Basically, the ACLI tends to represent the lowest common denominator in the life insurance industry. We try to be team players, but often we have to go out on our own."

3. Analysis of the company surveys revealed that external affairs professionals at Delta engage in less contact with the industry trade associations than do their counterparts in any of the other companies selected for intensive study.

4. Despite the fact that a primary means used by Delta for dealing with external affairs issues is to set up small, temporary task forces between company lawyers and actuaries, this company convenes task forces less frequently than any of the other companies in the comparative study, as revealed in the survey responses of external affairs professionals.

5. Membership on this top management steering committee includes the chairman and chief executive officer; the president; the senior vice presidents of sales, investments and agencies; the general counsel; and the corporate actuary.

6. After this vice president's retirement during the year following the site visit, his position was filled by a former Delta insurance agent and line manager who did not regard his primary area of responsibility as corporate external affairs.

7. Company survey results revealed that external affairs professionals at Delta spend less time per week exclusively engaged in external affairs activities than do their counter-

parts at any of the other companies selected for intensive study. For example, staff executives at Delta spend on average only 19.3 hours per week in external affairs activities as compared to an average of 33.8 hours per week by their counterparts in the other companies that received a best or mixed rating on overall corporate social performance.

8. A portion of the company survey examined the extent to which public affairs issues and events were important to people performing various line roles in the company. The specific survey question was, "Relative to other management topics, how important are public affairs issues and events to people performing the following roles in your company?" Based on the survey responses of senior line managers from all participating companies, Delta reported the lowest external affairs responsibility for its senior line managers, middle-level line managers, field managers, and insurance agents.

9. The low level of perceived career and advancement potential that Delta line and staff executives associated with external affairs activities was approached by their counterparts in only one other company in the comparative study. This company is Falmouth. These two companies are further distinguished from the other companies in the intensive study in that both are characterized as having chairman-dominated, external affairs functions.

10. On the eve of the site visit at Delta, a new position of president had been created and filled that reported directly to the chairman. The intention of this change in the organization structure had been to facilitate more delegation of operational decisions by the chairman. However, at the time of the visit the new president had not begun to assume his full duties; therefore, it was too early to ascertain what real changes in top management decision making would be realized. Even with this change, however, the policyholder review committee remained skeptical about the extent to which the company would be able to improve its effectiveness in the external affairs domain.

11. Daniel Hertzberg, "Life Insurers Start Offering Policies that Look More Like Investments." *Wall Street Journal,* February 23, 1983, p. 31.

12. Whether by plan or habit, the responses I received during the initial interviews with key members of Endicott's external affairs function provided additional confirmation on the company's individualistic/adversarial approach. During those interviews I was deluged with external affairs reports, company position statements, and public relations releases. Moreover, after reviewing the interview transcripts, I realized that I had barely been able to get a word in edgewise! Not once did these officials ask me about the purposes of my interviews or specifically about how the information I was collecting was to be used. In short, the interviews amounted to one-way communication exercises, the general nature of which may serve to capture Endicott's overall approach to external affairs.

13. In the comparative analysis of the company surveys Endicott was tied with two of the best-rated companies (Aetna and St. Paul) in having the highest degree of mutual influence among elements of the core external affairs function. Moreover, Endicott ranked third among the companies in terms of the extent to which external affairs professionals accorded high importance to their relationships with staff professionals in other core external affairs units.

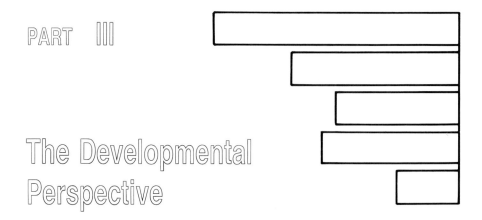

PART III

The Developmental Perspective

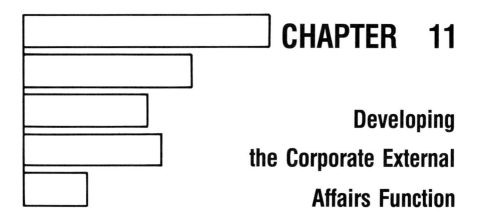

CHAPTER 11

Developing
the Corporate External
Affairs Function

External affairs depth has been shown to be an important factor affecting the way a firm approaches the task of understanding and managing the corporate social environment. Yet out of all the factors in the general framework, it is the least understood by executive leaders. Therefore, I would like to share some of the insights I obtained during five years of work as an action-researcher and consultant in the development of Aetna's Public Policy Issues Analysis Department (IA), the staff unit that was explicitly created by the company's executive leaders to facilitate managerial learning about the corporate social environment and to catalyze needed changes in the traditional business policies and practices of the company's line operations.

In addition, I have become increasingly excited about the prospects of the developmental perspective for enhancing both the theory and practice of organization and management.[1] Indeed, the entire comparative study summarized earlier in this book is a by-product of my original intention of tracking the creation and development of an innovative staff unit in an established organizational context. Thus, work began on the developmental study in the spring of 1978, shortly after the decision had been made to create Aetna's Issues Analysis Department, but before its cofounders had conceptualized its mission, developed its internal structure and process, and begun to build relationships with existing line and staff units.

I worked intensively with the cofounders of IA and their sponsor, Aetna's chief operating officer, for a period of two years before initiating the comparative study of corporate social performance in the industry. I entered the organization to learn about the practice of a subject I then referred to as organization–environment relations. I had studied this phenomenon from an outsider's viewpoint by focusing on how the tobacco "Big Six" corporations had responded to the smoking-and-health controversy.[2] But my outside-observer role in the cigarette industry study deprived me of the opportunity to learn about how corporate executive leaders managed their responses to the smoking-and-health controversy. At the same time, I was working with a faculty colleague on a book that we both hoped would stimulate the field of organization theory to pursue the development of organizations over time more seriously than was popular at the time. Thus, my initial reasons for gaining access to IA's creation was to observe at close range both the process by which large organizations adapt to a changing social environment and the creation and development of an innovative staff unit within an established organizational context.

However, as the following account of IA's creation and development will reveal, I quickly became a part of the developmental process I had intended to study. I worked closely with the cofounders of IA as they developed their work process, negotiated relations between their new department and established line and staff units, and launched their first activities. I also conducted surveys of the members of the corporate external affairs units and the business divisions at three points in time: during the first three months after creation of IA, three years later, and again during the comparative study of corporate social performance. The results of each survey were fed back into the company in the form of written reports and presentations to representatives of all relevant line and staff groups. They were followed up by focused group discussions with different units and divisions of the company that desired more in-depth discussions of the patterns and implications of the survey results.

During the first two years of my involvement with Aetna I also attended many of the important meetings that focused on the executive leaders' agenda to make Aetna more responsive to the corporate social environment and the development of IA. I debriefed IA's task forces for the purpose of helping the new department refine its task force leadership skills. Finally, I wrote a chronological description of the creation and development of IA, which appears in original form as Episodes II and III and was delivered to Aetna for circulation among its senior line managers and corporate external affairs professionals and subsequently used in my Harvard Business School classes.

But at the end of the first two years, I decided to take a more distant position with respect to the developmental process. First, it was obvious that IA's launch, although predictably difficult, had been successful. The department had effectively passed through the creation stage and was well into the developmental stage. Some time would have to pass in order to assess whether IA or its process would become institutionalized within Aetna. So I decided to periodically check on the progress of IA while waiting until the new department matured.

Second, having discovered how Aetna was organized to understand and manage the corporate social environment, I became intensely curious about *how well* it was performing this task. Working as I had with Aetna for two years gave me a considerable amount of insight into the insurance industry as a whole. By then I understood the language of the industry, the major business and social issues confronting it, and a good deal about the strategies that separate the major companies.

With all that industry-specific knowledge, and having to wait for the maturation of IA, I launched the comparative study reported earlier in this book.

As a developmental researcher, I got used to being asked over the next three years by my Harvard Business School colleagues, "How's the Aetna project coming along?" A few were perplexed when I replied that I was waiting for things to mature before concluding the project. The waiting, as it turns out, provided many insights that otherwise would have been lost in haste.

These insights reach into the advanced stages of IA's development, including its attempt to become institutionalized within the organization. And they apply not only to the creation and management of a high-depth, external affairs function, but also more generally to the creation and development of innovative staff units in established organization contexts.

ORIENTATION TO THE DEVELOPMENTAL EPISODES

The episodes that follow describe IA's development during its first five years.[3] Episode I summarizes the immediate context in which IA was created, identifies the precipitating factors in the event, and reveals some of the choices that were made for IA by executive leaders before the start up of this new department.

Episode II focuses on the creation of IA. It summarizes the early choices of IA's cofounders, the initiation of a work process, the negotiation of mission and turf with established line and staff units, and the reactions of IA members and their counterparts in other line and staff units to these choices and events. Episode III carries IA's development through its second year and focuses principally on reflections from various functional points of view about IA's progress.

Episode IV captures IA at the five-year mark; first summarizing developments during the preceding three years and then commenting on IA's efforts to become institutionalized within the company. These episodes illustrate what executive leaders and core staff professionals are required to do to ensure the successful launching of a high-depth external affairs function. The next chapter concludes the developmental study with a summary of the more general implications of the developmental analysis for the creation and management of innovative staff units within established organizational contexts.

EPISODE I: THE CONTEXT OF ORGANIZATIONAL INNOVATION

Aetna's decision in 1978 to create the new Issues Analysis Department was made within an organizational context that has been described in Chapter 7. But one fundamental aspect of that context is similar to the contexts that had evolved in most large American corporations at the time. The divisionalized corporate structure had emerged to meet the challenges posed by the operational scope and diversity typical of large, complex corporations.[4]

Divisionalized corporations, such as Aetna, operate on the basis of a separation of responsibilities between the corporate level and the divisional level of management. Executive leaders at the corporate level are responsible for setting the purposes, strategies, and policies of the corporation as a whole and for establishing and monitoring the performance standards and economic outcomes of the operating divisions. Under this organizational arrangement, the divisional profit-center executives are given considerable autonomy in determining how their line operations are going to meet the standards and policies established and monitored at the corporate level; and how well they perform these responsibilities largely determines their career and financial rewards. Importantly, the criterion for divisional performance are kept simple, since divisional managers are responsible for determining how their business objectives are to be achieved. This simplicity in the criterion for divisional performance, many believe, gives considerable motivational energy to the decentralized system of organization and management. This arrangement also attempts to place operating decisions at the level within the organization at which relevant business knowledge is greatest, while freeing executive leaders from the day-to-day operating decisions so that they can attend to corporate-level issues.

Although the divisionalized organizational structure has proved to be effective in enabling executive leaders to cope with the issues of huge scale and diversity in the large corporation, and consequently in facilitating corporate economic performance; this kind of organizational context also appears to be quite resistant to improvement efforts in the area of corporate social performance. Indeed, it tends to exacerbate a number of managerial dilemmas that are generally associated with the attempted reconciliation of economic and social demands imposed upon the large corporation.

An exploratory study of the attempts to increase the social responsiveness in two large, divisionalized corporations, that was conducted during the mid-1970s by Robert Ackerman, concluded that,

> For the chief executive of the decentralized corporation, the problem of securing responsiveness to social issues is compounded by the rules governing the interrelationships between corporate and division levels. The rules state that while the chief executive is obtaining and evaluating divisional results, he is not to meddle in the division's standard operating procedures. If he wants to change those procedures to coincide with the spirit of the new corporate policy, he presumably must attempt it directly by changing the standards for judging performance.[5]

It was in this kind of structural context that the decision was made to create a corporate staff unit that would be called upon to facilitate the process of managerial learning about, and organizational adaptation to, the corporate social environment. Moreover, it was no secret in Aetna that the company's executive leaders believed division managers and their subordinates had the most to learn in this regard and would experience the greatest pressure for change, in their attitudes and orientations as well as their traditional business practices.

The Precipitating Factors

Aetna executives point to four factors that precipitated the decision to create the Issues Analysis Department as a means of developing greater depth in the company's external affairs process.

First, as a multiple-line insurer Aetna had been impacted by most of the social issues confronting the industry as a whole. As the number and salience of industry-specific issues increased, Aetna's executive leaders found it increasingly difficult to stay abreast, much less ahead of emerging issues. As their zone of discretion narrowed, they searched for a mechanism that could help the corporation and its divisions respond to this new strategic contingency. To make matters worse, the company's business divisions, following the traditional principal of operating autonomy, were either ignoring these social issues or responding in a manner that created problems at the corporate level. In short, Aetna was experiencing for the first time in its long history a strong sense that there was a social performance gap.

Second, for half a decade the current executive leaders had pursued an agenda that called for better corporate-level control and integration of diverse operations at the division level. One of the organizational moves in this direction that was a precursor to the decision to launch an Issues Analysis Department was the creation of a Corporate Management Committee, made up of the executive leaders and the heads of all the company's divisions. Formerly, relations between the corporate and divisional levels had been conducted on a one-to-one basis between the CEO or COO and the individual who headed one of the divisional profit centers.

Another early move by the new executive leaders involved the initiation of a corporate-level strategic planning process. Business planning had been viewed as primarily the responsibility of the autonomous divisional profit centers and had been conducted at that level in a manner deemed appropriate by the division head. The creation of the Corporate Planning Department shifted some of the responsibility for this function to the corporate level and pressed the division planners for greater quality and uniformity.

A variety of other moves were initiated by the executive leaders that were aimed at reinforcing their agenda. For example, a management succession planning process was initiated at the corporate level to give executive leaders a better handle on their most critical human resources in the operating divisions. The plan included the identification of high-potential employees who might be given early opportunities to develop on a fast career track; one that also included rotational assignments at the corporate level or in other business divisions. Very little deviation from a vertical career progression within a single division had been tolerated under the traditional decentralized arrangement.

Finally, Aetna's executive leaders had created new units or assigned functions to the corporate level they felt warranted greater intensity and consistency of response across the various business divisions. For example, the chief executive officer created a Corporate Social Responsibility Department to decide where extra profits (from the divisions) could be allocated to corporate philanthropy and social investment projects. The Affirmative Action component was transferred out of the personnel department and its people were placed in a department that reported directly to the CEO. From that position he could have greater access to current information about each division's progress in achieving corporate affirmative action objectives.

Given the trend set by all these moves toward a better integrated corporation, the emergence of inadequate or conflicting responses to social issues by profit-center managers had the effect of turning the attention of executive leaders to yet another area of needed improvement in corporate-division relations. The creation of IA, therefore, became part of this ongoing process of adaptation within Aetna. Indeed, the coincidence of this episode of corporate development and IA's creation made it possible for the new department to obtain unusually strong support and sponsorship from Aetna's executive leaders. However, it did so at a cost. Line executives tended to view the decision to create IA in political as opposed to substantive terms—as evidence of further corporate-level encroachment into their traditional managerial prerogatives.

The first two precipitating factors, however, only served to raise the level of dissatisfaction with the status quo in the organization. In so doing, they reinforced the perceived need of executive leaders for a mechanism to catalyze learning and change about the corporate social environment.

Perhaps the greatest obstacle in the path of developing a high-depth, external affairs process—for that matter, any staff function that is both new and different relative to the organizational context in which it is created—was the fact that Aetna's executive leaders did not know what kind of mechanism was needed. Prototypes for creating a corporate-level staff unit (especially one within a traditionally decentralized firm) that could create and manage a purposive process of managerial learning and organizational adaptation were not readily at hand. Nor did field visits to highly exposed corporations in other industries produce such a prototype. (Presumably, the available academic literature on this subject was either silent or hopelessly obfuscated!) In short, Aetna's executive leaders were not sure that such a staff mechanism was feasible.

What they did recognize was that the kind of broad perspective needed to analyze and understand industry-specific, social issues would likely not be found among line managers, who had to deal with day-to-day business problems and whose career tracks prevented them from developing a broad corporate perspective. For many of the same reasons, members of the operating divisions, long accustomed to "business as usual," would be unlikely candidates as catalysts of change in business policies and practices that might be required as part of the corporation's response to social issues.

Aetna's executive leaders also believed that existing external affairs units would fare little better than line managers with this task. The skills and orientations of members of the Government Relations and Corporate Communications units were well suited to the tasks of protecting the status quo of the business operations and managing the "face" of the company to its publics; tasks that are quite different, and in many respects opposite, from those being sought. Nor was the Corporate Social Responsibility department well suited for this role. Its head was a nationally recognized expert on corporate philanthropy and its mission focused primarily on that task and other highly specialized areas.

Under these circumstances, the third factor precipitating the creation of IA derived from an experience the COO had on a public policy commission sponsored by the White House. It was during that experience that he became convinced that a diverse group of individuals could come together under the right circumstances and make significant progress on clarifying ambiguous public policy issues and developing practical recommendations for responding to them. He was particularly impressed with the work of the government staff that was assembled to support the work of the task force members. Indeed, he actually invited one of those staff members, whose career had been confined to government service, to join in the ad hoc issues-analysis activities at Aetna. Shortly after her arrival at the company, she commented on the COO's outside experience as follows:

> I think that, by and large, the COO was very impressed with the staff that we had on the Commission. This was a new experience for him. I think he was particularly intrigued by the idea that you could bring together a group of people to study what he would characterize as a social issue and come up with a balanced perspective. I think he, having seen the value of it in that context, felt that it was something that his company could also be carrying out.

Thus, the chief operating officer returned to Aetna not only with a conviction that a similar approach could feasibly be introduced into the company, but also with some definite ideas about what kind of mechanism would have to be created and how it would be staffed and evaluated.

The last precipitating factor in the creation of IA was a combination of social stimulus and organizational response. During the period the chief operating officer was working on the outside commission, Aetna was caught by surprise when a major social issue affecting one of its primary product lines emerged quickly and received the immediate attention of politicians, industry regulators, and the public media.

Aetna's tardy response was to appoint a task force headed by the COO's special assistant to study the issue and make recommendations for dealing with it. The outside allegations about the nonavailability of product-liability coverage for U.S. manufacturers eventually proved to be without merit and lost its salience in the public arena; but the shock of the event spurred Aetna's executive leaders to seek a more permanent approach than ad hoc task forces to deal with similar issues in the future. The scare also served to raise, if only modestly, the level of line-manager dissatisfaction with the status quo, and therefore opened a window for the creation of IA.

In addition, the task-force approach adopted in haste proved to be useful in several respects. On the eve of the creation of IA, the special assistant to the president who had headed the product-liability task force, sent the COO a memorandum in which he assessed the merits of the task-force approach to social issues analysis and management. He said,

> Whatever the judgment may be as to the usefulness of the task force's study, we can report that the *process* itself was, in our opinion, an unqualified success. Therefore, assuming continuing endorsement of the need for a more intensive effort by Aetna to provide industry leadership in addressing insurance related public issues, consideration should be given to the continuation of the task force concept as the problem-solving mechanism. With respect to the Product Liability Task Force, its constituency was a good blend of various talents, personalities, and skills. Whether by luck or design, it was this factor which was most important in making the task force a success.

> Apart from the benefit derived from the interdivisional nature of the task force, the educational aspect of this process to the participants should be of continuing value in another sense, as the problem-solving, analytical approach we employed will undoubtedly be translated into each member's day-to-day activity. It may be putting it too strongly, but it is quite likely that the participants may never approach new problems in quite the same way again. The importance of developing a factual underpinning in analyzing problems can probably only be appreciated after having gone through the actual process.

Together, these precipitating events (summarized in Figure 11-1) created the need for innovation in the way Aetna approached the task of understanding and managing the corporate social environment, and gave key individuals insights into the kind of mechanism that would be required to achieve a high-depth, external affairs function.

The Decision to Create the Issues Analysis Department

The decision to create the new Issues Analysis Department was made by the COO, who also served as president of Aetna's insurance operations. He felt that there was a need for a corporate-level department that could serve as a clearinghouse for company- and industry-related social issues;

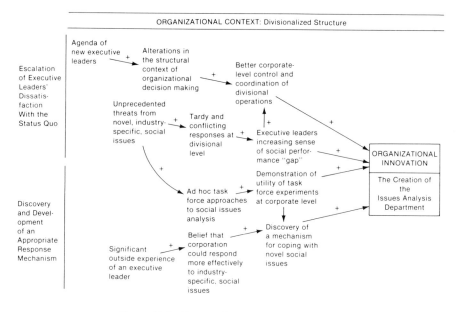

Figure 11-1   Context of organizational innovation.

one that would not only identify and and prioritize such issues, but when warranted would mount efforts to understand them and to help the company and its operating divisions cope with them. In fact, he believed that it would be possible for IA to serve as an agent of organizational learning *and* change.

The chief operating officer, Bill Bailey, promoted David Elliott, his special assistant as assistant vice president of the new Issues Analysis Department, and assigned Susan Bennett, the person he had brought to the company from the White House Commission, to assist Elliott in the design and implementation of the new department. Together, they were to build a corporate-level agency of managerial learning and organizational change with respect to the corporate social environment.

Bailey also made three decisions that members of the new department would have to live with. First, the divisional profit-center concept would remain. Second, he decided to evaluate the new staff department on two equal but potentially conflicting bases (1) the objectivity of its assessment of the nature and relevance of social issues affecting Aetna and (2) the extent to which its recommendations were implemented within the affected operating divisions. These criteria correspond to the learning facilitator and change catalyst roles envisioned for IA. Finally, Bailey decided that until IA established itself—a process that might take a few years—the new department would report directly to him.

**EPISODE II: THE CREATION OF AN INNOVATIVE STAFF
DEPARTMENT—THE FIRST YEAR**

During the spring of 1979, David Elliott, head of Aetna's Issues Analysis Department, was reflecting on the operation of his department that had been created only a year earlier. In particular, he was examining the initial choices he and Susan Bennett had made in designing and implementing the new department, the obstacles they had encountered, and the outcomes they had achieved or failed to achieve.

In general, David felt good about IA's first year, but he was concerned about the future of his department. By reviewing its short history, David was hoping to discover ways to enhance IA's contribution to the company and to sustain the early commitment and enthusiasm of its core members.

Initial Steps

Initial concerns (spring, 1978).   David was informed by Bill Bailey, the president of Aetna, in March 1978 that he would head IA. Looking back on the first few weeks following his assignment, Elliott recalled his major concerns at that time.

> . . . I was concerned, first of all, with attracting high-quality people . . . The most difficult job of this department would not be cranking out reports and doing the hard analytical work. It would be getting the confidence of the divisions and not being looked upon as just overhead that could be dispensed with very easily. My feeling was that to establish any credibility as a self-sustaining department, we would have to generate high-quality work . . . and the interaction of people with the divisional clients that we serve was extremely important. So I recognized the need to bring in some very analytical and intelligent people, but also people who could relate to others, gain their confidence, and establish some credibility.

> . . . Second, although the creation of this unit had the lip service support of the key corporate staff people at Aetna, it was possible they were merely going along with a decision they saw as inevitable . . . that the President wanted very much to create this unit. There was certainly a great deal of wonder as to the need for this type of unit.

> . . . Third . . . a turf consideration . . . The divisions probably felt that this type of staff unit was not needed and that they were doing an adequate job within the divisions on this type of work, because after all it is business related and it is their charge to focus on issues that impact their operations. But even if they didn't feel that they had these activities in place, they might very well feel that it shouldn't be a staff responsibility; that is should be a department located right within the division and controlled by each division head.

Note: The research assistance of Arvind Bhambri in preparing Episodes I and II is gratefully acknowledged.

. . . Fourth, at the corporate level there are two departments with which obviously there was a great deal of overlap; one being Government Relations—certainly the description of our department overlaps to a certain extent the government relations function. Second, the Corporate Planning Department would appear, probably to an outsider, to be the logical resting place for this department because of the nature of what it is doing.

Both David Elliott and Susan Bennett were also involved in follow-up work on the recommendations for organizational change proposed by a study of the "affordability" of insurance products that had just been completed by a task force within Aetna. Bennett described the reactions of senior line managers in the company's insurance divisions that compounded both her and David's concerns:

> The task force report, which was prepared largely by middle managers in the Property and Casualty Division, suggested that a lot of innovation take place in that Division. Even if the task force was philosophically opposed to some of the changes, we felt that they had to be accomplished if the insurance industry and Aetna in particular, were to gain any credibility with outsiders and to be perceived as a company that wanted change rather than resisted change. Almost without exception, people in the Property and Casualty Division would tell us that our report was excellent, that we did a good job, that we had solid analysis, and that we were concerned about the bottom line as well as about social responsibility; but, I think if there had been no Bill Bailey intervening, the Division might have read it, put it on a shelf, and just ignored it.

Initial decisions and priorities (early summer, 1978).   David and Susan translated these concerns into priorities for getting the new department off the ground and made two important decisions initially. First, they decided that the department would start small, and consist of the core group of professionals supplemented by part-time representatives from other corporate and divisional units who would serve on task forces led by IA members. As David explained, "I think there is a virtue in going slow at the beginning, to resist the natural tendency to let staff expand too fast." Second, they decided to get involved quickly in task force work, deferring the development of a comprehensive work plan for the new department until they had gotten IA off the ground. As they explained,

Susan Bennett:
The task force approach that has so far been employed has strong advantages—it utilizes experts from within the company in the areas being studied while including nonexperts for fresh perspective, and the composition of the task force makes it easier to "sell" the group's recommendations within the company. It also pays substantial dividends in terms of personnel development—it gives promising employees broader exposure to problems the

company faces, thereby not only making them better at their current jobs but also preparing them for more responsible positions.

David Elliott:
I wanted to have, immediately, some work to do in terms of task force projects. It was important to start with, I thought, not only an important project to establish credibility, but to try to balance the ledger a little bit by not necessarily dealing just with Property and Casualty Division issues, but also with the problems of other divisions.

They wasted little time before consulting with the Personnel Department and with Robert Clark, senior vice president of Corporate Administration, about staffing the department.[6] They were initially interested in attracting highly talented individuals who possessed strong analytical skills and represented different corporate and divisional perspectives. A few of the individuals they selected had been members of the early task forces, in which both David and Susan had had an opportunity to assess their performances and their orientations to this kind of work. Others were brought in directly from graduate school. The backgrounds of one core group they assembled are summarized in Table 11-1.

Initiation of public issues task forces (summer, 1978). Next they conducted a quick review of the major issues confronting the company, and decided to set up task forces for two of them. The first was the issue of insurance redlining in urban centers. It was surfaced by allegations that the insurance industry was denying casualty and property coverage to individuals and firms located in low-income urban areas; a practice that was at odds with public policy supporting urban renewal. Because Aetna's early success had been based on business in the major northeastern cities, its position on this issue was more critical than those of other major casualty insurance companies. The need to do something affirmative on this public issue, therefore, was felt not only by corporate management, but by managers in the property and casualty division as well.

The second issue selected for study was for the Life Insurance Division. It had not yet reached a critical stage and was more ambiguous. However, Dean Wolcott, senior vice president of the life division, had become concerned about the activities of regulatory commissions and public interest groups that focused on various issues involving the suitability of alternative forms of life insurance. In particular, there were allegations that the commissions paid to life insurance agents might not be justified in terms of the service they rendered. In addition, there was an active debate concerning the value of term as opposed to permanent life insurance. Spokespersons for outside interest groups saw more value in term insurance, whereas the insurance industry tended to promote permanent insurance

TABLE 11-1   The Core IA Staff: 1978

David Elliott (age 36).

Assistant vice president, Issues Analysis Department, a new department created in May 1978, to provide an analytical resource to the company on major public policy issues. David joined Aetna's Law Department in 1969 as an attorney in the casualty section. He was assistant to the president prior to his present position in charge of IA. David holds a B.A. in American studies and is a law school graduate.

Susan Bennett (age 26).

Joined Aetna in 1977 as manager, working on public policy issues under the president's office. She helped with the formation of IA in 1978. Before her employment at Aetna, she worked on a presidential study commission in Washington, where she was first recognized by Bill Bailey for her strong research and analytical skills. Susan holds a B.A. in American Studies.

Frances Callanan (age 40).

Joined Aetna in 1970 as a senior applications analyst in the Corporate Data Processing Department and from there became a systems administrator. In 1974 she was promoted to manager in the Corporate Accounting Department. Fran is presently manager in the IA Department. She received her B.S. in Mechanical Engineering.

Keith Stevenson (age 33).

Joined IA in October 1978 as manager after receiving his Ph.D. in Urban Studies from the Massachusetts Institute of Technology. He also holds a B.Sc. in Electrical Engineering, a B.A. in Engineering and Economics, and an M.S. in Operations Research. Keith had specialized in the health field and had served as consultant in health planning.

Jack Ericksen (age 30).

Joined IA during the summer of 1978 as a summer intern from the new Yale Master of Public and Private Management Program. After graduation in 1979 he became a manager in the IA Department. Jack holds a B.A. in Political Science and a Master of Social Work degree.

Mike Anstey (age 53).

Joined Aetna in 1968. He at first held the position of assistant secretary in the Personal Accounts Department of the Casualty Division in 1970, and in 1972 was promoted to director of the division's Planning Department. He joined IA as a director in 1978. Mike holds a B.S. in Business Administration.

Wes Stearns (age 35).

Joined Aetna in 1965 as a underwriting trainee in the Casualty Division. He joined IA as a manager in 1978. Wes holds a B.A. degree in Political Science and History.

policies. Therefore, Wolcott approached Elliott with a request to begin a study of these issues.

Each task force was led by an IA member and consisted of other IA staffers as well as part-time representatives from the line divisions, particularly the division affected most by the task force's analysis and recommendations. In the case of the redlining study, IA members screened potential candidates before approaching their superiors to obtain approval for their release. In contrast, the head of the life division made his own selection of his division's representatives to IA's task force study of alternative forms of life insurance. In both cases, the task force's representatives, from the divisions and from other corporate departments, received only partial release from their normal duties.

Analytical Framework of the Issues Analysis Department

Elliott and Bennett believed strongly that the broad analytical framework IA employed in analyzing public issues was not available elsewhere in the company. The business divisions were too preoccupied with the short-term operating performance of their profit centers and would, therefore, tend to justify the current business practices which had been built up over time in their divisions. The other corporate external affairs units, Elliott and Bennett believed, either were too focused on a particular segment of the outside world (e.g., Corporate Social Responsibility's charge to manage affirmative action and charitable contributions programs and the Environmental Analysis Group's focus on 5 to 10 year forecasts) or were oriented primarily toward influencing the environment as opposed to acting as a catalyst for organizational change (e.g., Government Relations and Corporate Communications).

I read several of the early task force reports to understand the basic analytical approach that was employed. It appeared that the frameworks took the general form of a medical analogy, and some of IA's final reports were organized using its components. The framework took the following form, adapted to the particular issue under study:

Phase I: Vague complaints about a product line or insurance business practice from various segments of the general public or institutional environment.

Phase II: Examination of the symptoms of the problem reported by industry critics.

Phase III: Diagnoses of causes of symptoms using data from interviews, work of other researchers, surveys of policyholders and field offices (e.g., commissioned studies by Cambridge Reports and Harris Polls), development of alternative scenarios, and the study of current Aetna business practices.

Phase IV: Prescription—conclusions and recommendations for company action.

The process memo. With members aboard and two task forces underway, the core group turned to the task of developing a comprehensive mission statement to guide its work processes. By the end of August, IA's process memo was complete.

The five key functions discussed in the Process Memo were[7]

1. *Issues Identification:* IA would serve as a clearinghouse for public policy issues for the company. It would prepare a general inventory of the

public issues that might affect the company and its business divisions. This would involve preliminary research to classify each issue on the basis of its relevance and immediacy. The initial issues inventory would be updated on a schedule compatible with the annual corporate and divisional planning cycle. Both internal and external sources would be used to build and update the inventory, and consistency would be maintained by assigning specific responsibility for the issues pertaining to one or more divisions to individual members of IA.

2. *Prioritization of Issues:* Next, IA would prioritize the issues in the inventory. A two-step process was to be used in setting these priorities. First, the issue would have to rank high in terms of its general importance (i.e., issues judged high on both relevance and immediacy). Second, issues surviving the first stage of selection were to be assessed by IA in terms of the impact an in-depth study of the issue would make in terms of potential contribution to company policy and public opinion.

3. *Selection of Issues for In-depth Study:* Taking into consideration the limitations of IA's staff and resources, each year the department would recommend to top management a list of public issues to be studied in depth. IA would also recommend some issues for study within the divisions. These recommendations were to be reviewed and approved by top management, and would serve as a guide to the research work for IA for the coming year.

4. *Issues Analysis:* The nature of the issue under study would determine the staffing pattern and framework of analysis for each task force. IA would draw heavily on the resources of the various divisions for task force members. Periodic status reports would be prepared for the divisions affected most directly by a given study.

5. *Implementation of Recommendations:* IA anticipated becoming an integral part of the annual planning cycle beginning with the spring of 1979. It also proposed a consulting role for itself that involved (1) assisting divisions in their efforts to implement recommendations for changes in their business practices, and (2) monitoring the extent to which divisions actually implemented the recommended changes.

In terms of the first three functions, ongoing liaison responsibilities with each of the major divisions would be assigned to core IA staffers. For the fourth and fifth functions, the task force leader, also a core member of IA, would assume a liaison role linking the work of the project to the affected division or divisions.

Because most outsiders only knew IA by association with the task force work that had preceded its creation, the purpose of the Process Memo was to clarify the broader mission of IA and to obtain the approval of senior corporate and divisional managers. As Elliott explained:

The document is really our internal creation. It has not been discussed with anybody other than Bill Bailey. So, this will be the first indication as to whether or not someone really has concerns, first, over the turf issues and second, even absent that, with what we should be doing or what (corporate and divisional management) expects us to be doing.

The process encounter (September, 1978). A meeting to discuss the Process Memo was held in Bailey's office in late September 1978. In attendance were Bailey, Elliott, Bennett, the divisional senior vice presidents, and Bill Yeats. The discussion was supportive although a few concerns were expressed.

Yeats, vice president of Government Relations, expressed some concern over the issues identification and prioritization functions outlined in the process memo. First, he felt that these functions might be too elaborate and might tend to drive out much of the hard research that IA was expected to perform. He indicated that his department also had an environmental scanning role that might also be classified as an issues identification mechanism. Second, Yeats observed that his department would need to stay close to the work of IA because of the lack of external awareness of IA's personnel, with the exception of Elliot.

Others at the meeting saw the need for IA to spell out what its role was going to be in the annual guideline planning process that involved the divisions and the Corporate Planning Department. Elliot replied that the development of IA was probably not far enough along to get involved in the divisional planning process (which was coming to a close during the time of this meeting); but that he intended for IA to get involved at the onset of next year's planning process, beginning in April of 1979, to review draft plans with divisional planners. "Next year," Elliott said, "if Bill Bailey finds fault with the divisions' guideline plans, he should direct it at IA as well as anyone else."

Next, the division senior vice presidents expressed concern about the last function outlined in the Process Memo. For example, Wolcott asked questions about how the IA-Division liaison system was going to work and emphasized that, "Everything rests on the quality of IA's work; otherwise the divisions may select to do the work themselves." He was also troubled by the implementation role IA had carved out for itself, and said, "I don't think IA's role should be 'monitoring.' It should be to serve as a resource to affected divisions."

A few days after the meeting, however, an insurance division manager, who was aware of the Process Memo, shared with me the following reactions to IA's planned implementation role:

> . . . The implementation [portion of the memo] said in so many words that once IA identifies the problem and comes up with recommendations, they expect to sit on top of the implementation process to make sure it gets done. We have operating people who say, "Who the hell is David Elliott to tell me how to run my

business. He doesn't have the responsibility for producing a rate of return of 15%–20% bottom line. He's not talking to customers out there. This is a bunch of bull . . . " David's heart is in the right place . . . this is a little bit of overswing . . .

Midyear Snags

Mr. Bailey's shock treatment (October, 1978). With the process hurdle out of the way, IA turned to its task forces and to the development of a company wide issues inventory. Liaison responsibilities for each of the insurance divisions as well as the Corporate Administration Division were parceled out to individual staff members. The thrust was on operationalizing and refining all five functions outlined in the Process Memo. By the time next year's divisional guideline planning process began (in early spring), Elliott wanted his department to be well positioned to assist the divisions in developing plans for coping with pressing public issues.

For the moment, relationships between IA and the divisional and corporate planners were still unclear. When asked in August 1978 what the relation was like between the Corporate Planning Department and IA, the planning department head replied,

We really wouldn't get too involved with David Elliott because he is more concerned with working on special projects. . . . [Our role is to] make sure that if there was an issue, it was in the plans. And, also, that there would be a discussion about its importance and what priority ought to be assigned to dealing with it.

Comments from David Elliott during this period also reflected an unclear relationship between IA and planners within the divisions themselves,

I think we would see our role . . . and this really isn't clear . . . as working directly with the divisions in focusing on their annual plans, for instance, with our liaisons and not necessarily through Corporate Planning . . .

. . . the [divisional planners] are not quite as tuned in to issues as they are to the quantitative [aspects of their annual plans]. For instance, one of the liaison members of IA had an initial meeting with the planning unit within a division and one member of that unit basically was extremely nonsupportive of the role of our department and said, "Why don't you work through Corporate Planning? Don't bother us with that stuff. Feed it through Corporate Planning." Now this person doesn't necessarily call the shots, but the individual is instrumental in the divisional annual guideline planning process.

As the 1978 divisional guideline planning process was moving toward final corporate review and approval, however, Bill Bailey intervened abruptly by asking IA to perform a quick critique of the responsiveness of each division's plan to "the issues." In what Elliott describes as a 24-hour crash program, IA generated a "very rough" critique and delivered it to Bailey. A few days later Elliott learned that the critique, submitted on the understanding that it was just an off-the-cuff report to Bailey, had been circulated to all the division senior vice presidents and had created somewhat of a furor. At the tail end of the planning cycle, the divisions were being asked by Bailey to modify their plans to address these issues before resubmitting them for final corporate review and approval.

Describing IA's critique as rushed and "nondiplomatic," Elliott assessed what one corporate planner later referred to as "Mr. Bailey's shock treatment on public policy issues" as follows:

> the short-term consequences were *disastrous* for us and nearly torpedoed all of the careful cultivation of relationships Susan and I had built up. . . .

A good deal of fence mending was required to reestablish relations only recently won with the operating divisions. To some extent, IA, working through its divisional liaisons, was able to assist in the reformulation of divisional plans that were subsequently approved.

Preoccupations.   By the fall of 1978, IA members were beginning to feel the pressures from the ongoing liaisons and task force activities. They began to express concerns about the heavy workload and the vague feeling that they were not in total control of the direction IA was taking. During this period, core IA members expressed the following concerns:

> We've been pretty much involved in front burner issues, which is not, as I understand it, where we want to go or, in my estimation, where we ought to be going. We're conscious of that and we are trying to do something about it . . . Until we get a process of our own in place for issue identification and prioritization, we're going to be *bombarded* constantly with suggestions from the outside for studies and we're not going to have any control over the pace or the direction of our work . . . . That's going to make things worse in terms of our staffing shortages . . . .

◇ ◇ ◇ ◇

> Right now IA's biggest problem is that we've gotten so involved with the two ongoing studies, that we are losing some perspective in another area of responsibility . . . which is to keep abreast of what's going on and to uncover new issues and to continue to monitor what's going on in the outside world . . . . I think that directing attention to emerging issues is a more important function to the corporation than actually doing a limited number of task force studies. I really haven't had the chance to discuss this with David Elliott as much as I should.

Elliott, too, had become concerned about these developments, as he confided in the researcher:

> One thing I am gradually gaining a greater appreciation of is the relative importance of the issue identification/inventory process as opposed to the project work. Our project work is still more visible to the outsiders in the company and there is not much of an appreciation yet of the role that we are expected to have in the guideline planning process and in shaping the division's plans. No one has really focused on or is really aware that we have this issue identification and inventory role, which is of equal importance.

Turf problems (December, 1978).   By late fall 1978, IA was finalizing its inventory of the public policy issues confronting Aetna and its divisions. Through an intensive screening process, involving company insiders and outsiders, IA personnel qualified and categorized issues into a 3 × 3 matrix, along two dimensions: company relevance and impact probability.[8] After completing the matrix, mini-analyses were conducted for each issue to decide whether it applied primarily to one division or was interdivisional in nature. The location of an issue in the matrix indicated what priority IA had attached to it. Issues high on both company relevance and impact probability required a major effort in order to understand and manage them. Issues high on only one dimension required substantially less effort, though they might be expected to be forced by events into the high-priority cell. Finally, issues in the low-low cell required only occasional monitoring and updating.

In general, the issues inventory was to guide the major study efforts in the company and to influence each division's annual plans. In addition to mounting major study efforts on the high-priority issues (or ensuring that studies within the divisions or in the industry trade association were underway), IA was responsible for keeping current on the other issues and updating the inventory in light of changing environmental conditions.

Much as in the case of the Process Memo, the first draft of the issues inventory was presented in early December 1978 during a meeting of senior corporate and divisional managers. At this meeting, people from the divisions and other corporate external affairs units were more outspoken.

For instance, Robert Clark, senior vice president of Corporate Administration, expressed his feeling that his IA function might be redundant with the annual legislative issues summary prepared by the government relations department. Elliott admitted that many of the issues in IA's inventory were legislative in nature, but argued that his inventory was broader and more analytical than the one prepared by Bill Yeats. Concerns of the duplication of work with divisional planners were raised as well, the implications being that more effective communications were required between all components generating different perspectives on public issues.

However, in a memo that the vice president of Corporate Planning forwarded to the members of the Corporate Management Committee (CMC) within a few weeks of this meeting, he emphasized the need to improve the process by which long-range plans were developed, with the objective of preparing the company's first comprehensive long-range plan by the second quarter of 1980. As he observed, "It is unlikely we could accomplish it in 1979 because we have not progressed far enough in assessing the impact on our business of public policy issues and other external trends and events."

He also said:

> All divisions, and in particular the Casualty Division need time to develop better linkages between the impact of specific external environmental pressures on the manner in which they conduct their businesses and on the results that might be expected.

> At the present time, a large number of people are engaged in monitoring trends—line management as relates to their own activities, and all staff departments with respect both to their functional responsibilities and, in varying degrees, to the activities of line operations. Those actively involved in monitoring trends include IA; government relations; corporate planning; and members of the environmental analysis group (EAG). The problem is how to organize and communicate the appropriate amount of this information in an efficient manner to the line and staff personnel that are or should be involved in solving or anticipating particular problems, and to senior management who need to maintain a broad perspective about what is occurring. This is a particular problem both with respect to (1) high-priority current issues that a large number of people need to know about in order to insure consistency of company viewpoints and (2) emerging trends that are not rocking the boat at the present time, but may have the potential to create a major crisis two to three years from now.

Coordination Among Business Divisions and Corporate External Affairs Units

Bill Bailey had given some consideration in his deliberations in early 1978 to consolidating many of the corporate external affairs units under one head. As part of this thinking he had also considered bringing in an outside superstar to head up Corporate External Affairs. This individual could represent the interests of all corporate external affairs units to the CMC and ensure the integration of the external affairs function. After discussing these possibilities with other senior managers, including Clark and Elliott, he decided to leave things as they were. Instead he created an independent Issues Analysis Department and let it, together with the other external affairs units, invent and develop processes for coping with their assigned responsibilities. Indeed, Bailey confided in me that he would tolerate a certain amount of redundancy for the time being in order for these units to mature, although he did not completely rule out the possibility of an eventual consolidation. With time, someone might emerge from the units in place who could assume leadership for corporate external affairs, thereby avoiding the need to bring in an outsider.

Under these conditions, the units were left to develop their own means of coordination. Government Relations, Corporate Communications, and Corporate Social Responsibility reported directly to Robert Clark, who also chaired the EAG and was a member of the Marketing Study Group (MSG). In addition, the MSG and EAG were made up of part-time representatives from the divisions and the major corporate-level units. David Elliott, for example, was a member of the EAG. Finally, Clark, Bailey, and the head of the Corporate Planning Department sat on the CMC, which met three to four times a month.

Much as IA had done, many of the corporate external affairs units had assigned divisional liaison responsibilities to their members. These individual liaison duties were complemented by the practice of sending memos to relevant units and divisions concerning current trends and work in progress within the external affairs units. Finally, an informal, bi-weekly Issues Luncheon had emerged in the spring of 1978. Depending on availability, the luncheons were attended by the division senior vice presidents and the heads of the corporate external affairs units, as well as by senior corporate executives. Initially these luncheon meetings were held without an agenda; instead, attendees were free to discuss their activities regarding emerging public issues. By 1979 this group had become more institutionalized under the label of the Public Issues Group (PIG). The PIG now had an agenda and a coordinator, Clark, with members preparing in advance to present to the group new developments and work in progress on public policy issues.

Relations with other units and divisions. A survey of relationships between corporate external affairs units and the insurance divisions was commissioned by Bill Bailey in the winter of 1978.[9] The results, summarized in Figure 11-2, which were reported to the company during February and March 1979, revealed that IA already had become a dominant player along with Government Relations in the external affairs domain. However, its importance to the insurance divisions, with perhaps the exception of the Property and Casualty Division, was not nearly so well established, as revealed in Figure 11-3.

In addition to establishing divisional liaison positions within IA and, so far, mounting task force projects for the Casualty and Life Divisions, Elliott was personally instrumental in maintaining IA's relations with other units. As Susan Bennett observed,

> David Elliott is very good in terms of being a facilitator of our contacts with other people in the company. He was well known to all the senior people before he

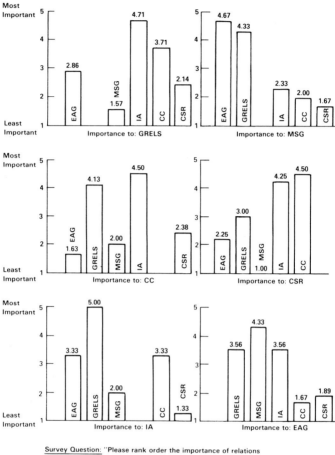

Figure 11-2   Survey responses by external affairs professionals on how important they feel relations with corporate external affairs units other than their own unit are.

took this position and, just by virtue of his personality, everybody really likes him and seems to view him as a very credible person . . . So, he spends a lot of time dealing with outsiders to the department; dealing with the mechanics of how things are going to happen; letting people know who the divisional liaison people are; smoothing the way for us before we get over there.

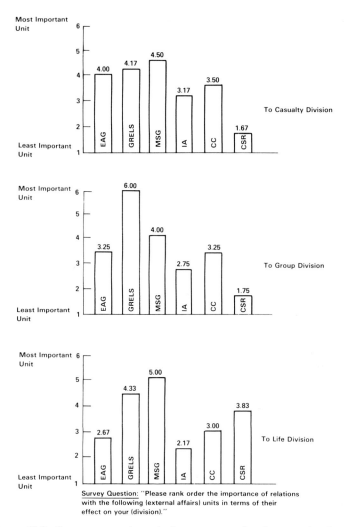

Figure 11-3 Survey responses by senior line managers on how important they feel relations with specific corporate external affairs units are to their business divisions.

Progress of studies.   By the winter of 1978, the insurance affordability project had become deep background. Although Elliott was somewhat disappointed with the limited extent to which its recommendations had been implemented, the report had been praised by groups outside Aetna for its analytical approach and general high quality. As Elliott recalled, "That gave us quite a bit of mileage for a while and helped us persuade people that this work was really valuable." The insurance redlining study was moving along nicely; its members were currently conducting field studies of Aetna's casualty operations in a number of major metropolitan centers. But the life insurance study, with its ill-defined cluster of issues and its members dominated by part-timers on assignment from the life division, had drifted aimlessly until a decision had been made in the fall of 1978 by Elliott, in collaboration with Dean Wolcott, to terminate it. As one IA member put it, the ill-fated life insurance study confirmed one of our assumptions in the issues inventory that,

> an issue that has not fully emerged is very difficult to deal with. You can't articulate it well. People who aren't issue-oriented [referring to divisional representatives] just can't deal with it all.

The initial life insurance task force was not a total bust, as Elliott explained, even though it was not prepared to resolve the large number of issues it uncovered in terms of either analysis or policy recommendations. Instead, its findings enabled Wolcott and Elliott to put together a follow-up task force focusing on a much broader conception of the issue of life insurance suitability. The new task force was making good progress, but Elliott admitted that in the initial effort "the process was horrendous and it could have been dynamite."

Progress in the Development
of the Issues Analysis Department

Assessments by core group members.   Jack Ericksen had this to say about his summer internship with IA, before returning for his second year in the Yale Master of Public and Private Management Program:

> . . . I'm really impressed that they've been able to do as much as they have in that amount of time as smoothly as they have. Internally it doesn't look smooth, but I know the results are.

Other core group members reflected on some of the internal departmental issues that had emerged during the fall and winter of 1978:

> I guess my expectations were in terms of a unit that would develop a process to identify issues about which management might be able to influence the outcome. If you can exercise some influence regarding the issue prior to the time it reaches a critical point . . . You may be able to head it off . . . . If you are trying to deal with an issue once it has converged and broken, I rather suspect you really don't need this department for that purpose.

◇ ◇ ◇ ◇

I think there are some morale problems and sort of office relations problems.
. . . Susan Bennett's productivity is hard for people to keep up with. It's a function of her productivity, and their relative progress in terms of age. . . . I've noticed that if there's something to be done at our staff meeting. . . . David Elliott will turn immediately to Susan and ask her to do it. . . .

◇ ◇ ◇ ◇

. . . there is less opportunity for getting together to discuss things. I think part of this is just the amount of work that is going on. Everyone is in the middle of something . . .

The results summarized in Figure 11-4 from the survey revealed how selected work outcomes of IA members stacked up against those experienced by members reporting directly to the heads of other external affairs units and the divisions.

Assessments from former task force members.   The effectiveness of the task force activities within IA had improved considerably over the first year of the department's operation. Beginning with the conclusion of the affordability study, I had been retained by Elliott to debrief members of task forces after their reports had been forwarded to the affected divisions.[10] Although my early debriefings surfaced a number of suggestions for improvement, by the spring of 1979 the development of the task force activity had reached a point that I had suggested to Elliott that debriefings be discontinued, except in the case of a novice task force leader desiring developmental feedback. Some representative comments made by former non-IA task force members in the debriefings were:

I think the whole group would tell you that this was an experience that was pressing on them and that we all learned an awful lot from it and from each other.

◇ ◇ ◇ ◇

Given that it is viewed as a high visibility situation and a promotional opportunity, people are *very* motivated to work hard on the task force. People are very committed.

◇ ◇ ◇ ◇

. . . for one thing, it exposes an individual to key members of the organization that one would never meet otherwise and it allows you to look at how the com-

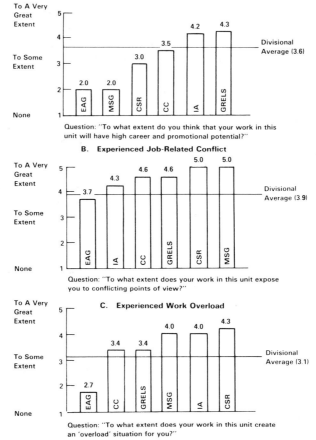

Figure 11-4 Some job outcomes experienced by professionals working in specific corporate external affairs units.

pany performs on a policy-making plane rather than a surface plane. . . . It was interesting, and I can see the possibility of working on intrinsically more important or interesting issues than the ones I had previously been dealing with. . . .

My debriefings also revealed that when asked if they would recommend working on an IA task force to their closest colleague in Aetna, the response of former task force members was unanimously positive.

Assessments from corporate executives and senior line managers. The controversy continued throughout the year over whether IA should be evaluated in terms of the quality and objectivity of its reports or the extent to which their recommendations were implemented.

The divisional point of view:

I think it should be judged on the basis of the quality of the report, and I guess I would think that just the discussion of the problems and the ideas and so forth could provide, hopefully, suggestions for how one might start arriving at some solutions. I wouldn't necessarily see the recommendations as being that critical. . . . I think it's easy to make lots of recommendations for changes, but I think the importance is in discussing the issues; coming to a clear understanding of the programs. . . .

The corporate point of view:

I think the "proof of the pudding" really is not the research itself, though that's critical; that's very important . . . but it is what the operating people will do in response to what comes out of the area. . . . If we don't get change out of it, then I guess you wonder was it really worth it. . . .

As far as David Elliott was concerned:

I am quite sure Bill Bailey believes that both the *quality* of our work and the acceptance of our recommendations are important. One indication was his reaction when I submitted a recommendation for a bonus for Susan Bennett because of her work on the Redlining Task Force Report. Bailey's reaction at the time was, "Let's wait and see how the report is received by the Casualty Division before we make that decision."

My reaction was that somebody who is running a task force and in charge of the quality of its report should be judged on the quality of that report as perceived by Bill Bailey and others and not on how it's received by the divisions. . . . If the division is unwilling to institute change, even though it might be the greatest report in the world and even though its recommendations made perfect sense, I don't believe that person should be penalized because the ultimate decision maker failed to see that. . . .

Task force successes (summer, 1979).   By the summer of 1979, IA had completed the work of the redlining task force. During the winter the life insurance suitability task force was being reconstituted and was making good progress. In addition, during the spring IA had developed a revised public policy issues inventory in collaboration with other corporate and divisional units. This inventory was now employed in conjunction with IA's liaison function to assist the development of the divisions' annual plans.

The recommendation of the Redlining Task Force had been well received in the Casualty Division. Reflecting on this process, David Elliott had this to say:

Bill Bailey has given very little feedback on the report itself and has had a hands-off policy and has let us work out the whole thing with the Casualty Division. The Casualty Division gave us very favorable feedback in terms of the report. Susan, as project leader, met with the Casualty Division staff and went through all the recommendations. The upshot was that about 95% of the recommendations have been agreed upon and, in many cases, the recommendations have already been implemented. The report is now being published and made available to the public.

Some of the changes resulting from IA reports were really fundamental. As Susan Bennett explained:

There are a number of things we got done to address the Redlining issue but probably the major one developed out of our meetings with consumer groups throughout the country. You have to understand that the way our Casualty Division distributes its products is through an independent agent system. The agents are not employees of the company, so there's a question of control when you talk about things like redlining. The allegations that were made by consumer groups centered around the fact that our agents were turning down applications for insurance based on the location of the property; the company never even got a crack at it. So, even if Aetna, through a review of its own files, could be said not to be redlining, our agents were doing that on our behalf and we viewed that as a serious allegation and one that was probably true.

From our meetings with the consumer groups, Bill Bailey said that he felt those charges had validity. In response, therefore, in six major cities, Chicago, New York, and others, we introduced a system by which our agents could not turn down an application for homeowner's insurance on our behalf. They had to submit all applications to the company for review; therefore, the agent could not turn down an application based on location. The company would have to evaluate the decision, which is a severe break from precedent with our distribution system. As a consequence, we have written a reasonable volume of business through that program in areas where we had not written before.

Elliott's Reflections on the First Year

In the summer of 1979, Elliott characterized the relationships between IA and the company's divisions as follows:

The status of our relationships now with the Casualty Division is excellent. The head of that division has said that we've overcome the problems that we faced initially and he has told us that he's very happy with what we've done. . . . Our relationships are very good with the Life, Group, and Corporate Administration divisions, but to some extent I would have to say there's probably a wait-and-see attitude on the part of the Life and Group divisions, pending the completion of the major studies that we are engaged in for them.

With respect to Corporate Administration, which includes Government Relations, Corporate Communications and Corporate Social Responsibility, as well as other departments, our relationships are very good. . . . I now attend Bob Clark's staff meetings. I gave a presentation to advise Bob's staff what IA has been doing and to answer questions. So I'm very plugged in there. [Before becoming part of Clark's staff meetings] this department was somewhat isolated [from the day-to-day operations of the company], although that could also be viewed somewhat as a blessing too, I suppose. Managing people as I do, however, I really needed to be plugged into these corporate time schedules and other things that are going on.

Although Bill Bailey had taken an active role in signalling the need for IA and making it a part of the planning process, he had begun to assume a less active role in IA's affairs in the fall after the conclusion of the affordability exercise. Reflecting on this situation, Elliott was aware that he had been cast adrift in a politically charged situation; but working for the ultimate boss without direct supervision was not inconsistent with Elliott's preference for working things out for himself.

He was, however, concerned about the inevitable turnover within IA. Already one member of the core group had rotated back to a division and others would likely follow in the months ahead as part of the general management development process. As one member still on board explained,

> . . . IA is not a place where one would spend the rest of his or her career, but a "developmental place." You know, a three-to-four-year place.

Although Elliott believed strongly in Aetna's recent emphasis on management development, the heavy investment required to bring a newcomer to the point where he or she should function effectively as a divisional liaison, a task force leader, and a public issues analyst caused him more than a little concern over the problems staff turnover would create for the development and persistency of IA's innovative approach. Indeed, paramount in his mind at this moment was the impending transfer of Susan Bennett to a line-management job in the casualty division.

EPISODE III: REFLECTIONS ON PROGRESS—THE SECOND YEAR

A year and a half after its creation, IA had managed to gain acceptance in the planning process and with the divisions. As Susan Bennett commented,

> One test of acceptance of the department is that divisions are now originating ideas for task forces and giving Dave Elliott candidates for studies that they would like to see done, and I think that, more than anything else, really indicates the extent to which divisions feel that our work products are useful to them.

David Elliott:

> . . . And I guess the other part of it is that we are now very much injected into the company's planning process. For public policy issues, the divisions are relying

upon us working together and coming out with a statement of the issue and a brief analysis of the issue to feed into their plans. . . .

Considering how IA's work had been evaluated, Elliott noted some areas for improvement:

It is very difficult, I would say, to evaluate our work because of the nature of the work. The area with which we have had the least amount of success has been the ability to pinpoint an issue, so to speak, before it becomes an issue. One of our objectives for this year is improving our environmental monitoring process. The issues we have so far catalogued are basically the issues we all know are pressing on us, but increased effort is going to be given to the identification of key issues for the future, beyond 1982, if that's possible. I'm not convinced that this is totally possible. Moreover, even if it is possible, and even if we have some certainty within our own department that an issue is going to be extremely important in affecting Aetna, I'm not sure that we could get the commitment within the company to spend the resources to mount interdivisional task forces to study it. It would be a heck of a job to persuade others unless they see the immediate need right in front of them.

The other part of our role though, the analytical role and the studies that we have undertaken, has been very successful and the feedback that we have gotten, both within and outside the company, has been extremely complimentary. This feedback has helped us perform this portion of the role that we carved out for ourselves. . . . Basically we evaluate ourselves through the feedback we get and the extent to which the divisions implement the recommendations.

Reflections and Assessments

In terms of what he had learned in his first managerial role, Elliott revealed that,

I've learned that even in a small department, it's very hard to assure that communications are open and complete . . . I found that you really have to work at it if you want to keep the whole department informed; that was my goal in the beginning. The pressure of day-to-day events, however, really dictates against that . . . I have learned there is a need for crystal clear directions and communication of expectations, depending upon level of competence, and there is a need for very frequent feedback.

In the beginning I had intended to have regular staff meetings. That was torpedoed almost initially . . . because of the pressure of work. Just yesterday I reinstituted a regularly scheduled staff meeting . . . to occur every Wednesday morning . . . There won't be a formal agenda, but these meetings will provide a chance to get together and raise concerns.

◇ ◇ ◇ ◇

I think I might tend to be more personally concerned than previously, but only because other people are involved in my venture . . . I'm responsible to some extent for the department and, therefore, for people's basic lives, jobs, and work products. I tend to be more aggressive in pushing the department vis-a-vis outsiders and defending it and its work products. I am more defensive than I would be if I was a one-person operation.

Also, I was thrown into a fairly unaccustomed role in terms of selling the concept of IA. My previous jobs had always been in the context that people would come to me because of *their* need and I wouldn't have to sell myself or sell the need for my services at least. Some people around here are not naturally sympathetic to the need for the public policy issues role that was carved out for IA, so I found myself in a very unaccustomed role of actually selling our services to people and resisting the tendency to say, "Look, we're offering something that should be very, very helpful to you. I can't understand why you wouldn't naturally accept it with open arms." I'd never been the salesperson type or thought that I'd ever want to be; but, in retrospect, I sort of enjoyed it and it has brought out something that I didn't think I had. That's been rewarding.

◇ ◇ ◇ ◇

I also discovered the importance of individual credibility, personality, reputation, or whatever you want to call it, in terms of the success of this whole process. I came to realize that these factors govern things to a greater extent than I had ever realized before . . . that these are qualities that are equally important, if not more important, than competence, and that certainly has been borne out here.

Reflecting back on Bill Bailey's late issues-oriented intervention into the 1978 guideline planning process, Elliott now saw that action in a different light.

I had to mend a lot of fences that had just been built. But the long-term consequences revealed that [Bailey's action] was a plus because this development and the flaps that ensued over senior management's opinion of the guideline plans, as presented initially, reinforced to the divisions corporate management's commitment and interest in public policy issues and their treatment in the planning process. . . . The whole episode helped to engrain IA in the entire process until we could prove our usefulness. And, indeed, at a time of uncertainty like that, from the divisions' standpoint, they came to rely upon our presumed expertise in the area. It helped us become established; so, ironically, it became a long-term benefit.

Observations from IA members on IA's development,

I think that we originally started with two main charges: one to serve as an issues clearing house and one to research a selected number of issues. The re-

search work is becoming our dominant work . . . When you have a specific research project to do, with deadlines and specific goals, it's hard to devote the
time to the issues monitoring, environmental scanning, futures work . . . We're
down to an annual issues inventory . . . There is one member of the department
who is extremely concerned over that and to the point where he is proposing
that IA be split into two functions and that one person officially head up the issues clearing house effort.

◇ ◇ ◇ ◇

Susan and David had a very unique relationship, and Susan is a very, very ex-
traordinary person . . . For a long while I felt like the odd person out because
there were many, many decisions being made to which I didn't even have an
awareness of. I certainly don't feel like an outsider anymore. I think I did for a
long time—6 or 12 months perhaps—but then I didn't feel as though I was privy
to what was going on in the department.

◇ ◇ ◇ ◇

IA is still exciting. There are always new problems. We have a number of
staffing changes and we are in the process of trying to find new staff members.
We have decided to create some new positions called research associates . . .
one for each of the insurance divisions to work on the issues inventory and on
specific task force efforts. That will help a lot. . . . Six months from now, in many
respects the character of the department will be significantly different because
of the almost doubling in size.

Before leaving IA in the late spring of 1979 to rejoin the Casualty Division,
Wes Stearns shared the following perception of IA's development:

> . . . the position of the department is becoming better understood by outsiders
> as more and more work is done. I think one of the big things that helped this
> was the release of the issues inventory. This brought in a lot of feedback . . . I
> still get back to my old divisional area, and people are beginning to understand
> the role of IA.

> . . . people looked at IA, at least from the Casualty Division, as an area that was
> going to be looking in on them; sort of checking up on them. I think this has
> gone by the boards now. IA is becoming more accepted.

By this time Susan Bennett had assumed her new role in the Casualty
Division and had completed the six-week casualty and property course, regarded by casualty veterans as intensive and rigorous. To no one's surprise,
Susan had finished first in her class and had been appointed by the head of
the Casualty Division as regional manager for one of the division's major
product lines. Talking about her perspective of IA as a line manager, she remarked,

I clearly feel very strongly, as I did when I was working with IA, that there is an overall value added to the company with this kind of operation and, in fact, my being here [in a line-management role] is deliberate in the sense that there is a lot that I can do within the division to further the work of IA and to help get recommendations implemented. Now that I'm making decisions that affect profitability, obviously there are times when I find myself resisting change or wanting to approach change in a somewhat different way. I think one tension that David Elliott's department will always have and will never be clearly resolved, even though they have certain kinds of expertise, is that when you're in a line job you are privy to and need to know a lot of technical information and the technical ramifications of issues that IA was not privy to when I was there, and probably never will be. Part of that is solved with the task force process but I think there will always be a healthy tension between the goals of the division, which are profit-oriented, and the goals of David's department, which are to make the profit-oriented divisions see long-term possibilities of issues rather than just short-term profit objectives.

Reflecting on the loss of Susan, Elliott commented,

What I'm most proud of is my ability to hopefully have developed and managed Susan well. It's definitely much harder to sustain the interest and motivation in somebody who is really as outstanding as Susan. I'm very proud that I've managed to sustain her interest. I hope she has learned as much from me as I have learned from her. . . .

We certainly had a very complementary and mutually supportive working relationship and her contribution to starting and sustaining the new department was literally immeasurable. She does so many things so well that her loss cannot help but have an adverse impact on the department's work product. There is a great amount of slack that others will have to try to take up. Luckily, I have some very talented people in the department and I am confident that we will all somehow manage to keep the momentum of the first year going. . . .

Elliott summarized the major obstacles to the development of his department as follows:

the suspicion of certain areas that we were going to intrude into their domain and what was the need for IA. Overcoming those turf problems and proving our utility. It's not by any means over. It's still a day-to-day thing. The main obstacle was the lack of appreciation for the need of an effort like this—the short-term outlook of the day-to-day business mentality versus the need to cope with longer term public policy issues. We have a selling problem to keep overcoming.

Finally, Elliott was asked whether he had experienced within the department any drift away from the early enthusiasm and commitment to the innovative mission of IA.

Naturally there has been some drift. But I think in my own personal case that will be offset for a while by the challenge that I will have when certain people leave. . . . I know that the year spent forming IA will always be regarded by me as a very special period in my life.

We have been very successful and I guess we will continue. But some of the new flavor has certainly gone out of it. . . . From a personal standpoint, it becomes repetitive and, therefore, loses some of its charm. . . . We'll make little fine tunings. You can begin to see a pattern in all these studies now that we've been through the task force process. And we certainly haven't meshed ourselves into the organization so that we can just sit back. . . .
Is that bad?

EPISODE IV: FURTHER DEVELOPMENT AND MATURATION— YEARS THREE THROUGH FIVE

1979 had been a big year for IA. The department had conducted six major task force studies, had assisted in over a dozen issue-oriented studies in the business divisions and other external affairs units, had become involved in the divisional planning process, and had developed an ongoing liaison system between its members and each business division. In addition, IA had become recognized for its work in the industry and had begun some outside consultation in the development or refinement of issues-oriented research units in the industry's trade associations. As the year came to an end, David Elliott commented on the progress of IA as follows.

While IA has been successful so far in becoming integrated into the corporate structure, there is room for improvement and "proving" ourselves is a daily challenge. We will continue to concentrate on this effort and to elicit an appreciation for our type of work—while still preserving our objectivity and broad perspectives.

At the end of 1980 Elliott reported that progress had been made on all of IA's functions. The issues identification and monitoring process, which had been somewhat upstaged by the task force and liaison work during the first two years, received more attention and a major revision of the issues inventory was circulated throughout the company before the end of the year. But perhaps the most significant aspect of IA's evolution was its intensive involvement in the development of social issues research functions in several of the industry trade associations. At year's end, Elliott was attempting to encourage greater involvement of IA in company issues "which are not purely or even primarily public policy related." He also had become concerned about the extensive participation of IA members in the research and analysis work going on in other staff departments and in the division. Because of the small size of IA relative to its assigned functions, he preferred to have IA in the leadership role when possible. However, he realized that the invitations

IA received to participate on divisional and staff task forces indicated a growing recognition throughout the company of IA's value and competence.

By 1981, Elliott had taken steps to create more of a career path for IA members and to clarify the roles of IA through an elaboration of the unit's structure. For example, IA now had three job levels below Elliott's position: research associate, director, and manager. Elliott had also divided the department into three subunits: research, issues management, and outside activities (such as IA's work in industry trade associations). He mentioned that the outside work was important from the department's perspective because it put IA members in touch with other issues-management professionals who could exchange experiences and approaches regarding common tasks and problems.

When Elliott was asked in the summer of 1981 how much support IA received from the business divisions, he said,

> When we staff our task forces we get support from the divisions. The harder question, however, is to what extent are we supported not in terms of staffing but in terms of general feelings, general recognition, or general appreciation of our work. I think that vacillates from time to time and has not stabilized, although we have made substantial improvements.

> But we are entering a very vulnerable period because of the current business downcycle, especially in the property and casualty business. There is pressure on profits. And there is a natural reaction when so much pressure is on market share and profits that attention to public policy issues is going to slip. So, I would say that IA is to some extent still proving itself and is in a somewhat precarious position. I suspect that some people perceive that the chief operating officer has not addressed these issues as much as he did when IA was started, and maybe the newness has worn off. He may feel that we've become institutionalized and, therefore, don't need his active support.

Follow-up Survey Results

1981 was also the year in which a follow up to the 1978 survey was conducted to assess both IA's progress and the progress Aetna's executive leaders had achieved on their agenda to make the business divisions more responsive to the corporate social environment. All managers reporting directly to the heads of the business divisions, as well as all staff professionals reporting directly to the heads of the core external affairs units (i.e., Government Relations, Corporate Communications, Corporate Social Responsibility, and Issues Analysis) participated in the survey. The results revealed that substantial progress had been made on both counts, despite the fact that competitive pressures on Aetna's business divisions had increased significantly over the previous three years.

First, mutual influence between the business divisions and the corporate external affairs units had increased from 1978 to 1981, as revealed in

Figures 11-5 and 11-6. Figure 11-5 summarizes the perceptions of external affairs staff professionals of the extent to which the business divisions influence the decisions made in their units, and Figure 11-6 indicates the perceptions of line managers about the extent to which their business divisions were influenced by the corporate external affairs units. Influence increased in both directions over the three-year period, signalling progress on the executive leaders' agenda.

Second, when the analysis was confined to relations among the core staff units in the corporate external affairs function, the results pointed to significant progress in the development of IA. For example, Figure 11-7 reveals that IA was second only to the Government Relations Department in terms of the extent to which it influenced decision making in the other external affairs departments. Importantly, IA has held this position since the first six months after its initiation, when the 1978 survey was conducted. Thus, IA has been able to achieve and maintain a leadership role in Aetna's external affairs function.

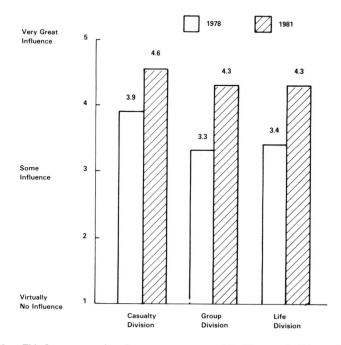

Note: This figure summarizes the average responses of the 25 external affairs professionals to the 1978 and 1981 surveys.

Figure 11-5 Average amount of influence of business divisions on decision making in the external affairs units (1978 versus 1981).

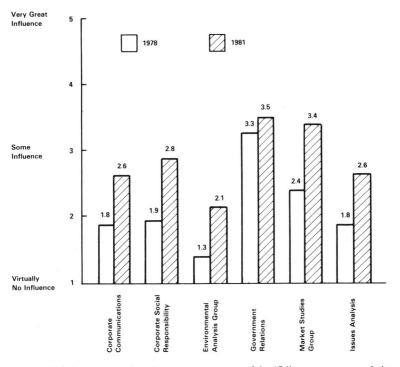

Note: This figure summarizes the average responses of the 17 line managers completing the surveys in 1978 and again in 1981.

Figure 11-6   Average amount of influence of external affairs units on decision making in business divisions (1978 versus 1981).

Finally, survey participants were asked to evaluate the core external affairs departments and the two line-based, external affairs steering committees on a number of performance criteria. In terms of the perceptions of members of other external affairs units (Figure 11-8), IA produced the highest quality work, was the most responsive to other core staff units, had the most competent members, provided the most practical recommendations, and exhibited the best ability to help other core staff units understand and manage the public affairs issues they faced.

Assessments from the line managers (Figure 11-9), however, were somewhat less positive and consistent. Although IA and Corporate Communications tied for the highest ratings of member competence, IA generally fell into third place behind Government Relations and Corporate Communications on most of the other criteria. (Recall that both Government Relations and Corporate Communications pursue missions that are oriented toward protecting and representing the traditional business practices of the business

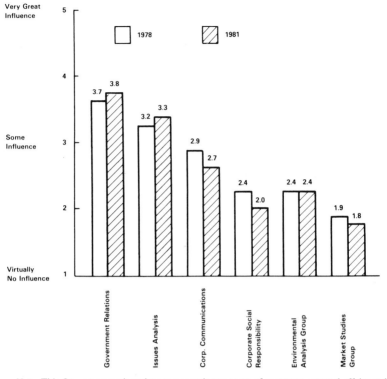

Note: This figure summarizes the average unit responses of corporate external affairs and professionals completing the surveys in 1978 and 1981.

Figure 11-7   Average amount of influence on decision making among external affairs units (1978 versus 1981).

divisions. These activities contrast sharply with the catalytic role imposed upon IA by Aetna's executive leaders.)

In summary, the results of the two surveys provided substantial encouragement to executive leaders at Aetna that progress was being made on both their agenda and the receptivity to IA within the company. These survey results were reported back to the company in a presentation I made to Aetna's PIG.

Subsequent Developmental Events

Toward the end of 1981 and into 1982, two changes took place in Aetna that had the potential for impacting IA's development. Both organizational events were responses to the increasingly competitive business environment in the U.S. insurance industry. Profits were down in several major lines of

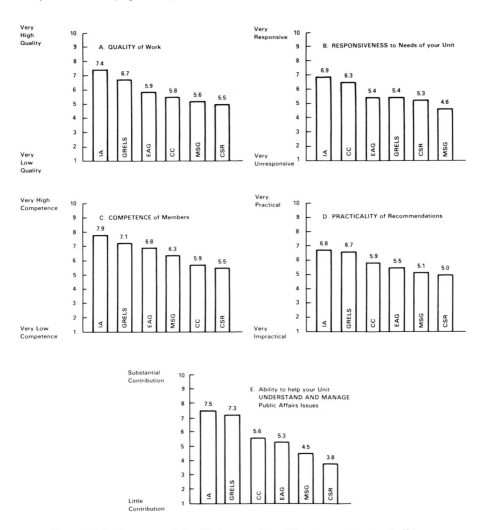

Figure 11-8 Assessment of the effectiveness of the different corporate external affairs units by members of all other external affairs units (1981). *Note:* The rating of 7.4 for the quality of work of the IA department is the mean rating provided by all external affairs professionals in the other five corporate external affairs units.

business, many firms were creating and introducing new products at an un-precedented rate, and most large insurers had moved into an austerity pos-ture with respect to corporate overhead expenses in an attempt to minimize profit erosion.

First, executive leaders reorganized Aetna's corporate structure, changing the traditional product-line divisions into market-oriented divisions. Product lines were unbundled and reassembled into product packages that

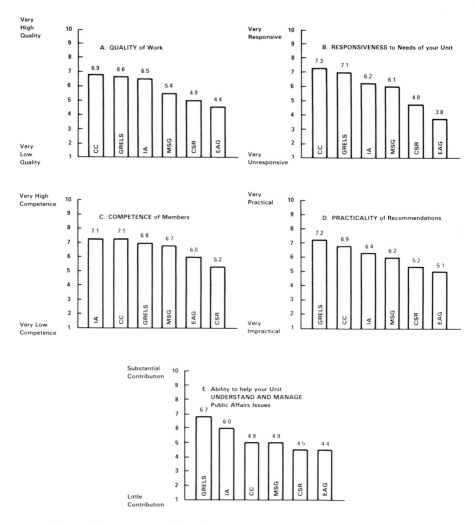

Figure 11-9 Assessment of the effectiveness of the corporate external affairs units by business division managers (1981).

were targeted for specific groups of insurance customers. Although the number of business divisions remained the same, considerable reshuffling of line employees had occurred. Moreover, one division head, who had resisted more than the others both the move to greater corporate-level integration of the business divisions and the catalytic work of IA, was offered and accepted early retirement. He was replaced by Bob Clark, the former senior vice president of corporate administration who had been heavily involved in the supervision of Aetna's corporate external affairs units and steering committees.

Shortly after the reorganization at the divisional level, there was a move to get better control over corporate staff expenses. As part of this move, the core external affairs units were consolidated into a new Law, Communications and Public Affairs Division.

By the spring of 1982, an Ad Hoc Synergy Committee had been created to investigate the possibility of better integrating the work of the core external affairs units. Many options were examined, including a merger of two or more of these units. However, by this time the work of IA had become well defined and was easily differentiated from the work of Government Relations and Corporate Communications. The committee's recommendation to allow them to continue as separate departments, but with better coordination, was accepted. 1982 was also the year in which David Elliott was promoted to the rank of corporate vice president; an event that brought his formal status in line with those of the heads of the other core external affairs units.

The first half of 1983 was more or less a continuation of 1982. Business performance was still down and discussion continued concerning the possible economies that might be achieved among corporate staff units in general, and the core external affairs units in particular. By this time, however, IA had become involved in several task force studies concerning basic business issues. There was even some discussion about whether to retitle the department as Corporate Issues Analysis.

RETROSPECTIVE

The early instincts of IA's cofounders had served the department well. IA had grown in maturity and company stature while containing its size to approximately a dozen professional and clerical members. Their early design choices, which were outlined in the Process Memo and which included the department's division of work, structure and processes, and boundary management activities, had been refined with experience. Similar refinements had been made in specific aspects of IA's mission, including the issues inventory process and the task force leadership activity; the latter being fine-tuned through both experience and the debriefings of former task force members.

David Elliott's sense of impending drift at the end of the first 18 months of IA never fully materialized. There remained a constant challenge because of the novelty of the social issues IA was called upon to address and the need to manage the development of incoming core staff members to replace those who moved on to assume normal line and staff jobs in the company.

By this time over 50 line managers, many of whom appeared on Aetna's high potential list, had rotated through IA task force assignments and were back on the job in the business divisions. IA had conducted several major studies of high-impact issues and many of its recommendations for change had been implemented in the business divisions. The department had also frequently assisted other line and staff functions with project work, and its liaisons were regularly consulted by divisional planners about the preparation of and progress on their annual business plans. Thus, the trauma caused by Mr. Bailey's 1978 shock treatment, together with IA's subsequent response, had facilitated IA's involvement in the annual planning cycle of Aetna's business divisions. Finally, IA had developed and regularized an annual issues inventory process that was based not only on its own environmental monitoring activities, but also on input systematically received from other line and staff functions. This inventory guided the allocation of resources within IA, and was updated on an ongoing basis through the liaison system IA had put into place during its first year of operation. Evidence that the issues inventory was achieving its purpose could be found in the sometimes intense debates that emerged among other units about whose issues should receive highest priority in the inventory.

Personnel turnover had been a planned event since IA's beginning, and most of the department's initial staff had moved to other departments or divisions by 1983. Susan Bennett had become an assistant vice president in one of the business divisions. Mike Anstey and Wes Stearns had also returned to operating jobs. Jack Ericksen was now a lobbyist in the Government Relations Department, and Keith Stevenson had left IA to form an issues analysis function in one of the business divisions.

Nevertheless, IA has continued to perform its mission at a high level of attributed competence. Personnel replacement decisions have been made very carefully, and new people are intensively groomed on the job. IA has become viewed as an important stop in one's career at Aetna. Moreover, IA has been successful in bringing in talented outsiders who could learn about the company and later move to more conventional jobs in the divisions and other staff departments.

Over the past five years, Elliott had developed a strong intuitive sense of the kind of person who could do well as an IA staff member. When asked to articulate the characteristics of such an individual, his initial response was "quickness of analytical ability and quickness of turning things around." He then referred to an "IA style" of doing things. He said, "It is not a breezy, highly communicative style; instead, it emphasizes very concrete support for one's positions, and it demands intellectual rigor and a fairly quick turnaround time in terms of producing written documents. It requires somebody to take criticism and comments, to understand clearly the nature of them, and then to be able to turn a document around that is perceived by our staff to be deficient. It requires rigor in understanding where people are coming from; something that's not native to certain people."

There also remained the problems of IA's assigned role in the company and the turf it had carved for itself among more established corporate staff units. The divisional challenges to IA's role divisions diminished in intensity as the worth of its work became more broadly recognized and as more and more rising line managers returned to their divisional jobs from IA task forces; but they never disappeared. Indeed, the divisional challenge seemed to vary in direct proportion to the perceived decline in the social contingencies confronting Aetna and to the perceived increase in the economic or business contingencies facing the enterprise. IA's selective involvement in general business issues, as opposed to public policy issues, however, had had the effect of reducing the threat posed by the occasional downcycles in the insurance business.

Similarly, the potential overlaps in the missions and work activities of IA and older corporate staff units, especially Government Relations and Corporate Planning, were never fully resolved; and attempts to consolidate these functions emerged every time divisional executives faced cost-reduction pressures from the marketplace.

FOOTNOTES

1. For an introduction to the developmental perspective on organization and management refer to John R. Kimberly, Robert H. Miles, and Associates, *The Organizational Life Cycle: Issues in the Creation, Development, and Decline of Organizations* (San Francisco, CA: Jossey-Bass, 1980); and Seymour B. Sarason, *The Creation of Settings, and the Future Societies* (San Francisco, CA: Jossey-Bass, 1972).

2. For a summary of this study refer to Robert H. Miles, *Coffin Nails and Corporate Strategies* (Englewood Cliffs, NJ: Prentice-Hall, 1982).

3. A summary of the context in which the Issues Analysis Department was created and of the role it plays in the corporate external affairs process is provided in the profile of Aetna in Chapter 7.

4. For evidence of this transition among large American corporations to divisionalized structures refer to Alfred D. Chandler, Jr., *Strategy and Structure* (Boston, MA: MIT Press, 1962); and Richard P. Rumelt, *Strategy, Structure and Economic Performance* (Boston, MA: Division of Research, Harvard Business School, 1974).

5. The broader implications of Ackerman's study for enhancing social responsiveness in divisionalized corporations are reported in Robert W. Ackerman and Raymond Bauer, *Corporate Social Responsiveness: The Modern Dilemma* (Reston, VA: Reston Publishing, 1976); quote from p. 125.

6. Robert Clark was regarded by many corporate-level managers as "the best all-round manager in the house." Elliott also revealed that, at a similar point in his own career, Clark had established an innovative operations analysis department at the corporate level, which had been disbanded after its techniques had diffused into the operating divisions of the company.

7. The original Process Memo has been reproduced in the Appendix.

8. The screening criterion are described in more detail in the Process Memo.

9. Focused group discussions of the survey results were conducted by the consultant with the senior management group of each requesting division or group. Among those requesting this activity were all the corporate external affairs units and the Group Division.

10. I also prepared a report, "Enhancing Task Force Effectiveness," after debriefing members of the early Affordability Task Force. It identified factors that might affect task force effectiveness and suggested ways that leaders and members could anticipate and manage common problems in task force work. This report was made available to all IA members, to senior divisional and corporate managers, and to individuals who subsequently joined IA task forces.

CHAPTER 12

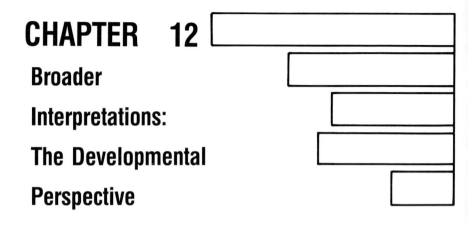

Broader Interpretations: The Developmental Perspective

The story of the Issues Analysis (IA) Department's creation and development has some important implications for the creation and management of innovative staff units within established organizational contexts. To obtain the most from the IA story, I will interpret that experience by contrasting it with the typical developmental experience of innovative staff departments

Although the developmental perspective on organization and management is relatively new, there are a dozen or so studies that have focused on various aspects of the life course of innovative staff departments. Among these studies, the work of Andrew Pettigrew, a British management scholar, has been the most programmatic.[1] By drawing upon his own field research on the creation and development of management science, organization development, internal consulting, computer programming, and systems analysis departments, as well as from the related work of others on the initiation of strategic planning and operations research departments, Pettigrew has constructed a model that describes the *typical* experience of an innovative staff department that is introduced into a larger, more conventional company setting.[2,3] The typical patterns provide a background for interpreting the creation and development of Aetna's Issues Analysis Department.

Such an interpretation will be made on five bases. The first three refer to different phases in the development of a staff unit: *creation, early development,* and *later development.*[4] The other two bases of comparison are: the *nature of the context* in which the unit is created and the *nature of the unit itself,* as expressed in its charter or mission, the functions it performs, and the way in which its performance is evaluated. Consistent with the developmental perspective, the patterns of typical units as well as those for IA will illustrate that the creation and development of innovative units within established organizational contexts is a manageable process and that critical choices made at various points in a staff unit's history powerfully shape the quality, organizational impact, and duration of its existence.

TYPICAL DEVELOPMENTAL PATTERNS

Creation

The development of typical innovative staff units, according to Pettigrew, may be scored into three phases that are not necessarily sequentially ordered.[5] Depending on the external contingencies encountered by the unit over time, as well as the choices made during different phases by the unit's leader, the unit may cycle back and forth between phases of development and self-doubt.

The creation phase is typically stimulated by a major political drama within a company, such as a transition in executive leadership or a reaction to a major change in the external environment. This drama serves as the immediate stimulus to the creation of a specialized staff unit that reflects an important agenda of the new executive leader or that is designed to engage the new contingency confronting the organization. According to the typical patterns observed by Pettigrew, "The essential characteristics of the conception are a sudden unplanned act of creation out of a combination of internal and external change."

The abruptness of creation often means that leaders of innovative units tend not to be carefully chosen. In many cases they are the trusted colleagues or protégés of the unit's original sponsor. The sudden and unplanned nature of creation also tends to cause new staff units to disregard many of the activities that are required to perform effectively as the unit begins to develop its niche in the larger organizational context. As sociologist Seymour Sarason has observed, "the necessity for anticipating problems and consequences [is] an activity or process notably absent or found in only diminished degree in the creation of most settings."[6]

Early Development

Soon after creation, new staff units move into the pioneering stage in which they wrap themselves around the task with considerable enthusiasm. Reflecting on the developmental histories of a variety of innovative staff units, Pettigrew has described the typical patterns of the pioneering stage as follows:

> Each of the units developed some of the characteristics of innovative sub-systems: high involvement and commitment to the task and the unit's goals, high energy given to the solution of a novel problem or set of problems, a strong sense of group identity and spirit leading to extensive in-group social contact in and out of the workplace, the development of group rituals often as ways of socializing new members and unconventional styles of dress and language (p. 8).

These developments within the typical new unit tend to increase the unit's ability to perform its novel tasks, but often at the expense of separating the unit and its members from their line and staff counterparts in the established organizational order. Often these opposing consequences are reinforced by the new unit's leader who tends to build a wall around his or her group to allow them to do the important internal development work without excessive outside interference. As Pettigrew has observed, "The group will not be aware of it at the time but this is the beginning of the unit's boundary and support problems (p. 8)."

As the pioneering phase unfolds, another typical pattern that emerges is an internal cleavage among the core members of the new unit. Pettigrew has identified the opposing forces as "pragmatists," who want the group to focus almost exclusively on the unit's tasks and getting the technical work out, and the "missionaries," who are oriented more toward developing and executing strategies intended to enhance the survival potential of the new unit. Put more generally, the pragmatists become preoccupied with enhancing unit efficiency, whereas the missionaries are motivated to create and maintain the legitimacy of the new and different unit among more established line and staff units.

An extension of the cleavage pattern during the pioneering phase of an innovative staff department is the tendency for one subgroup to prevail over the other. As Pettigrew has noted in the developmental patterns he discovered among innovative staff departments,

> In all cases the tactical approach of the pragmatists dominated the missionaries' concern for strategic thinking and the anticipation of the unit's future role and effectiveness . . . The supremacy of the pragmatists during the pioneering phase helped to ensure the later drift into self-doubt (p. 8).

Because of these internal-development tendencies, together with the leader's early attempts to seal off the boundaries of the new unit until it has perfected its tasks, Pettigrew has observed further that, "it is hardly surprising that the principal environmental reactions to the group [are] perceived to be disinterest, lack of awareness and silent skepticism from the body of the firm and, in some cases, more affirmative responses from those who thought they would benefit from the group's existence (usually the group's sponsor) and alarm from those who thought themselves just about to become the victims of change planned and initiated by a new group of specialists (p. 9)."

All of these typical developmental patterns reinforce the likelihood of early setback for the innovative staff unit. The preoccupation with task efficiency at the expense of underdeveloped relations with existing, potentially affected line and staff units, coupled with the avoidance tendencies of the new unit's leader, create an atmosphere of surprise for the client group. These surprises come about not only because the early initiatives of the new unit call for changes in the traditional status quo of other units, especially in the line operations, but also because the mission and functions of the new unit are poorly understood in other parts of the enterprise.

It is too often the process of enactment of that mission and those functions—often interpreted as encroachment by the new unit into previously well-ordered organizational domains—that enables clients to understand what the new unit is all about.

These early surprises, therefore, serve as poor substitutes for the neglected boundary-management activities of the new unit. They do create a new visibility for the unit whose mission and functions have typically been conceived and developed beyond the scrutiny of client and support groups in other parts of the organization. But potential problems associated with the new unit's mission and functions, which have been avoided during its early phases of development, are now forcefully pressed on the unit by resistant client groups. In addition, the surprises serve to alert suspicious but previously passive staff units that their turf has been violated by the new unit. This typical development episode propels the new and different unit into its first, and possibly last self-doubt phase.

Self-doubt

The self-doubt phase is reached when the euphoria of task development is replaced by doubt about the ability of the unit to efficiently deliver on its mission or to achieve legitimacy for its operations. The surprises associated with the typical start up serve as one stimulus to unit self-doubt, but there are others. The survival of some staff units is threatened when new contingencies bear down upon the host organization. These contingencies may require organizational responses that cannot be engaged by the new unit; and if they are strong enough, these contingencies may eclipse those that the new department was created to handle. Resources may, therefore, flow away from the new unit to other parts of the organization.

The new unit may also suffer from the withdrawal of its political sponsor. In the absence of an active and powerful champion, the new unit may find clients and other staff units less receptive to its intentions. Line managers may become more vocal about their resentment of the innovation unit's encroachments into their affairs. They may deny access to information about their operations that is critical to the work of the new unit and then criticize the unit's work as being incomplete or irrelevant. Professionals in more established staff units may view the acquiescence of the sponsor as vindication of their own functions and turfs and may, therefore, become less cooperative with members of the new unit. Some may even attempt to have the new unit absorbed into their own function as a way of controlling or neutralizing the threat it posed or of increasing the older unit's resource and power bases. Indeed, the withdrawal of the sponsor may encourage some line managers in the client groups to stimulate conflict among the new and older staff units as a way of getting better control over all of them.

Finally, for the truly new and different staff unit, there is always the problem of evaluating its performance. The inability to demonstrate performance effectiveness, or the unwillingness of client groups to agree with the unit about the criteria that are to be used to judge its effectiveness, also pushes the unit into self-doubt.

Thus, there are important internal, organizational, and environmental factors that can either separately or in combination push the innovative staff unit into self-doubt.

Pettigrew has described this phase in the development of innovative staff units as follows:

> The general picture of the self-doubt phase is of a group receiving its first real feedback from its environment, some of it positive and some negative but a great deal more of it confused and difficult to interpret, of the group over-perceiving the degree of threat in its environment and turning in on itself and its leadership system and, in effect, creating more uncertainty for itself rather than managing some of the original causes of doubt (p. 10).

Having reached the self-doubt phase, the way in which the unit responds to these threats is critical to its continued development and survival. Under pressure, the cleavage between unit members that develops in the pioneering phase can move to a higher level of internal conflict; the avoidance tendencies of the leader can become intensified as he or she attempts to build an even higher wall around the endangered unit; and career anxieties and task frustrations can lead to untimely turnover among key staff members.

During this phase, the patterns of typical units diverge as they select either adaptive or maladaptive coping strategies. Pettigrew describes the typical *maladaptive* response as "reacting to the symptoms of the problems they see and not the causes; withdrawing from sources of pressure in their environment rather than confronting them; living off their existing capital of credibility within their environment rather than taking some of the necessary risks to develop further capital, and producing a series of singular action plans to meet environmental contingencies (p. 10)." This response generally leads to unit demise or absorption by default.

By contrast, the *adaptive* response is associated with the continued development and institutionalization of the new unit. According to Pettigrew,

> The central thrust of adaptive strategies [is] towards the diagnosis of the causes of self-doubt, real and imagined, and the formulation, implementation and continuous monitoring of these strategies in such a way that the specialist unit deals both with problems in its internal make-up and across the boundaries of the unit to the market place of service it hopes to thrive in. The key-notes to this approach are diagnosis and anticipation, not carried out unilaterally but in relation to the needs and experiences of its potential and actual clients. In this way the unit might move from a state of familiarity to a state of awareness of its problems and hopefully to identifying new areas of opportunity and new forms of service for its environment (p. 10).

To be sure, the unit must develop direct and ongoing contact with its clients and other staff units, as well as with its political sponsors. But this overall strategy will not be sufficient unless it is coupled with an effective set of tactics for linking the new department to other line and staff units in the organization. The unit also needs access to important policy committees where its members can remain informed about the agendas and opportunities within the larger organizational context that can be engaged by the unit. Depending on the situation, there will often be a need for planned liaison functions that are assigned to specific members of the unit; for a strong personnel selection function within the unit, which is able to select core members who have high ability and who can collectively create a better image and higher visibility for the unit; for clients to have the opportunity to rotate through temporary or semipermanent assignments within the unit to foster mutual understanding and cooperation between the unit and its users; and possibly for the physical movement of core personnel, including the creation of satellite units, to bring them closer to the client system.

In summary, the maladaptive and adaptive responses typically exhibited by innovative staff units experiencing self-doubt differ principally in the feedback loops they create between the new unit and both clients and established staff units. The maladaptive unit closes off its boundaries in an attempt to mount a defense from within, whereas the adaptive unit opens up its boundaries and initiates a constellation of tactics that are designed to discover and work through conflicts and misunderstandings that may otherwise prevent it from obtaining the resources necessary to sustain itself.

The one issue that is overlooked in this analysis of typical response patterns under unit self-doubt is that it is possible for a new unit to become so accommodative to hostile clients and staff groups that in order to survive it becomes coopted by the interests it was created to influence or change. In such a case, the unit fails in its innovative mission and functions only at the pleasure of other line and staff units which, in turn, may have little to fear about further executive-sponsored, staff-initiated encroachments into their activities so long as the coopted unit appears to be making progress. Being adaptive without seriously compromising the unit's mission, especially if that mission is not only new and different but also *catalytic* in nature, may require the implementation of more intensive and more accelerated strategies and tactics than are suggested by previous comparative studies of the creation and early development of innovative staff units. Such was the case of IA.

THE ISSUES ANALYSIS DEPARTMENT'S DEVELOPMENTAL
PATH: Choices and Contingencies

The critical choices and experiences of IA's leaders and members depart in several important ways from those associated with more typical innovative units. Before discussing those choices and their consequences for IA's development, however, it is necessary to contrast the nature of IA with that of the typical innovative department and to isolate some factors in IA's context and prehistory that help explain its formation and development.

The Nature of the New Unit

New staff units that are introduced into established organizational contexts may be distinguished in terms of three fundamental characteristics. All are *new*, and must find some way to cope with the liability of newness.[7] Many are also *different*; meaning what they do is innovative, not conventional. They must find a way to manage the fact that they are both new and different. Finally, although almost all new and different units imply some change for more established elements in the organizational context in which they are created, only a few are *explicitly catalytic*.

I stumbled upon the first two characteristics in an earlier work in which I found it necessary to determine whether an organization is new but conventional versus new and innovative with respect to the context in which it was created. The following observations about new organizations appear to generalize fairly well to new units within organizations. For example, I contrasted the creation of new conventional organizations with ones that are both new and innovative as follows:

> Although accomplished competitors and other rivals for resources are an important part of the external environment of a new but conventional organization, much of the knowledge required to get the organization off the ground is in existence—all that the founders have to do is locate and tap it. In these settings new roles and relationships have to be learned but not invented. Relations with existing organizations must be developed, but much of their form and content will not be unique. The meaning of the new but conventional setting will be understood more readily, not only by its own members but by other organizations upon which the setting is dependent.[8]

The technical-efficiency and organizational-legitimacy issues confronting the founders of new organizations and units increase quite dramatically as one moves from the creation of a new but conventional unit to that of a new and innovative unit. In the new-innovative unit, tasks and roles must be invented, often through the process of trial and error. The new and different department has the initial problem of deciding how to perform its innovative mission and functions while struggling to demonstrate to the rest of the organization that it can do so in a cost-effective manner. This struggle on the technical side exacerbates the problems of creating legitimacy for the unit, which because of its deviant nature will draw out skepticism that ranges from passive resistance to outright sabotage, from established parts of the conventional organization context. Both of these difficulties tend to make the assessment of an innovative unit's performance problematic; a fact that may deprive the innovative unit from securing the slack in time and resources that are necessary to sort out its mission, perfect its tasks, and negotiate new relationships with essential supporters and clients and potential detractors. As I have observed in the creation of innovative organizations, "Experimentation and invention take primacy over technical efficiency in the start up of an innovative organization, and the amount of slack acquired by founders to permit these activities to go forward can be expected to covary with their venture's relative effectiveness as an innovation (p. 434)."

In terms of their fundamental natures, both IA and the typical units discussed in the preceding section must be characterized as both new and different. As innovative staff departments that were introduced into conventional, well-ordered organizational contexts, both IA and the typical unit had to find ways of developing and reconciling the efficiency and legitimacy aspects of the innovative tasks they were created to perform. However, at this point the fundamental nature of IA diverges from that of the typical innovative unit.

The basis for this divergence has to do with the degree to which a new and different unit is expected to be *explicitly* catalytic in initiating change in the status quo of the organization. The explicitness of a unit's catalytic role may be inferred from the intensity of disruption it is expected to create in the organizational status quo and the formal criteria by which its performance is to be assessed. On both grounds, IA's catalytic function is considerably more explicit than that of the typical innovative unit.

Many innovative staff units, for instance, are created with the intention that they will somehow enhance the efficiency of the organization's primary operations. If they are successful they will have created some modification in the way the host organization operates. But often their influence is primarily intended to facilitate the achievement of the line manager's day-to-day performance responsibilities. These units may fail in their attempt to help line managers and they may encounter resistance to the temporary disruption they cause in the line operations as they attempt to impose their innovation, but if they succeed then the line manager's job performance generally becomes more efficient.

In contrast, IA's interventions tended to reduce the line manager's operating efficiencies. In essence, IA was attempting to impose social constraints and contingencies, which are oriented more toward ensuring institutional legitimacy than short-term operational efficiency, on a well-oiled business machine. Consequently, IA's success made the line manager's job more complex and more difficult.

The performance criteria that were imposed on IA by Aetna's executive leaders reinforced its catalytic role. Not only did IA have to bring a high-quality and objective understanding to the social issues confronting the corporation, but it also had to ensure that line managers in the company's profit centers implemented recommended changes in their business policies and practices. Thus, IA was not only new and different; it was also *explictly* catalytic.

These three, as opposed to only two, explicit characteristics made the management of IA's creation, development, and persistence especially difficult. The inclusion of the explicit catalytic role exacerbated the normal issues of efficiency and legitimacy that are typically associated with the creation of new and innovative units, as illustrated in Figure 12.1.

Context and Prehistory

IA did not spring into the organizational world in a sudden reactive flurry as is more typical of innovative staff units. Instead, it was a conscious extension of the earlier task force experiments that had been sponsored by Aetna's executive leaders

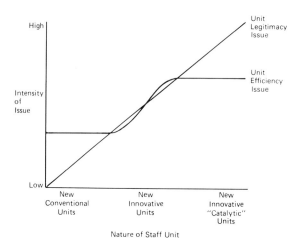

Figure 12-1 Managerial issues in the creation of new staff units in established organizational contexts.

to cope with a novel and potentially ominous set of contingencies that were bearing down upon the corporation. Indeed, one of the two projects that the department took on during the first few months of its life was a continuation of a task force study that had begun in earnest before the decision was made to create IA.

Because of this prehistory, some confidence and wisdom had already been accumulated in the task force approach to social issues analysis and management. Because the cofounders of IA had been instrumental in leading the task forces that preceded IA, they had already experienced the tension between technical efficiency (analytical quality and objectivity) and boundary management (operational relevance and receptivity) that would continue with even greater intensity after the formalization of its mission and functions. They were also in a good position to observe the work of members of the early task forces, and they used this knowledge to make important personnel selection decisions when they assembled IA's charter staff.

All of these elements of prehistory enabled IA's cofounders to launch the new department with greater confidence and less risk than is normally associated with the creation of an innovative staff unit in a conventional organization context.

The same benefits of prehistory applied to Bill Bailey, the executive leader who sponsored IA's creation. He had been able to observe the skills of IA's cofounders as well as the efficacy of the task force approach before making the decisions to launch IA and to appoint its leader. Moreover, his outside experience on the White House commission gave him the confidence in the utility of IA and its general approach that would be necessary to sustain his commitment to the new department during the initial period of high resistance from senior line managers and staff professionals whose autonomy and turf would inevitably be affected by the emergence of IA.

Finally, contextual factors figured heavily in IA's early success. The divisionalized corporate structure, with its traditional emphasis on line-manager autonomy and narrow career specialization, created considerable legitimacy for managerial resistance to the creation and development of IA. Counterbalancing this resistance, however, was the agenda of the new executive leaders and the emergent strategic contingency posed for the organization by the corporate social environment.

With regard to the agenda, IA went with the new grain that was being imposed on the organization by executive leaders. It was part of the new structural context for corporate decision making, and IA's importance in this context was rivaled only by the Corporate Planning Department that had been created by the executive leaders five years before IA. This fact, of course, did not go unnoticed by profit-center managers who were becoming increasingly uncomfortable with both the erosion of their traditional prerogatives and the general uncertainty about their roles and responsibilities during the transition toward more centralized corporate integration. Nevertheless, it was the new executive leaders who ultimately controlled the organizational context that determined the career fates of Aetna's line managers.

In addition, the particular form of strategic contingency confronting the organization also shifted the balance of power away from senior line managers toward IA and its sponsors. Responsibility for aligning Aetna with the corporate social environment resided principally with its executive leaders. Moreover, line managers had relatively little training and experience in dealing with social as opposed to business issues. Therefore, legitimacy favored IA and its sponsors for leading the corporate response to the unprecedented social threat.

In retrospect, I believe these elements of IA's context and prehistory were essential to its early success because of the unusually explicit role IA was assigned as catalyst of managerial learning and organizational change.[9] However, these elements of context and prehistory were not, as the following interpretation of IA's development will reveal, sufficient to keep the new department out of harm's way or to guarantee its vitality and persistence. These prospects for IA's existence depended critically on subsequent decisions made by its cofounders, on the symbolic and substantive actions taken on behalf of IA by its sponsor, and by developments that occurred within the organization and the larger economic and social context in which it is embedded.

Creation and Early Development

IA's early success may be attributed in part to the fact that its cofounders anticipated the self-doubt phase experienced by more typical staff departments at the time the unit was created. There is little doubt that the prehistory sketched above was an important stimulus to the early choices of IA's cofounders. Consequently the creation of IA was accomplished with a more conscious and intensive strategy from the beginning than is typical of innovative units even at later stages in their development. In essence, IA's cofounders greatly accelerated the developmental process by engaging in a variety of tactics that were intended to deal simultaneously with the pressure for task efficiency and the need to create legitimacy for the unit's mission and functions.

The split roles that the cofounders assumed shortly after the formation of the unit greatly facilitated IA's accelerated development. David Elliott, who knew the organization well, had developed during his career an extensive network of important relationships, had established an enviable track record, and was widely regarded as sincere and trustworthy. He spent much of his time linking IA to important elements of its context and smoothing the way for IA task forces and liaison roles that would soon follow. Susan Bennett, a relative newcomer to the organization with whom Elliot had worked on the ad hoc task forces that preceded IA, was an expert in public policy analysis. She was assigned the primary responsibility for leading the task-force studies and getting out the work of the department. Together they conceptualized how IA would perform its missions, collaborated on the selection of the charter staff, and kept each other informed about external and internal issues that warranted attention.

Other key decisions also facilitated the subsequent development of IA. The choice to keep the department small, by relying principally on members' skills as process facilitators, and to use the task force mechanism enabled IA to avoid early criticism about creating excessive corporate overhead expense. This choice also created a situation in which progress toward its dual objectives of rigor (i.e., analytical quality and objectivity) and relevance (i.e., the extent to which IA's recommendations for change were implemented in the business divisions) could be simultaneously managed within the IA process before its products were released into the corporation. By bringing talented middle-level line managers and representatives of other staff functions into the task forces on a part-time basis, IA was able to deal with their concerns from a position of strength. IA could also rely on the fact that ongoing feedback about its work-in-progress would be communicated through its task force members to senior executives in the line and staff units from which the members were drawn. IA was, therefore, able to avoid the surprises that typically beset innovative staff units during their early development.

The cofounders also chose to begin work immediately rather than wait until they had fully conceptualized the new department's function. (The IA Process Memo, which outlined the functions and work methods of the department, was not distributed to senior line and staff executives until six months after the creation of IA.) In addition, they decided to limit the initial work of the department to just two studies. They wanted to make sure they were well within their resources to ensure initial products that would be judged as both rigorous and relevant. They made this choice knowing that one of the three major business divisions would be neglected during much of IA's first year. (It is more than coincidental that several years later this neglected division created its own issues analysis function which is headed by its former liaison from IA.) Later, IA developed the issues inventory to enable it to serve as a clearinghouse for company-related social issues. This inventory also enabled IA to fend off excessive requests for assistance from other line and staff units that might jeopardize the quality of its work.

By placing boundary management activities and tangible work on two strategic contingencies confronting the corporation ahead of the complete articulation of all its functions, IA was able to concretely demonstrate that it was seriously in business before detractors had a chance to second-guess the decision to create it. Later, its cofounders were able to flesh out the Process Memo based on what they learned from the initial task force and boundary management efforts. The early task forces also kept IA open to its organizational context without inhibiting the development of enthusiasm, commitment, and group identity within the new department. The openness also ensured that the new unit and its members did not depart too far from the norms, language, and rhythms of the company as a whole.

By the end of the first year, IA's members did exhibit some of the tendency toward subgrouping into pragmatists and missionaries. A couple of staff members were concerned that all the initial efforts devoted to task-force studies and boundary management had tended to drive out other important departmental functions, such as monitoring the corporate social environment for emerging issues and managing the issues inventory. But the dramatic cleavage found in more typical staff units never materialized within IA. During the second year, IA refined its issues inventory and began to update it on an ongoing basis with inputs solicited from other line and staff units. During the second year, Elliott also began to assign specific responsibilities to core staff members to ensure that all of IA's functions were managed properly.

By the end of the first year, IA had also established specific liaison roles for its core staff members with each major line and staff unit in the corporation. It had commissioned me to provide interview and survey feedback on how it was perceived by other line and staff units and to debrief task force members. Information from these debriefings was used to improve the task force process, develop taskforce leadership skills inside IA, and capture the experience of non-IA task force members.

By the end of the first year, David Elliott was regularly attending the weekly staff meetings of the senior vice president of corporate administration. This forum put IA in touch with events going on in the corporation as a whole, and helped Elliott keep IA from drifting off into its own world. Elliott also sat on most of the external affairs steering committees, and his department was instrumental in the creation of the Public Issues Group, all of which were forums for discussion and debate that linked IA's leader to the most senior executives in the corporation.

Indeed, within its first year IA had developed a full blown development strategy that few typical staff units are able to approximate even at a much later stage in their development. By its third year IA's products were known throughout the industry and the external acclaim it received helped bolster the unit against the eventual shift in the corporation's strategic contingency from the social to the economic domain. By the middle of its fourth year IA had begun to create new capital. It had become involved in analysis and action planning in the area of traditional business issues and it was receiving requests for assistance from other line and staff divisions. Finally, because of the careful selection process IA had used to recruit both task force and core staff members, together with the intrinsically interesting work it offered, the department quickly developed and maintained a reputation as a developmental place that was associated with personal recognition and career advancement.

Important as they were to IA's creation and development, however, I do not believe that given its catalytic role, the department would have prospered on the basis of its prehistory and the early choices of its cofounders alone. The active role played by executive leadership rounds out the explanation of IA's early success.

Role of Executive Leadership

IA's sponsor played important *symbolic* and *substantive* roles in the early life of the new department. As the chief operating officer, Bill Bailey had risen from and now controlled all of the company's line operations. That he was regarded as a champion of corporate social responsiveness in the industry sent a powerful message throughout Aetna's business divisions that social issues are important. His active participation in a variety of external public policy forums reinforced his position on corporate social responsiveness.

When such an executive leader announced the creation of IA, along with the facts that it would report directly to him and that it would be evaluated on the unusual dual performance criteria, he communicated a strong signal to all of the company's line managers that they should be more responsive to industry-related social issues in the way they made decisions regarding business policies and practices. It may be stating the case too strongly, but even the chief executive officer, who had risen through the legal and corporate staff ranks, may not have been able to make as much of an impression as the COO on the company's line managers, had the CEO been the one to create IA.

But the symbolic role played by IA's sponsor did not cease with the announcement of the new department. Bailey missed few opportunities to reinforce the importance of IA's role. He did this in speeches to agents, in memoranda to line managers, in the topics he put on the agenda of the Corporate Management Committee, and in his active participation in the Public Issues Group that was formed shortly after the creation of IA. He even held the meeting in which IA presented the Process Memo to senior corporate executives in his office.

Soon after IA was off the ground and was evidently making progress, Bailey intervened boldly into the annual corporate planning process by having IA review the responsiveness of each division's plan to the social issues confronting its business. This shock treatment served to reinforce his agenda while creating a need for division planners to interact with IA in the formulation of their division's annual business plans. This intervention also served to insert IA into the corporate mainstream.

Later Bailey encouraged the formal incorporation of social goals in the corporate planning and review process. These moves significantly altered the structural context for decision making in the organization in a manner that favored both corporate responsiveness agenda of Aetna's executive leaders and IA's early development. Without these interventions, together with Bailey's active follow-through with the heads of the business divisions of IA's recommendations for business changes, it is doubtful that IA could have survived its catalytic role.

Finally, after the department had proven itself, its head was promoted to a rank equivalent to those of the heads of larger and more established, external affairs departments. Thus, active symbolic and substantive support of the sponsoring executive leader was essential during the launch of IA, and was a crucial factor that enabled the unit to encourage needed changes in the business divisions without running the risk of being coopted by them in the process. Without his support, the highly resistant divisionalized structure of the corporation would have made IA's early life more trouble that it was worth.

THE ESSENTIAL INGREDIENT OF SUCCESS

All of the foregoing factors have played an important role in IA's success, but one factor—IA's distinctive competence, or what IA has been able to do *particularly* well—if missing could have made all the difference in this innovative unit's progress. That factor is IA's ability to manage *process*.

It was not the broad perspectives and general framework that IA members brought to their tasks that resides at the core of IA's success, although these things were present and were necessary to the fulfillment of the unit's function. Nor was it the technical expertise in the specific social issue being addressed, although somehow—through internal or external consultants or from the specific experience of a line manager on loan to IA from a business division—this too was found in sufficient quantity and quality when needed. Nor did IA's leader exude a level of personal charisma that automatically captured the hearts of members of other line and staff units needed to support IA's development, although the leader did have the earned trust and respect of an unusually large number of important individuals within the company. (As one senior line manager said of David Elliott when the unit had encroached too heavily into his operations, "It's a bit of overswing, but Dave's heart is in the right place.")

What IA did particularly well is conceive of and manage its work as a process. The cofounders thought of IA's mission as facilitating a process of managerial learning and organizational adaptation with respect to the corporate social environment. Their early translation of IA's mission into specific tasks to be performed by the new unit was titled the Process Memo. Their analytical work was designed as an unfolding process, which involved line and staff managers in the task forces and provided for important linkages to other parts of the organization that might be affected by IA's recommendations or that might provide needed expertise and other resources at the right time to ensure a high quality product. They even conceived of the issues inventory as a process involving continual dialogue and update in interaction with all other important areas in the company.

Although the cofounders of IA felt strongly about the importance of process in launching and sustaining the new department, it was not until they encountered the difficult task of replacing core staff members that they were forced to test their guiding assumption. Through trial and error with new recruits, IA's leaders gradually discovered that it was process skills—the ability to lead task forces, to perform liaison roles and to link IA to other departments, to encourage others to respond to IA's recommendations, to deal with a variety of difficult one-on-one and group situations, to help one another learn and develop, and to make something positive out of criticism—that made the real difference between success or failure among incoming core staff members and ultimately in how IA was perceived and assessed by the organization as a whole.

Assessing Effectiveness

Finally, there is the matter of IA's effectiveness. Such an assessment must take into account three aspects of IA's performance

1. the extent to which it accomplished the tasks it was created to perform,
2. the extent to which its mission and functions have become recognized as legitimate,
3. the extent to which it has provided positive outcomes for those who have worked with IA either as a core staff member or as a part-time member of one of its task forces.

Given that Aetna was among the most highly exposed companies in its industry to the social and political turbulence in the late 1970s and early 1980s, the fact that this company became the most highly rated corporate social performer in the industry casts the tasks performed by IA in a very positive light. It is doubtful that without the response mechanism provided by IA Aetna could have achieved a leadership position in understanding and managing the corporate social environment surrounding this socially sensitive industry.

The evidence from the developmental history of IA also indicates that the unit quickly became the focal point for integrating the work of other elements of the corporate-level external affairs function. Moreover, the issues inventory process created and managed by IA served as an effective means of sorting and prioritizing the multitude of industry-related, social issues that impacted the company and was instrumental in helping executive leaders decide how to optimize the allocation of organizational resources earmarked for corporate external affairs activities.

Having IA in place also helped Aetna to avoid duplication and conflict in the way its decentralized business divisions responded to relevant social issues. Thus,

IA was able to contribute positively to the agenda of Aetna's new executive leaders who wanted a corporation that was better integrated and more responsive to society. Finally, there is considerable evidence that IA had had an impact in terms of helping line managers adapt their division's traditional business policies and practices to the changing corporate social environment. IA facilitated this adaptive process not only through the consulting it provided divisions in the implementation of task force recommendations, but also through the ongoing liaison roles it staffed and managed and its active involvement in the line divisions' annual business planning process.

For all of these reasons IA's performance of its assigned tasks must be judged as highly effective. Moreover, by relying on the task-force mechanism, IA was able to accomplish these difficult tasks with only modest additions to its annual budget and staffing levels during a time when corporate overhead expense had become a subject of serious contention within the organization.

In terms of the personal outcomes of part-time and core staff members on task forces, the record for IA is quite positive. Both line and staff members view work with IA both as a developmental opportunity and as a career-enhancing experience. Indeed, the line managers who were debriefed at the conclusion of task force work unanimously said that they would recommend a similar experience to their closest colleagues.

Such experience provided rising line managers an opportunity to tackle broad issues of strategic importance to their company and its industry and to develop a total corporate perspective relatively early in their careers. Many veterans of IA's task forces especially valued the unusually high degree of visibility and interaction IA work required them to have with senior corporate executives and with key managers in business and staff areas other than their own. The development of a company-wide perspective among line managers whose careers had been confined to a vertical promotion track within a single business division reinforced the new executive leaders' agenda of having a better integrated corporation. Having line managers become involved in a company-wide experience with IA also reinforced another part of that agenda, which called for the development of better overall corporate responsiveness to the changing social environment.

Finally, IA was successful in recruiting and socializing a number of fairly senior outsiders who could later assume more conventional jobs in other Aetna functions. Thus, IA was able to bring new talent into an organization that otherwise would have been highly resistant to outsiders. Moreover, the aging of IA has not led to much slippage in task challenge and member motivation. The principal reasons for its continued vitality are the novelty of the issues it engages and the planned turnover of its staff, not to mention the ongoing tension built into its dual-performance criteria.

The issue of IA's legitimacy is more difficult to gauge, although there is considerable evidence that the unit has been able to sustain its original mission and functions despite the removal of several props that were essential to its successful launch.

So far IA has survived the loss of its direct link to the chief operating officer who shifted the focus of his attention to the economic realities created by a severe and sustained business downcycle in one of the company's major product lines coupled with a long recession in the U.S. economy. IA has also remained intact during several cost-reduction programs that have been initiated within the company during the past two years.

During these developments, IA has begun to generalize its process to business as well as social issues, has continued to maintain its image as a developmental place, and been able to sustain its reputation despite heavy rotation of the core staff.

Just how long IA will remain in its original mission and form is difficult to predict. It has served its major purposes of enabling Aetna to lead the industry out of the social crises of the last half decade, of developing a broader sensitivity among line managers about the social consequences of their business decisions, and of facilitating a better-integrated and more responsive corporate approach to understanding and managing the corporate social environment. Its process has become regarded highly enough to be in demand throughout the corporation and one business division has even created an IA clone that specializes in the social issues affecting the division's product lines.

The most obvious contingency that IA will meet in the near future is the turnover of David Elliott, its leader and founder. Whether the unit can survive this event, given that virtually all of the original staff members have already rotated to other jobs, and whether the process IA has introduced into the organization will ever become institutionalized to the extent that only the memory of IA is needed, are questions that cannot be definitively answered at this time. They are, of course, contingent upon shifts that are yet to occur in the factors that have been isolated in this developmental history.

FOOTNOTES

1. The principal work of Andrew Pettigrew on the creation and development of innovative staff units is summarized in the following publications: Andrew M. Pettigrew, *The Politics of Organizational Decision-making* (London: Tavistock Publications, 1973); Andrew M. Pettigrew, "Strategic Aspects of the Management of Specialist Activity," *Personnel Review*, 1975, 4, no.1, 5–13; Andrew M. Pettigrew and D. C. Bumstead, "Strategies of Organization Development in Differing Organizational Contexts," in P.A. Clark, J. Guiot, and H. Thirry, eds., *Organizational Change and Development in Europe* (London: Wiley, 1981); Andrew M. Pettigrew, "The Influence Process between Specialists and Executives," *Personnel Review*, 1974, 3, no.1, 24–30; and Andrew M. Pettigrew, "Towards a Political Theory of Organizational Intervention," *Human Relations*, 1975, 28, no.3, 191–208.
2. Other studies explicitly included in Pettigrew's developmental model of specialized staff units are Michael Radnor, Albert Rubinstein, and Alan S. Bean, "Integration and Utilization of Management Science Activities in Organizations," *Operational Research Quarterly*, 1968, 19, no.2, 117–41; Bernard Bass, "When Planning for Others," *Journal of Applied Behavioral Science*, 1970, 6, no.2, 151–71; and Bernard

Taylor and P. Irving, "Organized Planning in Major UK Companies," *Long Range Planning,* 1971, vol. 3, no.4.

3. More recent studies of the development of innovative units within established organizational contexts include John R. Kimberly, "Initiation, Innovation, and Institutionalization," in J. R. Kimberly, R. H. Miles, and Associates, *The Organizational Life Cycle* (San Francisco: CA: Jossey-Bass, 1980), pp. 18–43; Richard E. Walton, "Establishing and Maintaining High Commitment Work Systems," in J. R. Kimberly, R. H. Miles, and Associates, *The Organizational Life Cycle* (San Francisco, CA: Jossey-Bass, 1980), pp. 208–90; M. Lynne Markus, "Implementation Politics: Top Management Support and User Involvement," *Systems, Objectives, Solutions,* 1981, Vol. 1, pp. 203–215; and S. C. Wheelwright and R. L. Banks, "Involving Operating Managers in Planning Process Evolution," *Sloan Management Review,* Summer 1979, pp. 43–59. The first publication refers to the creation of an innovative medical school in a conventional university; the second to the creation of innovative plants within traditional U.S. manufacturing corporations; and the last two publications refer to the development of innovative planning systems in established organizational contexts.

4. Pettigrew refers to these phases as the conception, pioneering, and self-doubt phases in the development of a specialized staff department.

5. Unless otherwise noted, the descriptions and quotes included in the summary of "Typical Developmental Patterns" are drawn from Andrew M. Pettigrew, "Strategic Aspects of the Management of Specialist Activity," *Personnel Review,* 1975, 4, no.1, 5–13.

6. Seymour B. Sarason, *The Creation of Settings and the Future Societies* (San Francisco, CA: Jossey-Bass, 1972), p. 17.

7. For a more complete discussion of the "liability of newness," refer to Arthur L. Stinchcombe, "Social Structure and Organizations," in J. G. March, ed., *Handbook of Organizations* (Chicago, IL: Rand McNally, 1965).

8. These quotes are drawn from Robert H. Miles, "Findings and Implications of Organizational Life Cycle Research: A Commencement," in J. R. Kimberly, R. H. Miles, and Associates, *The Organizational Life Cycle: Issues in the Creation, Transformation, and Decline of Organizations* (San Francisco, CA: Jossey-Bass, 1980), pp. 430–50.

9. Sarason, in *The Creation of Settings and the Future Societies,* has referred to these elements of context and prehistory in the creation of new organizations as "confronting history." For an in-depth treatment of the concept of confronting history refer to pages 37–43.

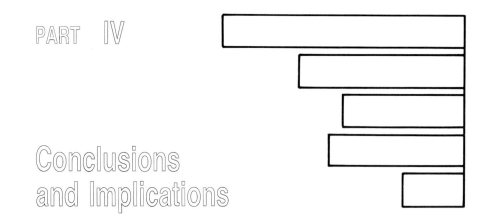

PART IV

Conclusions
and Implications

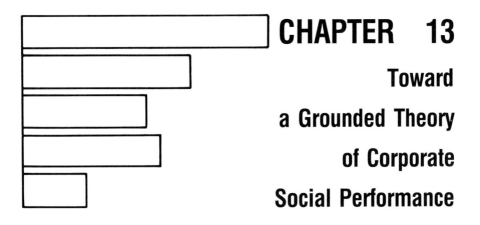

CHAPTER 13

Toward
a Grounded Theory
of Corporate
Social Performance

The information surfaced in the comparative and developmental studies provides an unusually rich empirical basis for the articulation of a grounded theory of corporate social performance. Such a theory requires the specification of a comprehensive yet parsimonious set of core concepts and relationships that explain a practically significant portion of the variance in the phenomenon of interest. Moreover, the concepts and relationships in such a theory must be clearly defined and easily measured. Finally, such a theory must be meaningful to relevant practitioners and scholars. It is intended as the basis for future improvements in practice and advancements in knowledge about corporate social performance.

The grounded theory advanced here consists of three categories of elements. There are *core concepts* and the *principal relationships* among them which are the immediate antecedents of corporate social performance. In addition, there are some important *contextual factors* that shape the core concepts and relationships. From an internal perspective, these contextual factors include corporate history and character and executive leadership. From an external perspective, these contextual factors are represented by the social and economic dimensions of overall corporate performance that are fed back into the corporation. The model of the corporation implied by the theory, therefore, is one of a system which is to varying degrees open to the outside environment. This systemic view reflects generally recognized tensions between environmental determinism and managerial volition as well as organizational rationality and politics. The nature of this system and the elements and relationships that make up the grounded theory are illustrated in Figure 13-1.

Before articulating the elements of this theory, it is important to recall that two different approaches and several measurement techniques were employed to be

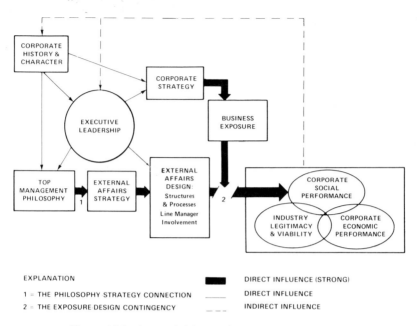

Figure 13-1 A grounded theory of corporate social performance.

able to reach this stage of theory development. Although there is remarkable convergence among these approaches and methods in terms of their implications for the construction and refinement of the grounded theory, the yield for some elements was greater for some approaches and methods than for others. For example, while all of the comparative methods tended to contribute in different ways to understanding and refining the core concepts and relationships, a large portion of the evidence on the role of corporate history and character came from the comparative case studies. Similarly, these case studies and the developmental study yielded a disproportionately large share of the insights into the role of executive leadership.

In this last chapter, therefore, an attempt will be made to bring all of these sources of information about the three sets of elements together in an articulation of the grounded theory. This process will take us beyond the general framework of concepts that was used to focus the study to include important relationships as well as the influences of contextual factors. Finally, an attempt will be made to reveal some of the important linkages between the social and economic dimensions of overall corporate performance.

CORE CONCEPTS

The grounded theory of corporate social performance that is being proposed consists of four core concepts (1) business exposure, (2) top management philosophy, (3) external affairs strategy, and (4) external affairs design, which includes the degree of line-manager involvement in this function.

Business Exposure

Exposure to the corporate social environment serves as a point of departure. Such exposure is a function of the business strategy a corporation explicitly or implicitly pursues, which in turn determines the businesses in which a company will operate and in what manner, and which is largely a product of corporate history and character and executive leadership.

Inherent in a corporation's business strategy are several dimensions, which not only define the company's product-markets, but also determine the degree to which its business policies and practices are exposed to social and political contingencies.[1] The most important and generalizable dimension of business exposure is a company's product mix. This term is intended as a broad dimension that encompasses the nature of a company's products and services as well as the manner in which they are produced and distributed. Moreover, close examination reveals two important underlying dimensions of product mix. The first is the luxury-necessity dimension; the other is the potential negative-contingencies dimension. In general, firms that produce products or services that are viewed as necessities by the general public and whose products or the processes by which they are produced or distributed entail substantial potential negative contingencies for the general public anchor the high end of the business exposure continuum. Business exposure to external social and political contingencies, therefore, declines to the extent that a firm's product mix consists more of luxuries or discretionary products involving minimal negative consequences for the general public.

In addition to product mix, there will be other elements of business strategy that contribute to overall exposure, but which will emerge more as a function of the specific nature of the company's business. In the study of the U.S. insurance industry these secondary dimensions of business exposure included customer mix and geographical mix. The latter is particularly applicable to this industry because of the state-level government regulation with which member firms must cope.

Degree of business exposure is presented here as the starting point for any serious inquiry or intervention into the realm of corporate social performance because the greater the degree of a corporation's exposure, the greater will be the need for executive attention and organizational resources in the area of corporate external affairs.

The next two core concepts involve the values and intentions that reside within the organization, which comprise the overall approach to corporate social performance.

Top Management Philosophy

Managerial values, herein described as *top management philosophies* about the role of the corporation in society, reveal the meaning attached to social performance within a corporation. Shaped by the confluence of corporate history and character and differences among executive leaders, as well as feedback on corporate performance, this value continuum is anchored at one extreme by an institution-oriented philosophy and at the other by an enterprise-oriented philosophy.

Executives in *enterprise-oriented* corporations tend to take a narrow view of the firm as an autonomous economic entity. For them, the public interest is served best when the firm is able to maximize the pursuit of its economic self-interests, free of industry-specific intervention by the general public or its agents. This orientation causes these executives to devote considerable energy and organizational resources to the process of protecting and buffering traditional business policies and practices from external social and political contingencies.

In contrast, executives in *institution-oriented* corporations tend to adopt a broader view of their firm, which they perceive as a social as well as economic franchise. They believe that a large, complex corporation not only has a duty to adapt its business policies and practices to changes in society, but also that because of the scope and pervasiveness of its operations such a corporation can exert nontrivial influences on society. Recognition of these interdependencies between the large corporation and society causes institution-oriented executives to be more willing than their enterprise-oriented counterparts to expose the traditional business policies and practices of the firm to external social and political contingencies.

It is worth noting that I have expressed the differences in the philosophical orientations of corporate executives less as a continuum and more as archetypes. That is, indeed, how they were found to exist in the host industry, where the overall exposure of firms is relatively high and where executive leaders and many other managers and staff professionals necessarily spend a significant portion of their time and resources dealing explicitly with external social and political contingencies. Such may not be the case in industries having less overall social exposure. There, these value-based differences may be more appropriately gauged using a philosophical continuum, with many firms reflecting a mixture of the archetypes. Such internal value contradictions may exist if for no other reason than they have not been tested by important social contingencies.

External Affairs Strategy

External affairs strategy is the third core concept in the theory. This concept refers to a company's overall approach to corporate external affairs, the function employed to understand and manage relationships between the corporation and the social environment to which it is exposed. The concept has two underlying dimensions. The first concerns the orientation of the firm toward external relationships with peer firms that share the same social environment. This dimension is anchored at one extreme by a collaborative approach, which recognizes both the shared fate condition of similarly exposed corporations and the implications of corporate self-interest for the longer term viability of the industry as a whole; and at the other by an individualistic approach, which asserts the prerogatives or self-interests of an individual firm. The other dimension concerns a corporation's orientation toward relationships with agents of the public interest, including government regulators, legislators, public interest groups, and individual members of the general public. This dimension ranges from a problem-solving approach, which attempts to keep the business operations of the corporation open to influence from the social environment, to an adversarial approach, which emphasizes the need to buffer and protect business operations from external social influences.

Finally, in highly exposed industries such as the one that hosted this study, these two dimensions tend to coexist in an internally consistent manner as archetypes of corporate external affairs strategies. Thus, firms—especially those in highly exposed industries—tend to pursue with varying degrees of explicitness either a collaborative/problem-solving strategy or an individualistic/adversarial strategy in their corporate external affairs activities. The former reflects a broader and longer view of effectiveness in the domain of corporate external affairs. The latter emphasizes the narrower and shorter-term consequences of corporate external affairs and reveres the preservation of the company's self-interests and maintenance of the status quo in its business policies and practices. Finally, these choices appear to derive directly from the philosophy held within a corporation about its role in society.

External Affairs Design

External affairs design is the final core concept in the proposed theory. It consists of the structures and processes that are put into place to implement the corporation's external affairs strategy. Together these structures and processes make up the mechanism by which corporations learn about and respond to external social and political contingencies affecting their businesses.

Several design dimensions are important in unraveling how well equipped corporations are to understand and manage these contingencies. External affairs *breadth* refers to the diversity of subfunctions within the overall external affairs function. The greater the breadth of the function, the better equipped the corporation will be to understand an increasingly complex social environment.

External affairs *depth* contains two components: (1) the diversity of perspectives that are allowed in the process of analyzing issues emanating from the corporate social environment, and (2) the range of responses that may be considered by external affairs professionals for dealing with these issues. The greater the external affairs depth, the broader will be the range of perspectives employed in the function to understand a social issue and the wider will be the range of alternative responses that may be chosen.[2]

Firms with little external affairs depth tend to take the narrow perspective of company self-interest when attempting to understand a social issue and to restrict the range of acceptable responses to those which engage elements and events in the external social environment without disturbing the status quo in the firm's business policies and practices. In contrast, firms with greater external affairs depth tend to take many perspectives in addition to their own self-interests (e.g., the perspective of peer companies and of the consumer or general public and their agents) into account as they struggle to understand an issue. They also tend to examine a broad range of response alternatives, including changes in the traditional business policies and practices that are engaged by the social issue. One important clue to whether a company possesses such depth is the existence of an important part of the structure of the external affairs function that has been assigned a catalytic role with respect to needed changes in business operations.

While the breadth and depth dimensions reflect how well the design of the external affairs function maps onto the complexity of the social environment to which a corporation is exposed, they ignore how well the environmental receptors in the function process the information they receive. To capture this aspect of external affairs design it is necessary to add two process dimensions, *integration* and *influence*.

For high-quality processing of information about the corporate social environment to occur, the breadth and depth represented by the mix of core subunits in the external affairs function must be integrated into a holistic perspective. Therefore, integrative mechanisms or processes must be developed to facilitate exchange among these subunits. In addition, to further minimize distortion in information processing, there must be a pattern of mutual influence among these subunits. Where large imbalances persist among subunits representing different perspectives on the corporate social environment, distortions will occur in the relative weights attached to different aspects of the social environment in how the corporation chooses to manage external affairs activities.

The final dimension of external affairs design refers not to the structures and processes of the core staff function itself, but to the degree of *line-management involvement* in corporate external affairs activities. Where line-manager involvement is low, three things are likely to happen. First, the perspective of line managers who run the businesses that are impacted by social and political contingencies is not represented in how the corporation attempts to understand the social environment. Consequently, external affairs professionals may develop naive or superficial responses to social and political contingencies that work at cross-purposes with the business operations. Second, when line managers are not involved in the external affairs process one may expect that their resistance to staff-sponsored interventions into their business policies and practices will be great. Third, line managers often serve as important receptors about business-related social issues.[3] Therefore, to minimize their involvement denies the core external affairs staff an important source of information about emerging social and political contingencies affecting or generated by the business operations. Consequently, corporations with staff-dominated external affairs functions tend to be deprived of the option of readily adapting business policies and practices to external social pressures.

But external affairs effectiveness can also be impaired if line-management involvement is too great. Where line managers dominate the corporate external affairs function, so does the perspective of the traditional business policies and practices of the firm. Line-management domination, therefore, distorts the corporation's perception of the importance and relevance of business-related, social and political events and trends, and biases the response choices in a manner that favors protecting and buffering the line operations from external social pressures. Moreover, these effects are amplified in enterprise-oriented companies.

Thus, at the extremes of this design dimension are line dominance versus staff dominance of the corporate external affairs function, both of which lead to predictable distortions in the information-processing activity as well as to predictable biases in the range of coping alternatives that are regarded as legitimate within the corporation. More sophisticated external affairs functions are characterized by the midrange on this design dimension, or what has been referred to as a condition of line–staff balance in the external affairs activities of a corporation.

Corporations vary, therefore, in the overall sophistication of the internal mechanisms they have developed for understanding and managing the social environment, depending on the extent of breadth, depth, integration, influence, and line-manager involvement that characterizes the design of their external affairs function.

PRINCIPAL RELATIONSHIPS

Having identified a core set of variables that need to be accounted for in understanding how large, complex corporations cope with external social and political contingencies, the task of explaining the variance among firms in coping effectiveness resides with a few key relationships among the variables. One relationship reflects the essential elements of strategy *formulation* in the corporate external affairs arena. The other relationship reveals how corporations *implement* their approach to corporate social performance through the choices made about organizational structures and processes.

Philosophy-strategy Connection

The first of these relationships, which has been referred to as the *philosophy-strategy connection,* represents the traditional Business Policy perspective on organizational effectiveness. Core business-policy concepts of managerial values and organizational strategy are translated in the corporate social performance arena as top management philosophies about the role of the corporation in society and the strategy executive leaders assign to the corporate external affairs function.

In the highly exposed host industry the connection between these two factors for most firms was quite strong. Executive leaders with institution-oriented philosophies had assigned collaborative/problem-solving strategies to their external affairs function. Executive leaders who held enterprise-oriented philosophies about the role of their corporation in society presided over external affairs functions that were explicitly or implicitly individualistic and adversarial in their approach to relationships with elements and events in the corporate social environment. Moreover, in such a highly exposed industry, it was relatively easy to understand these managerial and strategic differences and to demonstrate them through a variety of complementary measurement techniques.

On the surface this relationship between what managers believe and what they intend to do to realize their beliefs appears powerful enough by itself to discriminate between corporations at the extremes of overall social performance. Institution-oriented companies pursuing collaborative/problem-solving strategies in their approach to corporate external affairs occupy the high-effectiveness end of the social performance continuum, whereas lower performers are enterprise-oriented companies pursuing individualistic/adversarial strategies.

If a purely business-policy or strategy-formulation perspective had guided this theory-building effort, if the empirical evidence had been confined to companies residing only at the extremes of corporate social performance, and if the design of the organization as it relates to corporate external affairs had been outside the scope of the framework guiding the study, it would have been reasonable to expect the theory of corporate social performance to conclude with the finding that the philosophy-strategy connection is by itself both necessary and sufficient. However, by pursuing a framework with broader perspective and scope, as suggested by the early data-gathering efforts, and by expanding the sampling variation through the addition of firms distributed across the midrange of corporate social performance, it became clear that although necessary, the business-policy perspective is insufficient.

At best, the philosophy-strategy connection, which represents managerial values and intentions, serves as a gross discriminator of differences among firms in terms of their social performance. It takes the traditional perspective of Organization Theory, or a focus on the way in which a corporation's external affairs strategy is implemented, to provide the kind of fine-grained discrimination that diagnosis and intervention into the practice of corporate social performance requires. This additional perspective on corporate social performance, which reflects organizational capabilities, is provided by the relationship described as the exposure-design contingency.

Exposure-design Contingency

The *exposure-design contingency* focuses attention on the structures and processes that are part of the corporate external affairs function and the extent to which they are sophisticated enough to successfully engage the uncertainties imposed upon the corporation by its degree of exposure to external social and political contingencies. This relationship is an elaboration of the classical contingency theory of organization design, which asserts that organizational effectiveness is a function of the degree of congruence or fit between the complexity of the external environment and the design of the organization.

From this perspective, the external environments of organizations vary in the extent to which they create decision-making uncertainty within organizations. The task of organization design is to process information about the external environment in such a manner that decision-making uncertainty is brought down to manageable levels. Decision makers accomplish this task by adjusting the internal structures and processes of the organization to achieve the degree of specialization and the intensity of coordination that is required to effectively understand and manage the contingencies imposed upon the organization by its external environment.

These tenets of the contingency theory of organization design are adapted and elaborated in the exposure-design contingency within the present theory of corporate social performance. The breadth, depth, and line-manager involvement dimensions of external affairs design represent the variety of perspectives, or degree of specialization, that a corporation has in place for understanding the external social environment to which it is exposed. The integration and influence dimensions of external affairs design represent the degree of coordination that the corporation has achieved among the different, specialized perspectives represented in the external affairs function. Together these five design dimensions reflect the overall sophistication of the corporate external affairs function.

Other things being equal, the exposure-design contingency implies that corporate social performance is a function of the degree of fit between the sophistication of a firm's external affairs design and the business exposure of the firm. For example, corporations pursuing business strategies that expose them to intensive social and political contingencies must develop and resource external affairs functions with sophisticated designs in order to achieve high levels of corporate social performance. Corporations with lower business exposures require less sophisticated external affairs designs in order to effectively understand and manage the social environment.

When this contingent relationship was combined with the philosophy-strategy connection a fine-grained discrimination among the insurance companies that had achieved different levels of corporate social performance was obtained, as summarized in Table 13-1. The best-rated corporate social performers all exhibited institution-oriented philosophies, pursued collaborative/problem-solving external

TABLE 13-1   **Explanatory Powers of Business Policy and Organization Theory Perspectives**

Academic Perspectives	Traditional Perspectives	Core Concepts in Grounded Theory	Principal Relationships	Social Performance Discrimination
Business Policy	Corporate strategies	External affairs strategies	Philosophy-strategy connection	Coarse-grained
	Managerial values	Top management philosophies		
Organization Theory	External environment	Business "exposure"	Exposure-design contingency	Fine-grained
	Organization design	External affairs design		

affairs strategies, *and* had achieved a good degree of fit between their business exposure and the sophistication of their external affairs design. All of the other insurance companies exhibited enterprise-oriented philosophies and pursued individualistic/adversarial strategies, but the average performers had achieved a better exposure-design fit than had the worst corporate social performers. Taken together, then, the philosophy-strategy connection and the exposure-design contingency, which reflect the traditional perspectives of business policy and organization theory, respectively, do a much better job of explaining and predicting differences in overall corporate social performance than either relationship or perspective alone.[4]

CONTEXTUAL FACTORS

Three major contextual factors influence the operation of the core concepts and their relationships. They are

1. corporate history and character,
2. executive leadership,
3. feedback on corporate performance.

Company History and Character

I first recognized the importance of corporate history and character in a study of how firms in the U.S. tobacco industry attempted to cope with the social and political contingencies associated with the smoking-and-health controversy.[5] Included in *Coffin Nails and Corporate Strategies,* was an analysis of a quarter century of data on each of the "Big Six" tobacco firms, which revealed that corporate character was a subtle but powerful factor influencing both organizational decision making and corporate behavior in these exposed firms.

In that study corporate character was conceptualized as a mixture of organizational predispositions and competences and managerial values that are reflected in a consistent manner in the patterns of strategic choices that distinguished among the *behaviors* of corporations over time and across a variety of performance situations.[6] In all cases, an important part of the character of these large, complex organizations could be traced back to the founder's vision, some key decisions made early in the life of the company, and the patterns of successes and failures in the company's reinforcement history. The confluence of these factors often resulted in a contemporary reflection of corporate character in which all of the elements had become integrated. After examining the relationship between each firm's character and the choices made by its executive leaders to cope with an increasingly hostile social environment, I concluded that,

> the character of an organization sets limits on what it can do well, shapes the values that are pursued and the choices of what shall be done, and influences which behaviors are in the organization's repetoire and which are drawn from it (p. 247).

Tobacco companies that attempted to adapt to the smoking-and-health contingencies by resorting to strategies that were inconsistent with their character generally performed much lower than companies whose choices for strategic adaptation were consistent with corporate character.

Therefore, the tobacco industry study was useful in identifying the concept of corporate character and many of the subtle but powerful influences it had on organizational decision making and corporate behavior, but the insights it provided were limited because of my principal role as outside observer. In contrast, the present study, which placed me inside corporations, provided additional insights because of the variety of research methods that could be employed.

Among the national insurers several origins of corporate character could be isolated. In many cases of these large, old institutions the vision and ideals of the founder had been carefully preserved. Much of the corporation's contemporary statement of corporate mission and operating philosophy could be traced to the original statements or memoirs of the founder. As previously mentioned, one of the best social performers in the industry commissions a written history of the company every 25 years as a way of gauging its allegiance to its founding principles. In other companies, especially those pursuing an explicit philosophy and external affairs strategy, stories are shared about the deeds of executive leaders and about how the company coped in a value-consistent manner with major company and industry watersheds. Similar artifacts and stories focusing on the role of the corporation in society were not, however, found within the firms classified by their approach to corporate social performance as reactive.

Another feature of the development of corporate character among the major insurance companies is that shared values and hence, present-day top management philosophy about the role of the corporation in society tended to reflect the general purposes for which the company was created and the social and economic contingencies that were prominent during the era in which the company was founded.[7] For example, many of the large national insurers were founded shortly after the mid-19th century in direct response to public catastrophy. Such firms tend, therefore, to have been created for the principal purpose of satisfying a social goal. Others, many of which were founded during the first third of the 20th century, were explicitly created principally to pursue economic goals. For example, one of the companies that couched its approach to corporate social performance in terms of an explicit enterprise-oriented philosophy was founded by a group of industrialists whose shared objective was to reduce the insurance costs their manufacturing firms had been paying.

Thus, an important influence on the contemporary philosophies held within corporations about the proper role to play in society can be traced to the relatively enduring values embedded in the fundamental character of the enterprise, which in turn is in part a function of the values of the founder and the social context at the time of creation. Moreover, corporate history and character serve as major influences on the business strategies pursued by a large corporation. Basically, in the absence of influence from other contextual factors, corporations tend to pursue strategies in a value-consistent manner and that are congruent with the distinctive competences and reinforcement histories of the firm.

Executive Leadership

But such a deterministic explanation of top management philosophy ignores the important role played by executive leaders and by feedback on corporate performance in shaping and refining the prevailing view of the corporation in society and the approach it takes to corporate social performance. Here again, the quarter-century study of the tobacco companies is instructive.

First, the adaptive behaviors of the tobacco "Big Six" revealed an important influence of corporate character on executive leadership and hence, top management philosophy. Because many of the executive leaders in these firms had been socialized through long service before arriving at the top of the hierarchy, it was not surprising to discover that many of them served as agents of the traditional values embedded in the character of their corporation. But even when the traditional patterns of executive succession were preserved, noticeable differences in strategic orientation and risk-taking propensity could be observed in the firm within a short time after a new executive leader was appointed. Because of the limited scope of the tobacco industry study, it was not possible to inquire deeply into the individual differences between successive executive leaders to attempt to explain their refinements in corporate character and strategy. However, one individual characteristic was observable. Subtle yet potentially powerful modifications in strategic orientation and managerial values could be traced to differences in the functional career tracks of successive executive leaders. Put simply, executive leaders with marketing backgrounds pursued different values and strategies than did those with financial backgrounds, thereby signalling that individual differences in executive leaders could be reflected in the corporation's orientation and approach to the social and political contingencies associated with the smoking-and-health controversy.[8]

Similar patterns were discovered in this study of executive leaders in the insurance industry, where it was possible to examine more closely the influences of these executive leaders. They too were the products of long periods of socialization into the traditional corporate values and the philosophies and predispositions of their executive mentors. For that reason, each of the insurance company executive leaders presided over and reinforced a view of the corporation's role in society that, with few exceptions, bore the strong imprint of corporate history and character. But in all cases, executive leaders had been able to refine and elaborate top management philosophy and external afffairs strategy based on their own beliefs and experiences. Most of these influences took the form of directional rather than fundamental changes; many involved a shift along the implicit-explicit continuum toward greater clarity and attention-focus on external affairs strategy; and all included the modification of the mechanisms by which the corporation learned about and managed relations with external social and political contingencies.

Institution-oriented executives had logged far more extensive outside experiences in public forums than had their enterprise-oriented counterparts. To be sure, part of their motivation for doing this had been the influence of company traditions, career progression criteria, and role modeling by organizational mentors. But when the social environment surrounding the industry became more volatile in the 1960s and 1970s the rising executives who had greater exposure to public forums were influenced in two ways to a greater extent than their corporation-bound counterparts. First, they developed a greater awareness of the escalation of public and governmental expectations of their corporations and industry. Second, they became better acquainted with the innovative mechanisms that would be required to effectively cope with these new contingencies. As a result, executives with substantial outside public involvement tended to be more motivated and better equipped than other executives to exert their personal influence on corporate social performance. When they became executive leaders these sensitized individuals often were the ones to engineer transformations in external affairs strategy. Because of them, some responsible but otherwise passive corporations were able to also become responsive. Some reactive companies that lacked explicit strategies for dealing with social and political contingencies became proactive. And some companies that suffered from impoverished external affairs functions developed effective mechanisms for understanding and managing the corporate social environment to which they were exposed.

Executive leaders influenced the nature and quality of corporate social performance in a number of substantive and symbolic ways. Through their articulation and communication of the role of the corporation in society and its approach to external affairs, they created meaning for the organization and its members. Through the strategic choices they pursued, they defined the extent of corporate exposure to social and political contingencies. And through the design modifications they made to the corporate external affairs function they shaped the organization's capacity and capability for implementing their corporate social performance agenda.

This ability to alter the internal context of organizational decision making, which has both substantive and symbolic implications for the form and conduct of corporate external affairs activities and their relationship to the core business operations, serves as the primary basis of influence of executive leaders. As one general management scholar has observed, the internal context created by executive leaders,[9]

> shapes the purposive manager's definition of business problems by directing, delimiting and coloring his focus and perception; it determines the priorities which the various demands on him are given. Structural context has this role because it is the principal way in which the purposive manager learns about the goals of the corporation . . .

> Structural context is particularly important because all of its elements are subject to control by top management. Thus, management has in its hands the levers that influence behaviors of managers many levels below the top of the hierarchical organization (p. 73).

For these reasons, the influence of executive leaders on the form and conduct of corporate social performance tends to vary with the extensiveness of their alterations in the internal context of organizational decision making and the degree to which these interventions are consistent and mutually reinforcing.

But the magnitude of executive leader influence was not confined to setting the context. Executive leaders who had the greatest magnitude of influence also engaged in a variety of symbolic and substantive personal role behaviors that reinforced the context they had established, that signalled their commitment, and that facilitated the launch of innovative activities. Nowhere were these personal role behaviors more evident than in the companies that were moving toward a more explicit collaborative/problem-solving approach to corporate social performance. Implementation of this strategy exposes the core business operations of the firm to a high level of influence from the corporate social environment and involves a substantial expansion in the scope of responsibilities of line managers.

Executive leaders who successfully implemented such an agenda devoted an enormous amount of their time to corporate external affairs activities during the early stage of implementation of new or expanded strategies. They traveled far and wide to communicate the new approach, to explain why it was needed, and to clarify the expectations it imposed on line and staff managers. They inserted external affairs issues on the agenda of policy-making forums. They looked for early successes and made them public. They altered the reward and promotion systems for rising line managers to give them credit for involvement in and contributions to the external affairs process. They inserted social goals into the business planning and review process governing the operations of the business divisions and functions.

The successful executive leaders also created slack to enable the line organization to make the transition by urging senior line managers to grant release time to their most promising subordinates to become involved in the analysis of business-related social issues and in the implementation of needed responses in line operations. In some instance, high-potential line managers were assigned midcareer positions as heads of core staff units in the corporate external affairs function in hopes that these business managers would bring a line perspective to external affairs and that they would take the latter perspective back into the line function when their lateral rotation was completed. Indeed, in a few cases general managers of major business divisions or functions were fired in part because of their resistance to the call for greater line involvement and responsiveness.

They created and often presided over settings in which senior line and staff executives exchanged information on emerging social and political issues, particularly in the early stage of implementation of their agenda. They actively championed new external affairs staff units, often placing them conspicuously highly in the organizational hierarchy during their early stage of development. Moreover, they signalled the importance of these units by holding them responsible in part for actually implementing needed changes in business policies and practices. They reinforced their commitment by following through to determine whether line units were responding and by catalyzing such responsiveness when resistance was encountered. Many subordinates actually came to refer to these executive leaders as "industry activists."

By consistently and persistently performing these personal role behaviors, these executive leaders amplified the influence they exerted on subordinate line and staff managers as the result of modifications that had been made in the internal context of organizational decision making. To the extent that executive leaders possessed the credibility and skills to effectively exercise both bases of influence, they were usually able to implement substantial changes in the nature and conduct of overall corporate social performance.

Performance Feedback

The extent of influence of executive leaders will vary not only in accordance with their skills and credibility, but also as a function of the level of dissatisfaction with the status quo among organizational members. Perhaps nothing can be more difficult to change than a corporation that has been experiencing a prolonged period of successful performance. Under such a condition, organizational members will have little obvious reason to question the efficacy of traditional values, strategies, organizational arrangements, and employee orientations and skills. In the absence of credible data signalling imminent future performance problems, executive leaders will be hard pressed to implement major strategic and organizational change.

The influence of individual executive leaders, therefore, will be more pronounced to the extent that either the corporation is experiencing a sustained period of performance gap or there has been a major change in its performance context. Such was the case in this study of the U.S. insurance industry. When the major insurers either experienced a sustained period of shortfall between their expectations and their performance or encountered a major shift in the nature and intensity of the social and political issues, which potentially put future corporate performance in jeopardy, executive leaders were able to exert more influence on the form and substance of corporate social performance than under more munificent performance conditions.

The effects of real or potential negative performance feedback had several important effects on these companies. First, such feedback directly impacted the executive leaders who were ultimately responsible for corporate performance and who were in a position to reallocate resources and reorient the internal context in an attempt to help the corporation cope with the new situation. Second, negative performance feedback impacted the strategy-formation process by raising doubts about the wisdom of some previous strategic choices, thereby setting the stage for alterations in the business strategies of the firm and hence, in its level of exposure to external constraints and contingencies. Third, sustained performance shortfall or substantial alteration in the performance situation became part of each insurance company's reinforcement history, which in turn raised questions about the efficacy of traditional values, predispositions, and competences embedded in the character of each institution.

In summary, real or potential negative feedback on corporate performance can have a major influence on the character-formation and strategy-formation processes in organizations, and on the *magnitude* of influence exerted by executive leaders on the factors affecting corporate social performance. The extent to which this enhanced influence potential is realized depends, of course, on the skills and credibility of such leaders and the extent to which the changes they seek to make do not depart too far from the traditional character of the company. The specific *nature* of the responses selected by executive leaders to cope with negative performance feedback, however, will tend to be a reflection of individual differences which separate leaders, including such things as their political orientation and personal exposure to public forums. Enterprise-oriented executives will tend to seize opportunities such as these to intensify the protection of traditional business policies and practices from social and political intrusion; whereas institution-oriented executives will tend to view the same situations as opportunities to open the corporation to external influence and to increase line-manager exposure to the external affairs process.

Therefore, performance feedback represents the last of the factors that are included in the grounded theory of corporate social performance. Before moving on to an exploration of some economic consequences of corporate social performance, however, it is necessary to signal that an important underlying ingredient in a corporation's ability to manage new and different performance contingencies is its slack resources.[10] These are the resources possessed by an organization that are not consumed in the routine functioning of the business operations, and which may therefore be called upon to cope with nonroutine issues. Such slack resources take many forms, including financial reserves, underutilized capacities and skills, employee commitment and loyalty, and goodwill among external constituencies.

Not only may executive leaders redeploy existing slack resources to enable the corporation to cope with nonroutine contingencies, but if circumstances warrant they may also create slack resources by temporarily reducing the normal performance expectations of the firm or of some of its parts. The potential role of this factor is not highlighted in the present theory, which was constructed on the basis of evidence from, and is primarily intended for application to the large, complex corporations in society, most of which possess sufficient slack resources to effectively manage social contingencies should they choose to do so.

ECONOMIC CONSEQUENCES
OF CORPORATE SOCIAL PERFORMANCE

An important question that remains at the periphery of the primary objectives and methods of this study is: What are the implications of corporate social performance for corporate economic performance? Many studies have attempted to answer this question by examining the relationship between various indicators of corporate social performance and standard accounting measures of corporate profitability. The results have been equivocal for many reasons.[11] First, there has been little consistency in the choices of how to measure these dimensions of corporate performance. Second, most studies have failed to adequately control for the phenomenon of strategic choice. For example, within a sample of firms studied there may be companies that have chosen to pursue a growth strategy alongside those that have chosen to pursue harvest or profit-maximization strategies. All of these firms could have been performing these different business strategies equally well, but in any given accounting period their reported economic performance based on standard accounting principles could differ widely. Similarly, multiple-business firms may be pursuing cross-subsidization strategies which would not be obvious to a researcher who only had access to public information containing company-wide reports of financial performance. Third, none of the studies of this type have articulated a theory that specifies the relationship between the two dimensions of corporate performance or the time lag that might be expected between cause and effect. For these and many other reasons, it has been exceedingly difficult to pin down a simple pattern of association between rated corporate social performance and reported corporate economic performance.

The present study, because of the key choices made about primary objectives and research methods, can do little to provide this *type* of answer to the question. Its purposes led to the choice of a sample of firms whose business exposures and business strategies were different. The sample included property and casualty insurers and life and health insurers, as well as publicly and privately owned companies, all of which rely on different financial reporting systems, have different financial disclosure requirements, and pursue different accepted criteria of economic performance. In addition, only the largest national companies in the industry, presumably those with considerable market power and slack financial resources, were included in order to make it possible for the state insurance commissioners to have logged a long period of working experience with all of them. In the short run both the market power and financial slack of these large corporations, as well as the different business strategies they pursued, would tend to cause distortions in reported financial indicators of their economic performance. Finally, many of these firms operate in multiple businesses, where the internal processes of cross-subsidization and the business differences in economic strategy make it difficult to separate the economic outcomes of insurance versus other business activities. Thus, in order to maximize variation on business strategies and exposures, comparable indexes of reported financial performance were sacrificed.

Despite these study characteristics, it is possible to examine some important linkages between the economic and social dimensions of corporate performance in a less equivocal manner than the approach described above.

Industries vary considerably in terms of both their profit and growth potential and the critical success factors associated with effective economic performance. In general, executive leaders would prefer to operate in industries that offer better than average profit and growth potential and whose competitive factors can be successfully engaged by the business experience base within and the distinctive competences of the firm. Indeed, one of the most consistent findings from the research on corporate diversification is that companies that have pursued constrained diversification strategies, which means they have confined their strategy to only businesses that are closely related to their knowledge base and distinctive competences, have achieved substantially higher records of economic performance than have firms whose strategies have exposed them to new and different businesses and competitive factors.[12]

But as we have seen, industries and market segments also vary in their exposure to social and political contingencies. Indeed, some economically viable industries and market segments involve more business exposure to the corporate social environment than others. Corporations that can effectively understand and manage the inherent social and political contingencies are able to enter and remain in these highly exposed but economically attractive businesses; whereas firms that have not developed effective means for coping with these inherent noneconomic forces are over time forced to withdraw from or denied entry to these businesses. The impact of poor corporate social performance on corporate economic performance for the latter firms, therefore, is reflected in the costs of foregone business opportunities. Moreover, the economic consequence of this form of strategic flight or avoidance is exacerbated if such a firm is also forced to invest its resources in new and different businesses in which its executives have little experience. Evidence of such instances of flight and avoidance was found among the large insurance companies that had poor corporate social performance records.

During the half decade of this study, several major insurers were attempting to reconfigure their businesses strategies in an attempt to reduce their exposure to the corporate social environment. Some were reengineering their geographical mix by shifting their property and casualty insurance businesses away from the socially active, urban states in the northeast to more placid, but less dense markets west of the Mississippi. Two of the lowest-performing corporate social performers were in the process of phasing out all their automobile insurance business in a major urban state in the eastern United States, which for years had been a lucrative market under the jurisdiction of an activist insurance commissioner. Some firms were able to successfully operate property and casualty businesses in the nonurban areas of the country with a relatively small investment in corporate social performance activities. Executives in those firms readily explained that they avoided the denser markets in urban settings because they did not have sufficient sophistication in the corporate external affairs function to deal with the inherent risks of those markets.

Other major insurers were attempting to change the product mix in their business strategies. For example, some property and casualty companies were actively redeploying the earnings from their traditional business which they knew well into other insurance and noninsurance businesses which they knew less well but which appeared to expose them to less social and political risk. Essentially, all these poor corporate social performers were being forced to avoid or withdraw from economically viable businesses whose competitive factors they understood well and enter other businesses posing largely unknown economic risks but presumably lower social and political risks.

Given all of the vagaries of successfully moving into new and different businesses that have been revealed by contemporary research on diversification strategy, this trend among poor social performers provides one basis for the argument that executive leaders need to be concerned about developing the means to effectively understand and manage the corporate social environment.[13]

Another important linkage between the social and economic dimensions of corporate performance may be readily observed in highly exposed industries such as the one that hosted this investigation. Corporations in such industries have to cope not only with a large number of strategically important, industry-specific social and political contingencies, but also with a heavy canopy of industry-specific government regulations. The intrusion of these industry-specific contingencies into the business operations and the factors governing market competition is especially intense for the large firms in such industries.

In the U.S. tobacco industry, for example, government regulations and other public pressures associated with the smoking-and-health controversy virtually transformed the competitive marketplace for the manufacture and distribution of cigarettes.

The intensity and persistence of industry-specific, social and political contingencies caused a fundamental shift in the viability of this business from a tradition of high growth to one of stagnation and decline. Put into a position in which retained earnings could not be profitably reinvested in the traditional domestic market for cigarettes, the tobacco Big Six were forced to make investments in new and different businesses, both in the U.S. and abroad, about which they knew very little. Consequently, the historical financial performances of these corporations was replaced by a sustained period, lasting more than a decade and a half, in which the companies fell far short of their traditional earnings expectations. This connection between the business exposure and economic performance was also reflected in much lower than normal market prices and price-earnings ratios for the publicly traded stock of the cigarette manufacturers.

In addition to the overall consequences of failure to cope with social and political contingencies, there are many specific instances in the recent histories of the U.S. tobacco corporations in which important alterations occurred in the competitive marketplace as a result of new regulations that were implemented because attempts at self-policing by member firms failed. One clear example concerns the methods employed by the corporations to advertise their products in the public medium of television.

Agents of the public interest had become concerned that children were being exposed to too much cigarette advertising. Indeed, a large portion of the cigarette companies' advertising budgets was spent on family shows and sporting events that were broadcasted through television, both of which were popular among teenaged audiences. When the major firms in the industry failed to respond in a constructive manner to this public issue, the Federal Trade Commission enacted a ban on cigarette advertising in the public media. The result of this specific form of government intervention was that it transformed the competitive marketplace.

In a brand-sensitive market such as the one for cigarettes, advertising through the public media is extremely important for maintaining brand loyalty to an otherwise largely undifferentiated product. But even more important is the fact that cigarette companies depend heavily on public-media advertising to introduce and promote new products.

The timing of this specific intervention into the cigarette market was especially important for the tobacco Big Six, which were struggling to introduce new products that were allegedly safer for the consumer. Those companies that were able to develop and introduce filtered cigarettes and low-tar brands before the broadcast advertising ban were able to reap a competitive advantage that has sustained them for over a decade. They now are the market-share leaders. In contrast, companies that had been tardy in responding through new product development and introduction to the smoking-and-health controversy have greatly suffered from this government-initiated intervention into the marketplace. Because of the loss of access to broadcast advertising, these companies have experienced great difficulty in introducing new products that are viewed as responsive to the health issue, and most of them have suffered substantial market-share erosion as a consequence.

Evidence of similar economic or marketplace consequences of ineffective or tardy responsiveness to public pressure and government regulation is available from the experience of firms in the highly exposed U.S. insurance industry. State insurance commissioners often have wide latitude in the industry interventions they can make. Because they must safeguard the economic solvency as well as public responsiveness of the companies doing business in their states, most commissioners have control over both entry and exit barriers to the state insurance markets under their jurisdiction through the licensing authority they possess. Many have altered both the nature of competition among major insurers and the profit potential of their businesses through the exercise of approval authority over product design and pricing decisions. When companies cannot demonstrate that they have adequate financial reserves to meet their potential fiduciary obligations to customers, commissioners have placed constraints on how these companies allocate their resources. These government regulators even have a say about which customers the companies must serve, often forcing competitors to cooperate in insurance pools so that customers in need of coverage but who otherwise could either not afford coverage or not qualify for coverage under traditional private underwriting criteria. And at least one commissioner who was interviewed during this study was effectively running an insurance company that was in grave danger of mismanaging its fiduciary obligations!

Given this regulatory context, major insurers that have a broader perspective than strict company self-interest in debates on industry-specific, public policy issues, that value the maintenance of open and constructive relationships with government regulators and other agents of the public interest, and that have in place the internal orientations and mechanisms to support these perspectives and relationships, have generally fared much better in the highly regulated market for insurance products than have their counterparts pursuing more individualistic and adversarial approaches. Through their greater objectivity and preparedness, the former are often the first to be consulted when agents of the public interest are planning new regulatory models and legislative initiatives. Because of their willingness to suspend short-term gain and to seek compromise with other major firms that often lead to industry-wide positions on social issues, these firms have also been able to construct powerful industry coalitions to respond in substantive ways to important industry-related, social and political contingencies.

Moreover, executives in the firms that pursue a collaborative and problem-solving approach have often found that the constructive relationships established on the basis of trust and mutual respect with regulators pay dividends when it comes to obtaining support for the introduction of new products and services, appealing for rate adjustments, and dealing with consumer complaints that regulators bring to their attention. Their greater openness to the corporate social environment alone gives these firms a competitive advantage in being able to design products that meet new consumer needs and that accord with the public issues regulators, who rule on the acceptability of new products, want to resolve. In addition, their ability and willingness to become involved with regulators in the public policy formulation process has the potential for contributing to the improvement of the quality of government regulation, which is initiated and enforced by individuals who tend to vary substantially in their knowledge of how a particular business works.

This general approach to external affairs, therefore, appears to be well-suited to large corporations in highly exposed industries, and especially to those, such as the major insurers, which must cope with a powerful set of government regulators having considerable latitude in determining which companies will do business at what prices and with what products in their local markets.

In summary, two important linkages between the social and economic dimensions of the overall performance of individual corporations operating in highly exposed industries are highlighted in this study of major insurers. Failure to establish and maintain effective long-term relationships with industry peers and agents of the public interest and to effectively manage industry-specific, social and political contingencies is directly associated with both unsatisfactory market performance and corporate strategies of flight and avoidance. Both of these consequences translate into reduced economic performance for the corporation. For these reasons, the institution-oriented philosophy and an explicit collaborative/problem-solving approach to external affairs are favored for large firms with relatively high exposures to the corporate social environment.

By extrapolation, the longer-term viability and legitimacy of such an industry as a whole will be determined in large measure by the extent to which the population of firms it contains is dominated by one or the other approach to corporate social performance. To the extent that the population of a highly exposed industry contains a number of influential firms that pursue institution-oriented philosophies, it may be responsive and adaptive enough to avoid becoming hamstrung by excessive government regulation. But when such highly exposed industries become dominated by enterprise-oriented corporations, which prefer to win short-term victories in contests with agents of the public interest, the long-term viability and legitimacy of the private business mechanism are likely to diminish, with traditional private managerial prerogatives giving way to the exercise of government authority.

Nowhere has this longer-term pattern been demonstrated more dramatically than in the nuclear power generation industry in the United States. At this writing, the domestic nuclear industry has been brought to a virtual standstill because of its failure to deal with the intense social and political contingencies to which it is exposed. In contrast, the same industry is flourishing in the European Economic Community in part because of the ability of industry utilities and contractors to work effectively with representatives of the general public to find reasonable solutions for dealing with the industry's inherent potential for generating substantial negative contingencies.

BEYOND NAIVETE AND WISHFUL THINKING

This study has focused on how large, complex corporations in a highly exposed U.S. industry cope with industry-specific social and political issues. But because many corporations have never been as large in size and pervasive in influence in American society as they are today, even those which have traditionally operated at very low levels of business exposure to the corporate social environment are no longer afforded such luxury. Because they have become the ascendant social form in modern times, large and powerful organizations are increasingly looked upon by the general public and its agents not as free-standing economic instruments but as socioeconomic institutions in which evolving interpretations of the public interest are enacted and whose business policies and practices have nontrivial effects on the character and quality of American society.

Given these changes in the nature of corporations and in society, one of the most unsettling discoveries of this study has been that the majority of executive leaders in one of America's most highly exposed industries continue to deny or avoid the expanded corporate role that this new set of realities imposes. Instead, executive leaders in many of the largest and most pervasive companies in the U.S. insurance industry spend huge amounts of resources attempting to maintain what has always been a somewhat artificial boundary between their private prerogatives and the public interest.

As they attempt to reassert and defend what they still believe to be a "free" enterprise system, these executives fail to appreciate the fact that the general public through the instrument of government has always had a major role in determining the competitive conditions within most U.S. industries.[14] When such executives allow or encourage business policies and practices that are not congruent with the public interest to persist, they literally invite government to intervene on behalf of the public interest. Moreover, when the combined efforts of major firms within a highly exposed industry result in the perpetuation of gross inconsistencies between private business practices and important elements of the public agenda, they contribute unwittingly to the longer-term erosion of both the social legitimacy and the economic viability of their industry as a whole.

Hopefully this book helps to demonstrate the efficacy of another view of the role of these large corporations in society and a different overall approach to the management of corporate social performance. To capture the attention of executive leaders, an attempt has been made here not simply to argue, but to demonstate that this different perspective is more effective for highly exposed firms than the currently favored one, in terms of both private and public outcomes. In addition, what needs to be done within corporations by their executive leaders has been elaborated on. Moreover, this book has revealed how to implement such a perspective and what kinds of organizational dynamics are likely to be experienced as a result. All of these steps have been taken to create a theory from practice for practice.

Finally, the grounded theory is offered to scholars not only as an addition to the base of knowledge on corporate social behavior, but also as a demonstration of the benefits of relaxing the boundaries of tradition that have separated the fields of organization theory and business policy. Spanning this boundary at the current stage of development in these fields will involve some risks. For my part these risks have been far outweighed by the insights gained from a more holistic perspective on complex organizations. An institution is, after all, greater than the sum of the competing perspectives on it.

FOOTNOTES

1. It is important to distinguish between the objective external environment and the external environment as it is perceived by decision makers when one attempts to understand or predict organizational behavior and effectiveness. *Business exposure* represents one way to gauge the objective exposure of a corporation to the external social environment. Executive perceptions of this environment are colored by their values or philosophies and by the environmental information available to them. For a discussion of an early attempt to control for the objective exposure of corporations to external social and political contingencies, refer to Edward H. Bowman and Mason Haire, ''The Strategic Posture Toward Corporate Social Responsibility,'' *California Management Review*, 1975, 18, no.2, 49–58.

2. As the evidence in earlier chapters suggests, I have found it necessary to elaborate on the two fundamental design dimensions of contingency theory (Lawrence and Lorsch, 1967) in order to capture the important differences among corporate external affairs designs. *Differentiation* includes not only the degree of functional specialization (or breadth) but also depth; and *integration* is expanded to include the patterns of mutual influence among the specialized units within the external affairs function. Without making these explicit refinements in the traditional design concepts of contingency theory some important differences among the external affairs functions of corporations would be lost.

3. For an empirically based analogy linking the corporate external affairs function to the

human sensory system see Jeffrey Sonnenfeld, *Corporate Views of the Public Interest* (Boston, MA: Auburn House, 1981).

4. At a more general level, corporate strategy and organization design are the two principal ways in which executive leaders deal with the uncertainty created for the organization by its external environment. Through their influence on the formation of corporate strategy, executive leaders influence the *level* of uncertainty to which the organization is exposed. Through their attention to the issues of organization design they affect the *ability* of the organization to process the amount of information (or uncertainty) to which corporate strategy exposes the enterprise. Thus, from this information-processing perspective, managers may deal with environmental uncertainty through their influences on corporate strategy and organization design. They may, for example, choose a strategy that exposes the organization to a relatively simple, placid environment, thereby reducing the need for a sophisticated organization design. Or they may commit to a strategic choice that exposes the organization to a high level of environmental uncertainty and thereby create the need for the development of a more sophisticated organization design to effectively manage the greater external exposure.

5. Robert H. Miles, *Coffin Nails and Corporate Strategies* (Englewood Cliffs, NJ: Prentice-Hall, 1982).

6. It may seem curious to contemporary readers that I prefer the use of the term *character* instead of more popular terms such as organizational climate or culture. I have made this choice in part in hopes of rekindling interest in the pioneering work of Philip Selznick (*Leadership in Administration,* 1957), which argued for a developmental approach to understanding the role of executive leaders in large institutions. But my choice also reflects the broad meaning I attach to the concept of organizational or corporate character. Whereas climate is usually operationalized in terms of aggregations of employee self-reports and culture is often inferred from organizational stories, legends, and myths, character is deduced from the actual behaviors of an organization and the outcomes of its critical decision-making processes. In one sense, therefore, character may be conceived as consisting of climate and culture as well as organizational behavior and decision-making patterns. But when there is a contradiction between what employees perceive and say and what their organization actually does, I identify organizational character on the basis of the historical patterns of organizational behaviors and critical decisions.

7. This phenomenon of "organizational imprinting" is discussed at length in Arthur L. Stinchcombe, "Social Structure and Organizations," in the *Handbook of Organizations,* James G. March, ed., Chicago, IL: Rand-McNally, 1965, pp. 142–93

8. For a careful tracking of the influence of functional background and executive succession patterns refer to Chapter 6 in *Coffin Nails.*

9. Joseph Bower, *Managing the Resource Allocation Process* (Homewood, IL: Irwin, 1969).

10. Based on longitudinal and comparative studies of both simulated organizations and industry populations of firms, I have attempted to demonstrate that three important conditions for organizational learning and adaptation are (1) negative performance feedback, (2) catalytic leadership, and (3) the creation or utilization of slack resources. For a discussion of this evidence refer to Robert H. Miles and W. Alan Randolph, "Learning Styles and Early Development," Chapter 3 in John R. Kimberly, Robert H. Miles, and Associates, *The Organizational Life Cycle: Issues in the Creation, Transformation and Decline of Organizations* (San Francisco, CA: Jossey-Bass, 1980); and *Coffin Nails,*

esp. Chapter 6. For the early theoretical rationale on how organiations cope with nonroutine stimuli see James G. March and Herbert A. Simon, *Organizations* (New York, NY: Wiley, 1967).

11. The many studies that have attempted to correlate rated corporate social performance with reported financial performance have, themselves, been equivocal. For a recent review of this literature refer to Kenneth E. Aupperle, Archie B. Carroll, and John Hatfield, "An Empirical Examination of the Relationship between Corporate Social Responsibility and Profitability," *Academy of Management Journal,* 1985, 28, no.2, 446–63.

12. For a review of the literature on the efficacy of different diversification strategies, as well as an in-depth look at the diversification records of six large U.S. corporations, refer to *Coffin Nails,* Chapters 5, 6, and 7.

13. It must be emphasized that this study of corporate social performance was confined to the traditional insurance businesses of the largest U.S. insurers. In most cases, the sophistication in external affairs strategy and design that is associated with social and political contingencies surrounding the traditional insurance business is not matched when it comes to either their newly acquired insurance operations or their noninsurance business activities, even among the best-rated companies. It remains to be seen, therefore, if these companies do as well in terms of corporate social performance in their nontraditional operations as they do in their traditional insurance operations.

14. See for example the historical account by Paul R. Lawrence and Davis Dyer in *Renewing American Industry* (New York: The Free Press, 1983) of how governmental influences have shaped the nature of competition and the pattern of development of seven major U.S. industries.

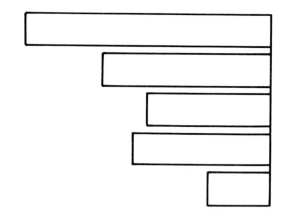

Appendix

THE PROCESS MEMO

The Process Memo, that accompanied the creation of Aetna's Issues Analysis (IA) Department, is reproduced below in its entirety:

INTEROFFICE COMMUNICATION

TO: Distribution

FROM: David Elliott, Assistant Vice President, IA

DATE: August 31, 1978

SUBJECT: SUMMARY OF OUR PROGRESS IN ORGANIZING IA'S WORK

This memorandum summarizes the progress of the IA staff in organizing the process by which public policy issues are identified and researched, and the resulting policies implemented. The purpose of this memo is twofold. The first is to serve as a tool for the staff in defining and planning IA's role within Aetna. The second purpose is to communicate our perception of this role to other key individuals and groups within the company.

Our discussions to date have made clear that there are numerous ways in which the responsibilities of IA and several other units overlap, and that cooperation between ourselves and these other units is essential. It should be stressed, therefore, that the decisions and plans embodied in this memo are open to discussion and revision. We will solicit comments from other Aetna units with the intent of revising and refining our plans in a manner that is sensitive to the interest of these units and that tries to maximize the efficient coordination of the company's resources.

Before proceeding to discuss the manner in which we will organize IA's work it is appropriate that a definition of "public policy issue" be set forth. We have developed the following working definition:

A public policy issue is

1. An issue regarding which the public (i.e., government and/or significant numbers of consumers) is or will be active in the foreseeable future;
2. An issue which currently has, or might foreseeably have, meaningful impact on Aetna's business.

There are five broad areas around which public policy issues research can be organized. These areas are Identification, Priority Setting, Selection, Analysis, and Implementation. The remainder of this memorandum defines the areas and describes IA's organization and processes relative to each category.

I. IDENTIFICATION

This category is limited to the processes by which issues are uncovered, given preliminary shape and periodically reviewed. The objectives of a successful issue identification process are

1. to avoid insular thinking in defining public policy issues relevant to Aetna;
2. to set boundaries on the issues identified;
3. to predict the emergence of future issues, as well as to inventory current issues.

To prevent insular thinking we will employ a variety of sources to discover potential issues. These sources include

Literature search (i.e., newspapers, periodicals, government documents);

Discussions with key managers and groups within the company (e.g., Marketing Study Group, Environmental Analysis Group);

Reference to corporate planning documents;

Meetings with trade association representatives;

Discussions with consultants;

Discussions with IA counterparts in other companies.

After reviewing these sources, an issue inventory will then be compiled, and some preliminary research on each issue undertaken. The purpose of this research would be to determine which issues should be studied further or monitored by the company. The preliminary research would primarily be designed to sharpen the *definition* of each issue. In addition, however, except for those issues immediately discarded from the list (e.g., an issue that on initial examination is not a public policy issue as we have defined it), the preliminary research should cover the three criteria included in first-level "Priority Setting." The research would also aim to determine, in a tentative manner, the *appropriateness* and *timeliness* of studying a given issue and the usefulness to Aetna of studying it.

The goal of this initial inventorying and research is to make IA serve as a "clearing-house" for public policy issues for the company.

Having inventoried and briefly researched all possible public policy issues, the priority-setting process, described below, will sort the issues into three categories:

1. those appropriate for study now by IA;

2. those now deserving study by another department/division within the company;

3. those currently requiring only monitoring over time by IA.

If IA is to serve effectively as a clearinghouse, the issue inventory must be shared with key executives and management groups in the company for additions, deletions, or suggestions. The issue inventory will be updated, on a schedule compatible with the corporate planning processes, by IA staff with the help of input from others in the company.

To insure continuity and consistency in our approach to the issue identification process, a divisional liaison system will be developed. Each IA staff member will be assigned one or more divisions with twofold responsibility. The first responsibility is to identify, do the preliminary research, and update the research on those issues that affect the company unit(s) to which he is assigned. Presumably, a staff person with responsibilities to particular company divisions will develop greater knowledge of the operation of those units and consequently enhance his ability to define and research each issue. To that end, publications, correspondence, and internal company communications will be selectively routed to the appropriate staff.

A second responsibility will be to serve as a liaison to the planning and operations people in the division. This function is important to all five categories of the IA department's work. The liaison function will promote a greater exchange of ideas and information between IA and the rest of Aetna than would a random procedure of building relationships and contracts.

We have also generally agreed that there should be some consultant input to the process of identifying issues. Consulting includes direct consultation with acknowledged experts on an issue-by-issue basis, as well as prepared information, reports, and packaged research available through several firms.

We need to insure that our consultants and publications represent a diversity of opinion, expertise, and competencies. It is generally agreed that reassessment of whether our consultants and publications represent the best available thinking should be a constant process.

In the early stages of IA's functioning, consultants will be used with some frequency to react to the preliminary research done on each issue identified. This review may take the form of adding to the list, shaping issues, or suggesting modification or deletion of certain issues. Consultant review will also be used as appropriate for priority setting. As the issue identification and priority-setting procedures mature, consultants may be used more sparingly.

II. PRIORITY SETTING

Armed with an issue inventory, we must then define the approximate order of importance of these issues to the company. We have decided that a two-level process is needed. The first level ascertains the general importance of an issue to Aetna. The second level attempts to define the relative profitability of studying these generally important issues.

Our methodology for determining first-level priority setting uses the following criteria, which help to establish, in a rough way, the relative importance of a given issue to the company.

1. What is the probability that an issue will develop into a *major* issue?
2. How *great* would its eventual impact on Aetna be (assuming, that is, that it does develop)?
3. *When* is this issue likely to peak?

The application of these three criteria allows us to develop some subjective probability of an issue occurring, when it will occur, and how significant it will be to Aetna. The probability and impact measures used will be qualitative (i.e., high, medium, low) rather than quantitative. Having decided at the first level the approximate general importance of a given issue, we will decide at the second level whether we can or should study this issue.

In other words, if the first level of priority-setting indicates that an issue is highly likely to arise in the near future and can be expected to have significant impact on Aetna, we then need to consider:

1. Can we expect to add any substantive information (from Aetna's perspective) by studying this issue? Has this issue been studied, either internally or exter-

nally, to the extent that the marginal benefit of our efforts will not be justified? If we already have a company position on an issue, can a study add documentation to our position?

2. Having already defined the timeliness of the issue, is there sufficient lead time to mount and complete the study so that it will make a contribution to company policy decisions? (e.g., is government regulation so far advanced that no flexibility exists?)

3. Has the issue matured and stabilized to a point that allows it to be framed for studying?

4. Will the study provide a direction for change? It may not be necessary for a study to result in a complete and permanent solution to a given problem, but there should be some reasonable belief before commencing that it will point in a coherent policy-making direction (e.g., not opposite to obvious regulatory trends).

5. Is there a reasonable chance that the study results will in actuality contribute to change?

6. Will the issue primarily affect Aetna or the insurance industry, or will its impact be more broadly diffused? If the latter, it may be that we can depend on other industries or trade groups to respond to the issue.

These are judgment-based criteria and some method of summarizing their application (quantitatively, graphically, or otherwise) will be required.

Priority-setting will initially proceed on a divisional basis. After this step is completed, overall priorities for *all* issues identified will be assigned.

We will need, of course, to review the rank-ordering of issues in the inventory on a regular basis. This can be done initially by the staff person originally assigned to research and track the issue, and then by the staff as a whole. Additionally, there should be significant input of consultants along the way.

Finally, considering the comments of other individuals and groups within the company in our priority-setting efforts is of paramount importance and we will solicit comments from them on a ongoing basis. Just as with issue identification, we will be flexible in doing this. Generally, in the interest of efficiency, IA staff will carry out a first level priority-setting process before soliciting comments from operating and planning personnel and groups. Additionally, only when the priority-setting process has advanced well into the second level, will top management be asked for their guidance.

III. SELECTION

The issue selection process may be viewed as a continuation of the priority-setting process. It will, in fact, involve marginal choices among issues that are found to be of very high priority to the company. The goal of the selection process is twofold: to determine what issues would be studied by IA over the course of a year or so; and to determine what issues should be recommended for study within the divisions. When these decisions have been made, the remaining issues will continue to be monitored by IA.

Clearly, an issue that is near the bottom of the list of priorities is not likely to be selected over one near the top. However, an issue grouped closely with others near the top of the list may or may not be selected for study for a variety of reasons. Among these may be current limitation on staff resources or other administrative limitations. More importantly, the choice and study of particular issues represent a commitment of resources, the outcome of which will affect the overall company position in the public eye. For this reason, as stated in the priority-setting section, this is the point at which agreement on priority and selection should be secured from top management (i.e., division heads and the President). It would seem appropriate that a final review on a periodic basis be conducted by the Corporate Management Committee.

All three activities described above—identification, priority-setting, and selection—will be carried out on a schedule that is compatible with the corporate planning processes.

IV. ANALYSIS

The analysis of issues will be done either through the use of task forces or solely by IA staff. Each issue will by its nature and scope determine which staffing pattern is more appropriate. The task force method of research has worked well where it has already been used, and IA will continue to draw heavily on the resources of the various divisions for task force members.

Periodic progress reports will be prepared by staff for the division and individuals most directly affected by a given study. This will also help to keep the study focused, or reveal the need for refocusing.

Another concern is the framework of the analysis. Obviously, the scope and range of IA studies will vary with topic. Consequently, study time and resource requirements will vary. Although the scope of analysis will differ depending on the issue to be addressed, our focus will always be on producing studies that are of direct usefulness to Aetna. Broader research will be undertaken primarily in those instances in which it is needed to put Aetna's or the insurance industry's practices in context or where an industry-wide analysis of a problem is essential to secure industry response to the issue.

V. IMPLEMENTATION

The process of implementation involves insuring that IA's work is used as an integral part of the overall policy-making process of the company. Monitoring the extent to which IA's work is utilized by the divisions is also an aspect of implementation.

Institutionalizing IA's studies requires assuring their use in the divisions' planning and in the work of Government Relations, Public Relations, EAG, and CMC. Top management directives and informal constituency building on the part of staff will be relied upon to achieve this end.

Periodic meetings with appropriate people from throughout the company and the liaison function previously described will be used to develop a mutually supportive relationship with other Aetna units. These efforts, coupled with a periodic communication by the President to his senior managers, should be instruments to achieve the following goals:

- reinforcing the view that IA's work should be an integral part of the planning and policy-making activities of all Aetna units;

- developing a consulting role for IA staff in the implementation of those policy recommendations that are endorsed by senior management;

- establishing a formal and informal feedback procedure to monitor the implementation of those IA policy recommendations that are endorsed. The routine forwarding from divisions and departments of memoranda, reports or correspondence relevant to the policies being implemented is one possible formal way of monitoring activities.

Bill Bailey has suggested that he and I meet quarterly with those on distribution to discuss the public policy issue research effort. I would like to have this memorandum serve as the subject matter for the first meeting, which I will try to set up at a convenient date in mid-September.

cc: W. O. Bailey
     (Distribution: Insurance division SVPs, Clark, Yeats, and Conrad)

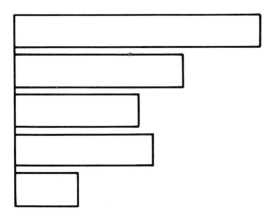

Bibliography

ACKERMAN, R. *The Social Challenge to Business.* Cambridge, MA: Harvard University Press, 1975.

ACKERMAN, R. AND R. BAUER. *Corporate Social Responsiveness: The Modern Dilemma.* Reston, VA: Reston Publishing Co., 1976.

AGUILAR, F. J. *Scanning the Business Environment.* New York: Macmillan, 1967.

ANDREWS, K. R. "Public Responsibility in the Private Corporation," *Journal of Industrial Economics,* April 1972, pp. 135–45.

————. *The Concept of Corporate Strategy* (revised edition). Homewood, IL: Irwin, 1981.

ASHBY, R. W. "Variety, Constraint, and the Law of Requisite Variety," ed. W. Buckley, *Modern Systems Research for the Behavioral Scientist: A Sourcebook.* Chicago, IL: Aldine, 1968, pp. 129–36.

AUPPERLE, K. E., A. B. CARROLL, AND J. HATFIELD. "An Empirical Examination of the Relationship between Corporate Social Responsibility and Profitability," *Academy of Management Journal,* 1985, 28, no. 2, 446–63.

BARNARD, C. I. *The Functions of an Executive.* Cambridge, MA: Harvard University Press, 1938.

BASS, B. "When Planning for Others," *Journal of Applied Behavioral Science,* 1970, 6, no. 2, 151–71.

Best's Insurance Reports, Life/Health Edition, 1981.

Best's Insurance Reports, Property/Casualty Edition, 1981.

BOK, D. *President's Report to the Board of Overseers.* Cambridge, MA: Harvard University Press, 1979.

BOWER, J. L. *Managing the Resource Allocation Process.* Boston, MA: Division of Research, Harvard University Graduate School of Business Administration, 1970.

BOWMAN, E. H. AND M. HAIRE. "A Strategic Posture Toward Corporate Social Responsibility," *California Management Review*, 1975, 18, no. 2, 49–58.

BRADSHAW, T. AND D. VOGEL, EDS., *Corporations and Their Critics*. New York: McGraw-Hill, 1981.

CARROLL, A. B. "A Three-dimensional Conceptual Model of Corporate Social Performance," *Academy of Management Review*, 1974, 4, no. 4, 497–505.

CHANDLER, A. D., JR. *Strategy and Structure*. Boston, MA: MIT Press, 1962.

CLARK, B. R. *The Distinctive College*. Chicago, IL: Aldine, 1970.

ENGLAND, G. W. *The Manager and His Values*. Cambridge, MA: Ballinger, 1975.

EPSTEIN, E. M. *The Corporation in American Politics*. Englewood Cliffs, NJ: Prentice-Hall, 1969.

FILER, J. H. "The Social Goals of a Corporation," eds. T. Bradshaw and D. Vogel, *Corporations and Their Critics*. New York: McGraw-Hill, 1981, pp. 269–76.

GHILONI, B. W. "The Corporate Scramble for Women Directors," *Business & Society Review*, Fall 1984, no. 51, 86–95.

GLASER, B. G. AND A. L. STRAUSS. *The Discovery of Grounded Theory: Strategies for Qualitative Research*. New York: Aldine, 1967.

GUTH, W. D. AND R. TAGIURI. "Personal Values and Corporate Strategy," *Harvard Business Review*, 1965, 43, no. 5, 123–32.

HARRIS, L. AND ASSOCIATES. *A Survey of Leadership and Public Attitudes Toward Various Aspects of Regulation of Insurance* (Study No. 805522). New York: Louis Harris and Associates, 1980.

HERTZBERG, D. "Life Insurers Start Offering Policies that Look More Like Investments," *The Wall Street Journal*, February 23, 1983, p. 31.

KASPER, D. "Note on Managing in a Regulated Environment" (1-379-032). Boston: HBS Case Services, Harvard University Graduate School of Business Administration, 1978.

KIMBERLY, J. R. "Environmental Constraints and Organizational Structure: A Comparative Analysis of Rehabilitation Organizations," *Administrative Science Quarterly*, 1975, vol. 20, pp. 1–9.

————— . "Initiation, Innovation, and Institutionalization," in J. R. Kimberly, R. H. Miles and associates, *The Organizational Life Cycle*. San Francisco, CA: Jossey-Bass, 1980, pp. 18—43.

KIMBERLY, J. R., R. H. MILES, AND ASSOCIATES. *The Organizational Life Cycle: Issues in the Creation, Transformation and Decline of Organizations*. San Francisco, CA: Jossey-Bass, 1980.

LAWRENCE, P. R. AND D. DYER. *Renewing American Industry*. New York: Free Press, 1983.

LAWRENCE, P. R. AND J. W. LORSCH. *Organization and Environment: Managing Differentiation and Integration*. Homewood, IL: Irwin, 1967.

LILLY, W. AND J. C. MILLER. "The New 'Social' Regulations," *The Public Interest*, Spring 1977, vol. 47.

LODGE, G. C. "Ideological Transformation of the United States," *The Journal of the Institute for Socioeconomic Studies*, 1983, 7, no. 1, 67–83.

————— . *The New American Ideology*. New York: Alfred Knopf, 1975.

MARCH, J. G. AND H. SIMON. *Organizations*. New York: Wiley, 1967.

MARKUS, M. L. "Implementation Politics: Top Management Support and User Involvement," *Systems, Objectives, Solutions,* 1981, vol. 1, pp. 203–15.

McGRATH, P. S. "Managing Corporate External Relations: Changing Perspectives and Responses," (Report No. 679). New York: The Conference Board, 1976.

————— . "Redefining Corporate-Federal Relations," (Report No. 757). New York: The Conference Board, 1979.

McQUAID, K. "Big Business and Public Policy in Contemporary United States," *Quarterly Journal of Economics and Business,* 1980, 20, no. 2, pp. 57–68.

MILES, R. E. AND C. SNOW. *Organizational Strategy, Structure, and Process*. New York: McGraw-Hill, 1978.

MILES, R. H. *Coffin Nails and Corporate Strategies*. Englewood Cliffs, N. J.: Prentice-Hall, 1982.

————— . "How Do State Commissioners Assess the Corporate Social Performance of Major Insurers?" *Best's Review* (Property/Casualty Edition), November 1981, 82, no. 7, 32–127.

————— . "Organization Boundary Roles," eds. C. L. Cooper and R. Payne, *Current Concerns in Occupational Stress*. London: Wiley, 1980, pp. 61–96.

————— . "Learning from Diversifying," (9-481-060). Boston, MA: HBS Case Services, Harvard University Graduate School of Business Administration, 1981.

————— . "Preliminary Report of the National Survey of State Insurance Commissioners," *Proceedings* of the National Association of Insurance Commissioners, 1981, vol. II, pp. 962–90.

MILES, R. H. AND A. BHAMBRI. "Organizational Maintenance and Adaptation: The Roles of Senior Line Managers and Corporate External Affairs Professionals," *Proceedings* of the 40th Meeting of the Academy of Management, Detroit, 1980, pp. 216–220.

————— . "Public Policy Priorities and Insurer Responsiveness: Comparative Views of State Commissioners and Company Executives," *Best's Review,* (Property/Casualty Insurance Edition), 1982, 82, no. 9, 20–24.

————— . *The Regulatory Executives*. Beverly Hills, CA: Sage Publications, Inc., 1983.

MILES, R. H. AND W. A. RANDOLPH. "Learning Styles and Early Development," in J. R. Kimberly, R. H. Miles and associates, *The Organizational Life Cycle*. San Francisco, CA: Jossey-Bass Publishers, 1980, pp. 44–82.

MILGRAM, S. "Behavioral Study of Obedience," *Journal of Abnormal and Social Psychology,* 1963, vol. 67, pp. 371–78.

MITNICK, B. M. *The Political Economy of Regulation*. New York: Columbia University Press, 1980.

Moody's Industrial Manual, 1982.

MOORE, D. G. "Politics and the Corporate Chief Executive," (Report No. 777). New York: The Conference Board, 1980.

MOSKOWITZ, M. R. "Company Performance Roundup," *Business & Society Review,* Spring 1980 through Winter 1984.

────────. "The 1982 Black Corporate Directors Lineup," *Business & Society Review*, Fall 1982, no. 43, 51–64.

NORMANN, R. *Management for Growth*. New York: Wiley-Interscience, 1977.

PETTIGREW, A. M. "Strategic Aspects of the Management of Specialist Activity," *Personnel Review*, 1975, 4, no. 1, 5—13.

────────. "The Influence Process Between Specialists and Executives," *Personnel Review*, 1974, 3, no. 1, 24–30.

────────. *The Politics of Organizational Decision-making*. London: Tavistock Publications, 1973.

────────. "Towards a Political Theory of Organizational Intervention," *Human Relations*, 1975, 28, no. 3, 191–208.

PETTIGREW, A. M. AND D. C. BUMSTEAD. "Strategies of Organization Development in Differing Organizational Contexts," eds. P. A. Clark, J. Guiot, and H. Thirry, *Organizational Change and Development in Europe*. London: Wiley, 1981.

PORTER, M. E. *Competitive Strategy*. New York: Free Press, 1981.

POST, J. E. *Corporate Behavior and Social Change*. Reston, VA: Reston Publishing Co., 1978.

PRESTON, L. "Corporate Power and Social Performance: Approaches to Positive Analysis," in *The Economics of Firm Size, Market Structures and Social Performance*, ed J. J. Siegfried, *Proceedings* of a conference sponsored by the Bureau of Competition, Federal Trade Commission, Washington, D. C., July 1980.

PUBLIC AFFAIRS COUNCIL. "The Fundamentals of Issue Management," Monograph 12-78, Washington, D. C., 1978.

RADNOR, M., A. RUBENSTEIN, AND A. S. BEAN. "Integration and Utilization of Management Science Activities in Organizations," *Operational Research Quarterly*, 1968, 19, no. 2, 117–41.

RUMELT, R. P. *Strategy, Structure, and Economic Performance*. Boston, MA: Division of Research, Harvard Business School, 1974.

SARASON, S. B. *The Creation of Settings and the Future Societies*. San Francisco, CA: Jossey-Bass, 1972.

SELZNICK, P. *Leadership in Administration*. Berkeley, CA: University of California Press, 1957.

SETHI, S. P. "A Conceptual Framework for Environmental Analysis of Social Issues and Evaluation of Business Response Patterns," *Academy of Management Review*, 1979, 4, no. 1, 63–74.

────────. "Dimensions of Corporate Social Performance: An Analytical Framework," *California Management Review*, Spring 1975.

SMITH, G. D. AND L. E. STEADMAN. "Present Value of Corporate History," *Harvard Business Review*, Nov.-Dec. 1981, pp. 164–73.

SONNENFELD, J. A. *Corporate Views of the Public Interest*. Boston: Auburn House, 1981.

STINCHCOMBE, A. L. "Social Structure and Organizations," in *Handbook of Organizations*, ed. J. G. March, Chicago, IL: Rand McNally, 1965, pp. 142–93.

TAYLOR, B. AND P. IRVING. "Organized Planning in Major U. K. Companies," *Long Range Planning*, 1971, vol. 3, no. 4.

Votaw, D. and S. P. Sethi. *The Corporate Dilemma.* Englewood Cliffs, N.J.: Prentice-Hall, 1973.

Wallace, C. "Protection for Sale: The Insurance Industry," NBC Special, April 17, 1982.

Walton, R. E. "Establishing and Maintaining High Commitment Work Systems," in J. R. Kimberly, R. H. Miles and associates, *The Organizational Life Cycle,* San Francisco, CA: Jossey-Bass, 1980, pp. 208–90.

Wheelwright, S. C. and R. L. Banks. "Involving Operating Managers in Planning Process Evolution," *Sloan Management Review,* Summer 1979, pp. 43–59.

Zenisek, T. J. "Corporate Social Responsibility: A Conceptualization Based on Organizational Literature," *Academy of Management Review,* 1979, 4, no. 3, 359–68.

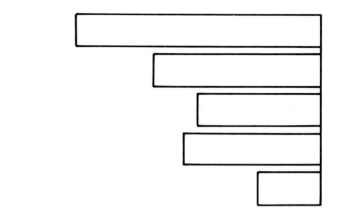

Indexes

Subject Index

Author Index